BEING GOOD
&
BEING LOGICAL

BEING GOOD

&

BEING LOGICAL

Philosophical Groundwork for a New Deontic Logic

James Wm. Forrester

M.E. Sharpe
Armonk, New York
London, England

Library of Congress Cataloging-in-Publication Data

Forrester, James W.
Being good and being logical : philosophical groundwork for a new deontic logic /
James W. Forrester.
p. cm.
Includes bibliographical references and index.
ISBN 1-56324-879-4 (hardover : alk. paper).—ISBN 1-56324-880-8 (pbk. : alk. paper)
1. Deontic logic.
2. Ethics.
I. Title.
BC145.F65   1996
160—dc20
96-15791
CIP

Printed in the United States of America

The paper used in this publication meets the minimum requirements of the
American National Standard for Information Sciences—
Permanence of Paper for Printed Library Materials,
ANSI Z 39.48-1984.

BM (c)   10   9   8   7   6   5   4   3   2   1
BM (p)   10   9   8   7   6   5   4   3   2   1

To Mary Gore Forrester

Without whose suggestions, criticisms, and encouragement

this book would never have been written

(including the parts she disagrees with!)

This book is dedicated

with respect and with love.

"Certainly, then, ordinary language is *not* the last word: in principle it can everywhere be supplemented and improved upon and superseded. Only remember, it *is* the *first* word."

—J.L. Austin

"A Plea for Excuses"

Contents

Preface

In a preface, it is customary to thank all those people who have helped in the writing of the book. I owe four major debts for this book; unfortunately, one of them I can never hope to repay in person.

While working on the first draft of this book, I learned of the death of Hector-Neri Castañeda. It was Hector who stimulated my interest in deontic logic and who strongly encouraged my work in the field. His unselfishness, his dedication, his immense critical abilities, and his constant desire to build rather than to destroy are familiar to all of us who knew him. For me, he was in all ways an example of what a philosopher should be.

I am also greatly indebted to an anonymous reviewer, who not only pointed out a number of faults in an earlier version of the work but also made some extremely helpful suggestions for clarifying my presentation. Chapter 2 and the present form of Chapters 3, 14, and 15 are the direct result of the reviewer's suggestions.

Professor Stephen Harris, who was a referee for the book, made suggestions that have led to major improvements in both clarity and content. Chapters 7 and 14 especially profited from his suggestions, and Appendix 2 was written at his urging.

My last major debt is to the book's dedicatee: my wife, Mary Gore Forrester. She has worked on deontic logic far longer than I have. We have talked for years about many of the points covered in this book; in fact, Chapter 4 began as a jointly written paper. The whole focus of the book changed because she made me see that a deontic logic using causal conditionals is the only sort that can hope to be true to our actual moral arguments. To have one's best and most constructive critic quite literally in-house is rare good fortune.

Many others have contributed to this book. Audiences at the University of Wyoming and at Colorado State University, to whom I read sections of the book in progress, proved both helpful and kind in their comments. Matthias Steup, a former colleague of mine, provided valuable input into what became chapter 4. Kenith Sobel, a student of mine, has provided valuable comments on Chapters 14 and 15. I read a version of what was to become chapter 16 to the Mountain-Plains Philosophy Conference, where I received valuable comments from Luc Bovens. And I am grateful for valuable practical advice to G. Nick Street.

For any mistakes, solecisms, and downright barbarisms that might remain, I am, of course, responsible. The others tried their best!

Introduction

The theologian Tertullian, denouncing those who would mix a little Greek philosophy with their Christianity, once thundered, "What has Athens to do with Jerusalem?" Similarly, I suspect, most people today would find highly unlikely the notion that ethics has anything much to do with logic. Ethics, whether one takes it as a matter of getting in touch with one's own feelings, with one's conscience, or with one's God, would seem almost a polar opposite from logic, that cold specialty of mathematicians. I would not be surprised to hear of someone who labels ethics a right-brain, logic a left-brain phenomenon.

But there is a long history of philosophers who have assigned logic a special place in ethics. And the twentieth century has seen the birth and rapid growth of deontic logic, a special branch of logic concerned with obligation and permission. Deontic logic has its own axioms and rules of inference; moral beliefs that run afoul of these are considered on a par with addition that runs afoul of the rules of arithmetic. The Athens of logic and the Jerusalem of ethics seem to be merging into a single deontic metropolis.

And yet, not all is well with deontic logic. There is a standard version of it — Standard Deontic Logic (SDL), put forward by deontic logic's founding father, G.H. von Wright — but sometimes it seems as though the standard is only a target for deontic logicians to snipe at. Alternative formulations are common, and there seems no way of telling which, if any, is correct. A related difficulty arises from what seems an ever-increasing set of deontic paradoxes. The special rules and axioms of deontic logic, supposedly neutral among ethical theories, seem to entail some unusual — perhaps in a few cases even unethical — results. For these reasons, even if in fact we do have reason to think the Jerusalem of ethics merely a suburb of the Athens of logic, our surveyors are having difficulty discovering just where that suburb is located.

Surely the cities are connected. At the least, ethics is a field of study; like other fields of study, it has a structure. Because of the structure of ethics, we can and do make logical inferences concerning ethical statements. But such a logic is a minimal one, consisting solely of the propositional calculus and special definitions. Ethics, I shall argue, needs more logic than those bare bones can provide.

I believe that there is also a special logic of obligation and permission. The rules of this special logic go beyond the propositional calculus, although they are less far-reaching than most deontic logicians have claimed. My main purpose in this book is to set out and justify that new deontic logic.

Attempts to connect logic and ethics have a long and checkered history. Plato — who was, after all, an Athenian — was probably the first philosopher to suggest an important role for logic in ethics. In the *Republic*, he claims that the Form of Good occupies a special place at the top of the ontological heap, and that one can somehow reason down from it to more mundane facts.

The philosopher who more than any other began the tradition of fusing logic and ethics was probably John Locke.[1] Locke, in his *Essay Concerning Human Understanding*, declared roundly: "Upon this ground it is, that I am bold to think, that *Morality is capable of Demonstration*, as well as Mathematicks."[2] Locke's "ground" has a whiff of twentieth-century Vienna about it, for he held that moral language does not describe anything in the world. According to Locke, we have no ideas of any entities, possessed of secret real essences, which answer to such terms as 'good' and 'right'. Rather, our moral ideas are our own creation; they are for the most part "such Combinations of *Ideas*, as the Mind puts together of its own choice." [Locke, 516]

Hence, Locke believed, nothing but negligence, perversity, or want of ingenuity can prevent us from gaining a clear and certain understanding of morality. All we have to do is to define our terms properly and, apparently, note whatever logical consequences follow from the defini-tions. "For Certainty being but the Perception of the Agreement, or Disagreement of our *Ideas*; and Demonstration nothing but the Perception of such Agreement, by the Intervention of other *Ideas*, or Mediums, our *moral Ideas*, as well as mathematical, being *Archetypes* themselves, and so adequate, and complete *Ideas*, all the Agreement, or Disagreement, which we shall find in them, will produce real Knowledge, as well as in mathematical Figures." [Locke, 565][3]

What we discover from our ideas must hold of any actions that sufficiently resemble those ideas. "If it be true in Speculation, *i.e.* in *Idea*, that *Murther deserves Death*, it will also be true in Reality of any Action that exists conformable to that *Idea of Murther*. As for any other Actions, the Truth of that Proposition concerns them not. And thus it is of all other Species of Things, which have no other Essences, but those *Ideas*, which are in the Minds of Men." [Locke, 566]

Locke suggested that some mental operations, over and above adequate observation of our man-made ideas, might be needed for a certain science of morals. "One part of *these Disadvantages*, in moral *Ideas*, which has made them be thought not capable of Demonstration, may in a good measure be *remedied* by Definitions, setting down that Collection of simple *Ideas*, which every Term shall stand for; and then using the Terms steadily and constantly for that precise Collection. And what methods *Algebra*, or something of that kind, may hereafter suggest, to remove the other difficulties, is not easy to fore-tell." [Locke, 552] Thus Locke envisioned, somewhat darkly, a mathematical method of reasoning as a means of making ethics perfectly clear.

It was Locke's determined anti-realism, then, that led him to emphasize the role of logic in ethics. If moral language does not pick out moral facts, its claims can be true — perhaps can be intelligible — only if they are analytic and hence necessary and demonstrable. I suspect that a similar argument underlay much of the concern with the logic of ethics among positivist philosophers in the first half of the twentieth century.

But although Locke, like his rationalist and positivist successors, saw ethical truths as part of the fallout from logical operations, neither he nor such rationalists as Price and Wollaston thought it necessary to construct a logic peculiar to moral argument. Locke found no special logic of obligation, of 'ought' and 'may', distinct from the ordinary logic of 'is' and 'must be'. Deontic logic, for better or worse, is a twentieth-century invention.

According to one standard book on the subject, Ernst Mally constructed the first system of deontic logic in 1926. [al-Hibri, 1][4] But the founding father of the subject is generally considered to be G.H. von Wright; the founding date is 1951, when his article "Deontic Logic" appeared in *Mind*. [von Wright 1] Von Wright put forward the basics of what is generally known as Standard Deontic Logic. Since von Wright, most deontic logicians have opted for a deontic theory that goes beyond the bare bones of the propositional calculus plus special definitions.

On the other hand, many ethical theorists such as R.M. Hare have followed the path Locke laid down: they have seen no need for a special deontic logic to account for the place of reason in ethics. Moreover, I believe that to most members of the community of moral philosophers, deontic logic is worse than useless: It has become an empty formal exercise, carried on by logicians more interested in questions of validity and completeness than in how people actually do their moral reasoning. In this way, deontic logic has fulfilled the gloomy prophecy of Ruth Barcan Marcus thirty years ago: unless deontic logic can give an account of the uses of 'ought' in certain sentences, "the development of deontic systems, however elaborate, may be misleading technical exercises." [Marcus, 582]

It is no exaggeration to say that deontic logic and moral philosophy have for some years been drifting apart. On both sides of the divide between ethical theorists and deontic logicians, I believe there are grounds for blame. In a well-known passage in *Fact, Fiction, and Forecast*, Nelson Goodman wrote: ". . . [R]ules and particular inferences alike are justified by being brought into agreement with each other. *A rule is amended if it yields an inference we are unwilling to accept; an inference is rejected if it violates a rule we are unwilling to amend.* The process of justification is the delicate one of making mutual adjustments between rules and accepted inferences; and in the agreement achieved lies the only justification needed for either." [Goodman, 64; his italics] But unfortunately, moral philosophers have been unwilling to throw out particular inferences that conflict with principles of deontic logic; deontic logicians have not for their part been willing to discard principles that lead to counterintuitive inferences. Goodman's delicate process of mutual adjustment has not taken place — to the detriment of both deontic logic and moral theory.

However, I believe the situation is improving, and those largely responsible for the improvement are deontic logicians. In the introduction to his *Introduction to Deontic Logic and the Theory of Normative Systems*, Lennart Åqvist suggests that an enriching of the resources of deontic languages might allow deontic logicians to regain their hope of contributing substantively to ethical and legal theory. [Åqvist 2, 11] In every respect, Åqvist's remark is good news: that deontic logicians wish to contribute substantively to moral theory, that they realize that shortcomings in deontic theory have stood in the way of such a contribution, and that they are willing to entertain major changes in deontic theory to accomplish a substantive contribution.

This book is an attempt at reconciliation from the philosophical side of the divide. My aim is first to show that standard systems of deontic logic, if we take them as attempts to codify our normal deontic reasoning, run into a number of difficulties. Then, I shall present a new system of deontic logic and argue that it is free from the shortcomings of standard systems. Finally, I shall sketch an argument for taking my new deontic logic to be a general logic of practical reasoning.

Part I of the book, an examination of standard deontic logic, consists of ten chapters. Chapter 1 tries to provide preliminary answers to some basic questions. Among these are: "What is deontic logic?"; "Are there any special principles of deontic logic?"; and "Why should anyone but a specialist care about deontic logic?" Chapter 2 is a description of standard deontic logics; it concentrates on propositions typically asserted by standard systems.

In my book *Why You Should: The Pragmatics of Deontic Speech*, I argued that it is best to take certain principles of deontic reasoning to be matters of pragmatics, not of logic. If so, there must be less to deontic logic than some have claimed. In Chapter 3 of the current book, I assess the situation of deontic logic in the light of my contentions in *Why You Should* and related claims by other philosophers. However, my assessment in this chapter is only a programmatic statement of what I shall be arguing for in the rest of Part I. This book's arguments must stand on their own, to complement rather than to lean on the arguments of my earlier book.

Chapter 4 is a key chapter, both in my argument against standard deontic logics and in my construction of a new deontic logic. In Chapter 4, I argue that there is a real difference in meaning and logical behavior between statements of what someone ought to do and claims that a particular state of affairs ought to be. Neither type of statement implies the other; at most they are pragmatically related. By taking the two sorts of 'ought' statements as equivalent, standard systems badly misrepresent our deontic reasoning.

In Chapter 5, I contend that both types of 'ought' statements are intensional. Hence, in view of the referential opacity of intensional contexts, any deontic logic that goes beyond the propositional calculus is crucially dependent on the presence of a workable deontic semantics.

Chapters 6, 7, and 8 constitute an assault on standard deontic semantics — or, as I shall call it, SDL semantics — as that semantics is applied to 'ought to do' statements. In Chapter 6, I argue that a drastic and highly problematic restriction of the set of deontically accessible worlds is unavoidable. In Chapter 7, I argue that a crucial semantic principle, the principle of backward translation, is unjustifiable. And in Chapter 8, I contend that various epistemic problems make SDL semantics, even if logically viable, useless to us.

In Chapter 9, I reassess the deontic paradoxes and questions of conflict of duties, in the light of the arguments developed in the previous three chapters. These older difficulties take on a new and sharper bite when they are combined with the problems set out earlier.

Chapter 10 turns to the SDL semantics of 'ought to be' sentences. Although the problems of 'ought to do' semantics do not, for the most part, raise difficulties for 'ought to be' semantics, the latter turns out to suffer from crippling disabilities of its own. The difference in semantical problems confirms the difference between the two types of 'ought' statement; but neither type of 'ought' statement lends itself to a viable semantics of the ordinary type. Hence, standard deontic logic fails as an account of our ordinary deontic beliefs and reasoning.

In Part II of this book, I turn to reconstruction.[5] My purpose is to develop and justify a viable deontic logic that does not suffer from the difficulties Part I raised for standard systems.

Part II consists of five chapters. In the first two chapters, I suggest that the distinction between 'ought to be' and 'ought to do' statements helps answer a pair of vexing problems in moral philosophy. In Chapter 11, I apply the distinction to an ancient and vexing problem in the theory of rights: the relation of rights to duties. Then in Chapter 12, I use the same distinction to defeat an argument that one ought to be beneficent even to the point of ruining one's self.

Chapter 13 argues that for certain reasons connected with moral realism, it is imperative that we try to construct a new semantics. The only alternative to a new semantics is a moral non-realism that has no adequate way of explaining an important feature of 'ought' language.

Chapter 14 presents my new semantics, based on the semantics of causal conditionals. I offer definitions of both "S ought to do F" and "State of affairs <p> ought to be," and I sketch out a semantics based on those definitions. I then argue that the objections which I brought against

SDL semantics in the first part of this book raise no difficulties for my new deontic semantics.

In Chapter 15 I look at the nature of the deontic logic, NDL, that falls out of the semantics of Chapter 14. NDL turns out to be a deontic logic pruned of dubious claims, but it is a logic fully capable of serving as the logic of ethics. Hence, it is justified both by what it does and should do, and by what it does not and should not do.

The third and final part of this book consists of a single chapter. In Chapter 16 I return to one of the questions raised in chapter 1: what is the value of deontic logic? I argue that my new deontic logic should be regarded as a general logic of practical reasoning, both teleological and deontic. If I am right, NDL should help solve one of the oldest and most pressing problems in the history of philosophy.

Appendix 1 presents the systems SDL and NDL succinctly. In a set of tables, I compare semantical rules, rules of inference, typical assertions, and typical non-asserted propositions for the two systems. Appendix 2 briefly considers whether NDL can be converted into a quantified deontic logic. I argue that it can, with some important restrictions.

Given the nature of my task in the present book, it cannot help but be more technical than *Why You Should*. Deontic logic in its various versions is a formal discipline, with axioms, inference rules, and a developed semantics. Any attack on standard deontic logics that deserves to be taken seriously cannot be entirely informal. The breezy, non-technical style of *Why You Should* was, I think, useful in developing and propagandizing for a new theory; although I hope the present book is readable, its style must be more technical. I wrote *Why You Should* for a wide audience; *Being Good and Being Logical* is unlikely to gain much of an audience outside the philosophical community.

However, I have not written a technical essay in deontic logic; rather, I have tried to provide a philosophical work about the foundations of deontic logic. This book is, as its subtitle suggests, *philosophical groundwork* for a new deontic logic, not a formal presentation of that logic itself. As a groundwork, *Being Good and Being Logical* should be of interest to philosophers in general, as well as to specialists in deontic logic.

Let us then see what logic there is to being good.

Part I

Problems of Standard Deontic Logic

Chapter 1: What Is Deontic Logic, and Why Should I Care?

In this chapter, I shall raise four basic questions about deontic logic. To the first question, I shall try to give a definitive answer. But to the other three, my answers will only be provisional; a full response can only come in the course of this book.

The four questions are:

- What is deontic logic?
- Why should anyone but specialists care about deontic logic?
- Is there any interesting way in which deontic logic diverges from ordinary logic?
- What can philosophers in general, and the author of this book in particular, hope to contribute to the study of deontic logic?

I shall take up these questions in turn.

Deontic logic, as a branch of logic, is the study of those rules and axioms which license a certain class of inferences. Because deontic logic is usually taken as a kind of deductive logic, the licensing procedure takes this form: if the premises of an argument are true, and if the argument is in accordance with the principles of deontic logic, the conclusion of the argument must be true. And for an argument to be in accordance with a set of principles, it cannot be the case that those principles are true and the individual steps in the argument false.[1]

My point in going over this well-trodden ground is that in any area of logic, the concept of truth is fundamental. A valid deductive inference is truth-preserving: the truth of the premises guarantees the truth of the conclusion. Even if someone should suppose deontic logic to be inductive, the concept of truth would still be central; the truth of the premises would establish a high probability that the conclusion is true.

A standard adjunct to any branch of logic is therefore a semantics — that is, a set of truth-conditions for the premises and conclusions that make up arguments. In ordinary propositional logic, the semantics usually employed is Tarski's Convention T: The statement 'S is F' is true if and only if S is F. To check on the truth of ordinary propositions, one need only check on how the world really is. At least in principle, that is easy to do.

But as David Hume observed long ago, it is not as easy as many think to derive an 'ought' from an 'is'. The statements typical of deontic logic concern the acts that people ought or ought not to do, the situations that should or should not exist, the acts that people may or may not do, and the situations that are or are not permissible. If Hume was right, then it is at least difficult and perhaps impossible to come up with actual states of affairs that can serve as truth-conditions for deontic statements.[2] And lacking a semantics, deontic logic would be at best a formal exercise.

Of course, it is open to deontic logicians to claim that certain actual, non-deontically described states of affairs do serve as truth-conditions for deontic statements. But then, the burden of proof is on them to provide such a semantics. And the experience of philosophers has been that Hume's skepticism seems well founded.

The objection to deontic logic that I have just sketched has a close counterpart in crude versions of ethical non-cognitivism. If moral language is no more than a sophisticated expression of people's feelings and attitudes towards other people, actions, and objects, then moral statements are neither true nor false; and being neither true nor false, moral statements admit of no logic.

If there is to be any useful study of deontic logic, then, deontic statements must be capable of being either true or false. That, in turn, means that deontic logic must have a semantics, a set of truth-conditions, that goes beyond Tarski's Convention T.

The development of modal semantics provided a way of escape from skepticism over the very possibility of deontic logic. For as with deontic statements, it is no easy task to come up with actual states of affairs that can serve as truth-conditions for claims about what logically must or can be true. But by allowing themselves to talk of what is the case in other possible worlds, however that talk is to be interpreted, modal logicians broke the impasse holding their subject back. The statement "Necessarily snow is white" is true if and only if snow is white in all possible worlds; the statement "Possibly snow is white" is true if and only if snow is white in some possible world; and the statement "Snow is white" is, as always, true if and only if snow is white in *this* possible world.

Deontic logic beats back its skeptics by employing the same device. "George ought to pay his debts" is true if and only if some state of affairs concerning various possible worlds is the case. A deontic logician will agree with Hume's gloomy assessment of the likelihood of finding truth-conditions for deontic statements in this world; that is why deontic logicians have espoused possible world semantics for their subject.

I shall argue in Chapter 5 that possible world semantics is more than just a convenient way for a deontic logician to respond to a skeptical, Humean objection. Without a possible world semantics, I maintain, deontic logic is literally impossible. But for now, it is enough to suggest that deontic logicians have had good reason to model their subject on modal logic and semantics.

Deontic logic, then, can be set out axiomatically or semantically. If it is set out axiomatically, it consists of a set of axioms and inference-rules, from which a set of theorems can be derived. If it is set out semantically, it consists of a set of relations between deontic statements and facts concerning certain possible worlds. In particular, the facts concerning possible worlds must warrant us fully in accepting the truth of every application of the axioms and theories of the axiomatic system. Thus axiomatics and semantics are connected.

However, in constructing deontic logic along the lines of modal logic, theorists have implicitly raised a point of major philosophical concern. Modal reasoning, like all propositional reasoning, is, in Aristotle's sense, *theoretical*: it is aimed at laying bare what is in fact the case. But much of deontic reasoning is rather *practical*: it is aimed at action, rather than at knowledge. If a form of practical reasoning can actually be construed on a model taken from theoretical reasoning, we are much further than we thought in the development of a truly practical logic.

Suppose that I reason as follows: "I ought to go to the store today; to get there, I can either walk or drive; but for reasons of health I ought not to drive; so I ought to walk to the store today." In this somewhat stilted but surely intelligible piece of reasoning, how should we understand the conclusion? It is an 'ought' statement, like the first premiss, and presumably we could give truth-conditions for it. But it seems more than a statement of fact. It expresses my *intention* to act in a certain way. I might have concluded equally well, "So I'll walk to the store today."

Likewise, if I reason in the same manner that you ought to walk to the store, my conclusion is generally more than just a statement that something is the case. Rather, it has an imperative flavor to it: if you are legally under my command, it would be a bad mistake for you not to walk to the store!

Not every case of deontic reasoning is practical, to be sure. We might reason about what ought to be the case, without any suggestion that you or I or anybody else should act in a certain way. Or we might reason about what people should do or should have done, even though we have no way whatsoever of influencing their actions. Hector, in Shakespeare's *Troilus and Cressida*, argues cogently that the Trojans should give up Helen; then, after announcing that this is in truth Hector's opinion, he advises them not to give her up.

But although not every case of deontic reasoning is practical, many are. Deontic reasoning seems to have a foot in both camps: the theoretical and the practical. And this dual role makes it possible for deontic logic to prove of great philosophical importance, by helping us understand practical reasoning.

We have passed to the second of the four questions with which this chapter began: Why should anyone but specialists care about deontic logic? My answer is that deontic logic gives us our best — in fact, I think, our only — chance of constructing a logic of practical reasoning. In the final chapter of this book, I shall defend this answer against some major objections.

As most philosophers know, Aristotle called attention not only to the theoretical syllogism but to what he called the practical syllogism. Whereas the conclusion of a theoretical syllogism is a statement, Aristotle claimed that the conclusion of a practical syllogism is an action.

Now clearly Aristotle was on to something: people do deliberate what they and others are to do. From our deliberation we reach decisions, form intentions, take action, issue orders. If there are rules to distinguish valid practical arguments from invalid, they would clearly be worth knowing.

Much practical reasoning seems to use counterparts of valid principles of theoretical reasoning. For example:

I must choose either plan of action A or plan of action B.
On balance, B is not as good a plan as A.
Therefore, I choose plan A.

My subordinate, Smith, can work on either the A file or the B project.
Smith's time will be worse spent working on the B project.
Smith, work on the A file.

These are clearly of a kin with examples of the valid theoretical principle:

Either p or q.
Not q.
p.

Hence, these two practical arguments and others like them themselves seem valid. We might generalize that a valid practical argument is one which has a valid theoretical counterpart.

But many of Aristotle's own examples of practical syllogisms lack this whiff of validity (slightly tangier than the odor of sanctity). For example:

I need a cloak.
What I need I can make.
Straightway, I make a cloak.

If this is parallel to any theoretical argument, it is to the invalid argument known as affirming the consequent.[3] And yet, as a *practical* argument, it does not seem that bad. Even worse, some highly dubious practical arguments seem parallel to *valid* theoretical arguments. It is this fact that puts the sting in the various deontic paradoxes. For example:

If you murder Sheila, you should murder her gently.
But you do, in fact, murder Sheila.
Therefore, you should murder Sheila gently.

Obviously, we cannot make the parallel to valid theoretical arguments our criterion of validity in practical arguments.

But finding the criterion of validity in practical arguments is a comparatively minor difficulty. A greater obstacle to finding principles of practical reasoning is that the job of any logic is to preserve truths from premisses to conclusion. If the conclusion of a piece of practical reasoning is an intention, a decision, an order, an entreaty, or an action, the notion of truth is inapplicable to such a conclusion. An action is not a statement, so it cannot be true or false. An order or an entreaty is an imperative statement, again neither true nor false. Statements of one's intention or decision are performatives: to respond "That is true" when someone says "I will drive into the city tomorrow" is to treat the person's statement as a *prediction* of his own actions, not as a statement of his intention. None of these outcomes of practical reasoning can be either true or false; none, therefore, can be truth-preserving. Hence, practical reasoning cannot be valid, at least not in the same way theoretical reasoning can. And since logic is built on the notion of validity, a logic of practical reasoning seems impossible on its face.

But deontic statements offer a way out of the difficulties. "I ought to give her money" and "You may go now" seem, like statements of intention and imperatives, to be *prescriptive*.[4] As such, they can serve as conclusions of practical arguments. One can easily amend my examples of practical arguments to end in deontic conclusions. However, unlike statements of intention and imperatives, deontic statements appear on their face to be capable of being true or false. "Please go now" cannot be true or false, but a speaker might long-windedly replace "You ought to go now" by "It is true that you ought to go now."

It seems, then, that ordinary deductive validity applies to deontic arguments, even though much deontic reasoning is practical. If, then, we can develop a valid deontic logic, its principles will cover a large part of practical reasoning. And perhaps we will have a method, or at least a model, for understanding the rest of practical reasoning.

In the final chapter of this book, I shall look at some difficulties in the argument I have just given. But I shall conclude that my system of deontic logic, NDL, can indeed serve as the basis of a logic of practical reasoning. If I am right, NDL gives us the key to understanding practical reasoning; and that makes deontic logic of concern to philosophers in general.

How important is it to philosophers that we find a logic of practical reasoning? An analogy might help. Some people, I am aware, teach critical thinking without letting students know that such principles as 'Do not affirm the consequent' are more than isolated rules of thumb. The 'rules of thumb' approach to critical thinking can be helpful, but it tends to break down in an unusual situation; and for that matter, many clever students tend to reject a step-by-step cookbook approach. I think the teaching of critical thinking benefits greatly when the teacher shows students that the principles of reasoning they are using form a coherent and consistent system, justifiable as a whole and not merely one by one.

Now in any practical ethics course the teacher's goal is surely to show the students how to apply moral principles to problematic situations — that is, how to engage in a form of practical reasoning. As with critical thinking, the teaching of practical ethics would profit if practical reasoning could be systematized, nor would teachers of practical ethics be so open to the charge of propagandizing for their own moral beliefs. For similar reasons, a systematization of practical reasoning should raise the quality of writing in ethics and other action-centered fields of philosophy. If deontic logic offers us a chance at systematizing practical reasoning, then deontic logic is of vital importance to all philosophers.

There is another reason why philosophers today should be concerned with deontic logic. I argue in the first part of this book that standard versions of deontic logic are at odds in important ways with our actual deontic reasoning. It is the task of Chapters 2 through 10 to reveal the extent of that battle. An examination of the fit between standard deontic logics and ordinary moral thinking shows a need for far-reaching amendments, either in deontic logic or in moral reasoning. Philosophers surely have a major stake in determining where the amendments should come.

Recall the quotation from Nelson Goodman in the introduction to this book. The principles of a logic must be checked against the actual reasonings which people make and think good; but people's reasoning must in turn be checked against the principles which have led to important correct results. This method of mutual adjustment, of reaching what Rawls was to call reflective equilibrium, will have a major role to play in the matter under discussion. If standard deontic logic fits actual deontic reasoning poorly, the chances are that both are in need of adjustment. And the likelihood of major adjustments to patterns of deontic reasoning ought to concern philosophers!

I turn next to the third of our four questions: is there any interesting way in which deontic logic differs from ordinary propositional logic? To answer this, let us look at some pieces of deontic reasoning:

(1) Tamino ought to go through one of the three doors. But he ought not to go through the door on the left, and he ought not to go through the door on the right. Therefore, he ought to go through the door in the middle, the only door remaining.

(2) Jane is monitoring a civil service exam. Her orders tell her she ought to behave as follows: if she sees cheating, to report it at once

to the authorities. She does see a case of cheating. So she ought to report it at once to the authorities.

(3) Pat ought to walk from Athens to Thebes. But necessarily, if a person walks from Athens to Thebes that person walks halfway from Athens to Thebes. Therefore, Pat ought to walk halfway from Athens to Thebes.

(4) There is someone who ought to take out the trash. Therefore, there ought to be someone who takes out the trash.

In case 1, the premisses and conclusion are all 'ought'-statements. In case 2, one premiss and the conclusion are 'ought'-statements, but another premiss is an 'is' statement, a statement of fact. In case 3, one premiss and the conclusion are 'ought'-statements, but another premiss is modal. And in the sole premiss of case 4, an 'ought'-statement occurs within the scope of an existential quantifier; in its conclusion, an existential quantification occurs within the scope of an 'ought' operator. Moreover, 4 infers a statement about what ought to be from a statement about what someone ought to do.

The reasoning in each case is parallel to accepted forms. In case 1, we have Sherlock Holmes's favorite form of propositional reasoning: if you've ruled out all alternatives to a hypothesis, what remains must be true. In case 2, the reasoning looks like good old *modus ponens*. In case 3, the parallel is to a *modus ponens* strengthened by making the conditional statement necessary. As for case 4, it looks like the case in which an existential quantifier precedes a universal quantifier: we can infer that the universal quantifier precedes the existential quantifier but not vice versa.[5] For instance, we can infer "Everyone has a mother" from "Someone is everyone's mother," but not vice versa. However, for all the parallels, there are problems with the reasoning in each of the four cases.

The reasoning in case 1 seems solid enough. Given the conditions of the case, we do think that Tamino ought to go through the remaining door. Nor do there seem any obvious counterexamples to the reasoning in this case. But suppose that we add two conditions: If Tamino does not please Sarastro, it is not the case that Tamino ought to go through the middle door; and Tamino does not in fact please Sarastro. We have now turned Tamino's story into a version of Roderick Chisholm's contrary-to-duty paradox, for we can infer that it is both true and false that Tamino ought to go through the middle door. Adding our two conditions to the original set of premises must have rendered them inconsistent; and yet they do not appear inconsistent.

Case 2 is much the same story. Here most people would indeed conclude that Jane ought to report what she has seen to the authorities at once. But the reasoning gives rise to a host of counterexamples, many of them variants of the well-known 'Good Samaritan' paradox. The law might say that I ought to behave as follows: if I murder Smith, to murder him gently. From that, and from the fact that I do in fact murder Smith, does it follow that I ought to murder Smith gently? Surely not.[6]

In case 3, the conclusion seems all right, if a little odd. Suppose that Pat has taken a vow to walk from Athens to Thebes. Pat has, however, taken no vow to walk halfway from Athens to Thebes. Still, we might well think that if Pat ought to do the first, Pat ought to do the second. But again, counterexamples arise. If we change the second premiss to read, "Necessarily, if Pat walks from Athens to Thebes, Pat has functional legs or prostheses," few would conclude that Pat ought to have functional legs or prostheses. And if the second premiss reads, "Necessarily, if Pat walks from Athens to Thebes, Pat exists," only Pat might conclude that Pat ought to exist.

In case 4, I do not know whether most people would think the inference good, but there are plausible counterexamples. Adolf Eichmann had orders to implement the Final Solution efficiently. Thus there was someone who, under the German chain of command, ought to have committed mass murder, but it is false that there ought to have been someone who committed mass murder.

We can conclude from these four cases that when deontic reasoning parallels accepted forms of standard reasoning, deontic reasoning can be good, bad, or not clearly one or the other. This conclusion holds whether our deontic reasoning uses deontic statements only or whether it mixes them with modal or non-modal propositions; it holds whether we restrict ourselves to unquantified statements or whether we mix in quantifiers.

In short, there is no royal road to deontic logic. We cannot see what works in other branches of logic and apply it to parallel deontic reasoning. That way lies paradox, at best.

It is possible for all I have said that by a judicious choice of predicates and definitions, one can get all the deontic inferences one wants, and none that one does not want, without introducing special rules and operators. But even if so, the step from ordinary logical inferences to their *seeming* deontic parallels would still be barred. Even if all the surprises of deontic logic can ultimately be explained without special rules or operators, those surprises are still there to trap the unwary. Deontic logic is, in a word, *different*.

Finally, deontic logic is a technical field. What can philosophers, as philosophers, hope to contribute to that field? This question takes on significance for me as I am a philosopher who is by no means a specialist in deontic logic. What's in this for me — and what is in my work for anybody else?

The answer should be obvious from earlier parts of this chapter. Philosophy as such gives no particular skill in working out the details of a deontic calculus. But by their examination of actual deontic reasoning, philosophers can help determine which systems of deontic logic are serious candidates for the role of a logic of practical reasoning.

Of course, all sorts of logics are of interest, whether they have practical application or not. But deontic logic promises to be something more than just another set of calculi. It promises to tell us important principles that govern at least a part of our practical reasoning. If that promise is to be fulfilled, more than an internal critique of systems of deontic logic is necessary. We need to know more than a system's consistency or even its completeness; we need also to know how well it corresponds to our reasoning. In determining that last point, the philosopher has an advantage over the specialist in deontic logic.

Or rather, the philosopher has an advantage over many specialists. Thanks, I suspect, to the influence of von Wright, who concentrated on norms as well as on logical calculi, the work of Scandinavian deontic logicians often embodies a lively awareness of the ultimate practical objectives of their subject. My complaint is only that people such as von Wright and Åqvist have not done enough philosophical spadework.

J.L. Austin put best the position I have adopted, in the words that serve as this book's epigraph: "Certainly, then, ordinary language is *not* the last word: in principle it can everywhere be supplemented and improved on and superseded. Only remember, it *is* the *first* word." [Austin, 130; his italics] I take Austin to mean, not that one must begin every investigation with an exhaustive account of the use of words in everyday speech, but rather that such an account is necessary at some point to determine the conditions under which new and supposedly improved theories should be judged.

The subtitle of this book announces that it presents a philosophical groundwork for a new deontic logic. I am trying only to indicate the general lines along which deontic logic should develop; if I am right, there is plenty of work left to do, and there are plenty of logicians more competent than I am to do that work. Philosophers, as such, should not pretend that they can do deontic logic better than can specialists. But they might — and I think I do — have a good and useful grasp of the practical criteria that deontic calculi should meet. Obviously, the proof of that particular pudding can only lie in the eating.

Enough, then, of preliminary questions. It is time to look at standard deontic logic.

Chapter 2: Standard Deontic Logic

As I indicated in the introduction, my chief purpose in this book is to argue for a non-standard deontic logic. In Part I, I shall argue that standard deontic logic (SDL) contains a host of vexing difficulties; a number of these difficulties are internal, such as the paradoxes of deontic reasoning, but I shall discuss most fully those problems which arise from a poor fit between SDL and ordinary deontic reasoning. Then in the second part of the book, I shall present my new deontic logic (NDL), and I shall show that NDL does not suffer from the difficulties that beset SDL. My conclusion will be that NDL is greatly preferable to SDL as a formalization of the principles which govern our ordinary deontic reasoning.

Why spend so much time on SDL, when most deontic logicians have left it behind?[1] There are several reasons. First, not every logician has abandoned SDL; of those who have abandoned it, many have taken up systems which are semantically similar to SDL and which face many of the same problems SDL faces. If SDL collapses under the weight of criticisms, it will take other systems down with it. Second, as we shall see, there is more to be said for SDL than is sometimes supposed. Finally, as I shall be arguing for a completely fresh start in deontic logic, I need first to show that the entire approach of SDL is wrong.

The first goal, then, is to exhibit the difficulties of SDL. In order to do this, I must present SDL itself. That is not so easy a task as one might suppose, for there are many different systems of deontic logic which have been called standard. One of the many virtues of Lennart Åqvist's *Introduction to Deontic Logic and the Theory of Normative Systems* is his systematic presentation of relations and differences among various standard systems. Why one system should be called standard and another not is often hard to determine.

A useful approach is that of Alan Ross Anderson, who spoke of a *normal* deontic logic as one in which certain claims were provable and certain others were not provable. [Anderson 3, 168] Similarly, I shall define a standard system as one in which certain propositions are asserted and certain others are not; in addition, a standard deontic logic has certain typical inference rules. Obviously, neither the list of asserted propositions nor the list of non-asserted propositions is complete. Nor does the list of asserted propositions distinguish between axioms and theorems, for the same assertion can be basic in one system and derived in another.

Systems of deontic logic are usually presented not only axiomatically but also semantically — that is, as a set of truth-conditions. Given those truth-conditions, one can prove that all the axioms and theorems of a system are logically true, as well as that a non-asserted schema comes out false on some interpretation. Standard deontic systems are similar both axiomatically and semantically.

Before listing and explaining the various asserted and non-asserted propositions that define a standard system axiomatically, I need to go over some preliminary ground.

It is typical of standard deontic logics that they express obligation and permission by means of two operators, 'O' and 'P'. These operators have in their scope entire propositions, either simple or complex. Thus, if 'p' stands for "Felix is happy," 'Pp' would stand for "It is permissible that Felix is (or: be) happy" or, more colloquially, "Felix may be happy." Similarly, if 'q' stands for "Jane assists Aaron," then 'Oq' would stand for "Ought (Jane assists Aaron)."

Many standard systems of deontic logic make use only of *unconditional* obligation and permission statements. "Ought (Jane assists Aaron)" is generally understood as "Ought-under-any-conditions (Jane assists Aaron)." Even a system such as Hector-Neri Castañeda's, which indexes the ought-operator to indicate a particular source of obligation, takes obligations to be unconditional. However, in recent years deontic logicians have turned more and more to systems of *conditional* obligation: "Given that condition *a* occurs, Ought (Jane assists Aaron)." I shall count as standard those systems of conditional obligation which assert counterparts to propositions typically asserted in standard unconditional systems, and which do not assert counterparts to propositions typically not asserted in standard unconditional systems. Thus in my reckoning, SDL includes both systems of unconditional and of conditional obligation, although the former will take up the greater part of my discussion.

I noted in the preceding chapter that, for good reason, deontic logic is usually regarded as a variety of modal logic.[2] The particular version of modal logic displayed by most systems of deontic logic is very weak: 'Lp → p' is not a theorem, as it is in the standard modal systems T, S4, and S5. Deontic logic cannot affirm its version of 'Lp → p', because people do not always do what they ought to do, nor is what ought to be always the case.

One result of considering deontic logic a type of modal logic is that the standard deontic logician takes such deontic words as 'ought' and 'may' to be operators, whose scope is a proposition and not merely a predicate. For instance, the sentence "John ought to help Joe" is regarded in standard deontic logic as "Ought (John helps Joe)." I shall argue in Chapter 4 that this reading fails to explain why a person who accepts "John ought to help Joe" as true is committed to the truth of "John exists."

'Ought' in standard deontic logic plays the role of the necessity operator 'L', while 'may' plays the role of the possibility operator 'M'. Now the semantics of modal logic holds that a proposition 'Lp' is true in this world if and only if 'p' is true in all possible and accessible worlds; likewise, 'Mp' is true in this world if and only if 'p' is true in at least one possible and accessible world. It follows from these truth-conditions that 'L' is definable as '~M~' and that 'M' is definable as '~L~'. If deontic logic is a kind of modal logic, we should expect that 'O' and 'P' are interdefinable, and that the semantics of deontic logic follows the pattern of the semantics of modal logic.

However, there are difficulties. First, in any strong modal system, the real world is a possible world, one to which we have access.[3] However, this is not the case in a weak modal system.[4] And in a deontic system, it must not be the case. For if 'Op' is true if and only if 'p' is true in all possible and accessible worlds, and if this is a possible and accessible world, then 'p' must be true in this world — that is, whatever ought to be the case is in fact the case. A logic which makes such an assertion is of no help in practical decision-making, since it suggests that whatever we do, we cannot go wrong. Moreover, if this is a possible and accessible world, every state of affairs in this world is permissible — a highly implausible supposition! But on the other hand, what sense does it make to say that this world is not a possible world, or that we lack access to the world in which we live?

A connected problem arises from taking the operator 'O' to be the necessity operator 'L'. If 'Op' is true, then 'p' is true in all possible and accessible worlds, in which case 'Lp' is true. That is, whatever ought to be is logically necessary. Even if one cannot infer from its necessity the existence of what ought to be, there do seem in the real world to be many alternatives to what ought to be. And once more, what practical value is a logic which tells us that what ought to be is necessary?

Standard deontic logic takes care of these and related problems with one move: the list of possible worlds to be taken into account in deontic semantics is a proper subset of the list of possible worlds to be taken into account in the semantics of a strong modal logic.[5] That is, there is a certain characteristic shared by some but not all possible worlds accessible to this one. 'Op' is true if and only if 'p' is true in all possible and accessible worlds *that have the given characteristic*; 'Pp' is true if and only if 'p' is true in at least one possible and accessible world *that has the given characteristic*. Because not all possible and accessible worlds have the given characteristic, it is not the case that 'Op → Lp'. And if we assume that the real world lacks the given characteristic, then the real world is not, for the purposes of deontic semantics, a possible world accessible to itself. I shall speak of possible and accessible worlds which have the given characteristic as *deontically accessible*. In what follows, when I use the phrases 'possible worlds' and 'possible and accessible worlds' to speak of the worlds considered in deontic semantics, my phrases are meant to refer only to possible and deontically accessible worlds. Worlds which lack the given characteristic I shall call *deontically inaccessible*, or *inaccessible* for short.

SDL semantics, then, is a modal semantics with a restriction on the group of possible and accessible worlds. Different versions of SDL semantics employ different characteristics to restrict the group of worlds. Some versions talk of *optimal* worlds, others of *permissible* worlds. One pioneer of SDL semantics, K. Jaakko J. Hintikka, spoke of *deontic alternative* worlds, worlds in which everyone does everything that he or she ought to do. [Hintikka 1, 185] So long as a deontic logic employs a semantics that limits the group of worlds under consideration to a proper subset of all possible and accessible worlds, but that otherwise follows the usual conditions of modal semantics, I shall say that the deontic logic employs a standard semantics.[6]

In putting forward typical rules and theorems of standard deontic logics, I shall indicate how these rules and theorems follow from SDL semantics. My purpose is to provide an early indication of a point I shall argue at length in Chapter 5: standard deontic logic is closely tied to SDL semantics; the two stand or fall together.[7] Since, as I shall argue in

Chapters 6-8, there are major objections to SDL semantics, we should expect those objections to raise difficulties for standard deontic logics.[8]

There are other consequences of regarding deontic logic as a weak modal logic. First, standard deontic logic incorporates the propositional calculus (PC): all well-formed formulae (wffs) of PC are wffs of SDL, all asserted propositions of PC are asserted propositions of SDL, and all inference rules of PC are inference rules of SDL. Second, standard deontic logic makes no distinction between 'ought to be' and 'ought to do' sentences. Whether "Ought (Jane assists Aaron)" should be understood as "It ought to be that Jane assists Aaron" or as "Jane ought to assist Aaron," SDL typically does not decide. Rather, it tacitly supposes that an 'ought to do' proposition and its parallel 'ought to be' statement are e-quivalent in meaning. In Chapter 4, I shall argue that a deontic logic which fails to distinguish 'ought to do' statements from 'ought to be' statements has gone badly wrong from the start.

With these preliminary points in mind, let us look at some assertions and inference rules typical of standard deontic logics. (I shall not include assertions and rules which SDL takes over from the propositional calculus.) For the reader's convenience, the complete list of typical assertions and inference rules of SDL is reprinted in Appendix 1, where SDL is compared point by point with my new deontic logic (NDL).

I begin with the conditions of SDL semantics:

SDLS1. If 'Op' is true in this world, 'p' is true in all possible and accessible worlds.

SDLS2. If 'p' is true in all possible and accessible worlds, 'Op' is true in this world.

SDLS3. If 'Pp' is true in this world, 'p' is true in at least one possible and accessible world.

SDLS4. If 'p' is true in at least one possible and accessible world, 'Pp' is true in this world.

SDLS5. Every possible world is in fact accessible to at least one possible world.[9]

Next, I list some propositions generally asserted in SDL:

SDLT1. $\sim(Op.O\sim p)$.

SDLT2. $O(p \rightarrow q) \rightarrow (Op \rightarrow Oq)$.

SDLT3. $O(p.q) \rightarrow (Op.Oq)$.

SDLT4. (Op.Oq) → O(p.q).
SDLT5. ~O(p.~p).
SDLT6. O(p v ~p).
SDLT7. Op ↔ ~P~p.
SDLT8. Pp ↔ ~O~p.
SDLT9. Op → Pp.

Next come two propositions that most SDL systems should assert:

SDLT10. OOp ↔ Op.
SDLT11. O(Op → p).

Next come four rules common in SDL:

SDLR1. If 'p ↔ q' is a theorem, and if '. . . p . . .' is a theorem, then '. . . q . . .', the result of uniformly replacing 'p' by 'q' in '. . . p . . .', is a theorem.
SDLR2. $\dfrac{\vdash p}{\vdash Op}$.
SDLR3. $\dfrac{\vdash p \rightarrow q}{\vdash Op \rightarrow Oq}$.
SDLR4. $\dfrac{\vdash p \leftrightarrow q}{\vdash Op \leftrightarrow Oq}$.

Finally, the following propositions are *not* asserted in SDL:

SDLX1. p → Pp.
SDLX2. Pp → p.
SDLX3. p → Op.
SDLX4. Op → p.
SDLX5. O(p v q) → (Op v Oq).
SDLX6. (Pp.Pq) → P(p.q).

I shall start our look at these propositions and rules with the five conditions of SDL semantics. After presenting some typical assertions of SDL, I shall discuss how these assertions follow from SDL semantics. After doing the same for SDL inference rules, I shall show that statements usually not asserted in SDL do not follow from SDL semantics.

The first four rules of SDL semantics provide a relation between the truth in this world of statements beginning with a deontic operator and the

truth in deontically accessible worlds of those statements minus their
initial operators. SDLS1 and SDLS2 have to do with oughts, while
SDLS3 and SDLS4 concern what is permissible.

SDLS1 asserts that an ought-statement, 'Op', is true only if the
statement 'p' is true in all deontically accessible worlds. SDLS1 then
licenses an inference from an explicitly deontic premiss 'Op' to a possibly
non-deontic conclusion, taken as holding in a set of worlds. Such
inferences are crucial if deontic arguments are to proceed. For instance,
suppose that we are given as premisses 'O(p → q)' and 'Op'. Lacking any
special rules for operating within the scope of deontic operators, we
cannot go forward. But in virtue of SDLS1, we can infer that both 'p →
q' and 'p' hold in all deontically accessible worlds, from which we infer
by *modus ponens* that 'q' holds in all deontically accessible worlds. I
shall refer to SDLS1 as a *principle of forward translation*.

However, in the sample inference I am discussing, it is unlikely that we
will be content with the conclusion that 'q' holds in all deontically
accessible worlds. If we started with deontic premisses, we are probably
looking for a deontic conclusion. We therefore need what I shall call a
principle of backward translation, to enable us to translate from claims
about what is true in deontically accessible worlds to deontic statements.
SDLS2 is a principle of backward translation, for it provides that if a
statement 'p' is true in all deontically accessible worlds, 'Op' is true in
this world. In our sample inference, we started with premisses 'O(p → q)'
and 'Op', and we inferred that 'q' was true in all deontically accessible
worlds. Now SDLS2 allows us to carry the inference one more step, to
'Oq'.

One might reasonably suppose that SDLS3 is a principle of forward
translation, SDLS4 a principle of backward translation. For SDLS3
asserts that a permissibility-statement, 'Pp', is true only if 'p' is true in at
least one deontically accessible worlds; and SDLS4 provides that if a
statement 'p' is true in at least one deontically accessible world, 'Pp' is
true in this world. Thus SDLS3 is the counterpart for permission
statements of the forward-translation principle SDLS1, while SDLS4 is
the counterpart of the backward-translation principle SDLS2. However,
in fact SDLS3 is a principle of backward and SDLS4 of forward
translation. For by SDLT7 and SDLT8, 'Pp' = '~O~p' and 'Op' =
'~P~p'. According to SDLS2, if 'p' is true in all deontically accessible
worlds, 'Op' is true in this world. Hence, if '~p' is true in all deontically

accessible worlds, 'O~p' is true in this world. By contraposition, if '~O~p' is true in this world, it is not the case that '~p' is true in all deontically accessible worlds. Therefore, if 'Pp' is true in this world, there is at least one deontically accessible world in which 'p' is true; and this is SDLS3. Conversely, SDLS3 holds that if 'Pp' is true in this world, 'p' is true in some deontically accessible world. It is then false that '~p' is true in all deontically accessible worlds. By substitution, it follows that if P~p, it is not the case that 'p' is true in all deontically accessible worlds. Hence, if 'p' is true in all deontically accessible worlds, '~P~p' — i.e., 'Op' — is true in this world; and that is SDLS2. Thus, since SDL asserts SDLT7 and SDLT8, SDLS3 is logically equivalent to SDLS2, a principle of backward translation. By similar reasoning, SDLS4 is logically equivalent to SDLS1. Hence, I shall call SDLS4 a principle of forward translation and SDLS3 a principle of backward translation.[10]

Any useful deontic semantics needs at least one forward-translation principle and at least one backward-translation principle. However, one can use *reductio ad absurdum* to establish certain conclusions without backward translation. For example, consider SDLT1: ~(Op.O~p). If SDLT1 is not asserted, then it might be the case that Op.O~p, whence Op and O~p. By SDLS1, both 'p' and '~p' would be true in all deontically accessible worlds; which is absurd. Thus SDLT1 can be proved without using principles of backward translation. But most semantic arguments for deontic principles require both forward translation, to allow us to use the semantics, and backward translation, to enable us to determine what deontic claims hold in this world.

In the argument of the last paragraph, there is a large gap. It is absurd that both 'p' and '~p' are true in all deontically accessible worlds only if there is at least one such world. If there are no D-type worlds, then any statements, including contradictory ones, are true in all D-type worlds. Hence, ordinary deontic semantics, to be useful, must contain a statement that in the real world, at least, at least one possible world is deontically accessible.

SDLS5 provides that needed statement. By supposing that at least one world is deontically accessible to every world, SDLS5 automatically assures that some world is deontically accessible to this one. By making no specific mention of the real world, SDLS5 allows us to use deontic statements supposed to be true of other possible worlds. Thus SDLS5 lets us consider what we should have done had conditions been different.

So much for standard semantical principles. We turn next to some typical asserted propositions of SDL.

SDLT1 says that for any proposition 'p', not both ought-p and ought-not-p. This is equivalent to saying that for any proposition 'p', either it is permissible that p or it is permissible that not-p. SDLT1 thus rules out the possibility of a person's being stuck in a dilemma where neither any action nor the failure to act is permissible.

SDLT2 asserts that for any propositions 'p' and 'q', if 'p' and 'if p then q' are both obligatory, so is 'q'. For instance, suppose that Smith should behave as follows: if Smith concedes the election to her opponent, she makes a gracious speech. SDLT2 says that if in fact Smith should concede the election to her opponent, then she should make a gracious speech.

SDLT3 and SDLT4 are often combined into a biconditional: 'O(p.q) ⟷ (Op.Oq)'. SDLT3 says that if the conjunction of 'p' and 'q' is obligatory, then both 'p' and 'q' are separately obligatory; SDLT4 says that if 'p' and 'q' are separately obligatory, so is their conjunction. SDLT3 supposes that if John has the duty to perform a pair of actions, he has a duty to perform the first and a duty to perform the second. SDLT4 supposes that if Jane has a pair of duties, she has a single duty to perform a pair of actions.

SDLT5 and SDLT6 are counterparts: SDLT5 denies that one ought to do the logically impossible, while SDLT6 affirms that one ought to do the logically necessary. SDLT5, often known as Kant's Principle, may also be taken as denying that a logically impossible situation ever ought to be. On either reading, the notion of *logical* impossibility needs to be stressed: for all that SDLT5 tells us, one might have duties to do what one is physically unable to do.

SDLT6 says that for any proposition 'p', it is obligatory that either p or not-p. That is, it ought to be the case that either a particular state of affairs or its absence holds; one ought so to act that one either performs or refrains from a given action. On either of those understandings, SDLT6 has little content: for it must be the case that either a particular state of affairs or its absence holds; and one must either perform or refrain from a given action. SDLT6 then says only that a logically necessary state of affairs is obligatory. It should not be confused with the proposition that either one ought to perform a certain action or one ought to refrain from that action. We shall see that SDL does not assert the latter proposition, which would rule out the possibility of morally indifferent acts.

SDLT7, SDLT8, and SDLT9 are all concerned with the relations between the ought-operator and the permissibility-operator. SDLT7 says that if 'p' is obligatory, then '~p' is not permissible. That is, if I ought to do something, it is not permissible for me to fail to do that thing. SDLT8 says that if 'p' is permissible, '~p' is not obligatory — i.e., if it is permissible for me to do something, I am not obligated to fail to do it. And SDLT9 says simply that what is obligatory is permissible. Combining SDLT8 and SDLT9, one can say that if a state of affairs ought to be, it is not the case that the state ought not to be: what is obligatory is not prohibited.

SDLT10 asserts that something ought to be obligatory if and only if it is obligatory. For instance, if it ought to be that Smith have the obligation of helping the sick, Smith has that obligation; and if he really does have that obligation, then that's the way it should be. SDLT11, in turn, asserts that it ought to be that whatever is obligatory is in fact the case.

Having looked at nine typical — and two fairly typical — assertions of SDL, let us see how they fall out of SDL semantics.

By SDLS1, 'Op' is true only if 'p' is true in every possible and accessible world. Hence, if 'O~p' is true, '~p' is true in every possible and accessible world. And if 'Op.O~p' is true, then 'p' would be both true and false in every possible and accessible world. Since, by SDLS5, there is such a world, this is absurd. Therefore, SDLT1 is a consequence of SDL semantics.

So are SDLT2, SDLT3, and SDLT4. Assume that O(p → q) and Op. Then by SDLS1, 'p → q' and 'p' are both true in all possible and deontically accessible worlds. Hence, in each possible and deontically accessible world, 'p' and 'p → q' are both true; so that in each such world, 'q' is true. Since by SDLS5 there is at least one such world, by SDLS2 'Oq' follows. By discharging of premises, SDLT2 follows.

Likewise, assume that 'O(p.q)' is true. Then by SDLS1, 'p.q' is true in every possible and accessible world. Hence, 'p' is true in every such world, and 'q' is true in every such world, and there is at least one such world; hence, by SDLS2, Op and Oq. Therefore, O(p.q) → (Op.Oq), and this is SDLT3. Assume in turn that 'Op.Oq' is true. Since 'Op' and 'Oq' are both true, by SDLS2 'p' and 'q' are true in all possible and deontically accessible worlds, of which at least one exists; in which case 'p.q' is true

in all such worlds. Hence, 'O(p.q)' follows by SDLS1 and '(Op.Oq) →
O(p.q)' follows by conditionalization; and this is SDLT4.

SDLT5, Kant's Principle, and its companion SDLT6 also follow from
SDL semantics. For a logical contradiction is true in no possible world,
by the very meaning of 'possible world'. Hence, it is false that 'p.~p'
holds in all possible and accessible worlds — so long as there is at least
one such world. But there is at least one such world, by SDLS5;
therefore, it is false that O(p.~p)— and this is SDLT5. Again, 'p v ~p' is
logically necessary, therefore true in all possible worlds, therefore true in
all possible and deontically accessible worlds. Since there is at least one
such world, by SDLS1 'O(p v ~p)' follows.

SDLT7, SDLT8, and SDLT9 also derive from normal deontic
semantics. Assume Op and ~P~p. By SDLS1, 'p' is true in every
possible and deontically accessible world; by SDLS3, it is not the case
that there is a possible and accessible world in which '~p' is true. 'Op'
and '~P~p' therefore say the same thing, as long as there is at least one
deontically accessible world. Since SDLS5 guarantees that there is,
SDLT7 follows. Again, assume Pp and ~O~p. Then there is at least one
possible and deontically accessible world in which 'p' holds; and it is not
the case that in every accessible world, '~p' holds. Since there is at least
one deontically accessible world, 'Pp' and '~O~p' say the same thing;
and SDLT8 follows from SDL semantics. Neither SDLT7 nor SDLT8
would follow from the semantics without SDLS5.

SDLT9's dependence on the principle that there is at least one
accessible world is also straightforward. If 'Op' is true, then by SDLS1
'p' is true in all accessible worlds. Then 'p' is true in at least one deontically accessible world — so long as there is at least one such world. By
SDLS5, then, 'Pp' is true, and SDLT9 follows.

SDLT10 is a consequence of any SDL semantics that allows iterated
modalities.[11] A standard system need not assert SDLT10 — or SDLT11,
for that matter — for one might rule that the deontic operator 'O' can
prefix only atomic propositions and truth-functional compounds of atomic
propositions. But without such a ruling, any standard system should
assert SDLT10 and SDLT11.

The expression 'OOp' might seem hard to make sense of, but if we take
one step at a time, SDL semantics makes the job easy. If we read the
expression as 'O(Op)' and apply SDLS1, we find that 'Op' holds in all

worlds which are deontically accessible to a given world w_0. Let us call the worlds deontically accessible to w_0 *worlds of range 1*, and let us take w_1 as any world of range 1. Then 'Op' holds in w_1. But by a second application of SDLS1, we infer that 'p' holds in all worlds which are deontically accessible to w_1. Call those worlds which are deontically accessible to worlds of range 1 *worlds of range 2*; then w_2, a world of range 2, is deontically accessible to a world deontically accessible to w_0. The semantic translation of 'OOp' is therefore: 'p' is true in all worlds of range 2.

With this translation, SDLT10 is plausible. If OOp, then 'p' is true in all worlds of range 2. But since all and only worlds of range 2 are deontically accessible to worlds of range 1, by SDLS2 'Op' is true in all worlds of range 1. But all worlds of range 1 are themselves deontic accessible to w_0; on one definition of 'deontically accessible', all inhabitants of any deontically accessible world always do everything they ought to do. If people in w_1 ought to do something, then they do it in w_1. But if 'p' is true in all range 1 worlds, then 'Op' is true in w_0. A conditionalization step leads to the following conclusion:

SDLIa: ⊢ OOp → Op.

Hence an expression prefixed by two or more 'ought' operators in SDL implies the same expression prefixed by a single operator.

However, the argument for SDLIa contains an ambiguous step: do all residents of w_1 do all they ought-in-w_1, or do they do all they ought-in-w_0? The argument for SDLIa requires that they do all they ought-in-w_1, but all that seems justified is that they do all they ought-in-w_0. The answer is that people in w_1 do as they should both in their own world and in w_0. For if people in w_1 do not act as they should-in-w_0, then their actions in w_1 are irrelevant to obligations in w_0. And if people in w_1 do not act as they should-in-w_1, it is hard to see how their actions, which are contrary to duty, could be of use in determining what anyone ought to do in w_0. If they fail either in duties in w_0 or in duties in w_1, they are bad models for the inhabitants of w_0 to follow. Hence, SDL semantics implies that deontically accessible worlds contain obligations which their inhabitants constantly fulfill, and SDLIa is a consequence of SDL semantics.[12]

By the same reasoning, the converse of SDLIa also follows from SDL semantics. For if 'Op' is true in w_0, 'p' is true in all worlds of range 1.

But the worlds of range 1 are alike only in that the inhabitants of each such world do all that they ought to do — that is, all they ought in w_0 as well as all they ought in their own world. Therefore, since 'p' is true in all worlds of range 1, 'Op' is also true in all such worlds. But in that case, 'p' is true in all worlds of range 2, and by backward translation 'OOp' follows. By conditionalization, we have the principle:

SDLIb: ⊢ Op → OOp.

Putting SDLIa and SDLIb together, we have ⊢ Op ↔ OOp — which is SDLT10.

If our deontic alternative worlds are defined as *optimal worlds* rather than as worlds where all people always do as they ought, SDLT10 still follows from standard semantics. For if a world w_1 accessible to us is optimal, clearly it is an optimal world accessible to itself; and therefore what is true in all optimal worlds accessible to w_1 is true in w_1. Therefore, SDLIa follows. Suppose again that 'p' is true in all optimal worlds accessible to us. Since those worlds are optimal, the fact that 'p' obtains in each of those worlds must be part of what makes them optimal. In that case, 'Op' is true in each such world; and SDLIb follows.

The argument for SDLT11 is much easier. Arthur N. Prior considered SDLT11 intuitively correct.[13] Ruth Barcan Marcus, on the other hand, argued that the supposed principle is simply confused: 'Op → p' describes a state of affairs, while the operator prefixed to 'Op → p' is supposed to prescribe an action. [Marcus, 580] My purpose here is to show that standard deontic systems should assert SDLT11, if their formation rules allow iterated deontic modalities. For if we define deontically accessible worlds as worlds in which all people always do what they ought, by definition whatever is obligatory in a deontically accessible world is the case in that world. If instead we define deontically accessible worlds as optimal worlds, so that 'ought' means 'productive of optimality', surely it would produce optimality if whatever would produce optimality actually existed. On either version of SDL semantics, then, we can use SDLS2 to infer that it ought to be that whatever is obligatory is true.

Therefore, given SDL semantics, all nine typical and both not-so-typical asserted propositions must hold. I turn next to typical inference rules of SDL.

SDLR1 is a version of an inference rule used by von Wright and later by al-Hibri.[14] Although it looks like a harmless substitution rule, it permits substituting for non-atomic compounds as well as for individual sentence-letters in theorems. One must remember as well that SDLR1 allows us to substitute equals for equals within contexts introduced by deontic operators. If such contexts are intensional, as I shall argue in Chapter 5, substituting equivalents will not always preserve truth. Perhaps for that reason, most deontic logicians have preferred to replace SDLR1 with inference rules that do not explicitly beg the question of intensionality.

The simplest such rule, SDLR2, has been called the rule of O-necessitation. From the fact that 'p' is an assertion, we can derive that 'Op' is asserted. For example, 'p v ~p' is a theorem of the propositional calculus, and hence of SDL. Hence, by SDLR2, 'O(p v ~p)' is asserted in SDL. And indeed it is: namely, as SDLT6.

With SDLR3, matters grow a bit more complicated. This rule states that from the fact that 'p → q' is a theorem, we can derive that 'Op → Oq' is a theorem. For an illustration, consider a variant of the one just given: 'p → p' is a theorem of the propositional calculus and hence of SDL. By SDLR3, then, 'Op → Op' is an assertion. And of course it is, being a substitution instance of 'p → p'.

SDLR4 adds to the complications. By SDLR4, from the fact that 'p ↔ q' is a theorem we can derive that 'Op ↔ Oq' is a theorem. Clearly, if a system includes SDLR3, it does not need SDLR4, which can be broken into a pair of uses of SDLR3; but it is not immediately obvious whether every system which employs SDLR4 can get along without SDLR3 or an equivalent (such as the combination of SDLT2 with *modus ponens*). To illustrate SDLR4, I note that 'p ↔ p' is a theorem of the propositional calculus; whence, by SDLR4, 'Op ↔ Op' is an assertion of SDL. And, of course, it is, since it is only a substitution instance of the theorem 'p ↔ p'.

Next we look at SDL inference rules as consequences of SDL semantics. With SDLR1, the substitution rule, no difficulty arises. Let 'O(. . . p . . .)' be a context introduced by the deontic operator 'O' and containing no other operators, and let 'p ↔ q' be a theorem. Then by SDLS1, ' . . . p . . .' is true in all deontically accessible worlds, and by SDLS5 there is at least one such world. Since ' . . . p . . .' contains no operators, in each deontically accessible world ' . . . p . . .' is extensional, and 'q' can be substituted for 'p' *salva veritate*. Hence ' . . . q . . .' is true in each deontically accessible world, and therefore, by SDLS2, it follows that O(. . . q . . .). A similar argument holds for contexts introduced by

'P'; and contexts in SDL not within the scope of deontic operators are extensional, and substitution of equals for equals should preserve truth. Thus SDL semantics supports SDLR1.

Of the three remaining inference rules for SDL, SDLR2, the rule of O-necessitation, is the most easy and obvious. From the fact that 'p' is a theorem, it is clear that 'p' is necessarily true. In that case, 'p' is true in all accessible worlds and hence in all deontically accessible worlds. Therefore, by SDLS2, 'Op' is true.

SDLR3 is almost as obvious. From the fact that 'p → q' is a theorem, it follows that 'p → q' is true in all accessible and hence all deontically accessible worlds. Now on the assumption that 'Op' is true, SDLS1 assures us that 'p' is true in all deontically accessible worlds. By *modus ponens*, 'q' is true in all deontically accessible worlds, and by SDLS5 there are such worlds. Hence, by SDLS2, 'Oq' is true, and by conditionalization, so is 'Op → Oq'.

As for SDLR4, we have no need to derive it separately from SDL semantics. For from 'p ↔ q' we can derive 'p → q' and 'q → p', whence by SDLR3 'Op → Oq' and 'Oq → Op', whence truth-functionally 'Op ↔ Oq'. Thus if SDLR3 follows from SDL semantics, so does SDLR4.

Therefore, all the typical theorems and rules of SDL are logical consequences of SDL semantics. If even one of these theorems and rules is unacceptable, so is SDL semantics.

Next, let us turn to the group of propositions that SDL does *not* assert. Obviously, in any logic there is a never-ending list of propositions that are not theorems; the list I have given contains only propositions that some might be tempted to assert. But SDL does not assert them, with good reason.

Take for instance SDLX1: p → Pp. This is not to be confused with an inference rule which would derive '⊢Pp' from '⊢p'. That rule is in fact valid in SDL, for it is easily derived from SDLR2 and SDLT9. But the proposition 'p → Pp' is not valid in SDL. For nothing in SDL semantics requires that every world is deontically accessible to itself or another world. Therefore, there might be a deontically inaccessible world w_1 (for instance, the real world) and a proposition 'p' such that both 'p' and 'O~p' are true in w_1. By SDLT8, then, both 'p' and '~Pp' are true in w_1; in which case there would be at least one world in which 'p → Pp' does not hold. Therefore, 'p → Pp' cannot be asserted in SDL.

Next, consider SDLX2: Pp → p. This proposition, the converse of SDLX1, is also not asserted in SDL. For take two worlds w_1 and w_2, such that w_2 is deontically accessible to w_1; and let 'p' be true in w_2 but false in w_1. Then in w_1 'Pp' is true and 'p' false, in which case 'Pp → p' is false in at least one world. Hence, 'Pp → p' cannot be asserted in SDL.

SDLX3 looks like the rule of O-necessitation, SDLR2, but SDLX3 is clearly not asserted in SDL. For suppose that it is asserted. By substitution, '~p → O~p' follows, whence by contraposition ~O~p → p. By SDLT8, there follows 'Pp → p', which is SDLX2. Hence, if SDLX3 is asserted, so is SDLX2; since SDLX2 is not asserted, by *modus tollens* neither is SDLX3.

A similar argument takes care of SDLX4, 'Op → p'. If it were asserted in SDL, then by substitution 'O~p → ~p' would hold; and so, by contraposition, would 'p → ~O~p'. By SDLT8 there follows 'p → Pp', or SDLX1. Since SDLX1 is not asserted in SDL, neither is SDLX4.

The last two unasserted propositions are not as blatantly off-base as the four that preceded them. SDLX5, especially, might look like common sense: if you ought to do one of two things, then either you should do the first or you should do the second. And it looks reasonable to suppose that if each of two acts is permissible, one may do them both. But common sense quickly runs into problems with these two propositions. Suppose, first, that I am obligated to choose between two alternatives; but the alternative that I pick is a matter of complete indifference. Then SDLX5 would be false. Suppose again that you are permitted to talk to John, but only if you do not divulge club secrets; and you are permitted to divulge club secrets, but only if you do not talk to John. Then both talking to John and divulging club secrets are separately permissible but not jointly so, and SDLX6 is false.

SDLX5 does not follow from SDL semantics. For if O(p v q), by SDLS1, 'p v q' is true in all deontically accessible worlds. This is compatible with there being at least one deontically accessible world, w_1, in which 'p' is true and 'q' false, and another deontically accessible world, w_2, in which 'p' is false and 'q' true. If w_1 and w_2 exist, neither 'Op' nor 'Oq' would be true, in which case 'Op v Oq' would not be true. Hence, we cannot assert in SDL that 'O(p v q) → (Op v Oq)'.

SDLX5 is logically equivalent to SDLX6, given SDLT7 and SDLT8.[15] Because SDLX5 cannot be asserted in SDL, neither can SDLX6. Thus

SDL is both internally consistent and externally true to our notions of good deontic reasoning in rejecting this pair of propositions.

That concludes my general survey of what SDL typically does and does not assert. To be sure, an axiomatic system is not just a set of isolated assertions. In any such system, some assertions are axioms, while others are theorems proved from the axioms by means of the inference rules. Now there are different ways to axiomatize SDL. But it is important for us to take one more look at the assertions and inference rules typical of SDL, to indicate some of the inferential relations that hold among them.[16]

The reason why this is important is no mystery. Suppose that if we assume Assertion A and Rule B, we can prove Assertion C. Suppose also that on independent grounds, we show that Assertion C is false. In that case, either Assertion A or Rule B, or both, must be false.

For example, if we take SDLT1 and SDLT3 as axioms, by substituting '~p' for 'q' in SDLT3, we have both '~(Op.O~p)' and 'O(p.~p) ⊃ (Op.O~p)'; whence, by *modus tollens*, we get '~O(p.~p)'. This is SDLT5, Kant's Principle. Now if we have independent reason to reject SDLT5, we must reject at least one of SDLT1 and SDLT3, the pair of axioms from which SDLT5 follows.[17]

Again, take as axioms SDLT6, SDLT8, and SDLT9. Since by SDLT6 'O(p v ~p)' is an assertion, by SDLT9 so is 'P(p v ~p)'; in which case, by SDLT8, '~O~(p v ~p)' is an assertion. Truth-functional rules therefore allow us to assert '~O(p.~p)', which is Kant's Principle, SDLT5. Hence, if we reject SDLT5, we must reject at least one of the trio SDLT6, SDLT8, and SDLT9.

Arguments against Kant's Principle, of which there have been many in recent years, are then much more than attacks on a single isolated claim of standard deontic logic. They are implicitly attacks on large portions of SDL. We shall look at some of these attacks on Kant's Principle in Chapter 3.

But first, we need to look at more of the logical relations among assertions and inference rules. Take first the SDL inference rules. If we assume SDLR1, SDLR3, and SDLT4, we can derive SDLR3. [al-Hibri, 12] Similarly, if we assume SDLR2 and SDLT2, it is easy to derive SDLR3. And given SDLR3, SDLR4 is obvious. Hence, systems that contain either SDLR1, SDLR3, and SDLT4 or SDLR2 and SDLT2 do not need SDLR3 or SDLR4 as original inference rules.

Versions of SDL have usually taken as axioms either SDLT3 and SDLT4 or SDLT2. For instance, von Wright and al-Hibri assume SDLT3 and SDLT4, from which they prove SDLT2. [al-Hibri, 13] On the other hand, the ten Smiley-Hanson systems considered by Åqvist in Chapter 3 of his *Introduction to Deontic Logic and the Theory of Normative Systems* assume SDLT2 and prove SDLT3 and SDLT4. [Åqvist 2, 90]

SDLT1 is an axiom in most versions of SDL, while SDLT5, Kant's Principle, is usually derived. However, a system that assumes SDLT4 can easily derive SDLT1 from an axiomatic SDLT5.

SDLT6 is not always an axiom of SDL, for it is an obvious consequence of the rule of ought-necessitation, SDLR2. But not all versions of SDL contain SDLR2; those that do not generally contain SDLT6,

SDLT7, SDLT8, and SDLT9 are often part of the definitions of 'ought' and 'permissible', not assertions of SDL.

In general, then, it seems that the crucial assertions of SDL, the assertions from which most theorems are derived, are SDLT1, SDLR1, SDLR2, and either the pair SDLT3 and SDLT4, or SDLT2. In Chapter 3, I shall look at some assaults on these crucial assertions.

But this chapter's look at SDL has yielded a further inference, which will be programmatic for much of the first part of this book. All the rules and typical assertions of SDL follow from SDL semantics. If, then, any portion whatsoever of SDL is to be rejected, so must SDL semantics. At least one of the five principles, SDLS1 through SDLS5, must be in error.

Suppose, on the other hand, that we discover independent problems in SDL semantics. Our discoveries do not rule out the possibility that the assertions and rules of SDL are valid; for the correct deontic semantics might, for all we know, imply SDL. But even if this outcome is logically possible, it is far more likely that a non-standard semantics will imply a non-standard deontic logic. In my new deontic logic, we will see this to be the case. That, however, is the work of Part II of this book; the task of the rest of Part I is to set out problems of SDL.

Chapter 3: What Is Left for Deontic Logic?

My purpose in this chapter is to look at some fairly familiar objections to a group of principles of Standard Deontic Logic. We shall look first at objections to SDLT5, Kant's Principle. Those in turn help generate objections to SDLT3, SDLT4, and SDLR3. I shall next look briefly at how similar objections can be made to SDLT6, SDLT2, SDLR4, and SDLR2, as well as to some non-standard systems of deontic logic. That I do not discuss other SDL principles in this chapter by no means indicates that I find those principles correct.

The arguments of this chapter are only preliminary. They all point to ways in which SDL appears to deviate from ordinary deontic reasoning. But, as I shall argue in setting up my new deontic logic, some of the deviations require only that we add a few conditions to SDL principles. And in any event, deviations from ordinary reasoning are the usual price for formalization of reasoning; adherents of SDL can easily claim that the price is in this instance not too high. Hence, to reject standard deontic logics, we need much more than the arguments of this chapter.

I begin, immodestly enough, with my own work. In a recent paper, "Conflicts of Obligation," I argued that whatever one might think about the status of moral dilemmas, there is no good reason to doubt that non-moral obligations can and often do genuinely conflict. [J. Forrester 3, *passim*] However, standard deontic logic rules out the possibility of any conflicts of obligation. For SDLT1 explicitly forbids this possibility; and, as I noted in Chapter 2, SDLT4 and SDLT5 together imply SDLT1 and thus the impossibility of conflicts of obligation. Similarly SDLT8 and SDLT9 together imply SDLT1.

As a colleague of mine has often remarked, one person's *modus ponens* is another's *modus tollens*. I noted in "Conflicts of Obligation" that some philosophers have made use of principles of standard deontic logic to argue against the possibility of moral dilemmas. But if there are in fact any irresoluble conflicts of obligation, the argument cuts in quite a different direction. For if the principles of standard deontic logic rule out not only moral dilemmas but all irresoluble conflicts of obligation, and if there are irresoluble conflicts of obligation, the principles of standard deontic logic must be false. In particular, SDLT1 is unacceptable, as are either SDLT4 or SDLT5 and either SDLT8 or SDLT9. Moreover, since these false principles follow from SDL semantics, that semantics is itself false.

There are two circumstances in which we would declare a set of principles false: the set might be internally inconsistent or inconsistent with established logical principles; or the set might, in a given interpretation, yield false results. It is the latter fault that I am attributing to standard deontic logic: "[B]ecause standard deontic logics cannot allow for irresoluble conflicts of obligation, standard deontic logics are inadequate accounts of our deontic beliefs and practices." [J. Forrester 3, 41]

SDL's refusal to allow for irresoluble conflicts of obligation is a relatively small departure from normal usage. Logicians have reconciled themselves to the differences between the ordinary reading of "if . . . then" and the version adopted by the propositional calculus — surely a much greater deviation from ordinary speech. But unnecessary deviations from normal usage are to be avoided: if we can find an acceptable system of deontic logic that allows for irresoluble conflicts of obligation, we should choose that alternative system.

We can draw the same moral from my book *Why You Should*. There I argued that the pragmatics of deontic speech rested on a group of eighteen maxims, which together gave content to the notion of rationality in deontic speech. Persons who follow the eighteen maxims in ascribing or imputing obligation and permission will, in almost every case, be proceeding in the most likely way to achieve the ends for which they are speaking. But for each of the maxims, there are situations in which disregard of the maxim is the best way for a speaker to achieve her purpose. Hence, none of the eighteen maxims is a likely candidate for the logic of deontic speech.

I doubt that deontic logicians would covet many of my eighteen maxims and try to claim them for logic. The maxim of Straightforwardness, for example, says: "Have as the goal of deontic speech that people behave in accordance with what your utterances say they ought, ought not, may, or may not do." This sounds like reasonable if rather obvious advice; but a person who goes against the maxim, one who uses deontic speech to promote a hidden agenda, seems reprehensible rather than illogical. Again, the maxim of Universalizability asks us to treat like cases alike. Universalizability is not the logical operation of universal generalization, which is in any case truth-preserving only if carefully restricted and hedged. There is no logical contradiction in describing someone's action as a failure to treat like cases alike, however reprehensible that failure might be. A logical contradiction is necessarily false, so that it cannot describe any actual state of affairs, but people do fail to universalize.

Thus my eighteen maxims of deontic pragmatics look like a supplement to deontic logic, not a threat to it. But a more careful examination reveals some genuine threats.

In Chapter 2 of *Why You Should*, I argued that Kant's Principle, "'Ought' implies 'Can'," does not always hold. In Augustinian Christianity, persons are thought to deserve eternal punishment for unavoidable, but forbidden, actions and omissions. In the law, persons occasionally find themselves through no fault of their own in situations where any action they can take, including the failure to act, is criminal. Kant's Principle is, I argued, a substantive and valuable moral principle; moreover, it is normally a necessary condition for effectively using deontic speech. But it is not a part of the logic of deontic speech. On pp. 151-152 of *Why You Should*, I argued that my eighteen maxims, seemingly rather toothless, imply a version of Kant's Principle. Thus Kant's Principle, I argued, should be regarded as a rule of pragmatics, not of logic.

I am far from the only person to have argued that Kant's Principle should not be regarded as a rule of deontic logic. Ever since E.J. Lemmon first suggested that Kant's Principle failed to do justice to moral dilemmas, attacks on the universality of that principle have been commonplace. [Lemmon, *passim*][1]

But as we saw in Chapter 2, Kant's Principle is SDLT5, one of the typical assertions of standard deontic logics.[2] SDLT5 says that the logically impossible is not obligatory, which is another way of saying that 'ought' implies 'can' (in the weakest possible sense of 'can', of course).[3] And I argued that Kant's Principle follows from SDLT1 and SDLT3, two more common assertions of standard deontic logics. If Kant's Principle does not legitimately belong to logic, either SDLT1 or SDLT3 must go.

It seems a reasonable move to give up SDLT1, the claim that obligations cannot conflict. For I argued in Chapter 2 of *Why You Should*, as well as in "Conflicts of Obligation," that a person might indeed have conflicting obligations, only one of which she is able to fulfill. If so, even though a person has a duty to do A, she might also have a duty to do not-A. Such conflicts of duties have been often discussed in the literature. Although my "Conflicts of Obligations" is, so far as I know, the first paper to concentrate on non-moral obligations, I am far from the first to note the problems which conflicts raise for SDLT1. Bas van Fraassen is one philosopher who has argued that because duties can conflict, SDLT1 is untenable, although he clung stubbornly to Kant's Principle. [van Fraassen, 15]

A person who accepts the argument of *Why You Should* will have no qualms about jettisoning SDLT1 along with SDLT5 as logical principles. But is jettisoning SDLT1 enough to prevent Kant's Principle from occurring as a theorem? And if SDLT1 goes, is there enough left to construct a useful deontic logic?

Take the second question first. Certainly, if we do give up SDLT1, not all theorems of Standard Deontic Logic (SDL) are lost, for not all theorems of SDL depend on SDLT1 or its equivalents. But more important, it is easy to construct counterparts of those theorems that do depend on SDLT1. For it is a standard derived inference rule of the propositional calculus that, if from the conjunction of the axioms and some proposition 'p' we can derive a proposition 'q', then from the axioms alone we can derive '⊢ p → q'. We can therefore replace every theorem '⊢ R' in SDL whose proof depends on SDLT1 with '⊢ [SDLT1* → R]', where 'SDLT1*' is an unasserted proposition whose content is identical either with that of SDLT1 or with that of a substitution-instance of SDLT1. The new system, which I shall call SDL*, has some interesting quirks. For example, where both A and not-A are obligatory, it is easy to show that neither A nor not-A is permitted.

But someone who accepts the argument of *Why You Should* will not be content with SDL*. For conflicts of duties are not the only sorts of case that threaten Kant's Principle. I noted in *Why You Should* that an Augustinian theologian who asserts that we have a duty — impossible to fulfill — to be perfect is not claiming that any duties conflict. Because the duty to be perfect cannot be fulfilled, the theologian must deny SDLT5. Since accepting SDL* entails accepting Kant's Principle, the

Augustinian theologian cannot accept SDL*. For since the axioms of
SDL normally include SDLT1 and SDLT3, the axioms of SDL* would
include SDLT3. Since SDLT5 follows from SDLT1 and SDLT3,
'SDLT1* → SDLT5' is a theorem of SDL*. An Augustinian need not
believe that duties ever conflict; and certainly, the Augustinian would find
no conflict arising from our duty to be perfect. We have, after all, no *duty*
to fall short of perfection. So our hypothetical theologian could and
probably would accept the claim that if we are obligated to be perfect,
then we are not obligated to be imperfect. That is, he can accept
'SDLT1*'. By *modus ponens*, if he accepts the axioms of SDL*, he must
accept Kant's Principle. Hence, since he does not accept Kant's Principle,
he cannot accept SDL*.

If my criticisms in *Why You Should* were correct, it follows that an
acceptable version of SDL must not only do without SDLT1 but must
also do without SDLT3 as well. About all that is left of SDL would be
whatever we could derive from SDLT4.

But SDLT4, the claim that whatever acts or states are separately
obligatory are jointly obligatory, faces a direct threat from the possibility
of incompatible duties. If there are in fact cases of incompatible duties,
SDLT4 assures us that these are cases of duty to do the impossible. If in
fact they are not cases of duty to do the impossible — whether because
one accepts Kant's Principle or for reasons peculiar to the case in point —
one must give up SDLT4.

Another of my examples from *Why You Should* shows how
incompatible duties raise problems for SDLT4. Suppose that a defendant
confides in his lawyer that he plans to perjure himself in court the next
day. The lawyer has a duty to her client not to do anything that will
prejudice the client's case; she has a duty to the court not to countenance
known perjury. Because of the law in at least some jurisdictions of the
United States, there is no way in which the lawyer can fulfill both duties.
Let us assume that she decides to keep silent during her client's perjured
testimony. She is brought up before the Bar Association and pleads that
she was required to do the impossible. The Bar Association is likely to
respond that the attorney was never required to do the impossible; rather,
she deserves punishment for failing in her clearly performable duty to the
court not to countenance perjury. That is, the Bar Association, by
allowing incompatible duties but not a duty to do the impossible, is

implicitly denying SDLT4. To find the Bar Association illogical requires grounds which do not beg the question by assuming the truth of SDLT4.

An important point about this and similar examples was suggested by Bas van Fraassen. [van Fraassen, 13] Van Fraassen argued that there is an important equivocation in the phrase "S ought to do the impossible." If we take the phrase to mean that S is genuinely required to intend to do what S knows to be impossible, then the presence of incompatible duties would, by SDLT4, lead to a situation which van Fraassen finds absurd. If, on the other hand, the phrase means only that S is required to intend to perform a task which turns out to be impossible, no absurdity follows by SDLT4 from incompatible duties. Persons have tried in the past to square the circle or to double the cube; so long as they do not know that one cannot perform such actions, they can surely intend — and be obligated to intend — to perform them.

But van Fraassen's point makes little difference to the case of the lawyer with a perjurious client. For both the lawyer and the Bar Association are well aware of the dilemma which the attorney faces. The lawyer and the Bar Association both know that she has incompatible duties. There is no equivocation: If the Bar Association accepted SDLT4, it would be claiming that the attorney ought both to do and to intend to do what the attorney and the Bar Association know to be impossible. Since the Bar Association explicitly denies that it makes such a claim, it can only be denying SDLT4.

Let us turn next to SDLR3, which says that from '⊢ p → q', '⊢ Op → Oq' follows. In Chapter 2, I noted that SDLR3 follows from SDLR1, truth-functional theorems and inference rules, and the axioms SDLT3 and SDLT4. If SDLR3 is no good, then either the inference rule SDLR1, the axiom SDLT3, or the axiom SDLT4 must be at fault.

Geoffrey Sayre-McCord finds many difficulties with SDLR3. [Sayre-McCord, *passim*] Since 'p → (p v q)' is a theorem, by SDLR3 so is 'Op → O(p v q)'. Then if Ralph ought to repay Tom, it ought to be that Ralph either repay Tom or shoot him. Given that Ralph really ought to repay Tom, it hardly seems right that Ralph can discharge his debt by discharging his firearm into Tom.[4]

As they had for SDLT3 and SDLT4, incompatible obligations also raise problems for SDLR3. If a person has incompatible obligations, by SDLT4 and *modus ponens*, 'O(p. ~p)' is true. It is a theorem of the propositional calculus that '$(p.\sim p) \to q$', for any value of 'q' whatsoever. Substituting in that theorem and applying SDLR3, we infer '$O(p.\sim p) \to Oq$'. From this and '$O(p.\sim p)$', 'Oq' follows by *modus ponens*. In other words, if someone is obligated to do the impossible, as *Why You Should* argued might happen, then everything is obligatory — which is absurd.

A simpler and more compelling objection to SDLR3 comes from Peter Schotch and Raymond Jennings, who point out that "We feed the starving poor" implies "There are starving poor." If SDLR3 is correct, "We ought to feed the starving poor" implies "There ought to be starving poor." If, as seems reasonable to suppose, we really ought to feed the starving poor, it hardly seems right to infer that poverty and starvation are conditions that ought to exist. [Schotch and Jennings, 151][5]

If in view of these problems one gives up SDLR3, one is faced with an unpleasant choice. We have already looked at some objections to SDLT3 and SDLT4; giving up SDLR3 might be taken to increase the case against these two principles. The only alternative is to give up SDLR1 instead. In any event, little seems left of standard deontic logic.

Next, I look at objections to several other important principles: SDLT6, SDLT2, SDLR4, and SDLR2.[6] The claim of SDLT6 that the logically necessary is obligatory is particularly likely to raise hackles. One problem arises from the cases of conflicts of obligation and of the Augustinian theologians which raised problems for Kant's Principle. For in Chapter 2 we derived Kant's Principle from SDLT6 along with the apparently innocuous SDLT8 and SDLT9. Hence, the objections *Why You Should* raised to SDLT5 apply equally well to SDLT6.

Moreover, SDLT6 has no value as an action-guiding principle. It does no good to know that one ought to do the logically necessary, or that what is logically necessary ought to exist. A logically necessary state of affairs will be the case, no matter what we do or say; and if our doing something is in fact logically necessary, then we are going to do that thing willy-nilly. Where the logically necessary is concerned, there is no choice; and where there is no choice, obligation and permissibility seem out of place if not unintelligible.

The same set of problems applies to the rule of O-necessitation, SDLR2, which allows us to infer '$\vdash Op$' from '$\vdash p$'. SDLT6 is a direct consequence of the rule of O-necessitation. Hence just as objections to Kant's Principle serve as objections to SDLT6, so do objections to SDLT6 in turn serve as objections to SDLR2. But such second-hand objections are not the only ones we can make to SDLR2. If a state legislature attempts to bar people from doing the impossible, and if it attaches various punishments to violations of the law, the legislature has made itself ridiculous. There is at best no point in prohibiting people from doing what they cannot do anyway. And yet, by SDLR2, from the undeniable "You are not going to do the impossible" we can derive either "You ought not to do the impossible" or "It ought to be that you do not do the impossible." And either derivation is as fatuous as my hypothetical state legislature.[7]

SDLR4 states that from the provable equivalence of two propositions, p and q, we can derive the equivalence of Op and Oq. SDLR4 looks unexceptionable because, for the most part, the examples of provable equivalence we can think of are cases of meaning equivalence. If 'p' means the same thing as 'q', then 'Op ↔ Oq' can hardly be doubted. But in fact, there is room to question SDLR4, for not every case of provable equivalence is meaning equivalence. The term 'provable equivalence' is something of a red herring; all that it means is necessary sameness of truth-value. For instance, the statements "This figure has exactly three sides" and "This figure has exactly three angles" are provably equivalent, but they do not mean the same. Now suppose, with Leibniz, that in a world as complex as this one there must logically be a certain irreducible minimum of evil, even though, this being necessarily the best of all possible worlds, there must also be a certain irreducible minimum of good. For every quantum of good, there is a certain quantum of evil, and vice versa; for every cloud there is a silver lining, and for every silver lining there is a cloud. Now even if necessarily a certain amount of good is present in the world if and only if a certain amount of evil is present in the world, the presence of good is something different from the presence of evil. And a Leibnizian could well claim that there ought to be a certain amount of good in the world without wishing to claim that there ought to be a certain amount of evil in the world. Thus SDLR4 does lead to some counterintuitive results.

Finally, we need to look briefly at SDLT2, which asserts: If it is obligatory that if p then q and if it is obligatory that p, then it is obligatory that q. Here the phrase "it is obligatory that if p then q" is hardly clear English; a more easily read version would be "it is obligatory that either not-p or q." Substituting 'not-p' for 'p', we have: If it is obligatory that either p or q and if it is obligatory that not-p, then it is obligatory that q.

But consider the following case: In the country of Freedonia, there are only two possible forms of government: rule by the people's choice from the candidates put forward by Party A and Party B; or military dictatorship. An impartial observer asserts that democratic rule is clearly better than dictatorship. For this reason, says the observer, it ought to be that either the candidate of Party A rules the country or that the candidate of Party B rules the country. However, thinks the observer, both candidates are equally rotten. Surely it ought to be that the candidate of Party A does not rule the country. But that hardly means that it ought to be that the candidate of Party B rules the country. And yet, given the terrors of military dictatorship, it ought to be that one or the other candidate rules.

The point of this example is that it is often best to have a choice, even if neither of the two choices deserves to be picked. From the mere fact that it ought to be that we do not pick the first, we can hardly infer that it ought to be that we do pick the second. To be sure, we are given that 'O(p v q)' is true. But we cannot infer that 'Op v Oq'; for that would be to assume the forbidden SDLX5. That it ought to be that either X is chosen or Y is chosen does not imply that either it ought to be that X is chosen or it ought to be that Y is chosen. Therefore, we cannot infer Y's fitness from X's unfitness to be chosen.

In sum, then, SDLT2 seems plausible only if we presuppose that 'oughts' can be distributed over disjunctions; and SDL does not allow any such presupposition. If we are looking for principles that are not counterintuitive, SDLT2 seems like a poor bet.[8]

To this point, I have looked at problems arising in straightforward monadic SDL. But Standard Deontic Logic is not all that deontic logicians have offered, nor is plain vanilla the only available flavor of SDL. If my claims in *Why You Should* are right, how do matters stand with some not-so-standard deontic logics? We should look at a few representative cases.

Perhaps the hottest recent trend in deontic logic is toward dyadic logics. In his recent book, *Introduction to Deontic Logic and the Theory of Normative Systems*, Lennart Åqvist cites five different dyadic systems dating back no farther than 1968 and then adds a sixth system of his own.[9] Dyadic systems are normally systems of conditional obligation.

Åqvist, in the course of arguing the relative virtues of dyadic deontic logics, makes it clear that the move from monadic standard deontic logics to their dyadic counterparts is hardly sufficient to remove all difficulties. Åqvist lists five problems the dyadic approach does not help resolve; these include the Good Samaritan Paradox and, more to our purpose here, problems revolving around Kant's Principle. [Åqvist 2, 77-83]

Bas van Fraassen, for example, argued that imperatives, a group which he takes to include 'ought' statements, are generally conditional in nature. [van Fraassen, 16] If I tell Jane that she ought to close the door, I am tacitly supposing that the door is currently unclosed. If it is open, Jane can neither fulfill nor violate my imperative. Therefore, van Fraassen constructs a logic of obligation-statements with dyadic operators 'O(p/q)' and 'P(p/q)', to be understood as "It ought to be that p, given q" and "It is permissible that p, given q."

In van Fraassen's conditional system, one of the rules of inference is a conditional version of SDLR3. This is rule RC2: "[I]f ⊢ A → B then ⊢ O(A/C) → O(B/C)."[10] But from RC2 and from '⊢ pq → p' and '⊢ pq → q', we can derive 'O(pq/C) → O(p/C).O(q/C)'. That is a recognizable dyadic version of SDLT3, and it would force an Augustinian to accept Kant's Principle. That is, RC2 would be unacceptable to an Augustinian theologian. Hence, by making his system of obligation conditional, van Fraassen does not escape the problems I posed in Chapter 2 of *Why You Should*, nor does he escape the objections Sayre-McCord posed against SDLR3. Thus Åqvist's point that the move from monadic to dyadic logic will not solve problems raised by Kant's Principle seems amply borne out in van Fraassen's system.

I agree with Åqvist that dyadic versions of standard deontic logics are real improvements over their monadic counterparts. They are much closer to what we actually mean by 'ought' statements. But one must depart much further from standard deontic logics than the mere introduction of conditional obligation statements to avoid the sorts of difficulties I am raising here. And we shall see in later chapters that the introduction of conditional obligation statements by itself does little to parry the objections I shall raise there.

An altogether different approach is that of Peter Schotch and Raymond Jennings, who worked out a deontic logic which starts from, but is clearly weaker than, SDL. [Schotch and Jennings, 158-159] Their two core principles are SDLR3 and SDLT5, which they call [RM] and [Con]. They explicitly reject SDLT4, which they refer to as [K], and have provided a semantics different from the usual, Kripkean kind from which the denial of SDLT4 falls out. As a result, Schotch and Jennings are able to allow for the possibility of conflicts of obligation, even though they not only accept Kant's Principle but make it central to their system.

From the standpoint of *Why You Should*, accepting the possibility of conflicts of obligation is clearly a step in the right direction. But conflicts of obligation were not my only reason for rejecting Kant's Principle. One must not forget St. Augustine and his followers, who were not worried at all about conflict cases. Bas van Fraassen quotes the Calvinist Synod of Dordt, as I quoted St. Paul, Augustine, Jansen, and Luther. [van Fraassen, 14] To persons of the Augustinian cast, humans ought to do certain things which, thanks to Adam's sin, they cannot do. If Kant's Principle were true, God's foreordination of any human to eternal damnation would be utterly unjust. Therefore, an Augustinian must reject Kant's Principle.

Quite aside from the problems of SDLR3, then, accepting the main arguments of *Why You Should* entails rejecting one of Schotch and Jennings's two core principles. Weakening SDL, as Schotch and Jennings do, does not then seem a plausible strategy in responding to *Why You Should*. What if one cuts loose from SDL altogether and tries a new sort of formulation?

Let us look briefly at the account of deontic logic which Hector-Neri Castañeda gave in *Thinking and Doing*. [Castañeda 5] Castañeda asserted that five chapters of the analysis of the logic of obligation-judgments yield as "purely logical results" a deontic system with the following, informally stated, four axioms:

(1) $\vdash$ (It is obligatory$_i$ that p) $\rightarrow$ (it is not obligatory$_i$ that not-p).

(2) $\vdash$ [(It is obligatory$_i$ that p) and (it is obligatory$_i$ that q)] $\rightarrow$ (it is obligatory$_i$ that p and q).

(3) $\vdash$ [(It is the case that p) and (it is obligatory$_i$ that q)] $\rightarrow$ (it is obligatory$_i$ that q while-it-is-the-case-that-p).

(4) $\vdash$ (For anybody it is obligatory$_i$ that he A) $\rightarrow$ (it is obligatory$_i$ that everybody A).[11]

The subscript following the word 'obligatory' indicates the system of obligation in which a particular action is obligatory.

Castañeda, by relativizing his axioms to individual systems of obligation, avoided any difficulty with conflicting obligations — so long as those obligations arise from different systems. Antigone's moral obligation to bury her brother might coincide in Castañeda's account with her political obligation to keep the brother unburied.

Castañeda's subscripting also yields a restricted form of SDLR3: If $\vdash_i (A \to B)$ then $\vdash_i (O_i A \to O_i B)$.[12] That is, from the assertion in system of obligation I that $A \to B$, derive the assertion in I that $O_i A \to O_i B$. It is not enough for this rule to work that '$A \to B$' be a theorem of the propositional calculus; it must also be a theorem of I. However, as Castañeda included in his system all general axioms for connectives, presumably every theorem of the propositional calculus will be a theorem of I. [Castañeda 5, 259] So the only restriction Castañeda placed on SDLR3 is to require consistent relativization of the deontic operators.

In sketching Castañeda's system, I need to emphasize its radical differences from SDL. For instance, Castañeda believed that what follows an 'ought to do' operator is not a proposition at all but an entirely different sort of entity, which he called a *practition*. The semantics of practitions is not that of propositions, as practitions cannot be true or false but can only have or lack legitimacy. Again, Castañeda cheerfully allowed conflicts of obligations, so long as those obligations stem from different sources. If SDL suffers from major problems and we are looking for a very different alternative, Castañeda's system is most attractive.

But if *Why You Should* presents difficulties for SDL, it presents many of the same difficulties for Castañeda's system. His first axiom is equivalent to: "It is not the case that both p is obligatory and not-p is obligatory under a given set of rules." That is, where there is a single source of obligation, there cannot be conflicts. But the case of the lawyer with the perjurious client presents a conflict of obligation which stems from a single source: the rules of the American Bar Association. Hence, *Why You Should* casts doubt on Castañeda's first axiom.

And the second axiom, "[(It is obligatory$_i$ that p) and (it is obligatory$_i$ that q)] $\to$ (it is obligatory$_i$ that p and q)," is a relativized version of SDLT4. Whether or not one accepts van Fraassen's characterization of SDLT4 as involving an equivocation, clearly if there are incompatible obligations, it follows from SDLT4 that Kant's Principle must be false. And although Castañeda's axioms do not imply Kant's Principle — for they do not include SDLT3 — his semantics does.[13]

Further, Castañeda accepted the following as an inference rule: "If '$A \to B$' is logically valid, so is *(It is obligatory$_i$ that A)$\to$(it is obligatory$_i$

that B)*."[14] This is a relativized form of SDLR3; relativizing it to a single system of obligation does not, so far as I can see, remove the objections which Sayre-McCord has brought against SDLR3. Likewise, to recall Schotch and Jennings's example, if "We ought to feed the starving poor" logically implies "There are starving poor," then by Castañeda's inference rule, if a system of obligation requires that we ought to feed the starving poor, that same system mandates that there ought to be starving poor.[15]

Hence, although Castañeda's system differs in important and basic ways from standard deontic logic, the arguments of *Why You Should* raise many of the same difficulties for it as for SDL. In general, if my claims in the previous book were correct, then neither Castañeda's system nor SDL adequately represents our deontic thought. For *Why You Should* questions SDLT5, SDLT1, SDLT3, SDLT4, and SDLR3; and any deontic logic I have seen that goes beyond the propositional calculus with special definitions, no matter how non-standard it might be in important respects, accepts at least some of these five axioms, theorems, and inference rules.

Sayre-McCord has suggested a way of saving deontic logic from such attacks as those I have just given. He advises that we give up the idea of a single deontic logic neutral among different moral theories. Rather, one first makes one's choice of moral theories and then works out the logic of that theory — which might be quite different from the logic of another moral theory. [Sayre-McCord 193-194] If one is not an Augustinian theologian, and if one's theory rules out incompatible duties, a version of SDL might be the preferable deontic logic; Augustinians and believers in conflicts of obligation should seek an alternative to SDL.

Sayre-McCord's suggestion does render the various deontic logics impervious to the arguments which I have given so far, or to any objections based on counterexamples, even though the neutrality of deontic logic might be a thesis which most deontic logicians would not willingly give up.[16] Sayre-McCord's proposal prevents me from asserting that arguments in *Why You Should* prove rich deontic logics impossible.

I could not make such a strong claim in any case, for the sword I have wielded cuts both ways. If Augustinian theology taken as a moral theory rules out Kant's Principle, then Kant's Principle rules out Augustinian theology taken as a moral theory. If one cannot accept both a standard deontic logic and the possibility of conflicting obligations, a defender of SDL would have no doubt which should go. From the standpoint of an upholder of SDL, there can be no genuine counterexamples to SDL. That my counterexamples do not seem logically impossible is no response; the existence of six types of regular solid in Euclidean space does not seem logically impossible, but it is.

Hence, deontic logicians might with perfect consistency maintain the truth of their favorite forms of deontic logic against all my counterexamples. For just that reason, in *Why You Should* I could show only that to regard Kant's Principle as a part of pragmatics yields a more promising, justifiable, and simple theory than to regard it as a part of deontic logic. [J. Forrester 2, ch. 13] Provisionally, we should accept the best available theories over their less promising competitors; but more than once in the past, new evidence has turned up to favor the more complex theory over the simpler, or the formerly unjustifiable account over the once justifiable one. For all I know, that might be the case with a theory that regards Kant's Principle as part of deontic logic.

Therefore, neither the counterexamples from *Why You Should* nor similar cases from Sayre-McCord, van Fraassen, and Schotch and Jennings provide an unanswerable argument against standard deontic logics. All the objections to a system of deontic logic that depend on theology or on incompatible obligations establish at best a probability that the system is false; and I suspect it is difficult at best to pin down that probability with any degree of precision. Even if one can, Sayre-McCord's gambit is still open to the friend of standard deontic logics.

Rather, I shall take the argument of *Why You Should* in this book as a marker. It indicates what I want to prove: that standard deontic logics are no good. But I need a new argument, independent of that in *Why You Should*, to prove my point. Chapters 4 to 10 provide that new argument.

My conclusions in this book, rather than leaning on the new analysis I presented in *Why You Should*, therefore provide new inductive support for that analysis. For if my argument here is correct, the usual ways of understanding deontic reasoning are wrong. A new analysis is needed, and *Why You Should* gives a portion of that new analysis. But since *Why You Should* provides only a deontic pragmatics, and part of any reasoning is logic and not pragmatics, *Why You Should* cannot and does not give an entire account of deontic reasoning. Thus this book, which offers a new deontic logic, and *Why You Should*, which offers a new deontic pragmatics, are independent of each other but complementary.

My present argument against standard deontic logic falls into two parts. First, I shall argue that 'ought to be' statements neither imply nor are implied by parallel 'ought to do' statements. Any logic, such as SDL, that treats the two kinds of 'ought' statements as equivalent is therefore badly flawed. I shall show that our tendency to accept certain of the principles of standard deontic logics arises solely from equivocating between the two types of 'ought' statements. This is the burden of Chapter 4.

Chapters 5 through 10 develop a different argument. I shall show first that any deontic logic requires a possible world semantics if it is to escape charges of unintelligibility. However, SDL semantics suffers from at least three kinds of major and irreparable flaws. To escape those flaws, we must erect a quite different sort of semantics; but any new semantics is likely to yield a set of principles not identical with those of SDL. As we shall see in Part II, this likelihood turns out, in the case of at least one such semantics, to be fact.

With the preliminaries out of the way, then, let us turn to my argument against standard deontic logics.

Chapter 4: 'Ought to Be' and 'Ought to Do'

My purpose in this chapter is to argue that there is an important distinction between 'ought to be' and 'ought to do' statements.[1] The distinction is so important that any deontic logic which treats the two kinds of 'ought' statements as synonymous cannot do justice to our ordinary deontic thinking.

I shall argue for the following points:

(1) An 'ought to do' statement and its 'ought to be' counterpart differ in meaning.

(2) 'Ought to be' and 'ought to do' operators differ in logical behavior. The 'ought to be' operator in ordinary deontic reasoning has entire propositions as its scope, but the 'ought to do' operator ranges over predicates only.

(3) An 'ought to do' statement and its 'ought to be' counterpart do not entail one another.

(4) The connection between 'ought to be' statements and their 'ought to do' counterparts is a matter of pragmatics, not of meaning or of logic.

I shall take up these points in order. The reader should keep in mind J.L. Austin's dictum, quoted as the epigraph to this book, that ordinary language, although not the last word on a subject, is certainly the first word. Deontic logicians are free to reject any feature of ordinary deontic speech and thought, including the distinction between 'ought to do' and 'ought to be' sentences. But all logicians should be aware that, the greater the divergence between their systems and the material they are trying to systematize, the less reason people have to adopt those systems.

1. THE TWO KINDS OF 'OUGHT' STATEMENTS DIFFER IN MEANING

Most deontic speech concerns what persons ought to, should, may, or may not do. We say that children should improve their table manners, that unauthorized persons may not enter, or that the president ought to veto a bill. Such statements claim that somebody may or should perform an *action*; I shall say that the 'ought' they contain is an 'ought to do'.

Deontic logic has tended to concentrate on 'ought to do' sentences, as one would expect from a logic of obligation and permission. For persons are obligated or permitted *to act*, or to fail to act, in certain ways. Deontic logic is above all intended to be a logic concerned with human actions; it is regarded as an important part of practical reasoning, and practical reasoning is in turn primarily a matter of determining one's actions. No wonder, then, that the deontic logician's basic sentences are usually understood as saying that someone ought, or is permitted, to do something. Thus K. Jaakko J. Hintikka, for instance, makes it clear that the individuals over which his variables are to range are particular acts. [Hintikka 2, 60]

What we ought to do is, in most cases, an act of a particular kind; the act which satisfies an obligation will, of course, have aspects which are independent of the kind in question. For instance, I ought to repay you what I borrowed from you; if I do so, I might pay by cash, by check, or by credit card. That I ought to repay you does not imply that I ought to repay you in cash. What we ought to do, then, is generally not so much to perform a particular action but to perform an action which has a given aspect. Moreover, 'ought to do' expressions are generally conditional, with the condition often stated or implied in the description of the obligatory aspect. "You ought to chew with your mouth closed" does not usually imply a duty to chew; the obligatory aspect is rather to keep one's mouth closed while chewing. Thus the proper reading of "You ought to chew with your mouth closed" is "You should act as follows: given that you chew, chew with your mouth closed."[2] Similarly, "I ought to repay you $5" means "I should act as follows: given that I borrowed $5 from you, I pay you $5."

Not all 'ought to do' sentences are conditional, however: e.g., "You ought to do the right thing, no matter what." This sentence might be taken as merely analytic, but even an analytic 'ought to do' sentence remains an 'ought to do' sentence. Therefore, a requirement of conditionality cannot be part of the meaning or logical form of 'ought to do' statements.

However, quite often our deontic utterances employ an 'ought to be' instead of an 'ought to do'.[3] An 'ought to be' sentence generally claims that the world would be improved if a given state of affairs existed or failed to exist. "There should be no more war" places no obvious obligations on anyone to act in any way; it says little more than that a world without war would be a better world than a world with war.[4]

'Ought to be' sentences range from the personal ("You ought to be ashamed of yourself!") through the societal ("There ought to be a law against that") to the truly universal ("The wicked should not be left unpunished"). In all these cases the listener is told that a certain state of affairs should obtain, but not — or, at least, not explicitly — that anyone should act so as to bring about that state. Such states might themselves be or include actions: "It ought to be that Jones runs for president," unlike "Jones ought to run for president," does not explicitly say what Jones should do.[5]

The states of affairs which we say ought to be, unlike the actions which we say people ought to do, often have no or few conditions attached. If I say that there should be peace on earth, I usually do not mean that there should, given certain existing conditions, be peace on earth. If it ought to be that you help a certain person, that might be because you promised to do so or because you were ordered to do so; but it might also be simply because helping that person is a good thing for you to do. If you ought to help that person, there is usually some condition in virtue of which you have that obligation. Hence, where 'ought to do' statements usually apply only given certain conditions, one can make no such generalization for 'ought to be' statements.

Although most theorists tend to interpret the 'ought' in propositions of deontic logic as an 'ought to do', they rarely do so consistently. One large reason is that deontic operators, like modal operators, govern entire propositions, and these propositions can be complex. Take a conditional obligation sentence, for example, such as: "If it rains, you ought to wear your raincoat." If we regard the entire conditional as lying within the scope of the deontic operator, how should we read the sentence? "You ought to do the following: if it rains, wear your raincoat?"[6] That seems dubious English; its raining is not something you do or ought to do. A more reasonable reading would be: "It ought to be the case that if it rains, you wear your raincoat." As this and more convoluted examples suggest, deontic operators whose scope contains truth-functionally complex propositions would seem best interpreted as 'ought to be' expressions.[7]

Or consider inference rule SDLR3:

$$\vdash p \to q$$
$$\vdash Op \to Oq.$$

If one person repays another a $100 debt, surely the government must have printed the money, or the bank must have issued a check, or something of the sort. But it is hardly plausible that if one person *ought* to repay another a $100 debt, the government ought to have printed the money, or the bank ought to have issued a check, or something of the sort. From one person's duty to repay a debt, SDLR3 would seem to license the inference that someone else unconnected with the debt has a duty as well. The only plausibility I can find in applying SDLR3 to the present example is if we read 'OA' as an 'ought to do' but 'OB' as an 'ought to be': in my example, if one person ought to repay another a $100 debt, then it ought to be the case that either the government printed the money, or the bank issued a check, or something of the sort. Thus SDLR3 makes sense in this example only if we can mix 'ought to do' and 'ought to be' expressions — that is, only if the two types of expression are logically equivalent.

Much the same is true of SDLT2: '$O(p \to q) \to (Op \to Oq)$'. It makes little sense to construe the antecedent as "George ought to do the following: if he cleans the cat box, he takes out the garbage." How can an if-then statement represent what someone ought to do? It is almost an irresistible temptation to construe the sentence as "If George cleans the cat box, he ought to take out the garbage." But in that construal, the obligation is conditional on George's cleaning the cat box; it is not the case that, as the antecedent of SDLT2 requires, the entire conditional expression is obligatory.[8] How much more plausible it is to read the antecedent of SDLT2 as: "It ought to be the case that if George cleans the cat box, he takes out the garbage." But if SDLT2 is used to derive theorems about what people ought to do, it can only be because 'ought to be' and 'ought to do' expressions are regarded as synonymous. And so they are regarded by standard deontic logic.

'Ought to do' and 'ought to be' expressions come paired together. If we can say there ought to be a law, we can say that someone ought to enact that law; if we can say that people ought to repay their debts, we can say that it ought to be the case that people repay their debts. I shall talk from now on of an 'ought' statement's *counterpart expression*: the 'ought to do' statement that corresponds to a given 'ought to be' statement, or vice versa.

It is my thesis that standard deontic logic is making a major blunder in failing to separate the two kinds of 'oughts'.[9] 'Ought to be' statements differ in meaning from their 'ought to do' counterpart expressions.[10] I shall argue in Chapter 15, however, that an 'ought to do' statement is equivalent to a claim that the agent exists and a non-parallel 'ought to be' statement.

That the two kinds of 'ought' statement are distinct in meaning might seem highly implausible. From a cursory look at the examples by which I have made a *prima facie* distinction between 'ought to do' and 'ought to be', one might think any distinction merely one of grammar. But that would be wrong. "You ought to be kinder to Mrs. Jones" claims that the person addressed should perform certain kinds of actions; I regard it as an 'ought to do', despite its grammatical form. Likewise, "Smoking is not permitted in this area" ranks as an 'ought to do', while "You should know the answer to that question" is an 'ought to be'.

In separating 'ought to do' from 'ought to be', I am not supposing that all 'ought' contexts fit into one category or the other. After all, many contexts using the English word 'ought' have little deontic or valuational flavor to them. Such contexts might use the words 'ought to do': "I reversed the antenna leads. That ought to do the trick." Or they might use the words 'ought to be': "That river down there ought to be the Colorado." But such contexts are at best marginally deontic or valuational; they do not prescribe actions, but they might have some overtones of the appropriateness which I take as the core meaning of an 'ought to be'. "That ought to be the Colorado River" seems to need a filling out, perhaps by "if I remember the topography of this part of the country correctly." Its being the Colorado fits with the remembered topographical outlines of the area. As such, it might count as an 'ought to be', if an anemic one; I shall regard it as neither an 'ought to be' nor as an 'ought to do'.

That we use the English words 'ought to do' or 'ought to be' in a sentence is therefore only a fallible clue to proper classification of the 'ought'. We can determine whether the 'ought' is deontic only by looking at the meaning of the sentence in context. In general, if the object of a deontic verb is a state, whether of persons or of the universe, that verb is an 'ought to be'; if the object is an action, the verb is an 'ought to do'. This is a highly incomplete formulation, however, for actions are a kind of state, and it ought to be that certain actions take place. The difference is something like this: if one says that Jones ought to vote for Smith, one is normally calling on Jones to act in the approved way. However, in saying that Jones's voting for Smith ought to be, a person is not directly calling on Jones to vote for Smith. After all, Jones might, all during Election Day, be trapped in her house by an unexpected flood; she had no chance to cast an absentee ballot, and she cannot now get to the polls.

As one might expect, there are borderline cases. "You ought to be ashamed of yourself" might be regarded as an 'ought to be' construction: your behavior is shameful, and it ought to be the case that you felt the proper shame. Or we might take it as an 'ought to do': you ought to show the proper apologetic behavior. With passive-voice constructions of the bureaucratic type, the 'ought to do' is usually poorly disguised: "Answers to the test questions ought to be completed by the end of the period" clearly means "Those taking the test should complete their answers by the end of the period." But not all passive voice constructions are so easily turned into the active; hence, it is sometimes difficult to tell whether a passive-voice 'ought' is an 'ought to be' or an 'ought to do'. Still, although there are borderline cases, we can usually tell whether a given 'ought' is an 'ought to be' or an 'ought to do'.

Clearly enough, the two types of 'ought' statements are *used* quite differently from each other. When we say that X ought to do A, we are generally doing one of three things: giving directions, making a judgment, or giving information.[11] But when we say that state S ought to be, we are ascribing some value to S, usually, although not always, in the wish that S come about. The wish might be strong or weak, practical or impractical. Thus, where uses of 'ought to do' tend to be directive, judgmental, or informative, uses of 'ought to be' tend to be optative.

Despite this difference in use, one might reasonably expect the two expressions to be related in *meaning*. To be sure, the exact meaning of 'ought' statements remains controversial, but most theorists agree that the meaning of all 'ought' statements involves the meeting of certain standards.[12] Certainly what ought to be should meet standards of what the world should be like, if the 'ought to be' is to describe conditions obtaining in an ideal or improved world. And perhaps the actions which we ought to perform should also satisfy standards, whether these are moral, legal, prudential, or required by a form of etiquette.[13] Thus the meanings of 'ought to be' and 'ought to do' statements might both involve the core notion of meeting standards.

But even if the meaning of 'ought to do' statements has something in common with that of 'ought to be' statements, the two meanings are not identical. For an 'ought to be' statement has implications that an 'ought to do' statement lacks, and vice versa.[14] We shall now look at some of these implications with respect to typical assertions of Standard Deontic Logic.

Consider first the old notion of evil serving to bring about a greater good. A certain complex state of affairs is, let us assume, most desirable. But the existence of that entire state of affairs requires the presence of certain of its component features which are either undesirable or neutral. For example, Mother Teresa's ministering to the beggars of Calcutta could not be unless there were beggars of Calcutta; neither could it be unless there were oxygen in Earth's atmosphere. Now it is reasonable to suppose that the desirable complex state of affairs ought to be: it ought to be that Mother Teresa ministers to the beggars of Calcutta. But it is false that each component — even each necessary component — of the complex ought to be: it is false that there ought to be beggars of Calcutta and false that there ought to be oxygen in Earth's atmosphere. Therefore, that the complex state of affairs <A and B> ought to be does not imply that <A> ought to be and that <B> ought to be.[15] Hence, SDLT3 is false, if we take it as a principle governing 'ought to be' expressions.

On the other hand, if a person S ought to perform a pair of actions <F.G>, surely S should perform <F> and should perform <G>. Even if <F> has no value in itself but is only a necessary step toward doing one's real duty, <G>, it still makes sense to say that S should do <F>. If I repay you all I have borrowed from you, I must first go to my bank. Therefore, if I ought both to go to my bank and to repay you, I ought to go to my bank. (Going to my bank is, of course, not all that I ought to do.) Hence, SDLT3, interpreted as a principle governing 'ought to do' expressions, is highly plausible.

SDLR3 permits us to infer 'Op → Oq' from the information that 'p → q' is a theorem. We might again turn to Mother Teresa for a counterexample to this rule, if the 'ought' is an 'ought to be'. That is, "If Mother Teresa helps the beggars in Calcutta, then there are beggars in Calcutta" seems a plausible theorem-instance; but "If it ought to be that Mother Teresa helps the beggars in Calcutta, then it ought to be that there are beggars in Calcutta" is unlikely. SDLR3 does better if the 'ought' is an 'ought to do': From "'S does F' implies 'S does G'," infer "'S ought to do F' implies 'S ought to do G'." Note that SDLR3 is plausible only if the same agent, S, is assumed to do both F and G. Apparent counterexamples arise whenever doing F is a qualified form of doing G: talking politely, for instance, implies talking; but from the fact that you ought to talk politely, no one would infer that you ought to talk. The problem disappears if we take your obligation as conditional: You should, given that you talk, talk politely. Hence SDLR3 as an 'ought to do' principle is reasonable.

Whichever kind of 'ought' we take up, SDLR4 raises problems. Suppose that humans, by their very nature, were logically compelled to feed the starving poor. Then it would be necessarily true that we feed the starving poor if and only if there are starving poor; but who would claim that it ought to be that we feed the starving poor if and only if it ought to be that there are starving poor? Or who would suppose that we ought to feed the starving poor if and only if the poor ought to starve — or we ought to starve them?

SDLT3 worked for the 'ought to do' but not for the 'ought to be'; SDLR3 failed for the 'ought to be' and was plausible for the 'ought to do'; SDLR4 worked for neither kind of 'ought'. With SDLT4, the result is much the same as with SDLR4. First, imagine a society in which all and only children should perform Task A, all and only adults should perform Task B, and there is a specific time, high noon on a person's eighteenth birthday, after which a person is an adult. Jenny, a member of this society, is an adult. There is a time at which Jenny ought to perform Task A, and there is a time at which Jenny ought to perform Task B. But there is no time at which Jenny ought to perform both Task A and Task B. Now we ordinarily consider 'ought to do' statements to have implicit time reference: we often talk of duties being canceled, becoming no longer applicable, coming into force, and the like. Hence, if one reads 'S ought to do F' to mean 'At some time, S ought to do F', then 'S ought to do A and S ought to do B' does not imply 'At some time, S ought to do A and B'. That is to say, SDLT4, regarded as a principle governing 'ought to do' statements, is false.[16] Nor are differently tensed 'oughts' the only sources of trouble here. If a cook ought to put cayenne pepper into a bland broth, and if she ought to put hot oil into the broth, it is surely possible that she ought to do only one of those two.

SDLT4 fares no better as a principle governing 'ought to be' statements. Imagine a problem in the world for which there are two quite different solutions. Either solution would lead to the world's being a much better place. However, if both solutions were to be implemented, the net result would be worse than if either one were implemented by itself. For example, suppose that too many people break the law by playing radios loudly on public transportation. Two solutions are proposed: confiscating the radios of offenders, and forbidding offenders to use public transportation. Either solution appears reasonable to the community leaders, but implementing them both seems much too harsh a punishment. Then a community leader might say: It ought to be that offenders have their radios confiscated; and it ought to be that offenders are forbidden to use public transportation; but it is not the case that it ought to be that both offenders have their radios confiscated and offenders are forbidden to use public transportation.

Sometimes, equally good solutions to a problem rule each other out. In such cases, one could well suppose that the first solution ought to be and that the second solution ought to be, but no one would think it reasonable to assert that both solutions ought to be.

Even if we say that any state of affairs ought to be only if it represents the *best* solution to a problem, many problems have equally optimal but mutually exclusive solutions. In such cases, it is false that both solutions ought to be. I find the supposed requirement of optimality implausible; to say that a solution ought to be, one need only think that the solution represents an improvement over existing conditions. But whether one holds to an optimality requirement or a mere improvement requirement, it is possible that a number of incompatible solutions to a problem ought to be. SDLT4 is therefore incorrect.

Consider another assertion of standard deontic logic, SDLT1: '~(Op.O~p)'. My discussion of conflicting duties in Chapter 3 indicates that SDLT1 is implausible as a principle of what we ought to do. If a person ought to do A and ought to do B, and if his doing B necessarily means that he will fail to do A, then it is plausible to say both that he ought to do A and that he ought to fail to do A. If such a situation is possible, SDLT1 is not true under all interpretations, in which case it cannot be a principle of logic — at least without important added conditions. On the other hand, conflicts of obligation are agonizing for those caught in them; we might well deny that it should be that S does F and that it should be that S not do F. Thus moral dilemmas and other conflicts of obligation seem to raise no difficulties at all for SDLT1, considered as a principle of what ought to be.

Consider SDLT6, 'O(p v ~p)'. As a principle of what ought to be, SDLT6 seems acceptable if a bit pointless: what must be the case ought to be the case.[17] But as a principle of what one ought to do, SDLT6 is more objectionable. An affirmative duty to perform the logically necessary makes little sense. How much energy does it take to carry out such a duty? Where there is no choice, there appears to be no duty.

The rule of O-necessitation, SDLR2, fares much the same as SDLT6. From the fact that 'p' is a theorem, can we derive that it ought to be that p? Well, if 'p' is a theorem, it has to be the case; saying that 'p' ought to be the case seems harmless if pointless. One can, I suppose, imagine a naive person's joy at being reassured that the Law of Non-Contradiction will continue to hold — "and well it should!" On the other hand, it seems logically necessary that if Smith acts at time t, then Smith does not fail to act at t. Can we infer that Smith ought to do the following: if he acts at t, he does not fail to act at t? That is an odd sort of obligation at best; if one can make sense out of it, not only is Smith totally unable to fail in this obligation, but succeeding takes no effort whatsoever on his part. An obligation to do, where there is literally nothing to do to fulfill that obligation, is implausible.

SDLT5, Kant's Principle, tells us that any logical contradiction is not obligatory. Now it seems all right, if pointless, to say that it is not the case that a contradiction ought to be; after all, no contradictions will be. But persons sometimes are told they ought to perform actions that are contradictory; sometimes they themselves believe that they should do so. These facts do not show that in fact we have some contradictory obligations; but they do show, I think, that the burden of proof lies on the person who claims that it never happens that a person ought to do what is self-contradictory. An argument, not an assumption, is needed.

Next, consider SDLT2. Considered as a matter of what ought to be, SDLT2 is intelligible but false. Suppose that it ought to be that p → q, and it ought to be that p. Can we reasonably conclude that it ought to be that q? Only if it ought to be that *both* p → q and p. And we can conclude that only if we suppose that from the fact that each of two propositions ought to be, their conjunction ought to be — that is, only if we suppose SDLT4 to be correct. And we have already said that SDLT4 does not hold for 'ought to be' statements. Hence, neither does SDLT2. On the other hand, SDLT2 is plausible for 'ought to do' statements: if you ought to do either F or G, and you ought not to do F, then you ought to do G. If Tamino ought to go through one of the three doors, and he ought not to go through the one on the left or through the one on the right, then he ought to go through the one in the middle.

Let us summarize these results. SDLT1, SDLT5, SDLR2, and SDLT6 all have some plausibility as principles of what ought to be, none as principles of what a person ought to do. Conversely, SDLT2, SDLT3, and SDLR3 are plausible as principles of what a person ought to do, not as principles of what ought to be. SDLT4 is false for both 'ought to be' and 'ought to do' statements; while SDLR4 is questionable for both kinds of statements. Therefore, standard deontic logic can uphold SDLT1, SDLT5, SDLR2, and SDLT6 with any appearance of faithfulness to ordinary deontic speech and arguments only by using one sense of 'ought'; it can uphold SDLT2, SDLT3, and SDLR3 only by using the other sense of 'ought'; and with SDLT4 and SDLR4, neither sense of 'ought' seems able to escape trouble. Such plausibility as SDL has therefore rests on an equivocation. I noted in Chapter 2 that the typical assertions and rules of SDL all follow from SDL semantics. If deontic logic is to be faithful to ordinary deontic thought, neither the semantics of 'ought to be' statements nor the semantics of 'ought to do' statements can be standard.

These are results that I shall come back to in the second part of this book, when it is time to formulate a new version of deontic logic. But for now, we can conclude that 'ought to be' and corresponding 'ought to do' statements differ in meaning, and that to conflate the two types of 'oughts' is indeed to equivocate.

2. THE TWO KINDS OF 'OUGHT' STATEMENTS HAVE DIFFERENT LOGICAL BEHAVIOR

A logician is unlikely to be worried by a mere difference in meaning between 'ought to do' and 'ought to be' statements. But there is worse to come. For the two kinds of 'ought' statements exhibit a substantive difference in logical behavior. And this difference is enough to justify separate treatment for the two 'oughts'.

Hector-Neri Castañeda found a major difference in logical form between the two kinds of 'ought' statements. Castañeda held that what ought to be is a state of affairs; but for him, the object of an 'ought to do' is neither a state of affairs, a proposition, nor a fact, but something completely different, which Castañeda terms a practition.[18] Although I do not adopt Castañeda's proposition/practition distinction, I think he was right to find a difference in the behavior of the two kinds of 'ought' statements. For the 'ought to be' is a *de dicto* operator, while the 'ought to do' is *de re*.

The distinction between *de dicto* and *de re* operators is familiar from modal sentences. The sentence "George can take out the garbage" presents an apparent *de re* possibility. It says that a certain possibility holds *of George*: George must exist for the sentence to be true. On the other hand, consider "It is possible that George takes out the garbage." This latter sentence presents a *de dicto* possibility, and George's existence is not required for its truth.[19]

Deontic operators can also be either *de dicto* or *de re*. "George ought to take out the garbage" can only be a *de re* deontic modality. It cannot possibly be true unless there is such a person as George. The sentence predicates a certain 'ought' *of* George. Thus the 'ought to do' operator does not operate on entire propositions, for the subject term is outside the scope of the operator. Rather, the 'ought to do' operator in ordinary deontic thought operates on predicates only.

However, "It ought to be that George takes out the garbage" is a *de dicto* deontic modality. In stipulating that a certain state of affairs should be, the sentence is in no way committed to the existence of any of its components. Even if there is not and never will be such a person as George, or even if no garbage is ever accumulated, it still might be true that it ought to be that George takes out the garbage. Thus the 'ought to be' operator in ordinary deontic thought operates on entire propositions, not merely on predicates.

Standard methods of deontic notation suggest no difference between quantification over object and quantification over agent. In translating into notation the sentence, "George ought to take out the garbage," the standard procedure is to begin by recasting the sentence as something like either "Ought (George takes out the garbage)" or "Ought (George to take out the garbage)."[20] Now if the context introduced by this 'ought' is such that one cannot quantify existentially over 'garbage' or 'George's-taking-out-the-garbage' while being sure to preserve the truth of the original sentence, it is hard to see how one could under the same conditions quantify existentially over 'George'.[21] All these terms are, on the standard construal, within the scope of the operator.

But in our ordinary deontic thinking, we are perfectly able to quantify existentially over the agent term of an 'ought to do' statement *salva veritate*. If George ought to take out the garbage, then surely somebody ought to take out the garbage. The term 'George' in the sentence "George ought to take out the garbage" appears to be in purely referential position. The subject term of an 'ought to do' sentence is therefore not within the scope of the operator; rather, the 'ought to do' operator is *de re* and operates on predicates.

Peter Geach reaches the same conclusion from a telling example. [Geach, 3][22] The sentences "John beats up Tom" and "Tom is beaten up by John" are equivalent. Prefacing each sentence with the same deontic operator should then yield equivalent expressions. But there is a large difference between "John ought to beat up Tom" and "Tom ought to be beaten up by John." The first sentence states what John ought to do, while the second states what Tom ought to suffer. A pacifist could with perfect consistency accept the second — "Tom has it coming" — and deny the first — "No matter what Tom has done, John should be above beating him up," or perhaps "It would be a work of supererogation on John's part to beat up the vicious bully Tom." Therefore, Geach concludes, it is bad logic to take all deontic operators as attaching to propositions.

But the attachment of operators to propositions, as such, is not the true source of philosophic error in Geach's example. Suppose that one accepts Hector-Neri Castañeda's contention that deontic operators attach to practitions. Still, the practition *John to beat up Tom* seems, so far as I can tell about those queer entities, to be equivalent to the practition *Tom to be beaten up by John*, in which case Geach's difficulty arises for Castañeda's system as well as for SDL.

The real moral to Geach's example is that the subject of an 'ought to do' sentence does not fall within the scope of the deontic operator, whatever one takes that scope to include.[23] That is, an 'ought to do' statement is *de re*. We should read "John ought to beat up Tom" as "John is such that he ought to beat up Tom," where the word 'John' but not the word 'Tom' is in purely referential position. Likewise, we should read "Tom ought to be beaten up by John" as "Tom is such that he ought to be beaten up by John," where the word 'Tom' but not the word 'John' is in purely referential position. Clearly these two statements are quite different from one another.

However, "John beats up Tom" is equivalent to "Tom is beaten up by John." Hence, the state of affairs <John's beating up Tom> is equivalent to the state of affairs <Tom's being beaten up by John>. To say that the first state of affairs ought to be is therefore to say that the second state of affairs ought to be, and vice versa. Therefore, the statements "It ought to be that John beats up Tom" and "It ought to be that Tom is beaten up by John" are equivalent.

Changing the active to the passive voice therefore makes no difference to an 'ought to be' statement, for the operator is *de dicto*; but the change from active to passive voice radically affects the meaning of an 'ought to do' statement, for the operator is *de re*. Hence, Geach's example illustrates the major difference in logical form between 'ought to do' and 'ought to be' statements.

Since the 'ought to do' operator is *de re* and operates on predicates, while the 'ought to be' operator is *de dicto* and operates on propositions; since the 'ought to do' operator presupposes the existence of the subject, while the 'ought to be' operator does not; then there is every reason to conclude that the two operators in counterpart deontic sentences are utterly distinct, not only in meaning but in logical behavior. Standard deontic logic, and any other deontic logic that does not distinguish between the two 'oughts', is therefore at a huge remove from our ordinary deontic reasoning.

3. THE TWO KINDS OF 'OUGHT' STATEMENTS DO NOT IMPLY EACH OTHER

Since 'ought to do' statements differ in meaning and logical form from 'ought to be' statements, it is likely that either an 'ought to do' does not imply the corresponding 'ought to be', or an 'ought to be' does not imply the corresponding 'ought to do'. I shall argue in this section that in fact, neither kind of 'ought' statement implies the other. That is, 'ought to be' statements are neither necessary nor sufficient conditions for their counterpart 'ought to do' statements.

First, I shall show that 'ought to be' statements do not imply their 'ought to do' counterparts.[24] This point should be obvious from the previous section. For since an 'ought to do' statement, being *de re*, implies the existence of the agent, it follows that if its counterpart 'ought to be' statement implies the 'ought to do', then the 'ought to be' statement would imply the existence of the agent. But an 'ought to be' statement does not imply the existence of the agent, for the 'ought to be' operator is *de dicto*. Therefore, an 'ought to be' statement does not imply its counterpart 'ought to do' statement.

Examples back up this conclusion. More than one theologian has believed humans inherently sinful but has nevertheless inveighed against sin. Many have no doubt taken literally Jesus' injunction (Matthew 5:48) to be perfect. Such thinkers suppose not only that it ought to be that humans are sinless, but that each human ought to make himself sinless. But if it is impossible for a human to make himself sinless, it seems at least pointless to say that any person ought to do so. Thus many readers have interpreted Matthew 5:48 as requiring only that each person try to be as sinless as possible. But in giving up a literal duty to become sinless, I suggest they are not giving up their ideal: it ought to be that humans are sinless. It is this ideal that inspires their supposed duty to try. Hence, in certain cases, one can consistently hold both that a certain state of affairs ought to be, and that no one ought to bring that state of affairs into being.

Again, many people have believed in utopias without supposing anyone to have the duty of bringing their utopias into existence.[25] Plato's Socrates affirmed that the ideal state of the *Republic* could arise only if philosophers became kings or kings philosophers; but not even he laid the duty on anyone or any group to perform this marvelous transmutation. To give an 'ought to be' without supposing an 'ought to do' might seem foolish to practical people, but it does not seem illogical.

Or again, consider "You ought to be a movie star." That sentence might be used to spur a person on to applying at studios, or to get movie moguls to help the person's cinema career. But it might be no more than an expression of a state of affairs for which the speaker at least pretends to wish. The speaker need hardly suppose that people should act to bring about that state of affairs.

For that matter, I see no objection in logic to an atheist's claiming that the wicked should not be left unpunished. The atheist might well believe that the best universe would be one in which reward is perfectly proportioned to virtue, but that there is no agency for bringing about that universe in all its perfection. She might believe that humans should work to make the world as close to her ideal as possible, but she need not believe even that. Her goal is perfect, shimmering, and utterly unapproachable.

One might object that my cases simply play off the distinction between *prima facie* and actual duties.[26] If one thinks a state of affairs ought to be, then, says the objector, to be consistent one must think that someone ought to realize that state of affairs — but the latter 'ought' is, in the objector's view, only *prima facie*. However, even if S has only a *prima facie* duty to do F, S must exist; whereas, even if it actually ought to be that S does F, S need not exist. Hence the *prima facie*/actual distinction is irrelevant to my claim that an 'ought to be' does not imply its counterpart 'ought to do'.

Moreover, consider supererogatory acts. Supererogation I take to be a matter of going above and beyond the call of duty: a soldier's diving on the live grenade to protect his buddies, for instance. These are the acts of saints and heroes, in Urmson's phrase. Clearly it ought to be that people perform heroic and saintly acts. But since going beyond one's duty is doing something that is not one's duty, it is surely permissible to fail to go beyond one's duty.

I believe it false that the soldier *ought* to dive on the grenade. Here a great many philosophers, including the one to whom this book is dedicated, would differ with me. But I think that in ordinary use, people do not make the distinction between 'ought', 'duty', and 'obligation' that philosophers have found useful. Moreover, I expect most people have no trouble in accepting SDLT7, 'Op ↔ ~P~p'. Now if it is permissible for a person to fail to perform a work of supererogation, then by SDLT7, it is not the case that the person ought to perform that work. But if I am right to regard supererogatory acts as acts that ought to be but as not acts that people ought to do, 'ought to be' does not imply the counterpart 'ought to do'. It does not even imply a *prima facie* counterpart.

These results are what one might expect. For, as I suggested, those who say what ought to be tell us what they think would be needed to achieve an improved or perhaps even an optimal world. These statements usually express a speaker's wish. But there are wishes that one knows to be idle, even as one wishes them. And one can affirm that a state of affairs ought to be without affirming that anyone ought to do anything.

Next, I shall argue that 'ought to be' statements are not implied by their 'ought to do' counterparts. Here again, we can derive this conclusion directly. I argued earlier in this chapter that 'ought to do' statements can conflict, but that 'ought to be' statements cannot. Although it is plausible to claim that a lawyer both ought to countenance and ought not to countenance perjury, it is implausible to suppose that it ought to be that she both countenance and not countenance perjury. However, if 'ought to do' implied 'ought to be', then a conflict of 'ought to be' statements would be possible. Hence, as the assumption that 'ought to do' implies 'ought to be' leads to an absurdity, the assumption must be false. Similarly, I noted that SDLT2, SDLT3, and SDLR3 all work with the 'ought to do' but not with the 'ought to be' — an impossibility if the former implied the latter.

Nevertheless, it looks counterintuitive to suppose that 'ought to do' statements do not imply their 'ought to be' counterparts. For surely, if John ought to mow the lawn today, there ought to be a state of affairs which includes John's mowing the lawn today. If Adam may not learn of good and evil, his having knowledge of good and evil is impermissible. The point seems trivially true.

The point is neither trivial nor true, however, as examples show. Suppose that a person ought to perform an action, because his doing so would meet certain moral or prudential standards. Nevertheless, the person would not perform that action if the world were better than it is. Perhaps the action, actually obligatory in the real world, is incompatible with the standards of a better world. What mother has not told her child: "You should apologize, but would it not be a lot better if you didn't have to apologize?"

Suppose that I have made a rash promise to act in a certain way. Had I thought things through, I would have realized that I had marginally better courses of action open to me than the one I promised. In a better world, I would not have made the promise in the first place; hence, it is not the case that it ought to be that I perform the action in question. However, given that in the real world I did make the promise, and given that alternative courses of action are only marginally better, I ought to perform that action.

In general, an 'ought to be' statement requires a broader setting than its 'ought to do' counterpart. Often a person ought to choose the lesser of two evils. But in such cases, it ought not to be that the person make that choice, for it ought not to be that the person be faced with such a choice. If other people had done what they ought to have done, and if nature, God, or whatever powers there be had acted favorably, what the agent ought to do at this time would be quite different. Hence, what the agent ought to do is not what ought to be.

For example: Brown's leg is gangrenous; the only way to save his life is to amputate the leg. Dr. Smith, the surgeon in charge of the case, consequently ought to amputate Brown's leg. But how did the leg become gangrenous in the first place? A drunken motorist ran over Brown, causing serious damage to his knee, as well as more obvious injuries. A well-meaning motorist stopped at the scene, picked Brown up, stashed him in the motorist's pick-up truck (further damaging the knee), and rushed him to the hospital. At the hospital, the overworked resident overlooked the injury to the knee joint. When Brown's knee became infected, the laboratory technician misread the tests on the microorganism causing the infection; as a result, Brown was given the wrong antibiotic. By the time Brown is referred to Dr. Smith, there is nothing she can do to save his leg after all the bungling that has occurred. In this situation, Dr. Smith surely ought to amputate Brown's leg. But it is equally clear that her amputating Brown's leg is an occurrence that ought not to be. For the situation should never have arisen. 'Ought to do', then, does not imply 'ought to be'.

It is sad but true that, on occasion, doing one's duty produces a comparatively poor result; it is equally true that a person who conscientiously tries to produce the best results will at times stray from the path of duty. Most of us try to find a rough-and-ready balance between teleological and deontological concerns: we are neither total precisians for duty nor complete result merchants. But if the meaning of "X ought to be" is, roughly, that X would occur if the world were better in relevant ways, then 'ought to be' is part of the language of teleology.[27] And since at least some 'ought to be' statements are teleological, there will be cases in which the ideals presented by those statements are incompatible with the performance of certain duties. If so, then in some cases one ought to do one's duty, even though doing so would result in a state of affairs other than what ought to be.

Nor should we have expected an 'ought to do' to imply its counterpart 'ought to be'. For what people ought to do is usually not what realizes ideals and thus brings about what ought to be, but what meets certain requirements. To bring about what ought to be usually requires more of an agent than to do what the agent ought to do. In fact, bringing about what ought to be often places impossibly stringent demands upon an agent. As a result, we do not in general take bringing about what ought to be as even part of what the agent ought to do.

Similar results obtain if we consider epistemic 'oughts'. Suppose that the available evidence amply justifies my false belief that p. Then it seems reasonable to suppose that I ought to assert that p, even though it ought not to be the case that I assert p. That is, I ought, in the light of the *available* evidence, to assert p; but since p is false, then the *total* evidence must show that it ought not to be the case that I assert p.[28]

For these reasons, an 'ought to be' neither implies nor is implied by its counterpart 'ought to do'. Hence, not only do counterpart 'ought to be' and 'ought to do' statements differ in meaning, but there is no logical connection between them.[29]

4. THE CONNECTION BETWEEN COUNTERPART 'OUGHT' STATEMENTS IS ONE OF PRAGMATICS

But 'ought to do' statements and their 'ought to be' counterparts are surely connected in some way. If Smith should have known better, then Smith should have found out the truth beforehand; if he should have found out, then he should have known. If there ought to be a law, then the appropriate agency should enact that law, and vice versa. Even with the universal 'ought to be', it seems tempting to translate "The wicked should not be left unpunished" as "God, or posterity, or some other agent should punish the wicked." Perhaps *some* 'ought to be' statements mean the same as their 'ought to do' counterparts; or maybe some 'ought to be' statements imply and are implied by their counterparts. Maybe we could find a rule to distinguish those cases where there is meaning-identity or mutual implication from those where there is not.

I see no reason to expect any such rule. For we can consider the main types of 'ought to be' statements:

(1) Some 'ought to be' statements have no clear connection at all with action or with values: "That ought to be the Colorado River down there."
(2) Some 'ought to be' statements reflect values but, as a rule, generate no prescriptions for action: "Philosophers should be rulers of the state." These are often like ordinary optatives: Othello said to his wife, "Would thou hadst ne'er been born."
(3) Some 'ought to be' statements both reflect values and usually generate at least some prescriptions for individual, group, or state action: "There should be no starving children in our rich society."

Statements of the first two types appear to have little if any connection with counterpart 'ought to do' statements.[30] Only with statements of the third kind is there some sort of connection: My examination focused on statements of this third kind; in looking at them, I found no relations of logical implication in either direction between a counterpart 'ought to be' and 'ought to do'. Where there is no mutual implication, there cannot be meaning equivalence. It might be reprehensible, but it is not illogical to believe both that there should be no starving children in our society and that no persons, individually or collectively, have a duty to relieve the starvation that exists.

The tie between 'ought to be' and 'ought to do' counterparts is therefore not one of logic, nor are the two kinds of 'ought' statement identical in meaning.[31]   And yet the tie is real.   I suggest that the connection between the two types of 'ought' statement is one of pragmatics. For normally, there is no point in making an 'ought to be' statement unless one is prepared to endorse some relevant 'ought to do' statements as well (including the counterpart expression). Those 'ought to do' statements might be vague and impractical, but without them the 'ought to be' would express a purely idle wish. And to state something purely idle is pointless.

Go back to the atheist who believes that the wicked should not be left unpunished. I claimed that she need not suppose that human efforts can begin to bring about that state of affairs. But suppose she flatly asserts that no human efforts, the only kind she admits, can make any difference at all in remedying the situation. She is not contradicting her ideal, but one wonders why she wastes her breath in stating the ideal at all. Certainly, the ideal does not guide her actions.

I am assuming that the usual role played by a picture of how things should or should not be is to guide actions — one's own directly, those of others indirectly.[32]   This role is normal whether the 'ought to be' is an ideal or a mere wish. An 'ought to be' without an 'ought to do' is incapable of playing the normal role, although it might have some other role to play.

If you assert that I ought to be ashamed of my conduct, you are not supposing that I can call up the appropriate feeling at will. Feeling ashamed is not an action to be performed. But surely you do think I ought to consider my conduct more carefully from the moral point of view. If not, why did you bother to make the assertion at all? You had your reasons, I suppose, but they certainly are not obvious. Or, of course, you could be trying to guide my actions, but you seem completely inept at figuring out how to do so. All sorts of things might be true, but I nevertheless have good reason, on hearing your assertion, to expect that you think I ought to do, or to refrain from doing, some action.

In a large bridge tournament, the game was late in starting, and players were wandering about the room. The tournament director announced: "All persons who have bought entries to this afternoon's session should be in their seats." No doubt, the point of the director's speech was to direct players to their seats. But his words did not imply that aim. He would not have contradicted himself had he added, "but I do not assert that players not in their seats should go there." The director's 'ought to be' only *implicated* an 'ought to do'. The connection was pragmatic, not logical.

Sometimes, of course, the user of an 'ought to be' has in mind actions that should have been taken some time in the past. If, looking at the ravages of ferocious strip-mining, you tell me that the land should be forested parkland, you might not be willing to assert that something should be done about it now, but you surely believe that the mining should have been prevented or made less destructive in the past.

'Ought to be' statements of the sort that reflect values and generate prescriptions are usually but not always meant to guide actions. One might put forward an 'ought to be' statement to change others' feelings or to vent one's own, where there is no possibility of altering anyone's conduct. This can be true even if the 'ought to be' statement is of the type that normally generates prescriptions for action. Or one might make such a statement in an effort to inform, or to express one's considered judgment. One could imagine using, "There ought to be no starving children in the world," in any of these ways, as well as to try to bring about action. Where the 'ought to be' statement is not used to guide actions, the speaker rarely has in mind the counterpart 'ought to do' statement.[33] When I inform you of my ideals concerning world hunger, if that is all I am doing, I am not implying anything about what anybody ought to be doing.

That 'ought to do' statements normally convey a picture of what ought to be is clear enough. To tell a child in all sincerity that he ought to practice the violin, while thinking all the time that it would be better if he did not, seems to be generally pointless. But one could easily imagine circumstances in which a parent would have good reason to make such a speech to a child.

All these considerations indicate that the connection between counterpart 'ought to be' and 'ought to do' statements is pragmatic. The connection, where it exists, depends on the purpose for which one makes an 'ought to be' statement. If that purpose is the normal one of action-guiding, we expect there to be an 'ought to do' statement in reserve. If there is none, the speaker has misled us but has not contradicted himself. And if the speaker's purpose is not to guide actions, then we have no reason to expect an 'ought to do' in reserve. Similarly, when the speaker attempts to guide action by making an 'ought to do' statement, we have reason to expect that she thinks a world with the action to be better than one without. Our expectation will not always be correct, but it will usually be so.

A pragmatic connection, a Gricean implicature, depends on the purpose of making an utterance. It holds normally, but not always. It creates a presumption; when the presumption is defeated, explanations are due. This seems exactly the sort of tie which exists between counterpart 'ought to be' and 'ought to do' statements.

Pragmatics, then, rather than logic or meaning-equivalence, explains the connection between 'ought to be' statements and their 'ought to do' counterparts.

But what then becomes of Standard Deontic Logic, if its 'ought' operator is so radically ambiguous? One might try the heroic step of banishing 'ought to be' statements from SDL. Such a move has some plausibility, for deontic logic would seem above all to concern actions. True, 'ought to be' statements are normally action-guiding, but so are many non-deontic utterances. And the appearance of the word 'ought' is hardly sufficient to make a context deontic. If, as I have suggested, 'ought to be' statements normally express desires and values, a general logic of action must take account of them. But a general logic of action would comprehend much more than deontic logic.

But if we read 'ought to be' statements out of deontic logic, many statements of Standard Deontic Logic become simply unintelligible. If we decide not to read 'OFa' as "It ought to be the case that a does F," how shall we read 'O(p → Fa)', or 'O(p ⊸ (q v Fa))', or some even more complex proposition within the scope of 'O'? No clear meaning attaches to "A ought to do the following: 'p' is true if and only if either 'q' is true or a does F." Nor are there any plausible rules by which we could attach a meaning to such a sentence. Yet the more natural 'ought to be' reading is, by hypothesis, barred. Iterated and nested deontic modalities would be unintelligible.

I suggest that deontic logicians, when faced with a complex proposition within the scope of a deontic operator, tacitly read the operator as saying: "The following state of affairs ought to be;" or perhaps as "It ought to be the case that . . ." Such a reading is permissible, given the removal of the 'ought to be' from Standard Deontic Logic, only if 'ought to do' sentences could be translated into or imply their 'ought to be' counterparts. But they cannot.

To be sure, logicians have done violence to natural languages in the past, and perhaps after years of staring, one might make sense of such a sentence as "A should do the following: 'p' is true if and only if either 'q' is true or a does F." The semantics of a natural language is rarely a static affair. But the fact that deontic logicians regularly employ expressions with no clear English equivalent, all as part of arguments which, among other things, transfer normative force from premises to conclusion, should give us all pause. The fact suggests what the deontic paradoxes suggest: something is rotten in standard deontic logics. Restricting SDL to the 'ought to do' will not rescue it.

Restricting SDL to 'ought to do' statements fails for more reasons than the unintelligibility of some of its statements. Consider again Schotch and Jennings's point that, in SDL, the fact that we ought to feed the starving poor implies that there ought to be starving poor. The absurdity of this result is even greater if we restrict SDL to 'ought to do' statements. How could our duty to feed the starving poor imply, without the addition of any supplementary facts, their duty to starve or anyone's duty to starve them? For that matter, how could my obligation by itself imply anyone else's obligation? Even if you are my slave, that I owe money hardly implies that you owe money. The gulf between standard deontic logics and our ordinary deontic thinking looks utterly impassible.

From arguments drawn from meaning, from individual cases, from the truth of standard SDL propositions, and from the logical form of 'ought' expressions, we have seen that 'ought to do' expressions differ completely from their 'ought to be' counterparts. Even when it ought to be that an agent perform a certain act, we cannot infer that the agent ought to perform that act; nor does the converse implication hold. There is at most a pragmatic connection between the two oughts; and of pragmatic connections, a properly constituted logic knows nothing whatsoever.

Chapter 5: Why Deontic Logic Needs a Semantics

In this chapter I shall explain why some type of semantics is essential to any deontic logic. In the five chapters that follow, I shall be looking at problems in SDL semantics. My overall aim is to show that deontic logicians, because of problems in SDL semantics, have no option but to provide a better semantics; to give up on semantics as an unnecessary part of deontic logic is to give up on deontic logic itself.

Let us start with an example. Smith ought to kill Brown. Unknown to Smith, however, Brown is the finest person in town. Does it follow that Smith ought to kill the finest person in town? Does it follow that there is someone who ought to kill Brown, a person whom Smith ought to kill, or a killing that ought to take place?

These questions raise the issue of whether deontic contexts are extensional. This issue is large and important; the range and power of deontic logic depend largely on how the issue is settled. For suppose that deontic contexts are not extensional but intensional. Deontic contexts are then like belief contexts or statements of possibility: one can no more deduce the existence of the Loch Ness monster from the truth of "John ought to kill the Loch Ness monster" than one can from the truth of "Jane believes that the Loch Ness monster is dangerous" or from that of "It is possible that Tillie was killed by the Loch Ness monster." In intensional contexts, terms that normally refer cannot be counted on to do so, even though the sentences containing such contexts are true. To use Quine's term, intensional contexts are referentially opaque.

But a referentially opaque context is, from the standpoint of normal logical operations, a closed book. Consider the following types of inference:

(A) John believes that p.
     If p then q.
     John believes that q.

(B) John believes that p.
     John believes that if p then q.
     John believes that q.

(C) It is possible that p.
     <u>If p then q.</u>
     It is possible that q.

(D) It is possible that p.
     <u>It is possible that if p then q.</u>
     It is possible that q.

All of these seem to be versions of the familiar *modus ponens* inference form; yet if regarded as such, each is clearly invalid. In A, John might not realize that if p then q; in B, John might not have drawn the reasonable conclusion from his beliefs. In C and D, for all we know, the falsity of 'If p then q' is a necessary condition for the truth of p.

In intensional contexts, then, one cannot confidently plow ahead, using standard logical operations, with any sure expectation that truth will be preserved from premises to conclusions. Quine's warning stands: "Intuitively, what occurs inside a referentially opaque context may be looked upon as an orthographic accident, without logical status, like the occurrence of 'cat' in 'cattle'." [Quine 1, 13] An opaque context, Quine warned, must be treated as a monolith; individual terms cannot be extracted from opaque contexts for the purpose of logical operations. Only a worked-out semantics will allow normal logical operations to proceed within such contexts.

If deontic contexts are extensional, deontic logic faces no special problems unless it has internal difficulties. But if deontic contexts are intensional, the very possibility of a workable deontic logic — or, at any rate, a logic that can work *within* deontic contexts, one that is not forced to take such contexts as entire unanalyzable blocks — depends on our ability to find a workable deontic semantics.

At first blush, it seems obvious that deontic contexts are intensional. After all, most deontic logicians stress a parallel between deontic and modal operators; and modal contexts are paradigms of intensionality. But Hector-Neri Castañeda has argued that one can both quantify existentially into a deontic context and substitute equals for equals in a deontic context, preserving the truth of the context in either case.[1] [Castañeda 5, 228-232] If he is right, then deontic contexts pass Quine's tests for extensionality.

I shall argue that Castañeda's claim is incorrect: deontic contexts are intensional. The fact that subject-terms in 'ought to do' statements have stable reference shows only that such terms do not occur within deontic contexts. Words such as 'ought (to do)' and 'may (do)' are wrongly taken as operators on entire statements; rather, their scope is the *predicates* of those statements.[2]

Castañeda, in the passage mentioned above, treats the question of existential quantification into deontic contexts separately from the question of substitutivity within such contexts. He even comes up with two separate extensionality claims: that deontic propositional functions are extensional with respect to quantification; and that deontic propositional functions are extensional with respect to substitutivity of identities.[3] [Castañeda 5, 229 and 231] I shall make use of Castañeda's distinction, for looking at both substitutivity and existential quantification reveals not only the fact but the degree of intensionality. Logically, one can do less with contexts that are intensional with respect to both existential quantification and substitutivity than one can with contexts that are intensional with respect to quantification alone.

Further, I shall treat 'ought to do' statements separately from 'ought to be' statements. In the sentence "It ought to be that p," 'p' stands for a statement that contains one or more purportedly referring expressions. If those expressions do in fact refer, one can happily engage in existentially quantifying over them and substituting equals for them, without fear of turning an originally true statement into a false one; if the terms do not refer, such operations are suspect.[4] I argued in Chapter 4 that, in the sentence "S ought to do A to B," the subject term 'S' is not in the scope of the deontic operator. The context within which 'S' appears is then extensional. But what about 'A', which purportedly designates an action-type, and 'B', which purportedly designates an object of the action? For the original sentence to be true, must 'A' and 'B' succeed in referring? If they need not, then 'ought to do' contexts are intensional.

I must therefore consider three sets of questions: one set concerning 'ought to be' contexts, and two sets concerning 'ought to do' contexts. For each set, I need to consider both the matter of existential generalization and the matter of substitutivity.

'Ought to be' contexts are clearly intensional, according to the test of existential generalization. If there ought to be a law, there need not be such a law now. If it ought to be the case that we preserve resources for our remote posterity, then no doubt both we and the resources exist, but the posterity need not. We often use the expression 'ought to be' to express a wish; and wishes might, but need not, concern actual individuals.

The test of substitutivity gives less clear results when applied to an 'ought to be' context. Consider the following case:

> (C1) Flo reaches the conclusion, amply justified by evidence available to her, that the person at the door ought to be her brother-in-law. Unknown to Flo, her brother-in-law has become the most recently recruited DEA agent.

Case C1 presents an epistemic 'ought'. Should Flo conclude from C1 that the person at the door ought to be the most recently recruited DEA agent? Clearly not. For the evidence that justifies her conclusion that the person at the door ought to be her brother-in-law does not license her to say that the person at the door ought to be the most recently recruited DEA agent. She lacks any evidence that would warrant the latter claim.

A similar situation might seem to occur whenever a set of rules and practices governs a non-epistemic 'ought to be'. For those rules play much the same role as did the available evidence in case C1. For example:

> (C2) According to the law, it ought to be the case that the rights of the defendant in this case are respected. The defendant is the tallest person in the courtroom. The law is silent on the rights of the tallest person in the courtroom.

In case C2, legal rules, precedents, and procedures are the basis of the statement that the rights of the defendant ought to be respected. Those same rules, precedents, and procedures do not warrant any conclusion that the rights of the tallest person in the courtroom ought to be respected. Substitutivity therefore appears to fail in C2.

But a closer look at C2 suggests that legal, moral, prudential, and etiquette 'ought to be' statements are not as opaque as the epistemic 'ought to be'. Although rules are silent on the legal rights of the tallest person, that hardly means that the tallest person lacks those rights. After all, the law grants rights to persons, not to persons-under-certain-descriptions. Therefore, if it ought to be that the defendant's rights are respected, it ought to be that the rights of that person, however described, are respected. Substitutivity in at least some 'ought to be' contexts appears not to fail.

And yet it does fail in other contexts. Consider the following:

(C3) It ought to have been that Christopher build St. Swithin's Cathedral in the heart of Little Gidding. He did in fact do so, and - thus produced the ugliest building in Little Gidding.

Here I find it reasonable to deny that it ought to have been that Christopher build the ugliest building in Little Gidding. And that is a failure of substitutivity.

The difference between C2 and C3, I suggest, is that the latter but not the former makes use of differently-tensed statements. At any time at which it ought to be that Christopher build the cathedral, the cathedral was unbuilt and thus was not identical with the ugliest building in Little Gidding. At any time that the cathedral was the ugliest building in Little Gidding, it was false that it ought to be that Christopher build the cathedral. Hence, if we time-index our statements, it looks as if we can substitute equivalents within an 'ought to be' context *salva veritate* — so long as the equivalence holds at the same time as the 'ought to be' statement.

Ruth Barcan Marcus, however, pointed out that the substitution of *extensional* equivalents in an extensional statement does not change the truth-value of the statement. [Marcus, 581-582] By this test, 'ought to be' contexts are clearly intensional. In Marcus's example, in a Manichaean world where each bit of good is exactly matched by a corresponding bit of evil, and vice versa, if it ought to be that you do something good, it does not follow that it ought to be that you do evil.

For 'ought to be' contexts, then, failure of existential generalization clearly establishes their intensionality. In non-epistemic cases, as long as we are careful about time-references, there is no failure of substitutivity for meaning-equivalents or for expressions designating the same object, but there is failure for extensional equivalents. Hence, the degree of intensionality is not as great in the case of moral and legal 'ought to be' statements as it is with epistemic 'ought to be' statements.[5]

The 'ought to be' context is therefore similar in its functioning to a context within the scope of a *de dicto* possibility operator. The scopes of both the 'ought to be' operator and the possibility operator are global: all the purportedly referring terms in a clause prefaced by either operator are within the scope of that operator. Now, of course, just as one can attribute possible situations to real people, so can one say that real people ought to be in certain situations. But in each case, we learn of the reality of the people only from collateral information, not from the modal or deontic statement itself.

Chapter 4 gave us reason to expect that 'ought to be' contexts are intensional. For these, I argued, indicate the speaker's vision of a better world, but such a world might contain some entities not to be found in the real world. Terms which purport to pick out entities in the improved world might well fail to refer to items in the real world. If so, 'ought to be' contexts must be referentially opaque. However, an improved world will be no different in some respects from the real world; the manner in which we refer to those objects in the improved world which are identical to items in the real world would seem to make no logical difference, so long as we are careful about time-references. Hence, although 'ought to be' contexts are opaque, substitutivity of meaning-equivalents is preserved.

I turn next to 'ought to do' contexts. When Castañeda terms these extensional, he has in mind such everyday examples as this:

(C4). I ought to help old Mrs. Brown across the street.

Here there are two persons (*a* and *b*) and a street (*c*), such that *a* ought to help *b* across *c*. It seems not to matter which terms a speaker uses to pick out those persons or that street: *a*, however referred to, ought to help *b*, however referred to, across *c*, however referred to. Case C4 is clearly extensional.

But not every 'ought to do' context is like C4. Consider the following example:

(C5). Christopher has contracted to build St. Swithin's Cathedral in the heart of Little Gidding. From the time of the contract onward, Christopher has a legal obligation to build St. Swithin's. Building the cathedral is a good thing, and Christopher has received payment; Christopher therefore has a moral obligation to build St. Swithin's. But the cathedral did not stand when the contract was made, and unfortunately Christopher dies before the work is well under way. St. Swithin's is never built.

Case C5 is an example of what I call the *creative* 'ought to do'. A person ought to (or may, or ought not to, or may not) act in such a way as to help bring about a given situation. The situation does not exist at the time the obligation is imposed and might in fact never exist. That is the case with Christopher's obligation to build St. Swithin's.

Note that time-indexing does not help with C5. The difficulty is not that St. Swithin's exists at a different time from that at which Christopher has his obligation. That is perfectly normal: one does not have a duty to build what already exists. The difficulty is that there is no time at which St. Swithin's exists. In case C5, it is true that Christopher ought to build a particular cathedral but false that there exists a cathedral such that Christopher ought to build it.[6] Existential quantification thus fails with respect to the *object* of the action that Christopher ought to perform.

Case C5 suggests an even more sweeping conclusion. For if a ought to do F to b, then the action-type a's-doing-F-to-b need not have tokens at any time whatsoever. A may at no time do F to b. Hence, if one allows quantification over events and event-types, one cannot count on the success of existential quantification in *any* 'ought to do' contexts. Existential quantification over the action-type might fail to preserve truth, then, in *any* ought-to-do context.

We must be careful at this point, however. A's-doing-F-to-b is, I have suggested, an action-type; different tokens of that type might exist. Now existential quantification over the action-type does not straightforwardly consist in positing tokens of that type. "There exists an action-type Q" does not clearly mean the same as "There exists at least one action of type Q." A platonist might well allow the existence of types without tokens. But where the object of the action-type does not exist, as in case C5, even the platonist will hesitate to allow the existence of the action-type. As there is no such thing as St. Swithin's Cathedral, how can there be such an action-type as Christopher's-building-the-cathedral?

With respect to existential quantification over both object and action-type, then, 'ought to do' contexts appear to be intensional. Nor are creative 'ought to do' contexts the only ones that suggest this conclusion, although they provide the clearest evidence. The following case is more open to question:

(C6). Robinson is charged with the general duty of uncovering covert Communists in a government agency. Robinson has convinced his superiors that there is a Communist with the code name 'Edith' in the agency. As a result, Robinson's superiors have issued him explicit orders to get the goods on Edith. However, there is no such person as Edith whom Robinson ought to get the goods on.

The problem illustrated by case C6 is that sometimes an imposition of duties is based on false beliefs. When that happens, what happens to the duties in question? If falsity of belief does not take away the reality or force of those duties, the preserving of truth in existential quantification becomes a chancy thing, as case C6 indicates.

Certainly, Robinson's superiors believe he has an obligation to get the goods on Edith. If he makes no effort to do so, the superiors will regard his inaction as a dereliction of duty. Even if they discover later that there is no such person as Edith, they are unlikely to regard Edith's failure to exist as licensing Robinson's failure to act. And if Robinson, in trying to carry out his orders, discovers and convinces his superiors of Edith's non-existence, they will still regard what he did up to that point as fulfilling his obligation.

People then regard assigned duties which turn out to be incapable of performance as binding at least to an effort at performance. The burden of proof lies on the person who believes that Robinson has no duty to get the goods on Edith.

One way of meeting that burden would be to invoke Kant's Principle: 'ought' implies 'can'. Because there is no such person as Edith, Robinson cannot do what, according to his orders, he ought to do; therefore, despite those orders, it is false that he ought to get the goods on Edith.[7] For the upholder of the principle that 'ought' implies 'can', then, there is neither a duty nor a difficulty. However, no philosopher today can afford to take Kant's Principle as a truism in no need of support.

Another reason for supposing that Robinson has no obligation is that sometimes those who issue orders are not so much factually mistaken as morally wrong. If one's superior officer in an army issues an order to kill civilians indiscriminately, one should not obey that order. Hence, the argument goes, entitlement and propriety are not sufficient to determine what one ought to do. Something else — moral rightness, perhaps — is needed for that purpose. I do not think this argument proves its point. The *a priori* assumption that obligations can never conflict is unnecessary unless one believes both that 'ought' implies 'can' and that an obligation to do A and an obligation to do B imply an obligation to do A and B. Both of these principles have been questioned; neither is obvious. Hence, if one obligation overrides another, we need not conclude that the overridden obligation lacks force.   Even if entitlement and propriety are not sufficient to determine one's obligation, that hardly affects the case of Robinson and his superiors. Unless one confuses factual mistakes with moral error, Robinson's orders to get the goods on Edith do not seem to partake inevitably of moral evil. Surely it is at least morally acceptable in some cases to ferret out subversives. The Robinson-Edith case is then unaffected even if one requires a moral component in all obligations. Absent a showing of actual wickedness, real obligations might stem from false beliefs.

A third way of arguing that Robinson has no obligation to get the goods on Edith would be to suppose that a real obligation is present only when performing the supposed obligation would result in the creation or preservation of something genuinely valuable.[8] Presumably, if there is no Edith, there is no value to getting the goods on Edith. But that is a very weak presumption. What if, in following his orders to get the goods on Edith, Robinson happens across a genuine subversive? Robinson's actions would then have value.[9]

The case of Robinson and Edith, therefore, provides some reinforcement for my treatment of the case of Christopher, the would-be cathedral builder. Both cases in different ways show the intensionality of 'ought to do' contexts.

I have argued to this point that 'ought to do' contexts are intensional with respect to existential quantification. I must next consider whether they are intensional with respect to substitutability *salva veritate*. Once again, as with the 'ought to be' contexts, substitutivity of meaning-equivalents or of expressions designating the same object is rather murkier than existential quantification.

I start with what might be thought of as a normal case:

(C7) Jane is morally obligated to help Susan. Jane does not know that Susan is secretly married to Arthur.

It seems perfectly reasonable to conclude that Jane is morally obligated to help Arthur's wife, even though she would not state her obligation in that manner.

But again, not all cases seem to work that way. Case C3 has an analogue:

(C8) Christopher had a duty to build St. Swithin's Cathedral in the heart of Little Gidding. He faithfully discharged his duty. That cathedral is the ugliest building in Little Gidding.

It is surely false that Christopher had a duty to build the ugliest building in Little Gidding. Hence, the term 'cathedral' is not in purely referential position, the context is intensional, and substitutivity fails.

But as did C3, C8 points the moral that we should time-index 'ought' statements. At the time when Christopher had the duty in question, St. Swithin's did not exist. It is false that when Christopher had the duty, St. Swithin's was the ugliest building in Little Gidding; and it is false that, now that St. Swithin's is indeed the ugliest building in Little Gidding, Christopher has a duty to build it. If we are careful about time references, C8 exhibits no failure of substitutivity in an 'ought to do' context.

Again, this is a result we should expect. For we normally consider that a person ought to act in a certain way with respect to individuals, not to individuals described in certain ways. If I ought to help Sonia, then I ought to help that person, however she may be described. I can substitute any referring expression for 'Sonia' in "I ought to help Sonia" and preserve truth, so long as the substituting expression holds of Sonia at the same time I ought to help her.

Marcus's point, however, holds for 'ought to do' statements as well as for 'ought to be' statements: substituting extensional equivalents in 'ought to do' contexts need not preserve truth value. In the world where all goods are exactly counterbalanced by evils, a duty to do good does not entail a duty to do evil.

Hence, the 'ought to do' operator, like its 'ought to be' counterpart, introduces an intensional context. However, in both cases, substitutivity of meaning equivalents or of expressions designating the same object is legitimate, so long as we keep time-references straight. Thus the degree of intensionality for both sorts of deontic operator is less than with epistemic oughts.

To sum up the discussion to this point: the opacity of 'ought' statements raises serious difficulties for rich deontic logics, which implicitly treat those statements as referentially transparent. Before the rise of possible world semantics, the opacity of 'ought' statements would have spelled the end of any but bare-bones deontic logic.

For, as Quine argued, a referentially opaque context must be treated either as an entire unit or not at all. [Quine 2, 143] One cannot perform logical operations on material within such a context. Consider what becomes of such a standard inference pattern as *modus ponens* within opaque contexts:

(P1) It is possible that p.
(P2) It is possible that (p → q).
(P3) Therefore, it is possible that q.

This inference is no good, for we do not know whether 'p' and 'p → q' designate, in Leibniz's language, compossible states of affairs. Perhaps the truth of 'p' rules out the truth of 'p → q' and vice versa. Similarly, consider this example:

(B1) Dorothy believes that p.
(B2) Dorothy believes that (p → q).
(B3) Therefore, Dorothy believes that q.

The inference is good only if we can trust Dorothy to recognize and properly apply *modus ponens*. As Dorothy is a human and not a machine, such trust is misplaced, and the inference is no good.

We should draw the same conclusions about such a deontic inference as:

(C1) Dorothy ought to do A.
(C2) Dorothy ought to do this: if A then B.
(C3) Dorothy ought to do B.

For, among other problems, it might be the case that no time at which C1 holds is a time at which C2 holds. Time-indexing would solve that difficulty, but others would be sure to arise.[10]

Someone might object that modal, epistemic, and deontic operators come in pairs, with one member of each pair being the stronger. Among deontic operators, 'ought' is stronger than 'may'. If so, 'ought' should be compared to the strong operators 'must' and 'knows', not to the weak operators 'can' and 'believes'. But this response will not rescue deontic logic from the opacity of deontic contexts, for several reasons:

(a) A strong operator can introduce an opaque context. Quine has argued that, if there are contingent identity statements — itself a vexed claim — one cannot substitute equals for equals within a context introduced by the necessity operator and be guaranteed preservation of the original statement's truth. Necessarily, whoever wins the race is the first person to cross the finish line; the red-haired kid is the first person to cross the finish line; but it does not follow that necessarily, the winner of the race is the red-haired kid. Similarly, George knows that the winner of the race is the first person to cross the finish line; but just because the red-haired kid is first to cross the finish line, it does not follow that George knows the red-haired kid is the winner of the race.

(b) The response depends on an analogy between 'ought', on the one hand, and 'must' and 'knows' on the other. An analogy is a rather weak basis for argument in logic; even so, the analogy is weaker than it should be. For what must be the case, is the case; and what I know to be the case, is the case; but what ought to be the case, unfortunately, often is not the case. Moreover, what I ought to do at times is left undone. In the semantics of deontic logic, this means that the real world is not a relevant possible world. If talk of strength of an operator has any content — as it must for the analogy to hold — 'ought' is significantly weaker than 'must' or 'knows'.

(c) Even though 'knows' is stronger than 'ought', we still cannot use it in a version of *modus ponens*. Consider Dorothy once more:

> (K1) Dorothy knows that p.
> (K2) Dorothy knows that (p → q).
> (K3) Therefore, Dorothy knows that q.

Is this inference any good? Only with an idealized sense of 'knows'. Dorothy could know that p and she could know that (p → q), but she might not ever have put the two together. Perhaps her knowledge is dispositional; she is actively aware that p only on weekdays and actively aware that (p → q) only on weekends. As a result, she has never drawn the conclusion that q, and she has no independent knowledge of the fact. One can save the inference only by taking 'knows' in the sense that a person who has learned the finitely many axioms and rules of inference of a calculus is said thereby to know all the at least denumerably infinitely many theorems which follow by the rules from the axioms. Such an idealized sense of the word is not what people usually mean by 'knows', and it can hardly be used to rescue the validity of an argument — such as the one about Dorothy — which uses the word 'knows' in its everyday sense.

If my contention that deontic contexts are intensional and opaque is correct, a logic that works within deontic contexts would seem to be impossible. Or so it would have seemed before the dawn of deontic semantics. If, as J.L. Austin joked, hydrosemantics is needed for books to be in running brooks, so deontic semantics is needed for there to be any possibility of a rich deontic logic. We need to see just how, thanks to semantics, the genie obligingly climbed back into the bottle.

Modal logic was once in the same desperate straits as deontic logic. Modal contexts are notoriously intensional; Quine thundered that modal logic was conceived in the sin of confusing use and mention.[11] [Quine 1, 175] But rather than accepting its illegitimacy and quietly dying of shame, modal logic is thriving today. Thanks to possible world semantics, the bastard is now legitimate.

To understand how possible world semantics rescued modal logic, we should start not with science fiction but with a much more down-to-earth notion: Carnap's concept of a state description. Suppose that we have a series of yes/no questions such that one particular set of answers would yield a complete description of the world. That set of answers is one state description; other state descriptions are different consistent sets of answers to the same series of questions.

Now to say that a statement 'p' is true in or at some possible world is at least to say that for some state description, the answer to the question 'p?' is 'Yes'. For a modal realist, the truth of 'p' depends on facts about various possible worlds; but even a modal realist will allow the bare-bones account that rests on state descriptions. To do modal logic, one need suppose only that the state description which tells us about the real world succeeds in describing a reality. Yet this simple notion of a state description is enough to allow logicians not only to define but to prove validity in the various modal systems.

SDL semantics, like standard modal semantics, need not affirm the reality of its several possible worlds. In SDL semantics, as we have seen, one restricts the sorts of possible worlds under consideration. Then 'A ought to do F' is understood as 'A does F in every deontically accessible world'. Since the set of deontically accessible worlds is a proper subset of the set of all possible worlds, the consistency of SDL semantics is assured.

A possible world semantics alone can keep deontic logic from falling under Quine's ban on doing logic within opaque contexts. In such a semantics, an opaque sentence is provided a counterpart sentence about possible worlds, and the counterpart is clearly extensional.[12] Whatever we discover about the counterpart and its logical relations, we attribute to the original opaque sentence and its relations. Thus some form of deontic semantics, whether standard or not, is necessary if deontic logic is to be possible.

We can see how semantics rescues deontic logic by looking at a particular inference. Suppose that Jane ought to keep her promises. Suppose further that Jane ought to do the following: if she keeps her promises, she takes care of her mother's cat.[13] Can one conclude that Jane ought to take care of her mother's cat? Not by *modus ponens*, since the conditional in the second premiss is within the scope of the deontic operator. Special rules are needed if the inference is to go through. Those rules will not work without fail in an opaque context; yet, if there is any validity in deontic logic, the inference must be valid. And under SDL semantics, the inference is indeed valid.[14] For by the rule SDLS1:

(A) In all deontically accessible worlds, Jane keeps her promises; and

(B) In all deontically accessible worlds, (Jane keeps her promises → Jane takes care of her mother's cat).

According to SDLS5, there is at least one world deontically accessible to this one. In each such world, according to A, Jane keeps her promises; in each one, according to B, the conditional holds. Hence, in each such world, we can use *modus ponens*. We conclude:

(C) In all deontically accessible worlds, Jane takes care of her mother's cat.

But since there is at least one deontically accessible world, there follows by SDLS2, the principle of backward translation:

(D) Jane ought to take care of her mother's cat.

Thus SDL semantics licenses a basic inference pattern of standard deontic logic — one that happens to be good common sense.

Failure to recognize the hopelessness of a rich deontic logic without deontic semantics allowed Peter Geach to mount a scathing attack on SDL semantics while casually accepting the following as an inference rule: "If given that an agent does A it necessarily follows that he does B, then if he ought to do A he ought to do B."[15] [Geach, 7] Such an inference rule, by working on terms within the scope of a deontic operator, is working within an opaque context. Geach's attack on deontic semantics therefore calls into question not only standard deontic logics but also his own preferred brand.

So much for the job that deontic semantics has been called upon to do. In Chapters 6, 7, and 8, I shall argue that SDL semantics is not up to the job.

Chapter 6: The SDL Semantics of 'Ought to Do' Statements I: Deontically Accessible Worlds

In this chapter, I shall examine some problems that deontically accessible worlds raise for the SDL semantics of 'ought to do' statements. Although different versions of SDL semantics give differing accounts of deontically accessible worlds, all versions suffer from a similar cluster of problems.

Particular persons ought to perform particular actions in particular circumstances. Change the persons, actions, or circumstances, and you have a different set of 'oughts' — or perhaps no 'oughts' at all. Joan borrowed $5 from Harry; she ought to repay him $5. Had she borrowed a different amount, she ought to repay that amount; had she borrowed from a different person, she ought to repay that person; had it been Jane who borrowed the $5 from Harry, then it is Jane and not Joan who ought to repay him; had Harry been acting as a loan officer, Joan ought to repay him $5 plus interest; and had nobody borrowed $5 from Harry, nobody ought to repay him $5. These common sense facts help determine what deontically accessible worlds can be.

Deontic alternative worlds are defined as possible worlds in which all people always do what they ought to do. We are assured by SDLS5 that there is at least one deontic alternative world. Such a world would surely be unlike this one, but, because of the humble facts mentioned in the preceding paragraph, the difference must not be too great.

First, a deontic alternative world must have people in it. For if "Joan ought to do F" implies "Joan does F in all deontic alternative worlds," then since a world without people is a world in which Joan does not do anything, it follows that it is not the case that Joan ought to do anything in the real world. We need, therefore, to specify that a world counts as a deontic alternative only if it contains people.

Second, anyone who ought to do anything in the real world must be a part of any deontic alternative world. For in a deontic alternative world that does not contain Joan, Joan does not do anything. Hence, if a world without Joan is a deontic alternative to this world, it follows from SDLS1 that there is nothing Joan ought to do; therefore, if there is something Joan ought to do, a world without her is no deontic alternative. This is a major difference between modal and deontic semantics. "All triangles have three sides" is true in every possible world, including worlds without triangles; hence, "Necessarily all triangles have three sides" is true. "This triangle has three sides" is not true in some worlds — worlds in which the item referred to is not a triangle, perhaps worlds in which the item referred to does not exist. Therefore, "Necessarily this triangle has three sides" is false. We do not have to restrict what counts as a possible world to account for necessity, but we do need such restrictions if we are to account semantically for the 'ought to do'.

Third, the conditions relevant to incurring and fulfilling obligations must be the same in deontic alternative worlds as in the real world. In a possible world in which Joan and Harry exist but dollars do not, it will be false that Joan repays Harry $5. Moreover, in a possible world in which Joan never borrowed $5 from Harry, it will be false that she repays him $5 — she might give him $5, but it would not be repayment. Therefore, unless the only deontic alternative worlds are worlds in which Joan borrowed $5 from Harry, "Joan ought to repay Harry $5" does not imply "Joan repays Harry $5 in all deontic alternative worlds," and SDLS1 would be false.

SDL semantics then requires that deontic alternative worlds must be all but indistinguishable from the real world. They and it must contain the same people, the same relevant circumstances, and the same obligations. K. Jaakko J. Hintikka shows his awareness of this point by his principle (C.OO*), which states that whatever ought to be the case in this world ought to be the case in every deontic alternative. [Hintikka 1, 185] Thus for Hintikka, who does not distinguish what ought to be from what people ought to do, a person in deontic alternative world w_n who does what would be her duty were she in this world, is doing her duty in w_n. This is sensible, for if she were not doing her duty in w_n, one might argue that she is performing a different action from the one she ought to perform in this world. For in w_n she would not be acting out of duty; that would make a huge difference to Kant, at least. Since for Hintikka the duties of this world must obtain in anything that is to count as a deontic alternative, the persons and circumstances of this world must also be part of any deontic alternatives, as he recognizes.

Perhaps deontic alternatives are much like this world, only richer. Although details of the real world must all be reproduced in deontic alternatives, alternatives might have persons, circumstances, and duties not present in the real world. The added richness of deontic alternative worlds would be one way of accounting for the fact that people's behavior is not the same in those worlds as in the real world. But a deontic alternative world cannot have too many features lacking in the real world, because obligations are rarely completely independent of one another or of circumstances. Suppose that in deontic alternative world w_n, Harry drops dead shortly after lending Joan $5, while in the real world Harry retains his health. Surely the nature of Joan's obligation is only temporarily the same in the two worlds; in w_n it becomes an obligation to pay Harry's estate $5. The more circumstances that arise in a deontic alternative world but not in the real world, the less likely it is that the obligations, persons, and circumstances of this world all continue to appear in the alternative world.

Hence, what counts as a deontic alternative world must be severely restricted. It can only be a world remarkably like this one, where the same people have the same obligations, the same circumstances, the same temptations, the same weaknesses, the same needs and wants as in this one. And yet, remarkably enough, in the deontic alternative world, they always do as they should. How is this miracle possible?

The only way I can make sense of worlds just like this one where people always do as they ought is to suppose that deontic alternative worlds branch from the real world. A deontic alternative is on this understanding identical to the real world up to a certain time t_1, when it diverges: presumably, after t_1, in the deontic alternative all do as they ought to do, but not in the real world,. Since we may and do use counterfactual conditionals, talk of branching worlds is equally legitimate.

The restriction of deontic alternative worlds to branching worlds makes sense of SDL semantics. If Joan has a present obligation to repay Harry $5, she repays the debt in all deontic alternative worlds that branch from the real world at this time. And since the worlds branch at the present time, Harry, Joan, and the $5 loan are all features of the branching worlds. Hence, branching worlds meet our demand that deontic alternative worlds share the obligations, persons, and circumstances of the real world.

By allowing that deontic alternative worlds branch from the real world at times other than the present, we can account for 'ought to do' claims about the past and future. Suppose I contend that Napoleon ought not to have invaded Russia. First, we must suppose that every 'ought to do' statement has a time reference: Napoleon ought-not-in-June-1812 to have invaded Russia; I ought-now to keep my promises; I ought-when-I-broke-that-promise to have kept that promise.[1] Call the time reference of an 'ought to do' statement the *ought time*; it is the time at which one has an obligation, not necessarily the time at which one is obligated to act. Then the deontic alternative worlds relevant for the semantics of a given 'ought to do' statement are those which branch from the real world at or during the ought time of that statement. In none of the deontic alternative worlds which branched from the real world in June 1812, did Napoleon invade Russia; therefore, I can say now that Napoleon ought-in-June-1812 not to have invaded Russia. In none of the alternatives which branch from the real world at the present time do I fail to keep my promises; therefore, I ought now to keep my promises.

If deontic alternative worlds are branching worlds in which people will always do as they ought, it is not necessarily true that they have done as they ought. The past of a deontic alternative world is as checkered as that of the real world — for it *is* the real world's past.

Moreover, the future in a branching deontic alternative world becomes increasingly irrelevant to this world as the ought time vanishes into the past. Once a world branches, changes engender more changes; the more radical the changes, the more rapid the divergence. The alternative world grows ever farther from this one. In the alternative world, Harry might soon drop dead; Joan might incur momentous new debts; the rules governing loans might alter drastically; and the whole situation will be different. For deontic alternative worlds to share the obligations, persons, and circumstances of the real world, they must have branched from the real world at or shortly before the ought time, and the branching must be restricted to alternatives in particular events, not in laws. Only in the specious present of the ought time are the distinctive characteristics of a deontic alternative world relevant to what we ought to do.

Perhaps SDL semantics needs no more than the short interval in which the duty structure, persons, and circumstances of a deontic alternative world are the same as those in the real world. On this account, "S ought at t_1 to do F" is true if and only if: (1) S does F in all worlds which branch from the real world at t_1; (2) the laws, descriptive and prescriptive, of any branching world are those of the world from which it branches; (3) S does F in a brief interval after t_1 in each of those worlds; and (4) each of those worlds is such that all persons always do what they ought to do.

Some arguments of Peter Geach bolster my conclusion that deontic semantics must restrict deontic alternative worlds to ones which branch for a short time from the real world. [Geach, *passim*] Geach first notes that the history of this world is filled with cases of people who failed to do what they should and did what they should not have done. No SDL semanticist could object: any world where people fail in their obligations is not its own deontic alternative. But, as Geach points out, many of our present-day obligations stem from past failures and misdeeds; in a world in which all did their duty, those obligations would not exist. Moreover, since most of us have ancestors whose existence stemmed from an act of sexual misconduct, few of us would even exist in a deontic alternative. Hence, what happens in such a world is hardly relevant to what we ought to do in this world.

Moreover, Geach argues, even those branching worlds in which people will from this point on do as they ought to do, are irrelevant to what we ought to do. For in the real world, people will continue to do wrong and fail to do right. In the real world, then, we will have obligations to help victims of future injustice and to repair, as much as we can, the damages caused by human misdeeds yet to occur. Since these obligations, which can be expected to form a major portion of our future duties, do not arise in worlds where all future duties are faithfully performed, such worlds have little weight in determining our future duties in this world.

Even worse, whether I rely on the doctrine of original sin or on simple induction, I have every reason to expect that I will be guilty in the future of doing what I ought not to do and of failing to do what I ought to do. I am not presently planning a career of wrongdoing, but I am well aware of my own moral fallibility. In determining what I ought to do, I need to take my fallibility into account, for I need to consider all relevant facts about myself and my situation. A world in which I am deontically perfect is simply too removed from the facts to be relevant to what I ought in reality to do.

Brian Chellas has noted that SDL does not reflect "the dependence of obligation on time." [Chellas, 196] Lennart Åqvist agrees: "There are strong reasons, then, for enriching the basic language of satisfactory deontic logics with explicit temporal resources." [Åqvist 2, 84] But Geach's arguments show more than a need for temporal subscripts. Obligations depend not on times but on what happened in previous times: fulfillments and nonfulfillments, choices, the occurrence or non-occurrence of states of affairs, causal connections and their absence. Geach's objection to the notion of a deontic alternative world is that any such world, understood realistically, lacks both a relevant past and a relevant future.

The assumption that in a deontic alternative world all obligations are met even though the same conditions, the same rules, and the same obligations hold as in reality, therefore fails, Geach argues. His arguments have a common thread: SDL semantics does not take account of the *interrelations* of obligations. We can add to Geach's arguments by noting that for one obligation to arise from the failure to do as one ought is not the only way in which obligations can be related. Sometimes a person ought to do one of a number of possible actions, each of which would create further obligations. For example: Jane has enough money to spare that she can help three needy people; but there are 100 available needy people, none of whom has a greater claim than the others. Suppose that any needy person Jane helps ought to be grateful to her. Then her helping A, B, and C would create one set of obligations, while her helping X, Y, and Z would create a quite different set. Given that conditions in any deontic alternative are like those in this world, so that Jane cannot help more than three, which duties, whether Jane's or those of others, are fulfilled in the deontic alternative world?

These arguments point the same moral I have been urging: The more remote deontic alternative worlds are from this one, the less relevance those worlds bear to what we ought to do.

Someone might respond to Geach that although our duties in this world might have been caused by various misdeeds, those duties *could have* been brought about by innocent means. If so, then there are other logically possible worlds, including deontically perfect ones, in which we have the very same duties as in this world. What happens in such worlds is surely relevant to what ought to happen in this one. Of course, neither I nor anyone I know is likely to be deontically perfect in the future, but that is hardly a matter of logical necessity. Hence, deontically perfect worlds where I have the same duties as in the real world are logically possible, and my actions in such worlds would seem relevant to my duties here.

But this response misses the mark, for we have good reason to doubt the possibility of worlds like the real world, but in which the same duties we have here stemmed from different causes. In any such world, no one would be the victim of racial discrimination; but somehow, all those who in our world suffer from racial discrimination suffer in just the same ways in those worlds. Perhaps the suffering would be caused by nature, not by humans — for if it were caused by human acts, those would be acts that humans ought not to perform. But such a world would be radically unlike this one. Not only nature but human nature would differ from their counterparts in this world. The very perfection of such a world would ensure that our motivational structures and their effect on our actions would be completely different; weakness of will would not exist, for example. Since human actions have repercussions which depend at least in part on the workings of nature, the effects of our actions in such a world would be very different from their effects in the real world. And persons are generally responsible for at least the foreseeable effects of their actions. Hence, even if I ought to perform the act of helping a victim in deontic alternative world w_2 that I ought to perform in w_1, I do not have the same obligation in w_1 as in w_2.

In essence, I am urging consistency in deontic semantics. If one supposes worlds that work very differently from ours, one cannot then ignore the workings of those worlds by imagining the same duty structure to hold as in the real world. For our duties are not so much to perform particular acts but to try to bring about certain results by licit means. If nature and human nature were radically changed, our attempts and available means would hardly stay the same. Even if the results we seek are the same from world to world, our duties would not be.

Moreover, the supposition that deontically perfect worlds could contain the same duties as this imperfect one is absurd. If Jane defrauds John of $1,000, she should make restitution of that amount to him. But how should she do it? Should she write him a check, or give him the cash in $20 bills, or give him a $1,000 bill, or sign over $1,000 worth of stock? If a check, which number should it bear? On which bank account should it be drawn? If Jane pays cash, what days, months, and years should the bills have been issued in? What serial numbers should they bear? Of course, these questions are silly: any of a number of actions will satisfy Jane's duty of restitution. That is, any action which Jane performs that satisfies the description "making restitution of the $1,000 of which Jane defrauded John" will serve to discharge the obligation.[2] What she ought to do, then, is not a particular act but an act that satisfies the description in question. I noted this fact in Chapter 4.

Now Jane's giving John $1,000 in bills might take place in a deontically perfect world. But in such a world, her doing so could not properly be described as making restitution to him. If Jane had a duty in a perfect world w_1 to perform an act under that description, she could not possibly perform it — in which case w_1 would not be deontically perfect. The obvious conclusion is that she can have no such duty. Geach is therefore quite right: Deontic alternative worlds are vastly different from the real world, and the duties we would have in such worlds are very different from those we have in the real world.

I am contending that the assumption of SDL semantics that one can have the same duties in a perfect world and in this world rests on a bad misunderstanding of the 'ought to do'. It is not the case that a person ought to perform a particular action; rather, the person ought to perform *some* token of a given action-type. Although the same action-tokens might exist in worlds with dissimilar pasts, the same action-types cannot.

Moreover, as Geach argued, the future of deontic alternative worlds is of little relevance to us. Deontically perfect worlds which branch from this one can share a common set of duties with the real world only for a very brief time.

Geach's arguments therefore point the same moral as my earlier arguments: Deontic alternative worlds, to be of any concern to us, must have branched within a short interval of the ought time from the real world and must share the same laws, obligations, persons, and circumstances with the real world.

Even if we make those severe restrictions on deontic alternative worlds, SDL semantics still faces major problems. First and most important, the restricted semantics provides no way of accounting for duties to be performed more than an instant after the ought time. If I promise you now that I will repay you at this time tomorrow, I ought now to repay you tomorrow. But in the next twenty-four hours, a deontic alternative world that branches from this one now will grow different in major ways from the real world, for people in the deontic alternative will behave differently from their counterparts in this world. They will do all they ought, and they will know that they will do all they ought; in the real world, we will fail repeatedly on both counts. The inhabitants of the deontic alternative world will therefore not incur certain obligations they would incur in the real world; they will probably also incur obligations they would not incur in the real world. Hence, if w_1 branches from the real world now, what I do in w_1 twenty-four hours from now is irrelevant to what I ought to do in this world twenty-four hours from now.

Most of our obligations are long term, not calls for immediate action. For example, I have a thirty-year mortgage on my home. Now if financial institutions knew that all those who borrowed from them would faithfully repay, they might decide to raise interest rates on loans: "It's safe to charge more." Alternatively, they might charge a lower rate of interest on loans: "We can be more competitive, and we won't get burned." Either way, my interest rate — and with it, the precise nature of what I obligated myself to pay my lender — would change. Hence, what I would pay in deontic alternative worlds would be materially different from what I ought to pay in this world. The relevance of a deontic alternative world to what I ought to do in this world is highly dubious.

Therefore, if we restrict deontic alternative worlds to ones which have recently branched from this one, we have no semantic account for almost all the 'ought to do' statements that we make. About the only way SDL semantics can escape this mess is to suppose that debts across time are continually self-renewing. But on that supposition, when I repay you in twenty-four hours, it will not be because of a debt I incurred just now but because of an obligation incurred just before the time of repayment. My giving you the money would then not be repayment.

The problem is not a mere technical glitch in SDL semantics. In both this world and any deontically perfect branching world we will be planning and providing for the future. But the nature of the planning and providing will be quite different in those worlds. People in deontic alternatives can rely on all persons' doing as they ought; we in the real world can rely on no such thing. Although the general description 'planning and providing for the future' looks the same from those worlds to this one, the sorts of actions that satisfy the description would differ widely. Hence, our present duties in the real world are not the same as our present duties in deontically accessible worlds, even if we put drastic restrictions on the kinds of worlds that are deontic alternatives.

A somewhat different although related difficulty is that if we severely restrict what is to count as a deontic alternative world, SDL semantics loses all explanatory value. Telling someone that she ought to do whatever she would do in all deontically accessible worlds, so long as they are just like this one,   means little more than: "Do whatever you would do if you did what you ought to do." That and fifty cents will no longer buy you a subway ride! The worth of SDL semantics, once we have restricted the deontic alternative worlds so severely, is very doubtful.[3]

My argument in this chapter has been predicated on the notion that deontically accessible worlds are deontic alternatives — i.e., worlds in which all people always do as they ought. But any alternative construal of deontically accessible worlds leads to the same sorry result. For however we think of deontically accessible worlds — whether as optimal worlds, perhaps, or as permissible worlds — it remains true that the real world is not a deontically accessible world. People in the real world do not always do what is best or even what is permissible. Deontically accessible worlds are by any definition worlds where people act in a consistently proper way, and the real world is not such a world. 'Op → p' is not a theorem of standard deontic logic; if it were, SDL would have no hope of representing our ordinary deontic thinking.

If in deontically accessible worlds people's behavior is not what it is in the real world, why should their behavior mean anything to us? It can do so, and the principles SDLS1 through SDLS4 can be correct, only if the population, the facts, the actions, and the duty structures of each deontically accessible world are the same as those of the real world. And that stipulation, as we have seen, is utterly implausible. Our future actions, for example, depend in part on our anticipations of future failures, our own and others, to follow the path of duty. How could a world reasonably be thought to contain those actions without containing those anticipated failures? And yet, how could an optimal or even a permissible world contain them?

Hence, the difficulties of SDL semantics which we have been investigating in this chapter do not hinge solely upon a certain definition of 'deontically accessible world'. Any version of SDL semantics will run into the same problems.

In this chapter we have seen ample reason to place severe restrictions on what will count as a deontically accessible world. But those restrictions do not account for obligations over time, and they leave the statements of deontic semantics with little discernible content. I conclude that this first set of objections to SDL semantics is highly damaging.

Chapter 7: The SDL Semantics of 'Ought to Do' Statements II: The Principle of Backward Translation

In Chapter 2, I introduced the principle of backward translation, SDLS2, which enables us to infer statements about what persons ought to do in this world from statements about what persons do in deontically accessible worlds. Without this principle SDL semantics would be crippled. One can fly on logical wings to deontically accessible worlds, and one might demonstrate much that people do in those worlds. But the entire enterprise is of little value unless we can use it to prove what people ought to do in this world.

We can see the importance of backward translation by looking again at a simple example of reasoning. Suppose that Jane ought to keep her promises. Suppose further that Jane ought to do the following: if she keeps her promises, she takes care of her mother's cat. Can one conclude that Jane ought to take care of her mother's cat? As I argued in Chapter 5, SDL semantics makes use of SDLS1 to translate the two premises of the argument into a pair of claims about deontically accessible worlds: in all deontically accessible worlds Jane keeps her promises; and in every deontically accessible world if Jane keeps her promises, she takes care of her mother's cat. SDLS5 assures us that at least one world is deontically accessible to this one. Therefore, in all deontically accessible worlds, Jane takes care of her mother's cat. But that is not the conclusion we were after. To conclude that Jane ought to take care of her mother's cat, we need the principle that if 'p' is true in all deontically accessible worlds, 'Op' is true in this world. And that is SDLS2, a principle of backward translation.

Perhaps there is a way to justify this inference and the underlying inference pattern *without* invoking SDLS2. I cannot preclude this apparent possibility, but I can show that the most likely procedure for justification without backward translation tacitly assumes SDLS2. The procedure in question is argument by *reductio ad absurdum*. I shall give a *reductio* argument for SDLR3, that from '⊢ O(p → q)' we can derive '⊢ Op → Oq'. For if not, it might be the case that 'Op', 'O(p → q)', and '~Oq' all hold. We cannot immediately translate these three statements into claims about all possible worlds, for '~Oq' is not an expression beginning with a deontic operator. (We can translate 'ought not', but not 'not ought'.) But we can use SDLT7 to transform '~Oq' into 'P~q', where 'P' is the permissibility operator. To say that 'P~q' holds in w_n is, by SDLS3, to say that '~q' holds in *some* deontic alternative to w_n. But since 'p' and 'p → q' hold in every deontic alternative to w_n, then there is some world in which 'p', 'p → q', and '~q' all hold. And there is our contradiction.

Unfortunately, the snake has entered the deontic garden. For when I introduced SDL principles of backward translation in Chapter 2, I showed that SDLS3 is in fact such a principle. Since no *reductio* can proceed without changing '~O' into 'P~', and since SDLS3 is the only SDL principle that gives a semantic counterpart for a permissibility statement, no *reductio* can succeed without assuming backward translation.

Hence, without SDLS2, SDLS3, or some other principle of backward translation, there is no *reductio* proof of the rule that from '⊢ O(p → q)' we can derive '⊢ Op → Oq'. It is then highly probable that all proofs of SDLR3 depend on a principle of backward translation. Nor is SDLR3 the only rule in the same predicament. It is a standard deduction theorem of the propositional calculus that '⊢ B' is derivable from '⊢ A' if and only if '⊢ A → B'. Any inference rule that allows us to derive '⊢ Oq' from '⊢ p' would then be justifiable if and only if '⊢ p → Oq'. A *reductio* proof of '⊢ p → Oq' could proceed in either of two ways: by assuming the denial of 'p → Oq' (i.e., by assuming 'p.~Oq'); or by assuming the denial of the consequent of 'p → Oq' (i.e., by assuming '~Oq'). In either case, we are stuck with an expression of the form '~Oq', for which we can find a semantical equivalent only if we turn it into 'P~q' by SDLT7 and apply principle SDLS3. But once again, SDLS3 and SDLT7 imply SDLS2, the principle of backward translation, which we are assuming not to hold. Hence, we cannot use SDLS3 and SDLT7, and therefore we cannot have a *reductio* proof of '⊢ p → Oq'.

Nor is a straightforward proof of an 'ought' statement from asserted premises possible without backward translation. For if we assume 'A', for example, our semantics might let us prove 'B' true in every deontically accessible world; but without backward translation, we cannot turn that result into a proof of 'Oq' in this world. Therefore, any special inference rule of any system of deontic logic — i.e., one which is not an inference rule of the propositional calculus — which purports to allow us to derive a statement of the form 'Oq', can be justified only if the semantics of the system licenses backward translation.[1] Without SDLS2 or a counterpart, all such inference rules are unjustifiable.

Likewise, many axioms and theorems of deontic logic would not survive the loss of backward translation. Any schemata either of the form '⊢ Oq' or of the form '⊢ p → Oq' or an equivalent cannot be justified either directly or by *reductio*, for the same reason that SDLR3 cannot be justified. As an example, take the theorem '⊢ O{[Op.(p → Oq)] → Oq}'. K. Jaakko J. Hintikka shows by a *reductio* argument that this theorem is a consequence of his six conditions for a deontic model system.[2] [Hintikka 1, 193] But because the entire expression is prefaced with an obligation operator, the expression he wishes to reduce to absurdity must itself be prefaced by '~O'. Hintikka can proceed only by converting '~O' to 'P~' by SDLT7 and invoking SDLS3. And doing so, as I have shown, presupposes the principle of backward translation.

Typical SDL assertions SDLT3 and SDLT4 show the same dependence on backward translation:

SDLT3: ⊢ O(p.q) → (Op.Oq);
SDLT4: ⊢ (Op.Oq) → O(p.q).

Both are assertions of SDL, often used as axioms. But, by the same argument I gave for Hintikka's theorem, neither SDLT3 nor SDLT4 can be justified by a semantics which lacks backward translation. Nor, for the same reason, can Castañeda's axiom, '⊢ Op → ~O~p'.

Shorn of axioms, theorems, and inference principles, would anything in deontic logic survive the loss of backward translation? Two typical assertions do so, for in them the obligation operator is negated:

SDLT1: ⊢ ~(Op.O~p); and
SDLT5: ⊢ ~O(p.~p).

A *reductio* argument for each is readily available without backward translation, for '~~O' = 'O'. The negation of SDLT1 is '(Op.O~p)', whence 'Op' and 'O~p'; therefore, by SDLS1, 'p' and '~p' hold in all deontically accessible worlds. Since, by SDLS5, there is at least one such world w_1, w_1 contains a contradiction — which is absurd. Similarly, the negation of SDLT5 is 'O(p.~p)', and by SDLS1 and SDLS5 we can derive the contradiction '(p.~p)' in some deontically accessible world.

Thus denying SDLT1 and SDLT5 leads to contradictions, and an SDL semantics shorn of backward translation will assert those two statements. Hence some deontic logic would survive if backward translation is ruled out. But without major inference rules, the two remaining assertions provide little basis for a useful deontic logic.

Therefore, any argument that raises problems for the principle of backward translation will also imperil the support which SDL semantics provides for SDL. SDL cannot afford to jettison backward translation, but even modifications to SDLS2 and SDLS3 are likely to present major difficulties. For typical SDL assertions, as I argued in Chapter 2, follow from SDL semantics; alter the semantics, and we have no reason to expect SDL itself to remain unscathed. In modifying SDL to disallow inferences we do not want, we might well be disallowing inferences we want. The future of standard deontic logic looks bleak indeed.[3]

2. 'OUGHT' AND 'NECESSARY'

There is a well-known difficulty that, I shall argue, calls for restrictions on backward translation. All deontically accessible worlds are, by definition, possible worlds. Necessary truths are, on standard modal semantics, true in all possible worlds. Therefore every necessary truth is true in every deontically accessible world. And by backward translation, that means that if Lp, then Op. But surely it is absurd to suppose that any 'ought' attaches to necessary truths. What we ought to do lies within the realm of choice, not of necessity; nor does there seem much sense in wishing that an inevitable state of affairs ought to be. Call this difficulty the problem of obligatory necessity, or PON for short.

PON might seem a paper problem, for no action is logically necessary. But the problem is perfectly genuine. For first, the 'ought' of SDL applies not only to actions but to states of affairs, and states of affairs are sometimes necessary. For instance, the state of affairs in which 'p v ~p' holds is necessary and hence, by SDL semantics, something that ought to be. Second, although no action by itself is logically necessary, a relation between two actions often is. It is contingent that you tie your shoes; but it is necessary that you either tie your shoes or not tie them. Hence, by SDL semantics, you ought either to tie your shoes or not to tie them.[4] Third, we can easily describe some logically impossible actions — that is, actions that an actor logically must fail to perform. For instance, in every possible world Edith does not square the circle. Therefore, by SDL semantics, Edith ought not to square the circle. Thus PON does arise in actual cases. When it does, it stretches the bounds of what most people mean by 'ought'.

Now PON should look familiar even to modal logicians who have little acquaintance with deontic logic. For PON depends upon the assumption that all deontically accessible worlds are possible worlds; that assumption licenses an inference from what holds in all possible worlds to what is true in all deontically accessible worlds. Yet parallel assumptions in other modal realms have caused problems.[5] Most notably, the so-called problem of logical omniscience (PLO) in epistemic logic arises from the assumption that epistemically accessible worlds are possible worlds. For suppose that 'S knows that p' is true if and only if 'p' holds in all epistemically accessible worlds relative to S, and suppose that 'p' implies 'q'. Since 'p' implies 'q', all possible worlds in which 'p' holds are worlds in which 'q' holds. But if all epistemically accessible worlds are possible worlds, then 'q' holds in all epistemically accessible worlds relative to S. By an epistemic version of backward translation, it follows that S knows that q. Hence, to know something entails knowing all the logical consequences of what one knows. But that result not only is empirically false but might even make knowledge impossible, as it seems to commit the knower to knowing a non-denumerable infinity of true propositions.[6] Therefore, PLO demonstrates at least the inapplicability of modal epistemic logic to ordinary epistemic thought, just as PON shows at least the inapplicability of deontic logic to ordinary deontic thought.[7]

But the resemblance between PLO and PON suggests a way of escaping PON without questioning the principle of backward translation. K. Jaakko J. Hintikka has suggested that we can consistently deny that what holds in all possible worlds must hold in all epistemically accessible worlds. [Hintikka 3, 477-483] If we adapt Hintikka's method to deontic logic, we might be able to block PON.

Using the urn models of Veikko Rantala, Hintikka constructs a semantics which seemingly allows for worlds that contain subtle inconsistencies — i.e., inconsistencies that do not show up at a certain level of analysis.[8] For instance, one might symbolize "The cat is on the mat and the cat is not on the mat" as 'p' or perhaps as 'p.q'; on neither of these versions does the inconsistency in the original statement manifest itself. But a subtly impossible world, since it does contain a contradiction, is not a possible world, and therefore what holds in all possible worlds need not hold in a subtly impossible world. Therefore, if we allow subtly impossible worlds into the semantics of epistemic logic, that 'p' implies 'q' and that 'p' is true in all epistemically accessible worlds does not imply that 'q' is true in all epistemically accessible worlds. Thus Hintikka concludes that PLO fails.

The same reasoning would take care of PON as well. If some deontically accessible worlds are not possible worlds, then a necessary truth might not hold in all deontically accessible worlds: 'Op' would not follow from 'Lp'.

Talk of subtly impossible worlds might appear ludicrous. Either a world is possible, or there is no world at all. Here, though, Rantala's urn models provide plausible theoretical backing for Hintikka's position. Suppose we want to consider a candidate world w_0. The available descriptions of w_0 come at different levels of complexity, which can be ordered. Take such a description with complexity-level n: uncovering successive degrees of complexity in w_0 is like removing a series of n balls from an urn; while the restrictions, if any, on making a removal represents the particular complexity present at the corresponding level. [Rantala, 457] If we now imagine that w_0 changes with each removal of a ball, we can allow that inconsistency arises only after a certain number of balls have been removed. That is, until we reach a certain level of complexity there literally is no inconsistency to be found; above that level, w_0 remains a possible world. Thus we have a model for the supposition that a contradiction may hold at one level of complexity but not at another. [Rantala, 459]

Hence, Hintikka's way of dealing with PLO is at least formally acceptable; whether it provides an adequate representation of our epistemic beliefs is a vexed matter that we need not consider. But whatever may be the case with PLO, I find a similar treatment of PON unjustified, for two reasons:

- Hintikka's introduction of subtly impossible worlds, however plausible it may be as an epistemic principle, seems unjustified as a deontic principle;
- Subtly impossible worlds provide no help in solving some related problems of SDL.

I will take these points in turn.

Hintikka has good intuitive reason to allow that not every epistemically accessible world is a possible world. For the worlds of epistemic logic are relative to a given knower, the S who knows that p; they represent formally the notion that 'p' will be true in that knower's epistemic world, whatever else might or might not hold. And surely the things one considers as holding or not holding do occasionally, after one has considered them, turn out to be subtly impossible. Hintikka's way of dealing with PLO is plausible, then, not merely because Rantala's urn models give him a formally acceptable way of defeating the argument, but because his method is consistent with our ordinary understanding of epistemic matters.

But if we put Hintikka's suggestion to use in dealing with PON, its intuitive plausibility is lost. Deontically accessible worlds are generally considered to be improvements over the world around us; otherwise, no one would appeal to such worlds to tell us what we ought to do here! But a contradictory world — even a subtly contradictory one — is in no meaningful sense an improvement over this world. It is certainly true that, in contemplating what one should do, one often does consider matters that turn out to be impossible. But deontic logic is not a logic of how we *determine* what we ought to do; it is a logic of 'oughts', not of thoughts. To confuse the two is as gross a mistake as is confusing real with epistemic probabilities. Only possible states of the world are relevant in determining either what we ought to do or what ought to be. Hence, there seems no plausibility in allowing deontically accessible worlds that are subtly impossible.

Let us next consider a different type of urn model. Suppose that we have an urn model of a constantly changing world, and suppose that successive draws from the urn represent not layers of complexity but successive states of the world. Such a model gives no help with PON; for each successive state of the world is a possible world, and hence a world in which all necessary truths hold.

This is not to say that urn models have no use for deontic logic. I shall argue in Chapter 9 that, to meet a paradox posed by Roderick Chisholm, deontic logic needs a semantics which allows for changes in worlds, and urn models provide such a semantics. My claim here is only that urn models give no help in resolving PON.

Moreover, PON is only one of a number of problems sharing the following general form: (a) a set of deontic statements is translated into talk of what is true in deontically accessible worlds; (b) inferences are made from these translations together with accepted modal or deontic principles; (c) the inferences are then translated into objectionable deontic statements. Let us call such difficulties *problems of form F.*

All problems of form F can be blocked by the introduction of subtly impossible worlds. For whatever follows logically from a proposition will hold true in all possible worlds in which the proposition itself holds true. But whatever follows logically from a proposition might or might not hold in subtly impossible worlds. Thus step b does not hold up, and the problem is blocked. But although this is a formally acceptable way of solving problems of form F, the solution loses much of its luster when we try to apply it to specific problems with SDL. We have seen this to be true of PON; it is true of other arguments as well. I shall look briefly at a well-known argument of this type: the Good Samaritan paradox.

From "S helps the person he will murder next week" we can derive "S will murder that person next week." Now if S ought to help the person he will murder next week, then in all deontic alternative worlds S helps the person he will murder next week. Hence, in all deontic alternative worlds S murders that person next week. Hence, S ought to murder that person next week.[9] But this result is, to say the least, unwelcome; given S's obligation not to commit murder, the result contradicts SDLT1.

If we allow subtly impossible worlds, we can answer the Good Samaritan. For all possible worlds in which S helps the person S will murder next week are indeed worlds in which S will murder that person next week; but since deontic alternative worlds need not be possible worlds, we cannot infer that all deontic alternative worlds in which S helps the person S will murder next week are deontic alternative worlds in which S will murder that person next week. In Rantala's terms, the world may change importantly between draws.

But although we block the paradox formally by allowing subtly impossible worlds, the difficulty posed by the Good Samaritan is as intractable as ever. For a world in which a person helps the person he will murder next week, but in which he does not murder that person next week, is not a subtly but a blatantly inconsistent world. Even if we allow that a world can change even as we investigate it [Hintikka 3, 478], there seems no change that can come over a world to make what will happen next week not happen next week. On any plausible account of an individual deontic alternative world, if S in that world helps the person S will in that same world murder next week, then S will murder that person in that world next week. Even if we allow 'impossible possible' worlds, we have every reason to think that the basic inference of the Good Samaritan will go through. The only plausible way of avoiding the Good Samaritan without jettisoning a great part of standard deontic logic is therefore to limit the possibility of backward translation. And that would jeopardize the arguments by which we derived SDL assertions from SDL semantics.

The Good Samaritan, PON, and other problems of form F can at least formally be dissolved by allowing subtly impossible worlds. In the next sections, I shall take up arguments which, I shall argue, SDL can deal with only by restricting backward translation.

3. ITERATED AND NESTED OUGHTS

In Chapter 2, I introduced two not-so-typical SDL theorems: SDLT10 and SDLT11. I argued that, so long as SDL formation rules accept iterated deontic modalities as well formed, both principles are consequences of SDL semantics.

However, SDLT10 — ⊢ OOp ↔ Op — represents a gulf between SDL semantics and ordinary deontic thought. One side of SDLT10, SDLIa, tells us that "It ought to be that S ought to do F" implies "It is the case that S ought to do F." SDLIa therefore licenses us to infer a statement of what is the case from a statement of what ought to be the case. Such an inference cannot be correct, for not all worlds are deontically perfect. The other side of SDLT10, SDLIb, permits us to infer from the mere fact that a state of affairs, S's obligation to do F, is the case that it ought to be the case — again, a bad inference because of imperfect worlds. Hence, SDLT10 is strongly counterintuitive.

The best way of exhibiting the counterintuitive status of SDLT10 is by examples. The most obvious sorts of examples are cases in which the iterated 'oughts' are true at different times. Suppose that we are founders of a club, writing bylaws that will, we hope, arrange in the best way duties for the club's officers. You suggest that it ought to be that the vice-president have the duty of keeping the books; I respond that it ought to be that the secretary have that duty. We are differing, then, on what it ought to be that officers ought to do. Now after the club has been founded and has elected officers, we have settled what the officers, under the bylaws we established, ought to do — but that in no way determines what it ought to be that they ought to do. Nor are the duties the officers ought to have necessarily duties they actually have. Hence, 'Op' neither implies nor is implied by 'OOp'.

Let us take the example more slowly. If we translate your original proposal into SDL semantics, as I proposed in Chapter 2, we get first the statement: "In all deontically accessible worlds accessible to the real world, the vice-president ought to keep the books." Translating further, we have: "In all range 2 worlds accessible to all range 1 worlds accessible to the real world w_0, the vice-president keeps the books." Since the vice-president keeps the books in every range 2 world, the vice-president ought to keep the books in every range 1 world; and since in any deontically accessible world all people always do as they ought, the vice-president keeps the books in every range 1 world. Hence, the vice-president ought to keep the books in w_0, as SDLIa provides. But in fact, the vice-president does not and, if my proposal wins the day, never will have that obligation. Hence, SDL semantics is wrong in inferring that the vice-president has the obligation to keep the books from your contention that it would be best if the vice-president had that obligation. Therefore, SDLIa, a necessary consequence of SDL semantics, produces a counterintuitive result.

Again, suppose that you win our debate and the vice-president is assigned the obligation to keep the books. Then in all worlds of range 1, the vice-president keeps the books. But that could be the case only if the vice-president ought to keep the books in all worlds of range 1. Therefore, the vice-president keeps the books in all worlds of range 2. By backward translation, it ought to be that the vice-president ought to keep the books. Thus the mere fact that you won our debate implies that you should have won it — another counterintuitive result.

The example might seem unfair, for it prefixes an 'ought to be' operator to an 'ought to do' operator. But the adherent of SDL semantics cannot make this response, for SDL makes no distinction between the two kinds of 'ought' statement; SDL has but one operator to cover all oughts. Despite SDL, it seems highly plausible to say that it ought to be that certain people have certain duties, without in the least implying that they actually have those duties; and the converse is also true.

SDL semantics has only four ways out of this difficulty without making major changes:

- One might try to deny that SDLT10 produces counterintuitive results. But it is unreasonable to suppose that in this world, what is implies or is implied by what ought to be.

- One might admit the counterintuitive result but suggest that counterintuitive results are only to be expected when ordinary thinking is logically regimented. SDL seems to have more than used up its quota of counterintuitive results, if it is to be a reasonably faithful formalization of ordinary deontic thinking.

- One might deny that inhabitants of deontically accessible worlds always do what in those worlds they should do. But then deontically accessible worlds are neither deontically perfect nor optimal nor even permissible.

- One might allow that if 'OOp' is true in w_0, 'Op' is true in all worlds of range 1 and 'p' in all worlds of range 2; but one might deny that the converse relations hold. That is, one might deny backward translation. And that, as I suggested at the start of this chapter, would be a true counsel of desperation.

The only plausible response for an adherent of SDL is to affix time-references to all 'ought' statements. If the two operators in 'OOp' have different time-references, then we cannot infer 'Op'. This would, of course, mean a large change in SDL semantics.

However, even if the two operators in 'OOp' have a single time reference, SDLT10 still infers an 'is' from an 'ought' and thus raises counterexamples. Suppose it the case that John will fight a sea battle tomorrow, although he is under no obligation to do so. If fulfilling one's obligations always improves the world — a debatable point — it might be true that the world would be better if whatever people do they ought to do. If so, then by backward translation, it ought to be now that John ought now to fight a sea battle tomorrow, but it is not true that John ought now to fight a sea battle tomorrow. Hence, 'OOp' does not imply 'Op', and SDLT10 is false. Hence, even when it ought-at-time-t to be that S ought-at-t to do F, we cannot infer that S ought-at-t to do F.

SDLT10 faces other difficulties as well. If deontically accessible world w_1 has its own duty structure and residents of w_1 always do as they ought-in-w_1, then w_1 is deontically accessible to itself. What is true in all deontic alternatives to deontic alternatives to w_0 is therefore true in all deontic alternatives to the real world. There is nothing intrinsically absurd here. But what does it mean to talk about a duty-structure in a deontic alternative world? Whatever people might do in such a world, they cannot ever act contrary to their obligation. Now people in a world of range 1 might still look to what holds in all worlds of range 2, including their own, to find out what they should do. But they would have no real reason to do so, for people in deontic alternative worlds have no opportunity and no temptation to fail to do what they should do. In the real world, people need to understand their obligations, to keep from going wrong; in a deontic alternative world, the inhabitants have no such need. The behavior of such literally unworldly creatures is hardly relevant to anyone's obligations in the real world.

The difficulty for SDL does not lessen if we substitute optimal worlds for deontic alternative worlds. There is a difference between saying that in an optimal world the vice-president keeps the books and saying that in an optimal world the vice-president ought to keep the books. Yet SDLT10 declares that the two statements are equivalent. Since an optimal world accessible to the real world is accessible to itself, whatever is true in all optimal worlds accessible to optimal worlds is true in range 1 optimal worlds. Likewise, one might suppose it optimal that all future actions will be optimal; it by no means follows that all future actions will in fact be optimal.

Similar difficulties beset SDLT11: $\vdash O(Op \to p)$. The only plausible way of reading this expression is to take the first 'O' as an 'ought to be'; SDLT11 then says that it ought to be that, if S ought to do F, then S does F. Once again, if the two operators have different time references, we will have no difficulty in finding counterexamples. Perhaps it would improve the world now if people fulfill their obligations a hundred years from now; and perhaps it would not. Certainly it is not the part of logic to decide otherwise!

However, as with SDLT10, stipulating that the two operators in SDLT11 have the same time-reference will not save the day for the theorem. A concentration-camp commandant had many duties, but we surely need not assume that it ought to have been that he carried out those duties. Doing as one ought sometimes, but by no means always, improves the world. If SDL admits SDLT11 as well formed, SDL is committed to SDLT11; and SDLT11 is far from being the intuitively obvious truth Arthur Prior thought it was.

Should standard deontic systems then adopt formation rules to block SDLT10 and SDLT11? The trouble with that suggestion is that, as my counterexamples suggest, these theorems do not look unintelligible. They appear applicable to real-world cases, but they lead to false conclusions.

Ruth Barcan Marcus was right to urge that an adequate deontic logic must provide interpretations for iterated and nested deontic modalities. [Marcus, 582] But those interpretations must be in reasonable accord with ordinary intuitions. SDL fails the test.

4. SOLT'S PROBLEM

Kornel Solt has argued that although the truth of 'Op' in this world implies the truth of 'p' in all deontically accessible worlds, the reverse is not true — because the real world might lack norms present in those deontically accessible worlds. [Solt, *passim*] It is therefore possible, Solt argues, for a statement 'p' to be true in all deontically accessible worlds but for 'Op' not to be true in the real world. If Solt's contention is correct, the hopelessness of SDL semantics is sure.[10]

So far as I can determine, Solt's argument in no way rests upon the supposition that deontically accessible worlds are possible worlds. It is not, that is, a problem of form F. Rather, Solt is directly assailing the possibility of backward translation. Therefore, urn models and subtly impossible worlds are irrelevant to Solt's argument.

In this section, I shall contend that Solt's argument is badly flawed. But in the following section, I shall transform it into a major problem for the principle of backward translation.

Solt's argument obviously depends heavily on the concept of *norms*. A norm in a given world apparently prescribes what people ought to do in that world.[11] I shall take this to mean that norms are necessary conditions for the truth of 'ought to do' expressions.[12] If we are to evaluate Solt's argument, we must get clearer on norms.[13]

It is something of a commonplace that there are no free-floating oughts. Whenever a person ought to do something, there are some facts in virtue of which the person should do the deed. The exact nature of those facts is a matter of dispute, but few would doubt that we have certain obligations because the world is a certain way. It is at least in part because there are starving poor that we ought to feed the starving poor.

Purely descriptive facts, such as the fact that there are starving poor, are not usually the only facts that bring about obligations. Often a system of rules — whether rules of law, morality, prudence, etiquette, or even of a game — generates a set of 'ought to do' statements when applied to a particular situation. Often an authority of some sort informs people of how they should behave, and often people learn what they should do from observing the behavior of those they take to be models. I shall group together rules, authorities, and models under the umbrella term 'institutions', a notion which I find clearer than that of norms.[14]

In the remainder of this section, I examine two related theses: (1) Whenever people make 'ought to do' statements, there are institutions standing behind those 'ought to do' statements; (2) The relation between an ought and an institution is a logical one, and hence there can be no non-institutional oughts. I shall argue that an amended version of the first thesis is true, but the second is false.[15] Because of the falsity of 2, Solt's contention that norms are a logically necessary condition for the truth of oughts cannot stand.

(1) Clearly, the only oughts which might depend on institutions are cases of the ought-to-do. Imagine a cave-dweller in Hobbes's state of nature, weary of the daily round of killing off his neighbors, who sighs: "There ought to be a law against killing." 'Ought to be' statements often indicate the speaker's desire that certain institutions would come into being; but they can hardly presuppose that those institutions have existed, do exist, or will exist. Hobbes's distinction makes sense: "The laws of nature oblige *in foro interno* — that is to say, they bind to a desire they should take place — but *in foro externo* — that is, to the putting them into act — not always." [Hobbes, Part I, Chapter 15] Without proper institutions, we can say that certain kinds of behavior ought to be, but it is at least questionable whether people ought to behave in that manner. What would be duty where institutions are present is supererogation in their absence.

The connection between 'ought to do' statements and institutions is clearest in conflicts of obligation. Perhaps the most carefully constructed such dilemma in literature is that of Orestes in Aeschylus's *Choephoroe*. Orestes's mother, Clytaemestra, has killed his father, Agamemnon; she and her lover, Aegisthus, rule in Argos. Orestes returns secretly from exile, gains entrance to the palace, and has no difficulty — physical or moral — in killing Aegisthus. But then Clytaemestra confronts Orestes. He clearly can kill her, but should he do so? Orestes ought to kill his mother, because he owes his father the deed of vengeance. But he ought not to kill his mother, for killing a parent is a terrible crime. As Aeschylus makes clear in the *Eumenides*, Orestes faces punishment from the avenging Furies, whatever he chooses to do.

Orestes's conflicting oughts are determined by the institutions of ancient Greek religion, as they affect questions of revenge, duties toward parents, and the status and claims of the dead. Orestes's dilemma would not have existed in a society that prefers public prosecution to private revenge.[16]

What holds in dilemmas is also true of everyday oughts. When I determine that I ought to do something, it is today's institutions — rules, authorities, models — that give shape to my 'ought' statement. As in Orestes's case, it is by means of those institutions that I attempt, if challenged, to defend my judgment. And, as in Orestes's case, it is by means of those institutions that others seek to determine whether my judgment was indeed correct. For the tie between 'ought to do' statements and institutions is not present in first-person decision-making alone. Institutions are vital in framing or determining what you ought to do, what he or she ought to do, or what they ought to do. Usually, the relevant institutions are those accepted by the speaker, not necessarily those accepted by the person supposed to be under an obligation. Sometimes, as when we ascribe religious duties to Orestes, a speaker does use the institutions of the potential actor's culture to make second- or third-person 'ought' claims. But whether speakers use their own institutions or those of the people about whom they are speaking, there seems a real link between second- and third-person 'ought to do' statements and institutions.

Orestes's situation is unusual, not because it was a conflict, but because it was a conflict of duties. More often, duties conflict with other items: usually desires, habits, or feelings. And these might, of course, conflict with each other. When duties conflict with desires, or habits, or feelings, what is the role of institutions? Jonathan Bennett's examination of Huckleberry Finn's decision not to turn Jim over to the slave-catchers is an excellent analysis of such a conflict. [Bennett, *passim*] Bennett stresses that morality, as Huck knows it, is all on the side of betraying Jim; on the side of saving him is, at most, inchoate feeling. Huck says that he knew very well at the time he lied to the slave-catchers that he was doing wrong, but he just could not bring himself to say the truth. We have no doubt that Huck made the morally right decision, but Huck had no doubt that his saving Jim was immoral.

The institutions of Huck's time and place could have led him to no other conclusion. Huck gives reason after reason why he should follow what he takes to be the moral path; he has no real reason for saving Jim. His feelings, fortunately, were too strong for his warped morality. But Huck does not evolve a new and better morality. He does not question that morality demands turning in runaway slaves. Rather, he resolves to pay no more attention to his conscience, the voice of morality. He is no moral innovator.

When desire wins out over moral beliefs, reasons are usually on the losing side. Lady Eldon, in the standard legal example, attempts to smuggle the lace because she wants it; legal and moral institutions give her plenty of reasons for not doing what she does. She might come up with a few justifications for her action, but they are likely to sound thin even to her. And the same thing is true when, through habit or inertia, persons fails to do what they thinks they ought.

It thus seems that where oughts are involved in any sort of conflict, institutions are also involved as giving body and point to those oughts. And where there is no conflict, where one quietly does what one ought, institutions provide the basis for explanation or justification. Even in cases of moral innovation, where a person claims that people should act in accord with new standards, the tie between 'ought to do' statements and institutions is present. I know no better example of moral innovation than the eighteenth chapter of Ezekiel, where the prophet, speaking for his God, announces that the old notion of children being punished for their fathers' misdeeds is false: persons are responsible for their own acts. "It is the soul that sins, and no other, that shall die; a son shall not share a father's guilt, nor a father his son's. The righteous man shall reap the fruit of his own righteousness, and the wicked man the fruit of his own wickedness."[17]

The prophet clearly is revoking, in the name of God, what God had said in Exodus 20, 5: that the children, even to the third and fourth generations, would be punished for the sins of their fathers.[18] The prophet, with almost painful doggedness, works out the notion of individual responsibility: he enumerates the various sins that one man might commit, his son avoid, his grandson commit; he concludes that the good shall live, the wicked shall die. This is genuine moral innovation.[19]

And yet, the innovation is clearly tied to existing institutions. First, of course, there is the authority of God, in whose name the prophet is speaking. But the author of the book of Ezekiel also refers to known characteristics of God: that he acts on principle (vv. 25-32); that he wants people to behave well and to live (vv. 23, 32). The innovation is solidly rooted in institutions which the listeners already accept.

Most cases of moral innovation are not so dramatic as Ezekiel 18. Usually, the innovation consists of a new application or a new extension of an old precept. Even philosophers who are out to transvaluate all values betray, by their rules for accepting new values, the old institutions which they accept. Moral innovation, the most likely case for the freedom of oughts from institutions, turns out to present no such thing.

In sum, then, it seems clear that the truth of 'ought to do' statements is indeed tied to the presence of institutions.[20]

(2) We must next consider whether the tie between 'ought to do' statements and institutions is a logical one. Solt presupposes that the presence of an institution is part of the meaning of an 'ought' statement, so that the truth of the statement logically implies the existence of the institution. I shall argue instead that some looser, non-logical tie connects 'ought' statements with institutions. If there can be any oughts without institutions, Solt's argument fails.[21]

The existence of relevant institutions is clearly neither necessary nor sufficient for ascribing oughts to people. There is no god Apollo, and there are no Furies; yet because Orestes believed in them and the codes they represented, his dilemma was real. Not even the institutions of ancient Greek religion must be real for Orestes to face a dilemma. There might be no institutions requiring vengeance: Orestes could have made a terrible mistake, and yet his dilemma would remain. Conversely, the gods and religious institutions might all be perfectly genuine, but an unbelieving Orestes would face no conflict. A person might take Lycurgus as his model, even though Lycurgus might never have existed. There might be a God who has genuine authority over us, but atheists do not derive any notion of what they ought to do from that authority. These examples all suggest that the ascription of oughts depends, not on the existence of institutions, but on people's acceptance of institutions.

But the ascription of oughts concerns what persons *think* they ought to do, not with what they *really* ought to do. Perhaps whenever a person really ought to do something, institutions backing up that 'ought' must in fact exist; only ought-claims depend on acceptance. I drew my examples of the preceding paragraph from the realm of ought-claims, not from genuine oughts. Cases of genuine oughts show the need for genuine institutions: thus it is false that Andrew Jackson ought to have fought the Battle of New Orleans, peace having been signed. Because Jackson was unaware of the peace, he did what he thought he should do, not what he actually should have done.

However, all the examples which I employed to show that 'ought to do' statements are tied to institutions also concern ought-claims, not genuine oughts. Orestes felt the tug of conflicting ought-claims; what he really should have done is quite irrelevant. Huck's conflict lay between his feelings and what he thought he ought to do. The prophet rooted his claims about individual responsibility in shared beliefs about God. I find no reason to think that genuine oughts are tied to real institutions. My examples show at most that there is a tie — and not a logical tie — between the *asserting* of 'ought to do' statements and the acceptance of institutions. The relation to an institution is not, then, part of the semantics of 'ought to do' statements.

A speaker's acceptance of relevant institutions is not even necessary for a person to assert an 'ought to do' statement. I might tell a naughty child that he ought to be good if he expects Santa Claus to bring him any presents. My child psychology might be reprehensible, but I can certainly make the assertion without sharing the child's belief in Santa Claus. To soothe the feelings of a religious relative, I might agree that I ought to attend her church regularly, even if I do not accept the creed of that church. Acceptance of relevant institutions is then necessary for asserting an 'ought to do' statement, but only so long as the assertion is a straightforward representation of the asserter's beliefs. Persons assert 'ought to do' statements for many reasons besides the straightforward one; when they do, they might or might not accept the relevant institutions.

Acceptance of institutions is then tied to the warranted assertibility for straightforward purposes of 'ought to do' statements, not to the meaning of those statements. We are clearly dealing with the pragmatics and not the semantics of 'ought to do' statements, for we are speaking of conditions of utterance, not of matters of meaning and truth-conditions.

Examples illustrate that matters of pragmatics are at issue here. Suppose that I decide that I ought to clean out the cat box today. My decision did not come out of the blue.[22] My acceptance of some sort of norm or institution underlies my decision. Perhaps I have decided or have been compelled to live by a code of rules that, together with some of my beliefs, leads me to conclude that I should do the dirty job. Or I might have followed the example of a saintly person who regularly cleans out her cat box. Or someone I regard as an authority in my domestic affairs — my wife or my cat — will have provided the basis for my decision. Third-person cases work similarly: If I claim that my wife ought to clean out the cat box today, my assertion is based on my acceptance of institutions.

Again, a tax attorney, consulted by a rich client about how to pay the smallest amount in taxes, advises her that, under the law, she ought to contribute a large sum of money to charity. She is ignorant of the law and will take the attorney's word for it. The attorney knowingly misstates the law, in the belief that the charity will make much better use of the money than the client will. The statement "You ought to give a large sum of money to charity" makes sense, even though no law requires or even suggests this. That the attorney does not suppose institutional support for his statement is irrelevant to the sense of the statement. He can even make his assertion in full knowledge that it has no institutional support, for his assertion is not straightforward but conceals a hidden agenda. No doubt the attorney deserves punishment, but not for being illogical!

I have argued that a person must accept relevant institutions for warranted straightforward assertibility of an ought-statement. But what is it to accept an institution? Certainly one must do more than suppose the institution's existence. A polytheist might accept the existence of many gods which have no authority over him. I accept the existence of the laws of Sri Lanka without expecting them ever to influence any of my 'ought to do' statements. Hence, warranted straightforward assertibility of an ought-statement requires also the belief that the institution has some degree of authority over the prospective actor. That is, the asserter must suppose that the prospective actor will — or at least should — recognize the authority of the institution. Thus the devious tax attorney does not straightforwardly tell his client that she ought morally to give money to charity, because he expects that she will not recognize the claims of morality.

To sum up: The connection between 'ought to do' statements and institutions is not a simple one. There is no meaning-connection and no logical tie. The connection is instead pragmatic: It links the straightforward warranted assertibility of an 'ought to do' statement with the asserter's acceptance of the existence and authority of a relevant institution.

We are finally in a position to assess Solt's argument. He had claimed that the presence of a relevant norm is a logically necessary condition for the truth of an 'ought to do' statement, and that therefore in the absence of a relevant norm, the 'ought to do' statement could not be true no matter what took place in deontically accessible worlds. Clearly, the argument is no good. For a relevant norm is a pragmatic condition on the assertion of an 'ought to do' statement, not a logically necessary condition of the truth of that statement. There can be oughts without norms.

5. THE ASSERTIBILITY PROBLEM

But although Solt's argument fails, my analysis of its failure provides the groundwork for a telling criticism of SDL semantics. I shall call this new argument the *assertibility problem*.

The assertibility problem is not difficult to state. The previous section showed that a person is in a position to assert an 'ought to do' statement only if the person believes in the existence and accepts the authority of some relevant institution or institutions in the real world. It is logically possible for a person to assert an 'ought to do' statement without being in a position to do so; practically speaking, however, this logical possibility will not be realized. Hence, a person might be in a position to assert 'p' in all deontically accessible worlds, but because of her non-acceptance of institutions in this world, she is not in a position to assert 'Op'. And this contradicts the principle of backward translation, which takes the assertion that 'p' is true in every deontically accessible world as a sufficient condition for the assertion of 'Op' in this world.

An example will clarify the assertibility problem. Jane has promised to give John a certain sum of money tomorrow. She knows that she ought to give him the money then, and she knows that she or her counterparts in all deontically accessible worlds will pay up tomorrow. But for her to pay up tomorrow, she must be alive tomorrow. She will therefore make every effort in all deontically accessible worlds to ensure that she is alive tomorrow. But in the real world, Jane believes in a strict interpretation of the scriptural injunction to take no thought for the morrow; she recognizes no norm, no institution requiring her to make every effort to ensure that she is alive tomorrow. Hence Jane is aware that in all deontically accessible worlds she will make every effort to ensure she is alive tomorrow, but she thinks that in the real world it is false that she ought to make every effort to ensure she is alive tomorrow.

Is Jane simply being irrational? I think not. Logic is simply not — at least not yet — a moral authority. That an 'ought' statement falls out of logic does not by itself provide an accepted body of rules, an authority, or a model to warrant her asserting that 'ought' statement. Logicians might think of their specialty as providing norms, but this seems no better than a bias on behalf of one's own field of interest. If acceptance of a norm is a necessary condition for warranted assertibility of an 'ought to do' statement, then without a norm, Jane would not be warranted in asserting that she ought to make sure she is alive tomorrow.

What does seem to be true in this example is that there *ought to be* a norm determining that Jane should make sure she is alive tomorrow. If the institution whose existence and authority Jane accepts does not hold that a logical consequence of binding claims is itself binding, that institution is at fault. Jane's lacking a proper norm for making sure she is alive tomorrow simply should not be. And in that case, it ought to be that Jane makes sure she is alive tomorrow. But, as I argued in Chapter 4, 'ought to be' does not imply the counterpart 'ought to do'. Neither we nor Jane would be warranted in asserting, in the absence of an accepted norm, that she ought to make sure she is alive tomorrow.

The example clarifies the dimensions of the assertibility problem. From the assertion that X performs an action G in every deontically accessible world, we can derive the assertion that it ought to be that X performs G in the real world. But we cannot derive from this source alone the assertion that X ought to perform G in the real world, for acceptance of relevant norms might be lacking. (I shall argue in Chapter 10 that the same difficulty does not apply in the case of 'ought to be' statements.) The principle of backward translation, SDLS2, therefore does not conform to our ordinary understanding of 'ought to do' statements.

Hence, the assertibility problem is a weapon against SDL semantics. If 'G ought to do p' is asserted in the real world, we can assert 'G does p' in every deontically accessible world; but *not* vice versa. If 'G does p' is asserted in every deontically accessible world, then we can assert in this world only the weaker statement that it ought to be that G does p. Backward translation is therefore severely weakened.

The assertibility problem is not a paper difficulty, for it ties in with the problems of iterated oughts discussed earlier in this chapter. If X does in w_n all the things she ought to do in the real world, then X does in w_n all that she ought to do in w_n.[23] Thus the duties in every w_n include all the real-world duties, but a deontically accessible world might contain a further set of obligations. Now suppose that F is not, but ought to be, a duty for S in the real world. If F ought to be a duty for S in this world, SDL semantics requires that it is a duty for S in all deontically accessible worlds; in which case, S will do F in all such worlds. But by backward translation, if S does F in all deontically accessible worlds, S ought to do F in this world — which contradicts our assumption. If we do not deny that everything that ought to be a duty is one, we can escape the argument only by denying that what a person does in all deontically accessible worlds he ought to do in this world — which is to say, by denying backward translation.

The preceding argument supposes that in every deontically accessible world, people do what it ought to be the case that they do. This is reasonable: after all, these deontically accessible worlds are supposed to be better than the real world. A world in which duty alone is done is not necessarily any better than the world in which we live; it might be quite a bit worse, even if the duties in each world are the same. For we in the real world sometimes fail in our duty, but we also sometimes go beyond it. We sometimes do not merely what we ought to do but what it ought to be that we do. A world in which people have no obligation to do what it ought to be that they do is perhaps be a morally impoverished world; deontically accessible worlds, however, cannot be morally impoverished. Therefore, we might be in no position to assert that whatever people do in all deontically accessible worlds they should do in this world.

One counter to the assertibility problem might come from a logician. Everything in my reconstruction depends on taking backward translation as a rule of inference, going from one assertion ("'p' is true in all deontically accessible worlds") to another ("'Op' is true in this world"). But by the standard inference rule of the propositional calculus, '⊢ A' implies '⊢ B' only if '⊢ A → B'. Hence, we need not worry about the conditions for asserting 'Op' in this world; all we need worry about is the validity of the statement "('p' is true in all deontically accessible worlds) → ('Op' is true in the real world)."

But the objection cuts both ways. If our assertion of 'p' in all deontically accessible worlds is not sufficient to allow us to assert 'Op' in this world, then we have no reason to suppose valid, and some reason to think invalid, the conditional proposition "('p' is true in all deontically accessible worlds) → ('Op' is true in the real world)." And simply to assume a debatable proposition as an axiom hardly shores up anyone's confidence in the ultimate triumph of SDL semantics. It is the sort of stipulation whose only advantages are, in Russell's famous phrase, those of theft over honest toil.

One might counter the assertibility problem by complaining that I have introduced concerns proper to pragmatics into a semantic discussion. Conditions under which a proposition may be asserted are irrelevant to the semantics of the proposition, and an argument about semantics should not introduce irrelevancies. I am not convinced that pragmatic and semantic concerns can be neatly and easily separated from one another. But in any case, it is the upholder of SDL semantics who needs to infer the assertion of a proposition in this world from the assertion of propositions in other worlds. It is SDL that first mixed pragmatics with semantics; my complaint is that the job was not done properly.

Another counter might be that the assertibility problem is no more than a bad pun on the word 'asserted'. True, SDL semantics seeks to infer "'Op' is asserted in this world" from "'p' is asserted in all deontically accessible worlds;" but the objector points out that the assertion here spoken of is not the act of asserting. After all, no positive human action, including that of asserting, follows logically from anything. Even if logic should demand that I act, perversity might well stay my hand. However, my argument speaks not of actual asserting but of warranted assertibility; it shows that, from the fact that we are warranted in asserting 'p' in deontically accessible worlds, it does not follow that we are warranted in asserting 'Op' in this world. The most we are warranted in asserting in this world is that it ought to be the case that p.

Again, an adherent of SDL semantics might try to turn against me my earlier contention that the connection between the assertion of 'ought' statements and the acceptance of norms is pragmatic, not logical. It is therefore logically possible to assert that X ought to do A without accepting any rules, models, or authorities backing up that assertion. But the mere logical possibility that a statement is asserted under certain conditions hardly proves that those conditions warrant such an assertion. To say that the proposition 'Op' *might* be assertible in spite of the absence of accepted norms is hardly enough to sustain the principle of backward translation. An adherent of SDL needs to show that the assertion of 'p' in all deontically accessible worlds is sufficient to warrant the assertion of 'Op'.

I conclude that the assertibility problem provides a powerful objection to the principle of backward translation. Unless the argument can be turned back — and I do not see any prospect of that — an important principle of SDL semantics contradicts our normal deontic thought and practice.

The effect of the assertibility problem on a dyadic logic of conditional obligation is curious. Such a logic would easily dispose of Solt's original argument by stipulating that the presence of a relevant norm is part of the condition for each obligation. On this stipulation, only those worlds where the conditions of each obligation hold — i.e., worlds in which the relevant norms are present — could be deontically accessible to one another. And if the conditions of a given obligation do not hold in the real world, one cannot assign any truth value to the obligation statement. Thus Solt would be wrong in supposing that 'p' could be true in all deontically accessible worlds but 'Op' false in this world.

But this quick solution of Solt's original problem does not defuse the assertibility problem. For if the connection between norms and oughts is only a pragmatic one, then one cannot suppose that a norm always forms part of the condition in a statement of conditional obligation. One can have the obligation without the institution, even if this is usually not the case. Hence, the conditions of a conditional obligation statement do not settle the assertibility problem.

Therefore, we have even more reason to doubt the viability of SDL semantics — and of standard deontic logic.

Chapter 8: The SDL Semantics of 'Ought to Do' Statements III: Epistemic Problems

Almost since the beginning of deontic logic, people have been raising objections. Many objections have come, so to speak, from the outside: neither the real world nor our moral reasoning is as the deontic logician says it is. Moral conflicts occur, institutions issue conflicting 'ought' claims, and the like. Other objections have come from within the structure of deontic logic, through the construction of paradoxes.

Yet such objections have not really threatened deontic logic in any major way — except that, as objections mount and devices for meeting them become increasingly *ad hoc*, the danger grows that deontic logic will end up like so many scien' ic theories, not disproved but disregarded. Still, objections from the outside can be met by rearranging one's principles, or by denying the lack of fit between one's principles and the world, or by claiming that deontic logic is a theoretical subject and that questions of applicability should arise only about the realized body of doctrine, not about its axioms. Paradoxes can be countered by a cheerful admission that the field of deontic logic is still young, its proper principles are not yet agreed upon, and the paradox-monger is only helping to sort out those principles.

The objections I developed in Chapters 6 and 7 are, I believe, not so easily met. The assertibility problem, difficulties of iterated modalities, and the need to restrict deontic alternative worlds to short-term branches of the real world all attack deontic logic in a vital spot: its semantics. If those arguments are right, SDL semantics badly misrepresents our usual deontic thought.

There is another important reason for my concentration on the usual semantics of deontic logic. The basics of SDL semantics are the same for dyadic as for monadic deontic logic. Thus David Lewis, in his survey of semantics for dyadic deontic logics, stipulates, "Then O(A/B) is true iff there is some permissible way to divide the worlds on which, non-vacuously, A holds at all ideal B-worlds." [Lewis, 4] That is, if A ought to be, given B, then 'A' is true in all ideal worlds where B is true. (Lewis makes no distinction between 'ought to be' and 'ought to do'.) That is a clear adaptation of an SDL semantics for monadic deontic logic; the only new stipulation is that the ideal worlds under consideration be worlds where the condition B holds. Similarly with Åqvist's semantic analysis of Danielsson-type truth-conditions: the conditional ought-statement is true "just in case some B-world where A holds is ranked above all B-worlds where A does not hold."[1] [Åqvist 2, 219] Here again, a standard-type semantics is limited only by the requirement that the condition B hold in all the worlds under consideration. Thus in raising problems for SDL semantics, I am raising difficulties for monadic and dyadic deontic logics alike.

In this chapter I open up a third line of attack on SDL semantics, one that stems from epistemic considerations. Because of unavoidable gaps in what we can know, SDL semantics and the logic that goes with it are in important ways incomprehensible. Even if a standard deontic logic is correct, we cannot hope to apply it to find out what we ought to do in the real world.

I shall first look at a problem in understanding the accessibility relation between this world and the various deontic alternative worlds. Then I shall turn to problems of circularity and lack of content in some characteristic claims of an SDL semantics. Both sets of problems are epistemic, for they raise questions about our ability to understand and use SDL semantics, not about the possibility of standard deontic logic and its semantics.

I begin our look at the accessibility relation with a quick general characterization of how SDL semantics works. All deontically accessible worlds, however one conceives of them, are possible worlds. Therefore, each deontically accessible world either is or is picked out by a Carnapian state description, and there is a modal accessibility relation between this world and deontically accessible worlds.[2] No matter what principle logicians might use to separate the proper subset of deontically accessible worlds from the set of possible worlds, conditions on the larger set are also conditions on the subset.

A state description gives an account of objects, their states, and their natural qualities. The real world provides one such state description — that man is happy, this desk is brown, and so on. From this state description, we can easily generate others: ones in which that man is not happy and this desk is not brown, for instance.

On Hintikka's formulation of the SDL semantics of 'ought to do' statements, a deontic alternative world is one in which all persons always do all that they ought to do. It might seem as though this semantics presupposes some sort of descriptivist theory of the 'ought to do', for only descriptive statements would seem true of worlds that are or are generated by state descriptions. No doubt that is true if deontic alternative worlds just are state descriptions. But a modal realist, who takes the deontically accessible worlds to exist in their own right, supposes that a state description is merely our device for coming to know of such a world. A world's content, for the realist, is not exhausted by its associated state description. Therefore, the realist can allow that people do what they should in a deontically accessible world without presupposing that a description of duties fulfilled is all that can be said of such a world.

As we have seen, the principle for selecting deontically proper worlds imposes an immediate restriction on the accessibility relation. For the list of worlds where all people at all times do their whole duty need not include the real world; as a matter of fact, it does not. The accessibility relation for SDL semantics is therefore non-symmetrical: if world w_1 is deontically accessible to world w_2, it does not follow that world w_2 is deontically accessible to world w_1. The model for a deontic semantics therefore cannot be the semantics of the modal system S5, where the accessibility relation is symmetrical; it must be some weaker system. However, if all in world w_2 always do what would be their duties in w_1 and are their duties in w_2, and if all in w_3 always do what would be their duties in w_2, then surely all in w_3 always do what would be their duties in w_1. And transitivity of the accessibility relation is the hallmark of modal system S4.

But because the real world is not an optimal world, nor one where all do as they ought, the real world is not deontically accessible to itself. (This is the semantic equivalent of saying that 'S ought to do F' does not imply 'S does F'.) Hence, the deontic accessibility relation is non-reflexive. In that case, some weaker modal system than S4 or even than T must serve as a model for an SDL semantics; for reflexivity of the accessibility relation is part of the definition of those modal systems.

However, many relations are non-reflexive, non-symmetrical, and transitive: 'larger than' is an example. I am aware of no *a priori* reason why a non-reflexive, non-symmetrical, and transitive relation might not serve as an accessibility relation in a semantics. So far, then, so good.

Less formally, though, some difficulties begin to arise from the accessibility relation. Hughes and Cresswell admit that talk of possible worlds raises among some people the fear that sober logicians have taken to science fiction. Their way of reassuring their readers is to note that our conception of other possible worlds is at least partly governed by conditions in the real world. They suggest that "a world, w_2, is accessible to a world, w_1, if w_2 is conceivable by someone living in w_1." [Hughes and Cresswell 1, 77] Thus a world which we can conceive of, with our imaginations restricted by the nature of the real world, is an accessible world — modally accessible, that is, but not necessarily deontically accessible. The purpose of requiring an accessibility relation is to ensure that we know enough about an accessible world to justify our claims that given statements are or are not true in that world.

But if, as SDL semantics requires, the accessibility relation is not reflexive, the reassurance that Hughes and Cresswell provide is not available. The real world need not be deontically accessible to itself; a staunch believer in the doctrine of original sin might say that it cannot be so related. We have done those things that we ought not to have done, and we have not done those things that we ought to have done; and if there is truly no health in us, perhaps we could not have done any better. At any rate, whether or not this could be an optimal world, it is not one.[3]

Under what conditions, then, is a deontically accessible world accessible to us in the real world? Not when we can conceive of it, as Hughes and Cresswell suggest. For if any world counts as conceivable by people in the real world, it is the real world. And if conceivability is sufficient for deontic accessibility, the real world must be deontically accessible from the real world. Since it is not, conceivability cannot be sufficient for deontic accessibility.

There is no major problem yet. After all, the reason the deontic accessibility relation is not reflexive is that the real world is not deontically accessible to itself. We need only add a condition: world w_2 is deontically accessible to world w_1 iff w_2 is conceivable by someone living in w_1 and w_2 is deontically accessible to w_1. Now our disciplined imaginations can tell us all the news of w_2, including whether the people of that world always do their duty. If they do, then w_2 is accessible to us; if they do not, then it is not.

This patch on the system works well enough, but it is ominous. For conceivability and hence accessibility are matters of degree. We can conceive of some worlds more clearly and distinctly than others. In general, the more like the real world w_2 is, the more clearly we can conceive it. But our patch commits us to supposing that we are able to conceive, clearly and distinctly enough to avoid errors, of worlds very different from our own. We are in danger of losing the discipline that Hughes and Cresswell saw the real world as exercising on our imaginations.

Conceivability, as a means of access to possible worlds, is itself a dubious tool. Take a counterfactual situation: what would have happened had Lee lost the battle of Chancellorsville? Would Joe Hooker have become president of the United States? If he had, would Woodrow Wilson have become president? One can imagine Hooker's becoming president and Wilson's not; perhaps each of those events is possible. But are they compossible with each other, much less with an entire world just like the real world until the battle of Chancellorsville? Conceivability at most shows the possibility of an isolated event; it cannot show that an entire world, one much like this one but containing that event, is possible.

Moreover, conceivability admits of degrees of clarity. Hughes and Cresswell suggest as much when they speak of the discipline which the real world exercises on the imagination. David Hume, whom no well-disciplined imagination could conceive as trying to draw a 'short and decisive reason' from 'an establish'd maxim in metaphysics' — but who nonetheless did so — states the maxim: *"That whatever the mind clearly conceives includes the idea of possible existence."*[4] The important point for us is Hume's inclusion of the word 'clearly'. His reason is obvious: one can fuzzily imagine somebody's squaring the circle. An upholder of Hume's maxim must say that we cannot imagine the precise steps of a circle-squaring argument. Accessibility, deontic or modal, cannot depend on mere conceivability: it must require conceivability with clarity and, perhaps, distinctness.

But how do we know when we have clearly and distinctly conceived of something? There seems to be no telltale mark exhibited by all and only clear conceptions. A perfectly sound argument proving that a certain geometric figure can be constructed might have the same psychological feel as an unsound argument for the same conclusion; the feel is therefore hardly enough to establish soundness. Perhaps the only test we have for clarity is that of Hughes and Cresswell: the closer our conceivings are to reality, the clearer they are. When we conceive of things as they are, we may be sure our conceptions are altogether clear. As our conceptions grow more distant from reality, they might for all we know still be clear. But we do not know if they are clear or not, and for the practical purpose of doing deontic logic, we need to know.

Once again, then, we find Hughes and Cresswell's suggestion that clear conceivability is sufficient for accessibility warring against the requirement that deontically accessible worlds must be, in at least one important respect, very different from the real world. It is this tension that gives point to Peter Geach's objections to SDL semantics, discussed in Chapter 6.

The problems with accessibility stem, not from formal semantics, but from an informal suggestion by Hughes and Cresswell. Perhaps we should get rid of the problems by dropping the suggestion. We might say that taking accessibility as disciplined conceivability works well for students who come to learn modal semantics, but it has no part in an understanding of deontic semantics. All we know, and need to know, of accessibility in SDL semantics is that it is a nonreflexive, nonsymmetrical, and transitive two-place relation. The problem with this maneuver is that deontic semantics is a purposive activity. From what is true in deontically accessible worlds, we infer 'ought' statements about this world. If we have no way of telling what is true in deontically accessible worlds, then we can make no such inferences. Hughes and Cresswell, by their suggestion of conceivability, have given us a tool, whatever its limitations, for putting modal logic to use. If we refuse that or any other tool — and no other seems to present itself — we might comfort ourselves that our own favored brand of deontic semantics has a place in Plato's heaven, but its earthly value is dubious.

Hence the accessibility relation in SDL semantics raises an epistemic problem. The accessibility relation is our way of getting a peek into deontically accessible worlds; without such a peek, SDL semantics is useless to us. If we do not know what is going on in a deontically accessible world, we cannot conclude that a given statement is or is not true in all such worlds. In that case, we cannot use SDL semantics to determine whether an 'ought to do' statement follows from certain premisses. Without an understandable and useful accessibility relation, SDL semantics is no support to deontic logic.

Certainly it is useless to claim that the proper deontic semantics is whatever fits best with the proper deontic logic. I argued in Chapter 5 that deontic semantics has the task of showing that there can even be a proper deontic logic. We cannot now assume the propriety of some form of deontic logic in order to find the correct deontic semantics. That would be building one's logical house on shifting sand.

The epistemic problem raised by the accessibility relation in SDL semantics is therefore not to be taken lightly. If the accessibility relation must remain obscure, we cannot really know what is going on in those deontically accessible worlds. And in that case, we cannot determine what we ought to do in this world, even if a correct deontic logic exists.

I now turn to epistemic problems clustering around the notions of circularity and emptiness of content, to show that the same gloomy conclusion should be drawn. I suspect that every newcomer to modal semantics has worried about the question of circularity. To say that "Possibly p" is true if and only if 'p' is true in at least one accessible possible world sounds initially like a blatant circle. After all, if you did not understand "Possibly p" to begin with, how could you understand the notion of a possible world? To be sure, circularity is not a logical vice, but it is an epistemic one. With a circular explanation, nothing really gets explained; no one can learn about the contents of a closed circle. To the tyro in modal semantics, the danger looms that he will spend his time in endless chasing of his own tail.

That is why it is so important, at least at first, to understand talk of possible worlds as simply talk about Carnap's state descriptions or Hintikka's model sets. With such accounts, circularity is not present, one can learn about possible worlds, and explanations in the field do really explain. Even a modal realist needs Carnap's or Hintikka's device to ward off misguided objections.

I suggest, though, that deontic logicians are not as well off as their counterparts in modal logic. Circularity is a real problem for SDL semantics, and a non-realist interpretation is not readily available to stave off the difficulty.

In Chapter 6, I noted one problem of circularity. If we restrict the list of relevant deontically accessible worlds to those which branch from the real world at the ought time, and if we allow ourselves to speak of those worlds only for the brief period in which their duty structure is the same as ours, then "Jane does F in all deontically accessible worlds" seems to mean "Jane, by doing F, does what she would do if she did what she ought to do." That is hardly a helpful translation of "Jane ought to do F."

The taint of circularity likewise attends Hintikka's account of deontic alternative worlds as worlds in which all do what they ought to do. To say that Helen ought to do F if and only if she does F in all deontic alternative worlds sounds impressive. But to say that Helen ought to do F if and only if she does F in all worlds in which all people do what they ought to do — that sounds more like a long-winded circle than an explanation.

The problem might be put this way: if deontic logic is to be of any use to us, it will presumably let us gain new information. Given deontic assumptions, we will derive new deontic truths, or at least we will find new reasons for accepting old deontic truths. For example, persons who accept the axioms and inference rules of Standard Deontic Logic will find themselves bound to accept Kant's Principle, whether or not they had accepted it before. But if we cannot specify the nature of deontically accessible worlds without presupposing knowledge of what one ought to do in this world, then the usefulness of deontic semantics is at an end. For it is useless to explain what we ought to do by what happens in other worlds, when we can explain what happens in other worlds only by what we ought to do.[5]

Therefore, if we cannot specify the nature of deontically accessible worlds independently of our specification of what we ought to do, deontic reasoning can do no more than repeat what we already know. It cannot tell us new deontic truths; it cannot even give us new reason to uphold old deontic truths. It is useless. And uselessness gives fangs to the circularity objection. It is no good reply to note that circularity is not a logical but an epistemic problem, a difficulty not *in* a logical calculus but *with* that calculus. For any field of logic to be useful to us, there must be a way of breaking into the charmed justificatory circle. Our talk of deontically accessible worlds need not be explanatory, but some of the talk deontic logicians engage in had better be.

We often try to escape circularity by retreating into relative vagueness. But giving less precise accounts of deontically accessible worlds raises problems of its own. Suppose, instead of speaking of deontic alternative worlds as worlds in which all do what they ought, in the real world, to do, we talk simply of *optimal* or *ideal* or *preferred* or *higher-ranking* worlds.[6] But if such phrases mean anything, they pick out worlds that are best in every way — worlds that ought to be. And from the fact that a set of actions — which is what a deontically relevant world consists of — ought to be, as I argued in Chapter 4, we cannot derive what anyone ought to do.

Hence, talk of optimal or ideal or higher-ranking worlds will do nothing to help determine the logic of 'ought to do' statements.

There is no logical contradiction in the claim that the various deontically accessible worlds are as real as this one. But anyone who makes such a claim should be prepared to answer epistemic questions concerning how we come to know about such worlds. Without an answer to the epistemic questions, the suspicion remains that circularity is endemic to SDL semantics. Persons cannot discover anything about deontically accessible worlds unless they already have knowledge about those worlds. Some child will sooner or later call out that the emperor has no clothes.

To be sure, there is an accessibility relation built into SDL semantics. But this relation merely says that we do have access to other worlds; it neither explains how this access takes place nor justifies the claim that it does take place. And as we have seen in the first part of this chapter, specifying the accessibility relation itself gives rise to epistemic problems.

The only promising strategy for answering the epistemic questions and thus avoiding circularity is to demonstrate an independent way of specifying the nature of deontically accessible worlds, a way not dependent on our prior knowledge of what people ought to do. This amounts to saying that an SDL semantics can be given a non-realist interpretation. Of course, deontic logicians have the right to be realists if they choose. State descriptions or model sets might be, in a logician's mind, only devices by which people can come to know the realities of other worlds. But unless a logician has a way of specifying deontically accessible worlds without appealing to what she considers their real and genuine nature, the epistemic questions remain unanswered.

Well, why should an adherent of SDL semantics not be able to find a non-realist interpretation of deontically accessible worlds? No less an authority than K. Jaakko J. Hintikka wrote a chapter (in *Models for Modalities*) that applies his technique of model sets to SDL semantics. [Hintikka 1, 184-214] What has been done can be done; since a model set is not a real world, Hintikka has freed other deontic logicians from having to worry about circularity. But worries about circularity do not go away just because we are told they do. It is one thing to say that one's theory can be given a consistent non-realist interpretation, quite another thing to show that such an interpretation is available. For what does it mean to say that 'Op' is a member of a deontic alternative model set?

Hintikka regards any such deontic alternatives as non-genuine worlds;
they are state descriptions, spelled out by Hintikka's standard
formalizations.[7] The sentences that go into such state descriptions are
either atomic sentences, identities, or truth-functional combinations of
these. 'Op' seems to be none of the above. One might regard 'Op' as an
atomic sentence. But Hintikka does not take this route: he says that 'O'
stands for 'it ought to be the case that' — i.e., a sentential operator.[8]
[Hintikka 1, 185] Since in Hintikka's axioms both 'Op' and 'p' occur in
the same formula — e.g., in his axiom (C.O*) — 'Op' is clearly meant
to be some sort of compound from 'p'; Hintikka says as much. [Hintikka
1, 188] Why, then, should Hintikka suppose that sentences of the form
'Op' have any place in a state description?

The difficulty is not merely formal. After all, there is no formal
impediment to Hintikka's enlarging his account of state descriptions to
include 'Op'. But given the normal meaning of 'O', which we have seen
that Hintikka adopts, is there any coherent notion of a state description
which includes 'Op' and which can do the epistemic job we need it to do?
That is, can an enlarged account of state descriptions give us non-circular
access to the 'worlds' thus described? The only way I can see is to accept
a thoroughly naturalistic version of descriptivism. Only such a theory
would yield a translation of 'Op' into the language of located observable
qualities. But quite apart from the implausibility of naturalism, an
ostensibly neutral deontic logic should not commit us to any such theory.

As I argued in Chapter 7, assertions of what people ought to do presuppose the acceptance of rules, authorities, or models. Inhabitants of the
real world can act or fail to act, obey or disobey rules, follow or ignore
authorities, imitate or ignore models. What people actually do has a place
in a state description, but there seems to be little place for whether they do
the right acts, follow the proper rules, and so on. After all, on at least one
common view, the sentence "John ought to play the piano" is, at least in
its main thrust, not descriptive but prescriptive. If the prescriptivist view
is correct, no set of descriptive sentences — and hence no state
description, or combination of state descriptions, or portions of state
descriptions — will be equivalent to 'Op'. Before he can allow 'Op' into
state descriptions, then, Hintikka must refute prescriptivism. That would
be an enterprise with which I have some sympathy, but it would be a
difficult one.

Moreover, even if the prescriptivist view is wrong and 'Op' stands for some sort of moral fact, it is by no means clear that any proposition stating that moral fact would be part of, or entailed by, a state description. Hintikka either must espouse a dubious naturalism or must broaden the notion of 'description' to include moral as well as natural facts. The latter course diverges widely from the Carnapian origins of the notion of a state description and is not obviously intelligible.

Hintikka therefore tries to escape the epistemic worry of circularity by leaning on the Carnapian notion of a state description. But by introducing 'ought' sentences into state descriptions, he raises a host of new epistemic problems. That is hardly progress.

One can always evade these difficulties by sticking resolutely to a modal realist view. Deontically accessible worlds are real; they have rules, and people perform actions in them. These worlds have some sort of duty structure. Hence, propositions such as 'Op' as well as 'p' can hold in those worlds. The modal realist view is consistent, although it has problems with the objections I raised in Chapters 6 and 7. The difficulty here is that the pure realist view is epistemically useless. It evades, but does not settle, epistemic problems.

The naive objection to modal semantics, that it involves a vicious circularity, was not well taken. But the same objection, when raised against deontic semantics, has a much greater force. For in an SDL semantics, unlike modal semantics, there is no readily available Carnapian device to provide an entrée into what appears to be a closed system.

The last three chapters have presented three different and, in a sense, practical objections to SDL semantics. In Chapter 6, I argued that one must so narrow the range of deontically accessible worlds as to render standard deontic logic feeble at best. In Chapter 7, I showed that the only justifiable principles of SDL semantics are too narrow for us to derive any useful deontic logic from them. And in this chapter, I argued that any consistent SDL semantics is epistemically useless. These three sets of objections allow for the existence of at least some form of SDL semantics. But if, as I believe, the objections are on the money, the truncated remains of SDL semantics will hardly be sufficient to justify an adequate deontic logic.

But if deontic semantics does not justify deontic logic, nothing can. Deontic logic acutely needs a new semantics to survive.

Chapter 9: New Light on Old Problems

In the previous three chapters, I have raised some major difficulties for the semantics of 'ought to do' statements. In Chapter 6, I found reason to mandate a drastic narrowing of the range of available deontic alternative worlds. In Chapter 7, I found that a major principle of SDL semantics is dubious. And in the last chapter, I noted that problems with circularity and with the accessibility relation make it doubtful whether deontic semantics and deontic logic can ever be of use to us.

In this chapter, I shall consider the effect of these three problems on some standard objections to deontic logic, including such puzzles as the Good Samaritan paradox and Chisholm's contrary-to-duty paradox. I shall also take a fresh look at some objections drawn from religion and from the possibility of morality; these objections were brought up in Chapter 3. I believe that all these objections, when we see them in the light of the difficulties presented in the three preceding chapters, gain considerably in strength. The usual replies given to the standard objections are no longer available; the objections, rather than being isolated difficulties to be met singly, hang together as a set. Standard deontic logic is therefore in a bad way.[1]

I shall start with Roderick Chisholm's paradox of contrary-to-duty imperatives, a paradox which James Tomberlin has rightly called seminal. [Chisholm 1; Tomberlin, 109] To my mind, Chisholm's paradox more than any other reveals the inadequacies of standard deontic logic.

Let us suppose the following plausible situation: Jane ought to contribute monthly to the upkeep of her elderly mother. It is best for Jane's mother to handle her own finances, which she is perfectly able to do; she has an account at the First Conglomerate Bank, right next to her house. Jane herself banks at an institution much nearer to her own home. Jane then ought to act as follows: if she contributes monthly to the upkeep of her elderly mother, she should deposit money regularly in the First Conglomerate Bank. But if she does not contribute monthly to her mother's upkeep, it is not the case that she ought to deposit money regularly in the First Conglomerate Bank. Alas, Jane fails to contribute monthly to her mother's upkeep.

Chisholm's paradox thus seems to embody four assumptions:

(A) S ought to do F.
(B) Ought (S does F → S does G).
(C) If S does not do F, not ought (S does G).
(D) S does not do F.

Truth-functionally, C and D together imply "Not ought (S does G)." But by SDLT2, A and B together imply "Ought (S does G)." That is, it is both true and false on SDL principles that Jane ought to deposit money regularly in the First Conglomerate Bank. Something has, it seems, gone terribly wrong.

And yet, even though A, B, C, and D generate a contradiction in SDL, there is something fishy about that supposed contradiction. Surely Jane ought to deposit money in First Conglomerate, so long as she is helping her mother; and surely she has no obligation to do so, as long as she is not helping her mother. If the rules and the formalizations claim this situation is logically impossible, either the rules or the formalizations must be faulty.

The situation appears made to order for the proponent of dyadic deontic logic. Such a person would formalize Jane's story as follows:

(A₁) S ought to do F, all things considered.
(B₁) S ought to do G, given that S does F.
(C₁) It is permissible that S fails to do G, given that S
       does not do F.
(D₁) S does not do F.

Now C₁ and D₁ do not truth-functionally imply that it is permissible for S to fail to do G. Nor must one's rules be set up in such a way as to require that the first two premises imply that S ought to do G, all things considered.

But, as James Tomberlin argued, a useful dyadic logic must have some rules to detach the condition from a conditional obligation statement.[2] And what is more likely than a rule that, when a condition is met, a conditional obligation or permission statement holds unconditionally? In that case C₁ and D₁ would imply that it is permissible for S to fail to do G.

And surely a system which reflects how we think would allow us to infer from A_1 and B_1 that S ought, all things considered, to do G. Hence it is likely that dyadic deontic logic can escape from Chisholm's paradox only by misrepresenting how we ordinarily think deontically.

Should Chisholm's paradox force us to give up the rules of standard deontic logic? That would be much harder than it might look. SDL semantics provides strong backing for the claim that A and B imply "Ought (S does G)." For by SDLS1, A implies that S does F in every deontic alternative, and B implies that in every deontic alternative if S does F then S does G. Hence, A and B together imply that in every deontic alternative S does G; while SDLS5 ensures that there is at least one such alternative. And by SDLS2, the principle of backward translation, that in turn implies that S ought to do G.

Restricting the set of deontic alternatives to worlds that branch at the ought time does not affect the support that semantics gives to the claim that A and B imply "Ought (S does G)." For what is true in each member of the wider set of worlds must also hold in each member of a proper subset. And, of course, C and D truth-functionally imply that "not ought (S does G)." No problem with deontic logic can affect the correctness of that implication. Hence, if there is any truth in standard deontic logic or in SDL semantics, even if we have modified the latter by narrowing the range of deontic alternative worlds, we must have wrongly formulated some member of the set A through D. Which one?

A, B, and D appear consistent with each other. Jane ought to but does not help her mother, and she ought also to act in this way: if she helps her mother, to put money into the First Conglomerate Bank. There is nothing contradictory in this situation at all. Nor is there any obvious problem if I add that should she not help her mother, it is false that she ought to put money in that bank.

Hence, the most likely candidate for a wrong formalization is C. The most plausible explanation is that C wrongly takes the ought operator to govern the consequent of the conditional. A better reading would take the operator as governing the entire conditional — i.e., as:

(C¹) Ought (S does not do F → S does not do G).

For from C¹ and D, 'Ought(S does not do G)' does not follow truth-functionally or in any system using SDL semantics. For SDLS1 allows us to infer from C^1 that in all deontically accessible worlds, if S does not do F, S does not do G. Since the real world, in which S fails to do F, is not a deontically accessible world, we cannot infer that in any deontic alternative world S does not do G. Hence, we cannot infer that S's failure to do G is permissible, and we cannot conclude "Not ought (S does G)." C^1 therefore seems the obvious way out of Chisholm's paradox.

But C^1 has its own flaws. Its semantic counterpart is "In all deontically accessible worlds, if S does not do F, S does not do G." That is equivalent to saying that in all deontically accessible worlds, either S does F or S does not do G: in all such worlds either Jane contributes to her mother's upkeep or she does not deposit regularly in First Conglomerate. But SDLS1, applied to A, entails that in all deontically accessible worlds Jane does contribute to her mother's upkeep. Therefore, in each such world it is trivially true that either Jane contributes to her mother's upkeep or she does not deposit regularly in First Conglomerate. By backward translation, then, C^1 is also, in light of A, trivially true.

However, we have no use for a version of C that is trivially true. Chisholm's point is that often duties carry with them subsidiary duties; if we fail to perform the primary duty, we are sometimes let off from performing the subsidiary one. This is a substantive fact about certain duties, not a necessary characteristic of all duties; after all, law courts sometimes convict a person of multiple felonies involved in a single act. Hence, C^1 gets us out of Chisholm's paradox only at the unacceptable cost of badly misrepresenting ordinary deontic thinking.

Perhaps my reformulation of C was wrong, and both the deontic operator and the negation should apply to the entire expression. That is:

(C^2) Not ought (S does not do F → S does G).

But C^2 is equivalent to "Permissible not (S does not do F → S does G)" and hence to "Permissible (S does not do F & S does not do G)." By SDLS3, we can infer that in some deontically accessible world, S does not do F and S does not do G — which contradicts the semantic counterpart of A, that S does F in all deontically accessible worlds. Hence C^2 does not escape paradox.

Suppose next that we reformulate C by using the permissibility operator:

(C^3): P(S does not do F → S does not do G).

By SDLS3, in some deontically accessible world w_0, S does not do F → S does not do G. But by the semantic translation of A, S does F in every deontically accessible world. Hence, it is trivially true that in w_0, S does not do F → S does not do G; and C^3, given A, is trivially true. But once again, Chisholm's original premiss C is not trivially true. Therefore, C^3 fares no better than its predecessors.

Let us try one more reformulation with a global permissibility operator:

(C^4): P(S does not do F & S does not do G).

By SDLS3, in some deontically accessible world w_0, S does not do F and S does not do G. But by the semantic translation of A, S does F in every deontically accessible world. Hence C^4, like C^2, perpetuates the paradox.

Reformulating C by having the deontic operator govern the entire conditional expression therefore does not afford a satisfactory resolution of Chisholm's paradox. But the failure of the four revisions of C does indicate a more satisfactory way of dealing with the paradox. For the difficulty with C^1 and C^3 stemmed from our taking "If S does not do F, S does not do G" as "S does not do F → S does not do G" — and therefore as "S does F or S does not do G." Likewise, the difficulty with C^2 and C^4 stemmed from our taking "Not(if S does not do F, S does (not) do G" as "~(S does not do F → S does (not) do G)" — and therefore as "S does not do F & S does (not) do G." The problems of C^1 through C^4 therefore arise from our regarding the conditional in C as truth-functional.

Chisholm's original premiss, however, suggests a *causal*, not a truth-functional conditional. It is Jane's hypothetical failure to contribute to her mother's upkeep that annuls her duty to deposit money in First Conglomerate. It is S's real-world failure to do F — a failure which, according to A, does not occur in deontically accessible worlds — which creates the permissibility of S's not doing G. Therefore, it is not permissible for S to fail to do G *until* S has failed to do F.

We can easily see now why Chisholm's paradox is such a major problem for SDL semantics. SDL semantics is truth-functional and atemporal, but Chisholm's paradox points the moral that deontic semantics must be both temporal and causal.

We found in Chapter 6 that in a semantics of worlds branching from this one at the ought time, deontically accessible worlds do contain derelictions of duty. Once S has failed to do F, S might well be permitted not to do G. That is to say, before the ought time S has failed to do F in the real world and hence in all deontically accessible worlds; after the ought time, S fails to do G in at least one deontically accessible world. The Geachian equivalents of A_s and B_s speak only of acts taken at or after the ought time. Hence, in the semantics of branching worlds, it does not look as if Chisholm's four principles will generate a paradox.

However, if we restrict SDL semantics to branching worlds, we still have not dealt with half the moral of Chisholm's paradox: that a correct deontic logic takes account of causal relations among obligations. Until we do so, the paradox remains troublesome. For one way a world w_1 can branch from a world w_0 at time t is for new causal laws to structure w_1 but not w_0 at t. Hence, in some possible worlds that branch from the real one upon Jane's failure to contribute to her mother's upkeep, quite odd results, possibly including some strange new duties, will come about. Less spectacularly, in some branching worlds other factors might combine to bring about the same duty in a different manner. Perhaps in one such world First Conglomerate will acquire a moral claim on Jane's funds. Therefore, it is not the case that in *all* deontically accessible worlds that branch from the real one upon Jane's failure to contribute, it will be false that she ought to bank at First Conglomerate. Temporal subscripts for obligations are therefore not enough to settle Chisholm's paradox.

For similar reasons, if we introduce into SDL semantics the changing worlds of Rantala's urn models, we avoid some but not all the difficulties raised by Chisholm's paradox. Urn models, like the restriction to branching worlds, make it possible that duties present at one time are not present at another. But they do not by themselves account for the ways in which our actions and inactions bring about a change in our duties. As a result, it is hard if not impossible to 'fine-tune' an urn model so that its worlds would change in just the right ways to avoid the paradox — unless we introduce the notion of causal laws and branching worlds into urn models.

A full answer to Chisholm's paradox must then wait for Chapter 14, when I present a new semantics for deontic logic. But for now, we can give a partial resolution of that paradox by counting it together with the arguments of Chapter 6. Like those arguments, Chisholm's paradox demands that we drastically revise ordinary deontic semantics, and hence deontic logic, by restricting the set of deontically accessible worlds to those which branch from the real world at the ought time. What else Chisholm's paradox requires of deontic logic, we must wait to see.

But if on the basis of the arguments of Chapter 6 and Chisholm's paradox we decide to adopt a more restrictive version of SDL semantics, another familiar deontic paradox raises its head. This is the basic Good Samaritan Paradox: X ought not to kill Y; but X ought to help Y, whom X will kill next week; therefore, by SDLT3, X ought to kill Y. If a person cannot have contradictory obligations, it is impossible that X both ought and ought not to kill Y. And even if contradictory obligations might exist, there is something deeply unsettling, although not strictly paradoxical, in the conclusion that X ought to kill Y.

The nerve of this argument is the move from "X ought to help Y, whom X will kill next week" to "X ought to kill Y." This move is justified by reading "X ought to help Y, whom X will kill next week" as "O(X helps Y.X kills Y next week)." One can then apply either SDLT3 or its equivalent: $\vdash O(p.q) \rightarrow (Op.Oq)$. It follows that X ought to kill Y next week, in which case X ought to kill Y.

The usual solution to the simple Good Samaritan Paradox is to claim that the paradox misreads "X ought to help Y, whom X will kill next week." The clause "whom X will kill next week" is not within the scope of the 'ought' operator; the sentence in question should be understood as "O(X helps Y).X kills Y next week." On such a reading, it does not follow that X ought to kill Y next week.

SDL semantics bears out the scope solution to the paradox. X helps Y in all deontically accessible worlds, but that X kills Y is a fact of this world but not necessarily of all deontically accessible worlds. In fact, if X ought not to kill Y, then X does not kill Y in *any* deontically accessible world. Hence, the conclusion that X ought to kill Y does not follow. Even if we narrow the range of available deontically accessible worlds to meet the arguments of Chapter 6, we still have no reason to suppose that X will kill Y in any, much less all, of those alternative worlds.

But introducing a semantics of branching worlds breathes new life into the Good Samaritan, so long as we speak of past rather than future injury. X ought now to help Y, whom she has unjustly harmed. Since the ought time is now, the available deontically accessible worlds for the semantic analysis of "X ought now to help Y, whom she has unjustly harmed" are worlds which branch from the real world at the present time. But if X harmed Y unjustly before now, then in all the worlds which branch from the real world at the present time X harmed Y unjustly. Hence, X ought to harm Y unjustly — or perhaps, to preserve tense distinctions, X ought now to have harmed Y unjustly. Either conclusion is most unwelcome.

We cannot escape the difficulty by noting that the action of X's harming Y was in the past. For, as I noted in Chapter 6, the ought time is the time at which the obligation holds, not the time, if any, at which the obligated action took place.

To escape the difficulty, we need another restriction on the semantics. One obvious potential restriction is to claim that there can be no duties at a time t to have performed some action before t. But although this restriction meets the current example, it is no help against a new variant.

Suppose that Y has been beaten and robbed and left lying in a ditch. X, an extremely bad Samaritan, comes along, notices Y, is disgusted by his pleas for help, and begins to throttle him. She is killing him at the very moment she should be helping him! All the worlds that branch from the real world at this very moment, the ought time, then include her throttling of poor Y — although in each deontically accessible world, presumably she immediately leaves off her wicked activities. Hence, X ought at the present time to be choking Y at the present time.[3]

Should we say that the worlds must branch at some time *after* the ought time? How long after? Since any segment along the time series is infinitely divisible, no two moments are next to each other. Hence, some interval must occur between the ought time and the branching time; and during that interval, at least in theory, some wrongful actions might occur, such as X's continuing to throttle Y. Those wrongful actions would then be features of every branching world, and the paradox would remain in force.

A more promising solution is to put a new restriction on SDLS2, the axiom of backward translation. After all, we care about what people do in alternative worlds only to the extent that their activities in those worlds help us determine what they should do in this world. S can, for all we care, run amok in other worlds, so long as backward translation does not produce a duty on his part to misbehave in this one.

One obvious way of restricting backward translation is by specifying the time of the act in question. We might try the following principle: If S does F at t_2 in all deontically accessible worlds branching from the real world at the earlier time t_1, then S ought at t_1 to do F at t_2.[4] The new restriction, that S do F after the ought time, blocks the paradox — but at an unacceptable cost. For X, who is choking Y now, has a duty now to help Y now. That is, X's present duty to help Y is not merely to perform a future action but to perform a present action. With our new restriction limiting backward translation to cases where the action is subsequent to the ought time, SDL semantics provides no alternative-worlds analysis of the clearly true statement "X ought now to help Y now."

Of course, I argued in Chapter 7 that the standard principle of backward translation faces problems of its own. If we give up backward translation altogether, we have removed the paradox for sure — along with the bulk of deontic logic! Blocking a paradox by tearing down the theory in which the paradox arises is like ridding a house of termites by burning the house to the ground.

Perhaps a different sort of restriction on backward translation will have better luck. After all, there is no logical connection between X's choking Y and her helping Y — unless one says that throttling is a rather spectacular way of failing in a duty to help. At any rate, throttling is not a logically sufficient condition for helping, nor is it a logically necessary condition. We then amend the principle of backward translation to read:

SDLS2^1.   If S does F in all deontically accessible worlds, and if doing F is logically necessary or sufficient for performing some known duty G, then S ought to do F in the real world.

Once again, the paradox is blocked; and this time, the cost might seem more acceptable. For as I have noted before, deontic semantics is purposive. From a set of 'ought' statements and from forward translation, we want to be able to deduce that certain non-deontic statements hold in all deontically accessible worlds. Let one of those non-deontic statements be: "S does F." If "S does F in all deontically accessible worlds" follows logically from a set of 'ought' statements, then those statements are logically sufficient for the truth of "S does F" in all deontically accessible worlds; and the truth of "S does F" in all deontically accessible worlds is logically necessary for the truth of the set of 'ought' statements. Similarly, the principle of backward translation itself allows us to deduce an 'ought' statement from the truth of "S does F in all deontically accessible worlds"; if backward translation is an axiom, then the truth of "S does F" in all deontically accessible worlds is logically sufficient for the truth of an 'ought' statement.   Therefore, restricting backward translation to cases where statements are logically necessary or sufficient for the truth of known 'ought' statements need not hamper the use of SDL semantics in proofs — so long as the 'ought' statements one is proving or working from are already known to be true! Deontic logic is not then a logic of discovery.

Circularity and related epistemic problems are clearly lurking in the weeds here. If we accept the new restriction to avoid the Good Samaritan, deontic logic is reduced to arguing from known deontic truths to known deontic truths. For those outside the charmed circle, there seems to be no good way to break in.

But there are worse problems than circularity. For several variants of the Good Samaritan paradox can meet the requirement of logically necessary or sufficient conditions — and still achieve paradoxical results. There are at least two such variants: Åqvist's paradox of knowledge; and my own paradox of gentle murders.

Lennart Åqvist's paradox depends on the familiar claim that knowledge strictly implies truth. [Åqvist 1, 366] If X knows that Y will commit a crime, it follows necessarily that Y will commit a crime. Assume that X ought to know that Y will commit a crime, perhaps because X is charged by her superiors with ferreting out crime. SDLR3 says that if A strictly implies B, and if OA, we can infer OB. Hence, Y ought to commit a crime.

One might discount Åqvist's paradox by pointing out that one person's duty to know hardly establishes another's duty to act. But that is a response to the example, not to the argument; it is easy to change the example to meet the objection. Suppose that X, the guardian, is the very same person as Y, the future felon. As a guardian, X ought to know that she will commit the crime; her knowing that she will commit the crime strictly implies that she will commit the crime. It is hard to avoid the conclusion that X ought to commit the crime.

Perhaps the fault lies in the principle that if A strictly implies B, and if OA, then OB. But as we saw in Chapter 2, SDL semantics bears out the principle SDLR3. To say that A strictly implies B is to say that in all accessible possible worlds, if A then B. All deontically accessible worlds are accessible possible worlds, so that 'A → B' holds in all deontically accessible worlds. Since 'OA' holds in this world, by SDLS1 'A' holds in all deontically accessible worlds. Since both 'A' and 'A → B' hold in all deontically accessible worlds, 'B' holds in all deontically accessible worlds; and by SDLS2, 'OB' holds in this world. Hence, SDLR3 must be correct if SDL semantics is right.

The preceding argument is similar to the PLO and the PON, which I discussed in Chapter 7. Like them, it depends on the assumption that deontically accessible worlds are possible and modally accessible worlds. Formally, then, one could get around SDLR3, and with it Åqvist's version of the Good Samaritan, by introducing Rantala's urn models. But, as I argued in Chapter 7, this maneuver is an implausible way of dealing with deontic problems. The world could not change in such a way that a known fact becomes false. For a person to know what is not so is blatantly, not subtly, impossible.

Giving up backward translation would jettison most of SDL. Nor does restriction of the set of deontically accessible worlds to ones branching at the ought time have any effect on Åqvist's problem, for what is true in the larger set of deontically accessible worlds is obviously also true in any subset.

Probably the most natural response to Åqvist's argument is to deny that X ought to know that Y will commit a crime. For in deontic alternative worlds, where all do as they ought, Y will not commit a crime. Therefore, in each such world X will not know that Y will commit a crime; hence, in the real world not only is it false that X ought to know that Y will commit a crime, but it is even true that X ought not to know that Y will commit a crime.[5]

But after this natural response, it becomes very hard to understand just what X ought to know. Surely she ought to know *something:* she is charged by her superiors with uncovering criminal plans. In deontically accessible worlds X would no doubt be out of work, but in the real world she has things to know. Åqvist's variant thus eloquently reinforces Geach's doubts about the relevance of the very different acts people perform in perfect alternative worlds to what they should do in this most imperfect world. Imagine that Y has already performed or is currently performing a criminal action. It is reasonable to say that X ought now to know what Y is doing or has done. For in all worlds branching from the real world at or after this time, Y performs the criminal action. If in all those worlds X knows what Y has done or is doing, then X ought to know that Y is or was performing a criminal action. Why should X's duty to know of future criminality have some status completely different from her duty to know of present or past criminality? To be sure, what is done is done and cannot be undone; but that fact hardly makes what is done logically necessary!

We can take matters the other way around. Suppose that X really ought to know at t_1 that Y will commit the crime at a later time t_2. Then by SDLS1, in all deontically accessible worlds that branch from the real world at or after t_1, X knows at t_1 that Y will commit the crime at t_2; in which case in all those alternatives, Y will commit the crime at t_2. By SDLS2, Y ought to do so. Thus if X really ought to know that Y will commit the crime, Åqvist's paradoxical result seems inescapable. Our restrictions of Chapter 6 strengthen Åqvist's paradox.

I blocked the plain Good Samaritan paradox by amending the principle of backward translation to read: If S does F in all deontically accessible worlds, and if doing F is logically necessary or sufficient for performing some known duty G, then S ought to do F in the real world. Well, if X ought to know now that Y will commit a crime, certainly Y's committing the crime is logically necessary for X's performing her duty. And in the semantics of worlds that branch at the ought time, if X ought to know now that Y will commit a crime, Y will commit that crime in all deontically accessible worlds. Hence, by SDLS2^1, if we can admit the premiss that X ought to know now that Y will commit a crime, we must still conclude that Y ought to commit the crime. Thus the added requirement of a logically necessary or sufficient condition, which blocks the standard Good Samaritan, fails to stop Åqvist's variant.

Perhaps our added requirement was too lenient: we should block the Good Samaritan, along with Åqvist's variant, by requiring a logically sufficient condition. Mere necessary conditions will not do. We then read SDLS2 in this way:

SDLS2^2. If S does F in all deontically accessible worlds, and if doing F is logically sufficient for performing some known duty G, then S ought to do F in the real world.

But SDLS2^2 runs foul of my paradox of gentle murders. [J. Forrester 1] That paradox derives from a supposed law which reads: if W murders Z, he should murder her gently. Since in fact W does murder Z, it follows that he ought to murder her gently — in which case, gentle murders being murders, he ought to murder her. One can make this a formal paradox by assuming a law against murder and axioms of SDL; but a duty to murder is nasty enough to work with.

Now an obvious problem with my paradox is the interpretation of the requirement that murders be done gently. To read this as "W murders Z → O(W murders Z gently)" would give us the unwelcome conclusion quickly, via *modus ponens*. All the more reason, then, not to adopt that reading. If we accept the variant reading "O(W murders Z → W murders Z gently)," it is by no means clear that the conclusion follows at all. It does in some systems of deontic logic, not in others.

SDL semantics reinforces one's skepticism about the argument. Suppose it true in all deontically accessible worlds that if W murders Z, W murders Z gently. If one ought not to commit murder, in all deontically accessible worlds it is false that W murders Z; therefore, by false antecedent, in any such world it is trivially true that, if W murders Z, W murders Z gently. That W murders Z in the real world shows only that this world is not deontically accessible to itself. That is, W murders Z in the real world — and only in this and other reprobate worlds; "if W murders Z, W murders Z gently" has only been shown to hold in non-reprobate worlds — and there only trivially. For all we know, there is no world at all in which W murders Z and the conditional proposition holds. Hence, there is no duty to murder gently, so long as SDL semantics is acceptable.[6]

But the Chapter 6 objections, Chisholm's paradox, and the resulting restrictions on deontically accessible worlds put new life into the paradox of gentle murders. For let us suppose that W, at this very moment, completes the act of murdering Z. In all worlds that branch from this world at this moment, he murders her. But in all deontically accessible worlds, if he murders her, he does so gently. Hence, in all deontically accessible worlds branching from this world now, W is murdering Z gently. And by backward translation, W ought now to murder Z gently.

I am assuming that the contents of the moment at which W finishes Z off are common to the real world and to any world which branches off at that moment. If not, if branching must always for some reason take place *after* the commission of a crime, one wonders whether branching could ever take place at all. As the old hymn has it, the world is very evil.

On the semantics of branching worlds, then, the paradox of gentle murders has a real bite to it. But the nastiest bite of the paradox comes from a standard truth of logic: any statement 'p' implies the statement 'q → p'. That is, 'p' is a logically sufficient condition for 'q → p'. Hence, "W murders Z gently" is a logically sufficient condition for "If W murders Z,

W murders Z gently." And our reading of a premiss of the paradox of gentle murders was: "Ought (if W murders Z then W murders Z gently)." Hence, the truth of "W murders Z gently" is logically sufficient for the performance of a known duty, *viz.* the conditional 'ought' statement. Since, as I have argued, W murders Z gently in all those deontically accessible worlds which branch at the ought time, and since the truth of "W murders Z gently" is logically sufficient for the performance of a known duty, SDLS2^2 yields the conclusion that W ought to murder Z gently. The plain Good Samaritan, Åqvist's version, and my version thus go together to subvert any form of SDLS2.

Thus the changes mandated in SDL semantics by the Chapter 6 objections and Chisholm's paradox make a real Frankenstein's monster out of the Good Samaritan Paradox. The only promising way of escaping the ordinary Good Samaritan with one's deontic semantics relatively intact is to insist that even if John does F in all deontically accessible worlds, he ought to do F in the real world only if John's performing that action is logically both necessary and sufficient for his performing his known duty G. If his doing F is merely a necessary condition of his doing G, Åqvist's paradox arises; if it is merely sufficient, my paradox stands in the way. But if his doing F is both logically necessary and logically sufficient for doing G, then his doing F and his doing G are not, at least extensionally, separate actions.

The two deontic paradoxes, Chisholm's and the Good Samaritan, turn out to be counterparts of one another. Chisholm's paradox complements our Chapter 6 objections in requiring a restricted semantics. But the Good Samaritan and its variants effectively complement the argument of Chapter 7 by raising what I believe are unanswerable difficulties for SDLS2. Taken together, and in the light of considerations raised in Chapters 6 and 7, both paradoxes have far more sting than before. I see no good answer to either one.

But the added sting is not the only important effect of our look at the standard deontic paradoxes. We have seen that each paradox attacks, not the generalized fact of deontic logic, but some major specific targets within standard deontic logic. With a restricted semantics of branching worlds, and with no principle of backward translation, there is little left of SDL semantics. Which means that, barring an improbable rescue by a radically new semantics that yields the propositions of SDL, there is little if anything left of standard deontic logic.

I turn from the deontic paradoxes to matters of contradictory obligations and obligations to do the impossible. Here, as I suggested in Chapter 3, there are two types of difficulty. The most common sort arises from what seem to be cases of conflicting obligations: S ought to do F, and S ought not to do F. Such cases, if allowable, directly contradict SDLT1, a basic principle of standard deontic logic. Other difficulties, primarily arising from the Augustinian-Calvinist strain in Christian theology, suggest that persons can have obligations to do what they logically cannot do. These difficulties directly contravene SDLT5, Kant's Principle that 'ought' implies 'can'. We can deal with both sorts of difficulty together.

So far as I can see, neither the arguments of Chapter 6 nor those of Chapter 7 have any bearing on contradictory or impossible obligations. As I noted in Chapter 7, SDLT1 and SDLT5 are obvious consequences of SDL semantics, and they can be proved without calling on the principle of backward translation. Thus the argument of Chapter 7 has no power over SDLT1 and SDLT5. Moreover, the semantic arguments for each principle depend only on showing that, were the principle false, in at least one world a contradiction would arise. Restricting the set of deontically accessible worlds in accordance with the Chapter 6 arguments means fewer worlds in which contradictions can arise, but one such world is enough for the argument to succeed — and SDLS5 guarantees that much. So the arguments of Chapter 6 and consequent semantic modifications have no effect on SDLT1 and SDLT5.

However, the *epistemic* considerations which I raised in Chapter 8 do have a major impact on SDLT1 and SDLT5. In Chapter 8, I argued that the accessibility relation, by which we supposedly 'see into' other possible worlds, provides in deontic semantics a peephole that is at best unreliable. Moreover, we found that questions of circularity produce doubts that anyone could ever come to understand 'ought' statements. Hence, deontic semantics will have great difficulty in serving as an explanation, much less a justification, for any supposed moral fact.

SDLT1 and SDLT5 both stand in need of such a justification, especially the former. For SDLT1 says that there are in fact no conflicting obligations. It might seem that Jane ought, as a citizen, to obey a certain law and that she ought, as a member of a certain religious group, not to obey the law. The upholder of a standard deontic logic must assure us that at least one of Jane's obligations is merely *prima facie*. Whatever

Jane's real duty, we are assured, it is not in conflict with other real duties. But as I argued in "Conflicts of Obligation," there seems no good basis for this assurance. [J. Forrester 3, *passim*]

Similar questions arise with SDLT5. As I argued in Chapter 2 of *Why You Should*, Augustinian Christianity presumes that all people except Adam, Eve, and Jesus ought to do the impossible. An adherent of a standard deontic logic must respond that such a presumption is simply false. Whoever believes in the precepts of Augustinian Christianity — and millions do — is, at least with respect to one of its tenets, mistaken. Whence comes the standard deontic logician's assurance that they are wrong and he is right? Merely saying that standard deontic logic works is hardly enough. After all, there are plenty of versions of deontic logic. And if the working of a particular version is simply a matter of formal consistency, or adherence to the rules of modal logic, or some other such matter, the deontic logician provides little reason to think that his version codifies our ordinary deontic thought.

SDL semantics provides the only available basis on which we can reasonably conclude that Augustinian Christianity must be wrong, as well as that genuine duties do not in fact conflict. If the Augustinians were right, says SDL, then some possible world would contain a contradiction. But no possible world can contain a contradiction, so the Augustinians cannot be right. And neither, for the same reason, can the supposition that genuine duties can conflict. SDL semantics, then, is needed to explain and justify the claim that SDLT5 and SDLT1 apply to real-world situations. Neither SDLT5 nor SDLT1 is self-evident; some situations in the world would seem to violate one or both of them. Only deontic semantics can rescue the situation. But, as I have argued, SDL semantics is so beset with epistemic problems that we cannot make a practical use of it. Hence we have no good reason to think that SDLT5 and SDLT1 apply to this world.

In Chapter 7, I argued that SDLT5 and SDLT1 would be just about the only survivors among the principles of deontic logic if, in response to the argument of Chapter 7, we deprive SDL semantics of backward translation. Now I am suggesting that, because of apparent counterexamples and the epistemic problems of SDL semantics, even these two principles are doubtful.

Chapter 9 exhibits a nice symmetry with the previous three chapters, for they present three kinds of difficulties for SDL semantics: epistemic problems, problems of restricting deontically accessible worlds, and problems with backward translation. Chapter 9 argues that each of those three difficulties has a familiar, and reinforcing counterpart among the recognized objections to deontic logic. And among them, the six problems at the very least render dubious every principle of SDL.

What then is left of the standard deontic logic of 'ought to do' statements? Very little; perhaps nothing.

Chapter 10: The Semantics of 'Ought to Be' Statements

The version of SDL semantics most appropriate for 'ought to do' statements is probably Hintikka's semantics of deontic alternative worlds — i.e., worlds in which all persons always do what they ought to do. For the semantics of 'ought to be' statements, a version whose worlds are *optimal* or *permissible* is more plausible. For, as Chapter 4 indicated, 'ought to be' statements suppose ways in which the world might be improved. To see what would make this world better, it seems reasonable to look at better worlds.

To set up an optimal world semantics for 'ought to be' statements, we take a proper subset of the set of all possible worlds accessible to this one. The proper subset consists of worlds in which everything is just as it ought to be; these are the optimal worlds. Then "It ought to be that p" is true in this world if and only if 'p' is true in all optimal worlds, and "It is permissible that p" is true in this world if and only if 'p' is true in some optimal world. If Thelma helps John in all optimal worlds, and if there is at least one such world, her helping him is just how things should be in this world. But since 'ought to be' does not imply 'ought to do', we cannot infer that Thelma ought to help John in this world. Hence, if backward translation is in order, we can infer 'ought to be' statements but not the corresponding 'ought to do' statements from optimal world semantics. Optimal-world semantics of this kind seems a plausible way to give truth-conditions for 'ought to be' statements.

A permissible-world semantics works in the same way as an optimal-world semantics. A permissible world is one in which every action is licit. Since, by SDLT9, every optimal act is permissible, every optimal world is a permissible world; what is true in all permissible worlds is then true in all optimal worlds. The converse is not logically necessary, but it is plausible. For we might well understand what ought to be the case as what is permissible *no matter what*. Walking across a lawn is permissible in some cases, not in others; but no matter what happens, one may always help those less fortunate than one's self. That is, one performs optimal actions in all permissible worlds, but there is at least one permissible world in which a less-than-optimal act is not performed. If so, all and only what one does in all optimal worlds is performed in all permissible worlds, and a semantics of permissible worlds should give the same results as a semantics of optimal worlds.

However easy it is to set up an optimal-world or a permissible-world semantics, difficulties quickly set in. In a truly optimal world very few of us would have a place, for we cannot be counted on to act for the best in all situations. An optimal world would have different people, different situations, different everything. We might learn from such a semantics how worlds in general should be, but not how this world should be.

To rescue the relevance of optimal world semantics, we need to recall Leibniz's doctrine of the best of all possible worlds. Those possible worlds which are optimal not only might but must have some faults, Leibniz claimed. Two states of affairs, considered in isolation, could each be optimal; but the existence of one optimal state often logically excludes the existence of another. An optimal world might therefore contain us and what we do. Optimal worlds are then not worlds where everything is as it should be; rather, they are worlds where as much as possible is as it should be. We need not agree with Leibniz that this is the best of all possible worlds; we need only say that what ought to be in this world is what will help to make this world as good as possible.

Since optimal worlds are possible worlds, not every state of affairs in an optimal world will be optimal. The very notion of a world which is not a possible world is incoherent.[1] A world, to be possible, must contain no logical contradiction; and a logical contradiction implies any proposition. Hence, if an optimal world were not a possible world, all propositions would be true in such a world — and if so, no coherent description of that supposed world could be given. What I shall call the *Leibnizian construal*, which takes optimal worlds to be ones in which as much as possible is as it should be, is the only way to make sense of optimal-world semantics. On the Leibnizian construal, we might speak of *optimized* rather than optimal worlds.

One might seek to avoid the Leibnizian construal by supposing that a certain optimal world w_1, accessible under modal accessibility relation R, is not accessible under modal accessibility relation R'. Then the fact that a proposition 'p' is true in an optimal world would not imply that it is true in a possible and accessible world, because w_1 is not a member of the set of possible worlds defined by R'.[2] In this way an optimal world might not be an accessible possible world.

However, even if one allows alternative accessibility relations, the Leibnizian construal is unavoidable. For if optimal worlds are possible worlds under *any* accessibility relation, presumably descriptions of them are not self-contradictory. But if Leibniz was right, an entire world where every detail is as it ought to be would be self-contradictory. Hence w_1, even though not a possible world accessible under R', can be optimal only in Leibniz's sense: evil is at a minimum, not non-existent.

There is therefore no good alternative to adopting the Leibnizian construal: Only by doing so can we account for the presence of us and our actions in optimal worlds. But the SDL semantics of 'ought to be' statements then faces a major difficulty. If there is evil in optimal worlds, a state of affairs present in all optimal worlds might be no more than a necessary evil. And one would hardly say of a necessary evil that it ought to be — although SDLT6 would commit us to just that absurdity. Therefore, SDLS2, the SDL principle of backward translation, is indefensible. From the fact that a state of affairs holds in all optimal worlds, it does not follow that the state of affairs ought to be in this world.

A semantics of permissible worlds faces the same Leibnizian problem, for a state of affairs that occurs in all permissible worlds need not itself be permissible. It might instead be the minimal amount of impermissible evil consistent with maximal permissible good. Hence, that 'p' is true in all permissible worlds does not imply that it ought to be that p. Likewise, if a deontic alternative world is one where people do as little as possible of what it ought not to be that they do, what they do in all such worlds may not be what it ought to be that they do here.

So far as I can determine, SDL semantics has no good answer for the problem Leibniz posed. Even if worlds containing nothing but good are possible, they would be so different from the real world as to be of no use in determining what ought to be the case here. If such worlds are not possible, then the question of usefulness does not even arise.

Problems with the Leibnizian construal are not the only ones to bedevil the SDL semantics of 'ought to be' statements. A difficulty discussed in Chapter 7, PON, has a counterpart in the semantics of 'ought to be' statements. For in all possible worlds, and hence presumably in all optimal and all permissible worlds, all necessary truths and the denials of all necessary falsehoods hold true. Therefore, it ought to be that all triangles have three sides, and it ought not to be that 2 + 3 is equal to 6. Swallowing both these propositions seems likely to choke anyone. SDL semantics can avoid these results only by implausibly denying that every optimal world is a possible and accessible world.

Perhaps the worst problem for the SDL semantics of 'ought to be' statements once more invokes a Leibnizian theme: that many situations lack optimal solutions. Even when such solutions are available, what ought to be need not be optimal — and might not even, in some circumstances, be permissible. There is then a large gap between our ordinary understanding of what ought to be and the supposed truth-conditions for 'ought to be' statements.

Let us consider *morally* optimal worlds: in such worlds, as much as possible is for the morally best. Now sometimes we do indeed suppose that what ought to be is what would be morally the best course. More often, though, what we think ought to be the case represents only an *improvement* on what there is. Anybody whose ears have been assaulted on a city street by the loud squalling of a boom box has no doubt thought that there ought to be a law against playing those infernal devices in public places. But is the presence of a law really the optimal solution? People do not always obey laws, and laws are not always vigilantly enforced. There would be satisfaction, no doubt, in seeing a malefactor apprehended, but that satisfaction would come only after having listened to highly amplified howls. Surely in a truly optimal world boom boxes would never have been invented. Or else, a truly optimal world would contain no one with the inclination to subject others against their will to his own musical taste.

This example suggests three points:

- To say that a situation ought to be is not necessarily to say that the situation would be optimal if it occurred. The situation might represent only an improvement on the existing state of affairs.
- There might be no optimal solution to a problem: any of several alternatives might improve the situation, but none would do away with the problem entirely.
- There might be quite different and possibly even conflicting optimal solutions to a given problem. In some optimal worlds there are no boom boxes; in other optimal worlds there are better people.

The first point should lead us to talk, not of optimal, but of improved worlds. An improved world is one which is better than this one in some respect: namely, one relevant to the situation at hand. And an improved world cannot be one which is better in one relevant respect and worse in others; it must be better overall. But because there might be more than one optimal solution to a given practical problem, and since every optimal world is an improved world, it cannot be true that what ought to be the case is the case in *every* improved world. In some improved worlds there are no boom boxes and hence no laws regulating their use; in other improved worlds people need no laws regulating the use of boom boxes. Only in *some* improved worlds is there the kind of law that we think ought to be in this world. These worlds must, of course, be *relevantly* improved: the improvement must have to do with the problem of boom boxes.

Let us change the semantics, then, to the following: "It ought to be that p" is true if and only if 'p' is true in at least one relevantly improved world. Will that be sufficient to meet all objections? It will not. For if slavery is evil in itself, a world with marginally less slavery is a relevant improvement over a world with marginally more slavery; but neither world represents what ought to be. Hence, we need to add a further condition: "It ought to be that p" is true if and only if 'p' is true in at least one relevantly improved world and 'p' represents a positive good.

But our amended semantics is far from out of the woods. With SDL 'ought to do' semantics, it was obvious that the real world was not deontically accessible to itself. This is not a world in which all people always do as they should. But it *is* a world in which sometimes things are as they should be. Consider the first declaration of the final paragraph of the American Declaration of Independence: "That these United Colonies are, and of Right ought to be Free and Independent States." They are, and they ought to be. To say that a situation ought to be therefore does not rule out the possibility of its actually existing.

Therefore, even an improved world semantics will not do. If in a certain respect the real world is as it ought to be, then any world improved in that respect would differ from the real world, so that by improved world semantics the real world would not be as it ought — which contradicts our assumption. Improved world semantics therefore works only for what ought to be in this world but unfortunately is not. Adding another condition to our statement of improved world semantics seems unlikely to help. For the added condition would leave us saying something like this: "It ought to be that p" is true if and only if: (1) 'p' is true in at least one relevantly improved world or in the unimproved real world; and (2) 'p' represents a positive good. Condition 1, however, is a mere consequence of condition 2. If a state of affairs is a positive good, then either it holds in this world or its holding would improve this world; for if a positive good not present in this world would not improve this world, it would not hold true in a *relevantly* improved world. So condition 1 is otiose, and our semantics is left with condition 2 alone. Our semantics now claims that a state of affairs ought to be the case if and only if it is a positive good.

That is not much of a semantics. Even if it is a positive good that perfect human beings inherit the earth, we could not infer that there are perfect human beings such that it is a positive good that they inhabit the earth. "It is a positive good that p" is therefore intensional with respect to existential quantification. Again, suppose that the best person for the job happens to be the last applicant. If we allow that it is a positive good for the best person for the job to be hired, must we infer that it is a positive good for the last applicant to be hired? The answer is not obvious. "It is a positive good that p" is therefore at least as intensional and referentially opaque as "It ought to be that p." Our original appeal to semantics allowed an escape from the opacity of 'ought' sentences. If the semantics to which we appeal turns out also to be opaque, the escape was only an illusion.

Therefore, optimal world semantics cannot rescue the logic of 'ought to be' statements from opacity and worthlessness. Permissible world semantics fares no better, for we often suppose that different and incompatible solutions to a given practical problem ought to be. There ought to be a law against boom boxes, and there ought to be no boom boxes. But it is at least plausible to suppose that if there were no boom boxes, a law against boom boxes would be otiose, and that otiose laws are not permissible. Hence, there ought to be a law against boom boxes, even though such a law is not present in all permissible worlds.

Moreover, just as we found that 'optimal worlds' had to be weakened to 'improved worlds' and finally to 'relatively good worlds' in order to give plausible truth-conditions for 'ought to be' statements as we usually understand them, so too 'permissible worlds' can mean no more than 'relatively good worlds'. For suppose the world contains evils which can only be palliated but not removed. Then, if evils are impermissible, the palliated versions of such evils would not exist in any permissible worlds, even though it surely ought to be that the evils of this world are lessened. The only reasonable solution to this difficulty is to define 'permissible' in such a way that an irreducible minimum of evil is permissible — which is to say, to define 'permissible' as 'relatively good'. Once again, then, the sentences giving truth-conditions for 'ought to be' statements are as opaque as the statements themselves. Hence, permissible-world semantics does no better than optimal-world semantics in accounting for 'ought to be' statements.

The objections I have raised against SDL semantics of 'ought to be' statements have little or no force against the SDL semantics of 'ought to do' statements. Doing what one ought to do often does not produce a positive good, much less an optimal state. Therefore, worlds in which all people always do as they ought might perfectly well contain evil. Although PON is a difficulty for the semantics of 'ought to do' statements, there is no reason to consider opaque any statements about worlds in which all people always do as they ought. Hence, the semantics of 'ought to do' statements escapes most of the difficulties of the semantics of 'ought to be' statements. I shall next argue that the converse is true: the semantics of 'ought to be' statements escapes most of the problems that we have seen bedevil the semantics of 'ought to do' statements. That SDL semantics faces a different set of problems with each of the two types of 'ought' statement strongly indicates that SDL semantics was wrong to give a single theory for all 'ought' claims.

In Chapters 6 through 9, I considered six difficulties with the SDL semantics of 'ought to do' statements:

(1) Problems with SDLT1 and SDLT5;
(2) Epistemic problems, clustering around circularity and the accessibility relation;
(3) Problems with backward translation;
(4) The Good Samaritan paradox;
(5) Arguments requiring restrictions on deontically accessible worlds;
(6) Chisholm's paradox.

We must now examine whether these difficulties afflict the semantics and logic of 'ought to be' statements. I shall take the six in order.

(1) Suppose that, in line with the Leibnizian construal, we restrict optimal worlds to improved worlds, possibly including the real world. Since every improved world is a possible world, and since the real world is a possible world, no contradiction holds in any such world. Hence, by SDL semantics for 'ought to be' statements, it is false that there ought to be a contradictory situation. Moreover, for the same reason, it cannot be the case that both 'Op' and 'O~p' are true. Thus the 'ought to be' equivalents of both SDLT1 and SDLT5 are at least consistent with the semantics of 'ought to be' statements.

But do both SDLT5 and SDLT1 actually hold true in the logic of 'ought to be' sentences? SDLT5 is plausible enough. Certainly, if somebody claims that a certain situation ought to come about, we usually think it a sufficient answer to point out that the situation is in fact impossible. Normally the impossibility involved is physical, but it can be logical: if two units of good will accrue in a given situation should event F occur, and if one unit of good will accrue in that situation should event F not occur, it is easy to respond to anyone who thinks there ought to be three units of good that accrue in that situation. However, as I suggested in Chapter 4, 'ought to be' statements are often used to make wishes, and wishes are not always restrained by rules of possibility — for instance, if persons are unaware of or unconvinced by the claim that what they want is not possible. People in the twentieth century have tried to prove Euclid's parallel postulate from his other axioms and postulates, just as people through the centuries have tried to square the circle or to give a precise finite numerical value for pi. And no doubt, some of those people thought that there ought to be a proof for the parallel postulate, a way to square the circle, a method of precisely calculating pi in a finite number of decimal places.

To many people, considerations of possibility are quite separate from their thought of what should be. For instance, in her introduction to Anthony Trollope's *Doctor Thorne*, Elizabeth Bowen says this about the title character: "The doctor despises pretension, honours tradition. Taken all-in-all, he realises, I imagine, Trollope's sense of what a man not only should be but also *could* be." [Trollope, xvii] Ms. Bowen's implication is that some other character might fit Trollope's sense of what a person should be but not his notion of what is possible. Such a view of things fits the Augustinian Christianity which I mentioned in Chapter 3. Since we are all slaves to lust and sin, we cannot be what God's law says we ought to be. We ought to be perfect in every way, but that goal is unreachable. After all, Utopia is quite literally nowhere. Plato, in the *Republic*, has Socrates say that the ideal city will not be realized on earth except in the unlikely event that philosophers become kings or kings philosophers. If we could convince Plato that this event is not only unlikely but impossible, would that force Plato to give up the opinion that his city is the one that more than any other city *ought* to exist? Probably not. For Plato, and not just for him, the existence of ideal archetypes does not depend on anything's following those archetypes.

We can put the same point in Leibniz's language of compossibility. Not all separately possible good things are compossible, and therefore the best of all possible worlds might contain necessary evil. Someone might well think the world that ought to be is far better than the best possible world, for in the world that ought to be there is much good and no evil at all. That such an ideal is unreachable is no objection to its status as an ideal. For this reason, Kant's Principle, when applied to 'ought to be' statements, is by no means an obvious truism.

Nevertheless, there is something ludicrous about an impossible ideal, at least as an action-guiding principle. There can be reason to wish for what cannot be, but not for what one knows cannot be. Although SDLT5 is not above dispute as a principle governing 'ought to be' statements in their ordinary meaning, then, it is not obviously false. An adequate semantics of 'ought to be' statements might, but need not, include a version of SDLT5.

An adequate semantics of 'ought to be' statements might also include SDLT1, although again it need not. Certainly it ought not to be the case that both it ought to be that S does A and it ought to be that S does not do A; in a better world, it would not be the case. But as we saw in Chapter 7, to reduce these iterated modalities would require us to infer an 'is' from an 'ought'. There ought to be no contradictions among 'ought to be' statements, but for all we know some might exist.

The story of the lawyer with the perjurious client, mentioned in Chapter 3, illustrates this point. The lawyer ought not, as an officer of the court, to countenance perjury; but she ought to do her best to help her client win; and in the present situation, she does her best to help her client win by countenancing perjury. We have a conflict between one 'ought to do' and another, and there is no clear basis for backing up the claim that at most one of these oughts is genuine. If we speak of what ought to be, the situation seems at first blush different. Perjury will never even be contemplated in an optimal world — and possibly not in a better world — so that in no such world will the lawyer even consider countenancing perjury. Hence, in the real world, it is false that it ought to be that the lawyer countenances perjury. However, it still ought to be the case that the lawyer does the best for her client. In the real world, she does this by countenancing perjury. Hence, she has a conflict between one 'ought to be' and another in the real world; that there ought not to be such a conflict is irrelevant.

Notice that the lawyer's dilemma depends on the substitution of equals for equals in an 'ought to be' context. If semantics allows such a substitution, the lawyer's dilemma casts doubt on SDLT1; if it does not allow the substitution, semantics seems of little service to deontic logic.[3] Thus SDLT1, like SDLT5, is a questionable principle of 'ought to be' statements.

But although SDLT1 is questionable, it is not obviously false. It is not entirely irrelevant that the lawyer ought not to be in a dilemma. For even if she ought to divulge her client's perjury and she ought not to divulge that perjury, neither divulging nor not divulging represents the lawyer's ideal or even the lawyer's wish. So, quite possibly, neither divulging nor not divulging — much less both — ought to be. If so, the lawyer's dilemma and similar problems, not being conflicts of what ought to be, raise no trouble for SDLT1 as part of the semantics of 'ought to be' statements. An adequate semantics for 'ought to be' statements could, without losing touch with our ordinary reading of such statements, accept both SDLT1 and SDLT5. If an adequate semantics for 'ought to do' statements would not accept those principles, at least without modification to take care of such matters as Augustinian theology and the lawyer's dilemma, the semantics of 'ought to do' statements must differ from the semantics of 'ought to be' statements.

(2) We turn next to the epistemic problems of circularity that beset the semantics of 'ought to do' statements. The chief of these difficulties was that we have no way of specifying deontically accessible worlds without already knowing what persons ought to do in this world. The same problem does not arise with the semantics of 'ought to be' statements, for we can specify which worlds will count as relevantly good without first specifying all that ought to be the case.

Certainly a world that ought to be is one that contains at least as much good and no more evil in relevant respects as the real world. The same Leibnizian considerations which I raised earlier in the chapter serve the cause of SDL semantics here. For in imagining what ought to be, we construct our visions by, in the words of the song, accentuating the positive if not totally eliminating the negative. I am suggesting that, instead of taking our picture of a good world from our vision of what ought to be, we normally eliminate the middleman and construct the picture of a good or better world by mentally emphasizing the goods around us. We build our picture of a better world out of the same materials as we use to build our picture of what ought to be; there is therefore no circularity in using one picture as a check on the other. Two identical newspapers do not corroborate one another, but two different reports by the same correspondent, printed on the same paper with the same ink, can do so.

Therefore, epistemic objections do not pose a difficulty to the SDL semantics of 'ought to be' statements.

(3) I considered three major problems of backward translation: PON, iterated and nested oughts, and the assertibility problem. PON, I have noted, does have a counterpart in the semantics of 'ought to be' statements, but the assertibility problem does not. For that problem, as we saw in Chapter 7, arises from the premiss that assertion of an 'ought to do' statement requires the acceptance of relevant institutions; and the premiss does not hold with 'ought to be' statements. Even in Hobbes's state of nature, totally without institutions, law and order ought to be.

Consider an old chestnut of book reviewers: "This book should be required reading for anyone interested in the field." A literal reading of this cliché apparently commits the reviewer to asserting that there ought to be a law or rule requiring interested people to read the book. But the reviewer is hardly committed to the proposition that such a law is actually in force in this world, or that institutions supporting such a law do, to the best of his knowledge, exist. No doubt, the reviewer holds that in a better world there will be a rule requiring interested parties to read the book — and, of course, all interested parties will do as they ought. But the assertibility problem depends on the acceptance of rules in this world, not in other worlds. Hence, the assertibility problem does not bedevil the semantics of 'ought to be' statements.

With iterated oughts the situation is more muddled. If w_1 is an optimal world accessible to w_0 — in the language of Chapter 7, a range 1 world — then w_1 is surely an optimal world accessible to itself. Hence, we should conclude that what is true in all range 2 worlds is true in all range 1 worlds, and 'OOp' implies 'Op'. SDL 'ought to be' semantics is therefore committed to supposing that an 'ought' implies an 'is'. And that result looks counterintuitive.

Perhaps with iterated 'ought to be' operators the supposed implication is not counterintuitive. If it ought to be that it ought to be that the secretary keep the books, one might well allow that it ought to be that the secretary keep the books. Perhaps an adequate semantics of 'ought to be' statements might accept '$\vdash OOp \rightarrow Op$', in which case iterated 'ought to be' statements would present no problem for SDL semantics. But as in Chapter 7, causal and temporal considerations strongly indicate otherwise. Suppose that if state of affairs X ought in 1950 to be in 1950, good results would obtain in 2000 — perhaps by giving hope or encouragement to the people of 2000. Then it ought to be in 2000 that it ought to be in 1950 that X obtain in 1950. But this state of affairs is consistent with the supposition that X's occurrence in 1950 is a bad thing for 1950, however good it may be for 2000. In that case, it might be false that it ought to be in 1950 that X obtain in 1950.

Does 'O_tO_tp' imply 'O_tp', where the expression 'O_tp' means "It ought-at-time-t to be that p?" It does not, for the same reason that a counterpart failed in Chapter 7. Someone might assume with reason that it would improve the world if preaching would make the world better. In that case, 'O_tO_tp' is true. But not everything that would improve the world does improve the world; perhaps preaching doesn't help anything. Hence 'O_tO_tp' does not imply 'O_tp'. Thus SDLT10 fails for 'ought to be' statements, even when the deontic operators all have the same time-reference.

'Ought to be' versions of SDLT11 — $\vdash O(Op \rightarrow p)$ — face similar objections. It might or might not improve the world of today if what ought to be in a hundred years is the case then. Where operators have different time-references, SDLT11 gives rise to many reasonable counterexamples. If the operators have the same time-reference, SDLT11 is more plausible. However, in the *Provinciales*, Pascal reports that the Jesuit Escobar defined 'sloth' as "grieving that spiritual things are spiritual, as if one should lament that the sacraments are the sources of grace."[4] One who is thus slothful might presume that the sacraments ought to be, but that it ought not to be that they ought to be. The slothful person would probably deny that what ought to be is real, but he would certainly deny that it ought to be that what ought to be is real. Hence, the slothful person provides a counterexample to SDLT11.

(4) The simple form of the Good Samaritan paradox does not arise with 'ought to be' statements. For suppose that it ought to be that X helps A, whom X will murder next week. If the phrase "whom X will murder next week" is within the scope of the 'ought to be' operator, the SDL semantics of 'ought to be' statements tells us that the complex state of affairs <X helps A & X murders A next week> is a positive good, true in all optimal worlds. In that case it is true in all optimal worlds that X murders A next week. Given that in fact it ought not to be that X murders A next week, and that therefore it is false in all optimal worlds that X murders A next week, it follows that either the phrase "whom X will murder next week" is not within the scope of the 'ought to be' operator or that it is not the case that it ought to be that X helps A, whom he will murder next week. In either case, there is no paradox.

Likewise, the variants of the Good Samaritan raise no problem for the semantics of 'ought to be' statements. An adaptation of Åqvist's problem would assume that it ought to be that X knows that Y will do something wrong. But in a relevantly better world, Y will not do something wrong, and therefore in such a world X will not know that Y will do something wrong. Hence, it is false that it ought to be that X knows that Y will do something wrong — even if it is X's duty to know of Y's wrongdoing. Nor is my paradox of gentle murder any obstacle to the semantics of 'ought to be' statements. For suppose it true that in any branching world where W murders Z, W murders Z gently; nevertheless, any branching world where W murders Z is no improvement over the real world, nor can we see in the branching world a relevant positive good.[5] Certainly there is nothing optimal about worlds with unnecessary murders, however gentle they may be.

(5) Peter Geach pointed out that many of our duties in this world are brought about by the wrongful actions and inactions of ourselves and others. We owe duties of reparation and restitution to innumerable injured parties. Worse yet, we can expect this sad pattern to continue into the future. Others will continue to do wrong, and even with the best will in the world, so will we ourselves. Duties caused by wrongful acts have

been, are, and will continue to be features of this world. Any deontically accessible worlds having the same duty structure as this one, if they are worlds in which all do their duty, must branch at the now time and be relevant for only a short time. Thus Geach's objections require a drastic curtailment of the deontically accessible worlds needed by 'ought to do' semantics. But the same objections have no force against the SDL semantics of 'ought to be' statements.

For it is indeed a fact that wrongdoing is past, present, and future, but, as Leibniz suggested, that same sad fact might well obtain even in optimal worlds. Hence, many actions and states of affairs in optimal worlds could be predicated on the presence of evils in those worlds. We would not need to restrict the list of such worlds to account for what ought to be the case in this world. Likewise, 'ought to be' statements, unlike their 'ought to do' counterparts, do not presuppose that relevant possible worlds contain the same persons, situations, and obligations as the real world. Hence, arguments such as Geach's do not affect the SDL semantics of 'ought to be' statements — as long as SDL semantics accepts the Leibnizian construal.

(6) Finally, Chisholm's paradox, if adapted to 'ought to be' statements, consists of four assumptions:

(A) It ought to be that S does F.
(B) It ought to be that (S does F → S does G).
(C) If S does not do F, then it is not the case that it ought to be that S does G.
(D) S does not do F.

In SDL semantics, A and B clearly do imply that S does G in all optimal worlds, however those worlds are constituted. Therefore, it ought to be that S does G.[6] Since C and D imply that it is not the case that it ought to be that S does G, and since D is clearly unimpeachable, once again C must be the villain of the piece.

But the 'ought to be' version of C is a villain easy to overthrow, provided that we take the deontic operator to govern only the consequent. If it ought to be that S does G, and if indeed S does not do F, then C is simply false: it is a conditional statement with a true antecedent and a false consequent. And indeed C is false: if it truly ought to be the case that S does G, then this ought to be the case no matter what might actually happen.

I argued that in the logic of 'ought to do' statements, we can escape Chisholm's paradox only if we realize that S's failure to do F creates the permissibility of his doing G. As do Geach's arguments, Chisholm's paradox requires us to include wrongful acts within the worlds envisioned by the SDL semantics of 'ought to do' statements. The inclusion of any wrongful acts in turn mandates a semantics of branching worlds. We find no such outcome in the semantics of 'ought to be' statements. For since optimal worlds are not necessarily ideal, they need not branch from the real world to contain evil. Chisholm's paradox therefore does no harm to the semantics of 'ought to be' statements.

Of the six objections that I found devastating to SDL 'ought to do' semantics, only PON and questions of iterated and nested modalities are problems for SDL 'ought to be' semantics. But SDL 'ought to be' semantics has won only a Pyrrhic victory, for it faces its own formidable objections. The moral of the story is that of Chapter 4: the logical behavior of 'ought to be' sentences is very different from that of 'ought to do' sentences. SDL, in confusing the two, succeeds in answering objections only by an untenable equivocation.

I conclude that standard deontic logic, whether taken as a logic of 'ought to be' statements or as a logic of 'ought to do' statements, is unsatisfactory. The way is open for a new deontic logic that avoids the difficulties I have explored in Part I of this book, and that fits well with ordinary deontic thought and language. In Part II, I shall construct such a new deontic logic.

Part II

A New Deontic Logic

Chapter 11: Rights and What Ought to Be

The first part of this book has been an extended argument aimed at showing that standard deontic logic, whatever its merits as a formal calculus, fits poorly with our usual deontic speech and thinking. The negative tone of the preceding chapters has been unavoidable; I do not apologize for it. If some people have, in Berkeley's phrase, raised a dust and then complained they cannot see, it is no small thing to have helped allay the dust. But points made earlier in this book allow us to deal positively with important philosophical issues. After the demolition, it is time for reconstruction.

In this second part of the book, I hope to show that being logical does in fact have a great deal to do with being good. Chapters 13 through 15 will attack this question head on. In this and the following chapter, I shall show how the distinction between what ought to be and what someone ought to do throws light on a pair of vexed questions in ethics.

In this chapter, I take up the difficult matter of *natural rights*. Americans are told by their Declaration of Independence that they possess and cannot give away certain God-given rights. But rights, unlike most possessions, are not apparent to the naked eye; one does not declare them at border crossings. What is it to possess a right?

Legal rights can easily be thought of as entitlements. I have a legal right to vote in the next election because I meet all the qualifications set out in the relevant election laws. The laws, either by what they say explicitly or by what they do not explicitly rule out, entitle all who meet the qualifications to vote. If anyone questions my right, I can always point to the written laws.

Natural rights, such as those mentioned in the Declaration, are not such an easy matter. Even if there is a natural law written on all our hearts, a law which entitles each of us to certain benefits, attempts to cite chapter and verse in that law have caused much controversy. Laws passed by a governing body might need interpretation, but one can hardly doubt their existence, nor is their general tenor usually a matter of debate. The realm of natural laws is much murkier. Many thinkers, from legal positivists to utilitarians, have doubted their existence; many others, from Aquinas to Hobbes to Locke to the present day, have given widely varying accounts of the specific requirements of natural law.

Hence, rights theorists have for some time sought an account of their subject that covers both legal and natural rights — an account that does not depend on assuming a particular version of natural law theory. A standard method for accounting for rights is to employ what I shall call the correlativity thesis (CT):

> **CT:** Person X has a right to a if and only if each person in a position to affect X's a-ing has a duty to act or to refrain from acting in a certain way with respect to X's a-ing.[1]

If correlative duties are spelled out by the law of a particular jurisdiction, X's right is legal; where the duties are moral, X's right is natural. Thus citizens of most nations have both a natural and a legal right to life.

CT states, in a long-winded way, that rights are correlated with duties. For Jane to have a right is for each member of a group of persons, possibly including Jane herself, to have a certain duty. Since what we ought to do is presumably knowable, we can know whether persons do or do not have the relevant duties. Hence, we can be justified in claiming that persons do or do not possess certain rights.

The correlativity thesis is part of ordinary moral thinking, not just the plaything of rights theorists. A phrase such as "all rights reserved" is clearly a warning that others should not trespass. The language of the United Nations' Universal Declaration of Human Rights seems to move freely from claims about the rights of humans to claims about what humans should or shall do.[2] A bizarre example of CT in a context that is neither legal nor philosophical comes from the American writer Garry Wills. [Wills, 285] Wills quotes the Marquis de Sade as claiming the right to force any woman into sexual submission: "Has not nature proved to us that we have this right, by allotting us the strength necessary to force them to our desire?"[3] Wills's summary of the passage is: "For Sade, it is the *duty* of any woman to submit to any man's sexual desire at any time and in any form that attention takes."[4] Thus Wills turns Sade's improbable Hobbesian claim of a right based on strength into the even more absurd assertion of a woman's duty, presumably based on her comparative weakness. Only a commentator for whom CT is plain common sense, not to be questioned or even thought about, would unhesitatingly draw such a conclusion on his author's behalf.

Although the correlativity thesis is common sense, it gives rise to some difficult problems. In a number of cases people assert the presence of rights, especially positive rights, but not of correlative duties. To look at these cases, let us first divide CT into two theses — one about negative and the other about positive rights:

CT1: Person X has the negative right to *a* if and only if each person in a position to affect X's *a*-ing ought to refrain from acting in any way that would prevent X's *a*-ing.

CT2: Person X has the positive right to *a* if and only if any group of persons in a position to affect X's *a*-ing ought to act in such a way that X is, so far as possible, enabled to *a*.[5]

According to CT1, *negative rights* are rights whose correlative duties are duties to refrain from action. These negative rights include what Locke, among others, believed the most fundamental rights of all: life, liberty, and property. To say that I have the right to life is to say that everyone ought to refrain from acting in a way that would keep me from living. To say I have the right to liberty is to say that everyone ought to refrain from detaining me. And to say I have the right to possess and enjoy property is to say that everyone should refrain from interfering with my possession or enjoyment of what I own.

According to CT2, positive rights, also known as welfare rights, carry with them correlative duties to act and not merely to refrain from acting. If Jane has the right to a living wage, those around her ought to do more than refrain from preventing her from getting that living wage. They ought to act in such a way that she is able to receive the living wage. Potential employers ought to offer her an adequate salary; those who are not potential employers should apply whatever pressure they can to bring about a living wage for Jane.

Many, especially libertarians, have raised objections to the duties that CT2 correlates with positive rights — and hence to positive rights themselves. Those correlated duties are often thought either impossibly restrictive, and thus a violation of the negative right to liberty, or so vaguely spelled out as to accord with any conduct whatsoever. We can understand these criticisms by looking again at Jane's supposed right to a living wage. If Adam, the pin manufacturer, is able to pay her that wage, CT2, unless it is impossibly vague, states that he ought at least to offer to do so. If Adam is tired of manufacturing pins and wishes to liquidate his business, he may not do so, for then he would be unable to pay Jane as he ought. Hence libertarian critics often suggest that in a world of positive rights, the wealthy are deprived of liberty for the benefit of the poor. The assertion of welfare rights means a diminution of basic negative rights — an unjustifiable exchange.

Even though I think the libertarian indictment of positive rights overdrawn, the difficulties it raises are not easily dismissed. It is hard to understand what either Jane or Adam has done that would give her a genuine claim against him. She might have a claim against society, but it is Adam who supposedly ought to provide her the living wage. Similarly, it is hard to see on what grounds she is entitled to a certain amount of his funds. Yet with neither claim nor entitlement clearly on Jane's side, the supposition that Adam ought to provide her a living wage is certainly open to question.

CT2 gives rise to other objections. If Adam is not yet in a position to offer Jane and others a living wage, he should act in such a way as to be able to make that offer. Thus Adam might, while building up his pin factory by robber-baron methods, claim that he is merely upholding CT2. CT2 is so vague as to permit and perhaps even require any actions that might fulfill presumed duties.

Just as Jane is not the only potential employee around, so is Adam not the only potential employer. CT2 might therefore mean that each potential employer has duties to each potential employee, or it might mean that prospective employers as a group have a collective duty to prospective employees as a group. But as I argued in Chapter 4, subject terms of 'ought to do' sentences are not within the scope of the deontic operator. Hence, since 'ought to do' operators are *de re*, if all employers have a certain duty, and if Adam is an employer, it follows that Adam has that duty. Even if we suppose some more mystical sort of collective duty, so that we cannot infer a duty on Adam's part, there is still a duty for *someone* to perform.

These consequences are hard to swallow. If Adam already employs Jane, perhaps he does owe her a living wage; but someone who does not employ her would not seem to have any such obligation. If Jane is currently unemployed, does Adam owe employment at a living wage to her, as well as to all other unemployed persons? If not, who does owe employment at a living wage to Jane and the other unemployed? Someone must, if CT2 is correct; and yet, nobody seems to.

Considerations such as these have led some to reject the entire notion of positive rights. Perhaps the rich man and the poor man *do* both have the same right to sleep under the bridge, and that is all there is to rights. But I suggest that the root of the difficulty cannot lie with the notion of positive rights. For negative rights are not immune from the same difficulties that beset positive rights. Because CT1 faces similar problems to those facing CT2, merely dismissing positive rights will not avoid objections.

The problems of CT1 arise because, on any sane theory of negative rights, the duty of others to refrain from interfering is only *prima facie*. If a violent murderer poses an immediate danger to people, they may surely take away his ax, his freedom, and possibly even his life. His right to life, according to the Declaration of Independence, is inalienable; but even if the murderer retains his right, it does not seem true that all others should refrain from interfering with his exercise of the right to life. Again, a soldier in wartime has a right to life, even though soldiers on the other side have a duty to try to take his life. If CT1 is true, how can a person retain natural rights when others lack the correlative duties to refrain?

One plausible answer is that rights, like duties, come in two flavors: *prima facie* and full strength.[6] A *prima facie* right is correlated with *prima facie* duties, a full-strength right with full-strength duties. Our duty not to interfere with the murderer's life and liberty is overridden whenever he poses a grave threat to others; the murderer's rights to life and liberty are overridden in the same circumstances. But this answer raises difficulties. William Frankena infers from the common supposition that only stronger duties can override duties, that only when a stronger *prima facie* right supervenes is a *prima facie* right overridden. But that conclusion is false. The soldier's *prima facie* right to live is not overcome by anyone's stronger right to shoot him; after all, the soldier's buddies have no obligation to refrain from interfering with the exercise of that supposed stronger right![7] More important, people usually think that universal human rights cannot fail to obtain. An overridden *prima facie* duty is not my duty, but a right not respected remains my right. If a society such as that of ancient Carthage practices infanticide without apparent qualms, it seems implausible to maintain that a Carthaginian priest of Moloch had a duty to refrain from killing children. If a priest did refrain, his act would be beyond the call of duty. Yet despite the priest's lack of a duty to spare the infants, one can still affirm that the infants had a natural right to live. Thus the assumption that natural rights are only *prima facie* does not smooth the path for CT1.

Joel Feinberg considers two other ways in which CT1 can be squared with the seemingly absolute nature of human rights. [Feinberg, 251-255] First, one might regard the claim that S has a negative right as shorthand for a much longer statement that S has a right unless one of a list of conditions should occur. But as Feinberg points out, not only are people unlikely to agree on the composition of any such list, but there seems no good reason to suppose that all possible exceptions can be specified. Nor is there anything remotely self-evident about such carefully hedged rights. [Feinberg, 252] Feinberg's second alternative is to suppose that sometimes there is justification for infringing on a person's actual rights. This seems not so much an answer as a restatement of the problem. For, as Feinberg points out, this alternative plus CT1 entail that sometimes people are justified in not doing what they ought to do — i.e., in not refraining from interfering. Even if this is so, one wants to know why!

Hence, CT1, like CT2, asserts that people ought to act in circumstances where rights but not duties seem to be present. To do away with positive rights will not remove the difficulties CT faces. The trouble must lie either in the very notion of natural rights, or in CT. I believe that it lies in CT.

The problems of CT stem from an obvious truth about obligations: What a person ought to do in a particular situation usually depends in part upon the conditions under which the person acts.[8] This point I made in Chapter 4: 'Ought to do' statements are usually conditional. Carthaginian society, beliefs, and practices formed the conditions under which a priest of Moloch should have acted, just as the beliefs and practices of Jane, Adam, and their society form the conditions under which Adam should act either granting or denying Jane a living wage. Even if the rules governing what people ought to do are unconditionally binding, those rules are general in nature. One cannot spell out exactly what a person should do without applying the rules to the person's particular circumstances. Since we are obligated to perform an action of some type, but we actually perform a particular action, the conditions of actions inevitably are part of the specification of the actions a person should take. However, the objections to CT1 and CT2 suggest strongly that rights are not as dependent upon existing conditions as are obligations.[9] If I have the natural right to liberty, the fact that a state unjustly deprives me of freedom does not abrogate my right, even though the law of the land might release my guards from their duty to let me go free. Thus conditions that prevent others from respecting my genuine rights might cancel others' duties, but they do not cancel my rights. Thus we can have rights without correlated duties, and CT is false. Of course, unless conditions that cancel others' duties are unavoidable — so-called 'acts of God' — they ought not to be. But an 'ought to be' does not imply its counterpart 'ought to do'.

The degree in which rights and duties depend on existing conditions provides the clue to a better version of CT. For just as natural rights have relatively little dependence on actual circumstances, so do many claims about what ought to be. As I argued in Chapter 4, most 'ought to do' claims are conditional but many 'ought to be' claims are not; from a seemingly unconditional statement of what ought to be, one cannot reasonably infer hidden conditions. It ought to be the case that a priest of Moloch not have slaughtered infants, because the slaughter of infants is not good — even though we cannot say that, given the laws and customs of ancient Carthage, the priest ought not to have slaughtered infants. Hence, rights and what ought to be are importantly similar — and unlike what someone ought to do — in their relative independence of particular circumstances.

I therefore propose that we try the effect of making rights correlative, not with duties, but with what it ought to be the case that people do. The revised Correlativity Thesis reads as follows:

CT*: Person X has a right to *a* if and only if it ought to be that each person in a position to affect X's *a*-ing either act or refrain from acting in a certain way with respect to X's *a*-ing.

And, of course, we can split CT* into two parts, one for negative rights and the other for positive rights. These parts would be:

CT1*: Person X has the negative right to *a* if and only if it ought not to be the case that anyone acts in such a way as to prevent X's *a*-ing.

CT2*: A person X has a positive right to *a* if and only if it ought to be the case that persons who can enable X to *a* do so.

I shall first discuss CT* as a whole; then I shall turn to the effect of my revised Correlativity Thesis on the distinction between positive and negative rights. I shall conclude the chapter with some remarks about problems for CT*.

CT* arose from our noticing that rights-claims, like 'ought to be' statements, are less dependent on circumstances than are 'ought to do' statements. A statement of what ought to be cannot, on pain of at least incredibility, cut entirely loose from fact. Pie in the sky when you die is one thing, pie in the sky here and now quite another. What ought to be might be idealized, but it is rarely ideal. Similarly, even though rights do not logically depend on circumstances, there is some non-logical connection between, say, the right to life and the mundane fact that one human being is able to kill another. However, the assertion of what someone ought to do is far more dependent on actual conditions than is the imputation of rights or the assertion of what ought to be. The examples of Jane, Adam, and the Carthaginian priest make this point clear. What ought to be is an idealized and not always actual state, just as rights are not always recognized, but what one ought to do is an actual duty. Thus it makes sense to correlate rights with what ought to be, not with what one ought to do.

If we do so, we gain at least one major advantage. For CT*, unlike CT, is able to explain precisely why we are sometimes justified in infringing upon others' rights. Let us see how it does so.

In Chapter 4, I argued that an 'ought to be' statement does not logically *imply* but pragmatically *implicates* its counterpart 'ought to do' statement. Anyone who claims that it ought to be that Mary slaps John will normally be prepared to assert that Mary ought to slap John. But normal conditions do not always obtain. Perhaps in a better world, Mary could slap John and get away with it; in this world, if she does so, she will be battered. The special circumstances that do not stop me from asserting what ought to be in Mary's case might well prevent me from claiming that Mary ought to slap John.

According to CT*, rights are strictly correlated with what ought to be. If a Carthaginian child has the right to live, it ought to be that nobody interferes with the child's continuing to live. Under normal circumstances one would conclude that a priest of Moloch ought not to take the child's life. But since the normal circumstances did not obtain in ancient Carthage, the argument for this conclusion is defeasible — and, I have suggested, defeated. Therefore, because 'ought to be' statements only pragmatically implicate 'ought to do' statements, one can possess a natural right in circumstances where others do not have correlated duties.

CT* entails, then, that rights are strictly correlated with what ought to be but only loosely and pragmatically with what someone ought to do. It ought to be that nobody interfere with another person's life and liberty, but the circumstance of that person's being a murderer defeats any notion that people ought not to interfere.

We can use the double correlation of rights with oughts in order to understand the institutionalization of natural rights.[10] Because I have a natural right to life, it ought to be that others refrain from taking my life. Under normal circumstances, then, other people ought not to take my life. Both of these 'oughts' are moral, as is my natural right. But because I live in a society which grants me a legal right to life, the society has specified when circumstances are to count as not normal, and it has prescribed sanctions for violations of my legal right. Hence, because I have a legal right to life, others ought not to take my life, except in specific circumstances, on pain of sanctions. The law, in converting a natural right into a legal right, thus converts *prima facie* moral obligations into binding legal requirements.

The difficulty many find with positive rights stems, I suggest, from the distinction between natural and institutionalized rights. The proposition that Jane has a moral right to a living wage is plausible, as is the correlated claim that it ought to be that Jane receives a living wage. Such matters have a place in a declaration of universal human rights. However, if the state converts Jane's natural right to a living wage into a legal right, it makes the provision of that wage a binding requirement on actual people. Thus a reasonable claim about a moral right is converted into a tendentious placement of an apparently open-ended legal burden upon all possible employers. Some natural rights, I suggest, are best left uninstitutionalized and in the form of ideals — that is, of what ought to be. With rights as with duties, moral correctness is insufficient to prove legal appropriateness.

There is a second major reason for correlating rights-claims with 'ought to be' statements. As Chapter 4 indicated, to say that S ought to do F commits the speaker to S's existence; to say that it ought to be that S does F does not make that commitment. That is because what a person ought to do is, in a way, personal: Actual people have obligations, whereas what ought to be might call for quite different people. One could say that it ought to be that the government of a poor African country ensure that all who live within the country's borders have enough to eat and drink, but it seems foolish at best to say that the actual government, given the actual lack of provisions, should do so.

Rights, I suggest, are like 'ought to be' claims in not making imputations to specific people or groups. This is clearly true of positive rights. One can claim that Jane has a right to a living wage without supposing that Adam or anyone else has a duty to pay her that wage. But it is also true of negative rights: the soldier has a right to life, even though we do not impute to his enemies a duty of non-interference. Thus the 'ought to do' is personal, while the 'ought to be' and rights-claims are not. We therefore have a second good reason to correlate rights-claims with 'ought to be' and not with 'ought to do' statements.

There is a third consideration which supports the correlation of rights with what ought to be: the continual discovery and acceptance of new rights. This has been especially true of positive rights in the past century. Since we began to frown on what we consider dehumanizing and alienating aspects of people's lives, we have excluded those aspects from our picture of how the world ought to be; as a result, we have been more prone to impute a natural right to be free of what is dehumanizing and alienating. Similarly, only since people started to find serious harm in invasions of their privacy have they asserted a right to privacy. Thus the assertion of rights seems tied to a picture of how the world ought to be, not to any clear notion of how people ought to act in order to bring that world about.

We next look at whether the revised Correlativity Thesis does justice to the difference between negative and positive rights. Negative rights-claims, according to CT1*, assert that it ought to be that others not interfere; positive rights-claims, according to CT2*, assert that it ought to be that others take positive steps. Under CT1*, persons might have negative rights even in cases where nobody recognizes or even possesses a duty of non-interference. Local circumstances might help determine what a person ought to do, but they do not alter what ought to be the case.

Therefore, by CT1*, they cannot affect a person's negative rights. Hence, CT1* does better justice to the Carthaginian case than did CT1.

CT1* also makes slightly better sense out of the strange claims of the Marquis de Sade than did CT. Perhaps Sade was thinking of a right as, in Hobbes's definition, a "liberty to do or to forbear." [Hobbes, Chapter 14] He considered that his power over a woman gave him the liberty to do as he wished with her, and interference with a person's liberty is surely wrong.[11] It should not be the case that even the woman herself resist. But even Sade might allow that the woman could have a duty to resist — a duty that had, no doubt, been impressed on most women of the time by their moral instructors. Sade could only say that in a better world — one in which he retained his advantage in brute force over women — they would not resist.

CT1* therefore seems to do justice to negative rights. We turn next to CT2*, which says that Jane has a positive right to a living wage if and only if it ought to be the case that someone able to provide her that wage does so. CT2* clearly escapes the libertarian objection which CT2 faced. Even if Adam, the pin manufacturer, is the only person who can give Jane a living wage, her right to a living wage entails only that it ought to be that Adam gives her that wage. CT2* does not imply any duty on the part of Adam to do so; rather, it is perfectly consistent with the absence of any such duty. And if Adam is only one of many who can give Jane a living wage, he can even say, "It ought to be that someone give her a living wage — but not me!"

Adam would be right. Suppose it true that it ought to be that someone give Jane a living wage. It might still be false that someone is such that it ought to be that he give Jane a living wage. For 'ought to be' statements do not imply the actual existence of any individuals. Hence, by CT2*, Jane's positive right to a living wage does not even imply that Adam or anyone else is such that it ought to be that he pays it to her, much less that anyone ought to pay it to her. And this conclusion seems appropriate, for we can easily imagine a situation in which Jane's right to a living wage coexists with Adam's having a duty *not* to give her that wage. Suppose that Adam knows Jane to be a saboteur, bent on destroying his pin factory. He knows that, if the pin factory is destroyed, nobody will receive a living wage. He therefore, quite reasonably, takes it to be his duty not to employ Jane, even though she has no other chance to receive a living wage. Now if Jane has a right to a living wage, surely it ought to be the case that Adam hire her at that wage, just as it ought to be the case that she not sabotage his factory. Since she will engage in sabotage, it is surely false that he ought to hire her at a living wage.

CT2* therefore does not generate those duties to act which restrict the liberty of the actor. And it also escapes from the other troubles which CT2 faces. For under CT2*, there is no question of distributing a collective duty. It ought to be the case that someone enables X to a, but it is false that someone must have a duty to do so. Similarly, under CT2* people are not presumed to have a duty to do what they can to enable X to a; so that Adam, if he is presently unable to pay the living wage, has no license to engage in robber-baron methods to build up his pin factory.

One objection to CT2* is based on the fact that, for the most part, fewer and less important preconditions are needed for a person to refrain from action than for a person to act. To read a book, I need a book, decent eyesight, and reading ability; to fail to read a book, I need very little. Hence, most of the time more conditions must be met for a positive right to have any practical value in a given situation than for a negative right.[12] Since it was the relative absence of preconditions for the application of rights that led us to formulate CT* in the first place, one might conclude that although negative rights are correlated with what ought to be, positive rights are not. Nevertheless, there are fewer preconditions for positive rights than for positive duties to act. It would be at least pointless to say that a starving child has a positive right to food if there is no food available; but the remediable lack of an adequate system for delivering food to the child would not obviate the right. On the other hand, if under current conditions a health officer has no way of delivering food to the starving child, we would not impute to her a duty to do so. Hence CT2* seems reasonable.

To this point, it sounds as if CT* is clearly preferable to the original Correlativity Thesis, but like CT, CT* faces some objections. For one thing, since statements of what ought to be are generally wishes, to make rights correlative with what ought to be appears to locate the source of rights in mere wishful thinking.[13] But the objection misses the target: although we often use an 'ought to be' statement to express a wish, we saw in Chapter 4 that the meaning of 'X ought to be' is not 'I wish that X'. Rather, to say that X ought to be is to say that the world would be better off if X is than if X is not. The source of rights lies, if CT* is correct, in a picture of how the world could be improved.

Another likely objection is that under CT*, the concept of rights seems to have lost all its teeth. What is the use of Jane's having a right to a living wage if nobody ought to provide it to her? What is the point in a child's having a right to life if other people have no duties to refrain from interfering? I suggested earlier that what ought to be is an idealization. But rights-bearers live in an actual, non-idealized world; that they would be treated in a certain way in a different world seems irrelevant. The objection has force, but a pragmatic tie is still a tie. Although assertions of rights do not logically imply claims of duties to do, the former are generally pointless without the latter. And people do not normally engage in pointless activities.

Is a mere pragmatic tie strong enough to put real teeth into CT*? Under CT*, there is little point in anyone's asserting that children in ancient Carthage had the right to live, for the normal conditions under which one would assert that people ought not to interfere with the children's lives did not obtain. But unfortunately, whether or not one accepts CT*, an assertion of rights in this situation is pointless. One cannot now change the children's fate, and the Carthaginians have no duties left to perform. Nor is it reasonable to assert the children's right as a way of indicting the Carthaginians for neglect of duty, unless one can show that the Carthaginians were or should have been aware of the right to live. One might make the assertion as grounds for a wider claim — by saying, perhaps, "*Even* in ancient Carthage, all children had the right to live." Or one might have some special reason for indicting ancient Carthaginian laws and practices. But without duties to do or to have done, the assertion of negative rights has little point to it — whether one accepts CT* or not. Thus the objection is not to CT* but to the way of the world.

Positive rights without positive duties might seem especially hollow. If Adam is able to pay Jane a living wage, and if he has no good reason not to do so, and if he is in the best position to do so, to assert that Jane has a right to a living wage has little point without the assertion that Adam ought to offer her a living wage. Where we are not willing to assert his duties, an assertion of her rights is logically permissible but practically useless. But on the other hand, if we assert that, under current conditions, Adam does have a duty to provide Jane a living wage, again libertarian objections arise. It is small comfort to Adam, after all, that his duties are merely pragmatically implicated and not logically implied by Jane's rights. Am I not diminishing Adam's freedom to meet a supposed right which rests on no obvious entitlement or claim?

I believe two considerations should take away at least some of the force of these libertarian objections. First, the duty to provide Jane a living wage falls on Adam only under limited circumstances: that Adam is able to give her a living wage, that he has no good reason not to do so, and that he is in the best position to do so. These circumstances are restricted enough that one can hardly generalize and say that Adam has the same duty to all the unemployed. If there is nobody able to give Jane a living wage, or if everybody has good reason not to do so, no one is likely to assert that Jane has a right to a living wage.[14] It is not Jane's poverty as such that binds Adam but that poverty combined with a set of specific circumstances.[15]

Second, nothing in CT2* requires that Jane actually has a positive right to a living wage — or that anyone has any positive rights. There is little point in ascribing positive rights without ascribing some positive duties; if we are justified in not ascribing duties, we are likewise justified in not ascribing rights. Should there be widespread disagreement over the ascription of positive duties, we would expect no agreement on the ascription of positive rights. If the Adams of a society are neither willing nor required to take on duties toward Jane and those like her, there is no point in claiming that Jane has a positive right to a living wage.

It might seem that these two considerations have once again widened the gulf between positive and negative rights. Negative rights seem to be present everywhere, despite what people in a given situation might think; positive rights are present only in particular situations, and their existence seems to depend on a kind of common consent. To assert that it ought to be that people not act in a certain way is a very different matter from asserting that it ought to be that people act in a certain way. But the gulf has in fact been narrowed, not widened. For negative rights are not universally applicable. Although there are fewer preconditions for their application than there are for the application of positive rights, preconditions there are. The difference between negative and positive rights is, on my reading, only a difference in degree. Moreover, to say that it ought to be that X does a is not to say that X ought to perform any action. Positive nor negative rights are alike in not entailing that any person ought to take or refrain from any action; they are again alike in pragmatically implicating that under normal circumstances someone ought to take or refrain from action.

I suspect that those who find a large gulf between positive and negative rights think that the former, unlike the latter, require of people onerous duties. It is no imposition on me to require that I not murder or imprison Brown, but it is an imposition to require that I provide Brown at my expense with certain goods. Since on my account both positive and negative rights implicate but do not imply duties to act, much of the impetus for strongly differentiating negative from positive rights should disappear.

Thus the distinction between what ought to be the case and what someone ought to do has proved to be of solid value in untying a major problem in metaethics. In Chapter 12, we shall find that another consideration raised in Part I helps solve a difficulty in practical ethics.

Chapter 12: Can Duties Be Multiplied Beyond Necessity?

From a reputable agency, Norma receives a long list of starving children. As her eye happens to light on the name of a boy in a refugee camp, an agency official informs Norma that her payment of $20 per month will keep the boy from starving. It is reasonable to believe that Norma, who can afford to give the money, ought to do so. For it is reasonable to suppose that Norma has a general duty of beneficence, and the starving boy is obviously in need of help. Any help that Norma ought to give the boy clearly derives from the fact that he, in company with the others on the list, is starving, not from any unique feature of the boy or his situation. He is not present, and it is surely morally irrelevant that his name, rather than one of the others, caught her attention. But if the boy's starvation gives Norma a duty to help him, then the starvation of each other child on the list gives her a similar duty to that child. That is, Norma ought to aid each of the starving children. Unfortunately, her income is not close to being equal to so huge a task. No matter how generous Norma is, no matter how she might beggar herself, most of her duties will remain unfulfilled.

I shall call the above argument the multiplied beneficence argument — for short, the MBA. The MBA has been much discussed in recent years and has been accepted by some, most particularly Peter Singer. Those who embrace the MBA acknowledge that what might at first seem a duty of minimal beneficence will, when one considers the requirements of the MBA, mushroom to huge proportions. The only question for Norma is whether she ought, as Singer at one point suggested, literally to beggar herself to the condition of a Bengali refugee. [Singer, 33]

Others, most particularly James Fishkin, find the reasoning of the MBA unexceptionable but its conclusion unacceptable. If so, the MBA must depend on at least one false assumption. But Fishkin suggests that the assumptions on which the MBA rests are deeply rooted in ordinary ethical thought. "Either we must give up some element of the basic structure of individual morality or we must give up general obligations."[1] Neither alternative is particularly inviting.

I shall argue that neither the heroic action which Singer contemplates nor the fateful decision which Fishkin believes we face is required of us. For, I shall argue, the reasoning of the MBA is fatally flawed. Minimal altruism does not in fact mushroom into duties to millions.[2] I shall first show that we have good reason to look for a flaw in the reasoning of the MBA. For the MBA, if it were sound, would be even more problematic than Singer and Fishkin have supposed.

The usual response to the MBA is to find some sort of cutoff point in the multiplication of duties. Norma should support a certain number of starving children, but beyond that number it is not the case that she ought to give. One might, with Singer, calculate the cutoff point on the basis of marginal utility: if helping the nth starving child would cause as much harm to Norma and her family as it would good to that child, then she has no duty to help that child. [Singer, 33] Others might include in the calculation considerations of the quality of one's life: the cutoff occurs when Norma would, by helping a starving child, do serious and irreversible damage to the kind of life which she and her family lead. Those who look for a cutoff point grant the multiplication of duties which the MBA supposes, but they believe this multiplication must come to a halt somewhere.

But the MBA gives no justification for cutoff points, however determined. If there is a cutoff point, Norma ought to help each of n children but not child $n-1$ or any other child. In the first place, one wonders just how Norma should count starving children. Of the perhaps millions on the agency's list, how should she decide which are to be counted among the lucky n? She ought, at least in the period of time before she helps the nth child, to help each of the millions. Although, in feeding n children, she is doing her duty, she is failing in her duty with respect to millions more. Moreover, what becomes of her duties to the millions once she has reached the cutoff point? Do the duties silently disappear, perhaps on the grounds that 'ought' implies or implicates 'can'? Or do they remain, unfulfilled and unfulfillable? Neither alternative seems plausible.

Suppose first that duties disappear at the cutoff point. Then Norma, before helping the nth child, has millions of duties. By performing just one, she wipes her moral slate clean. This happens in no other case than the nth; only there does her gift of twenty dollars a month have the magical effect of wiping out not merely one but millions of duties. That seems improbable. Certainly, one has in no way satisfied the millions by helping the nth child; it would be hard to explain to any of them why Norma, who once ought to give him money, no longer ought to, even though Norma has given him nothing.

The principle that 'ought' implies or implicates 'can' is itself problematic when used in conjunction with the MBA. For Norma can help any of the starving but she cannot help them all. Before she helps the nth child, she can help child $n-100$; by the MBA, she ought to. After she helps the nth child, she cannot help child $n-100$; hence it is no longer the case that she ought to. What happened to her duty to child $n-100$?

Suppose next that Norma, having reached the cutoff point, retains her duties to the starving millions. Then Norma has far more duties than she can possibly fulfill. Even if this is logically allowable, what point could there be in supposing her loaded with such a burden?[3] Further, why should she fulfill her duty to the nth child, when this is a mere drop in the bucket compared to what remains undone?

If Norma retains her duties after reaching the cutoff point, more problems arise from the so-called agglomeration principle of Standard Deontic Logic, SDLT4: if X ought to do A and X ought to do B, then X ought to do A and B. If Norma ought to help starving child #1, and if she ought to help starving child #2, and so on, then she ought to help all the starving children. And yet, of course, she cannot; it is no better than pointless to say that she should. To be sure, SDLT4 has its own difficulties; I shall argue in Chapter 15 that a proper deontic logic lacks a counterpart to SDLT4. But it is hard to see how we could get along without some way of amalgamating separate nonconflicting duties into a single framework of what one ought to do. The problem is that Norma's duties are not jointly fulfillable; even a modified agglomeration principle should not allow us to amalgamate them.

One might suppose that Norma's duties are general; she has no particular duties toward each starving individual. But that supposition will not stop the MBA, for the MBA does not presuppose that Norma has duties to individuals. The MBA argues that she ought to help the starving boy, not that she owes her help specifically to him. Nor can we escape the MBA by supposing that Norma's duties are specific to her and might differ from the duties of others in her position.[4] For agent-specificity, as such, does not prevent the multiplication of duties of beneficence. Only certain kinds of agent-specific duties would avoid the MBA — usually by including a cutoff. And to all such agent-specific duties of benevolence, the difficulties I have raised for cutoffs apply.

Therefore, one cannot accept the MBA as a valid argument but dismiss its results as an odd but acceptable theoretical result. Either one should try to identify the assumptions behind the MBA which one can somehow give up, or one should attack the reasoning of the MBA itself. Fishkin takes the former course; I shall take the latter.

Fishkin himself provides the best argument against his method of dealing with the MBA. What he calls "the central dilemma" that results from the MBA takes the form of a modified inconsistent triad:

(1) Morality is logically coherent.

(2) There are principles of general obligation, including some duties of beneficence.

(3a) Some actions are morally indifferent.

(3b) Some actions are 'beyond the call of duty'.

Holding 1 and 2, Fishkin argues, requires one to give up either 3a or 3b and perhaps both.[5] Likewise, holding 1, 3a, and 3b requires one to give up 2. And holding 2, 3a, and 3b requires a person to give up 1. [Fishkin, 153-171] Taking any of these courses of action would do extreme violence to morality, as most of us conceive of it. Fishkin's proposal, as he realizes well, is a counsel of desperation, to be taken only if we find nothing better.

Since attempts to work out a satisfactory position while conceding the solidity of the MBA's reasoning are so unpromising, we should tackle the MBA head on. I shall start with an analogous situation.[6] Let us suppose it necessary, in some unspecified sense, that Norma help everyone whose name is on the list; suppose also that Tomas's name is on the list. We cannot infer that it is necessary that Norma help Tomas. For I have not specified that it is necessary in the same sense, or necessary at all, that Tomas's name be on the list. If his presence on the list is accidental, it can hardly be necessary that Norma help him.[7] We cannot infer that it is necessary for Norma to help Tomas, because modal statements are intensional. The truth of a sentence containing an intensional context is not sufficient to guarantee the reference of terms occurring within that context; failures of substitutivity and existential quantification might occur. Tomas's name is on the list in this world, but it is not on the list in all possible worlds. Hence, the 'necessity' analogue of the MBA fails.

What is true for the analogue holds for the MBA itself. For I argued in Chapter 5 that the context following an 'ought to do' is intensional and opaque. Hence, from "Norma ought to help everyone whose name is on the list" and from "Tomas's name is on the list," "Norma ought to help Tomas" does not follow.[8] That "Norma ought to help Tomas" does not follow from the other two statements does not, of course, mean that it is false. But because 'ought to do' statements are intensional, "Norma ought to help everyone whose name is on the list" and "Tomas's name is on the list" do not provide deductive justification for the conclusion that Norma ought to help Tomas. In light of the absurdities engendered by the MBA, we have good reason to think that conclusion not only unjustified but false.

Because 'ought to do' contexts are intensional, the MBA fails as an argument. One can allow that Norma ought indeed to help all the starving children without inferring that she ought to help each starving child on the list.[9]

Moreover, as Chapter 5 argued, one cannot quantify existentially into deontic or other opaque contexts *salva veritate*. If Governor Duck ought to write all the laws for the state of Euphoria, one cannot infer that there are laws that he ought to write. Even if Norma ought to help all the starving children, it does not follow that there are specific children whom Norma ought to help. Further, if the MBA were valid, we could infer from a general duty a host of particular duties by specification from a universal quantification. Such inferences are acceptable only if 'ought to do' contexts are extensional. Since they are not, the MBA fails, and the dire consequences Fishkin foresaw are no danger.

My diagnosis of the failure of the MBA might raise more questions than it settles. It seems peculiarly bloodless and technical, not at all likely to be of help with a pressing practical problem. Perhaps the MBA is not logically valid, but a deductively invalid argument can still have plenty of force. Nothing in my diagnosis appears to make the MBA any less persuasive than it had been.

I think this response misses the point of my objections to the MBA. For look again at the meaning of the sentence "Norma ought to help the starving children on the list." If in asserting that sentence we do not suppose that Norma ought to help the first child, the second, and each of the others, what are we supposing? Can Norma fulfill her general duty without fulfilling a host of particular duties? I believe she can; and when we see how she can do so, we will understand the failure of the MBA.

Suppose that Norma has a duty to help precisely three children from a list. Fortunately, there happen to be just three names on that list. Ought she to help those children? Clearly she should, for she has no other way of fulfilling her duty.[10] Norma ought to help the three children, not because of what logically follows from her general duty, but because she has available only one way of performing that duty.[11] The reasoning is causal, not logical.

We can verify this by changing the example. Suppose that Norma has a duty to help precisely three children, but there are four children on the list. Now Norma has precisely four ways of doing her duty. She can help A, B, and C; or A, C, and D; or A, B, and D; or B, C, and D. Clearly, she ought to pick one of those ways. But just as clearly, it is false that there exists a particular way which she ought to choose. This failure of existential quantification demonstrates anew the intensionality of 'ought to do' statements. But more importantly, the example indicates that one might and often does fulfill a general duty by doing something that is not itself a particular duty.

We can generalize the point: Let n be an integer greater than 0, and let m be an integer equal to or greater than 0. Suppose that Norma ought to help n children and that there are $n+m$ children on the list. Then the number of ways Norma can fulfill her duty is the number of distinct n-tuples in $n+m$. So long as that number is greater than 1 — i.e., so long as m does not equal 0 — it is not the case that there is a particular n-tuple of children whom Norma ought to help. If she does as she should, we should not conclude that she owes anything to the n-tuple she helps, any more than to an n-tuple she does not help.

Now we can make sense of the intuitively reasonable notion of a cutoff point. Suppose that Norma's finances and moral principles lead to the conclusion that she should help precisely n children, where this number is less than the total number of children on the list. Then again, she ought to help n children, even though there is no particular group of n children whom she ought to help. The general conditions of the problem do not determine how many children she should help, and her general duty does not bind her to helping any particular children. The general duty is deter-

mined by facts and moral principles; it includes a cutoff point, in the form
of a statement of how many children Norma ought to help. Once Norma
has taken *one* of the ways of fulfilling her general duty, her duty is
discharged.

I have suggested that circumstances and principles determine how
many children Norma should help to fulfill her duty of beneficence. But
beyond that, I suspect that the duty of beneficence is agent-specific: quite
possibly, someone else in Norma's situation might have a somewhat
different duty. For instance, someone with Norma's means but a far more
miserly temperament — call him Ebenezer — would find it harder than
she does to help the same number of children. Perhaps Norma's cutoff
point is different from Ebenezer's, and perhaps it is not. Certainly, as
Mary Gore Forrester has pointed out, one's penchant for charity is not
usually the major determinant of how charitable one should be, but it
might be a determining factor. For instance, someone might argue that
precisely because Ebenezer finds it harder to be charitable, he should do
more.

In any event, the general duty of beneficence does not entail duties to
show a particular degree of beneficence, nor does it entail duties to be
beneficent to any particular people. Not only is there no entailment, but
the duty of beneficence by itself provides no basis for determining how
much beneficence to bestow or on whom to bestow it. The MBA is
formally invalid; moreover, unlike many other invalid arguments, the
MBA proves on close inspection to be entirely unpersuasive.

The clue to my analysis of the MBA was the intensionality of 'ought
to do' contexts. That might have seemed in Chapter 5 a matter of interest
only to theorists, to be reserved for deontic logicians — nothing that could
impinge on matters of practical ethics. Yet we have seen in this chapter
that the intensionality of deontic contexts provides a refutation of the
MBA. And the MBA, if sound, would have implications that a leading
practical ethics textbook claims are "practically bothersome because it
becomes extremely difficult to pin down and discharge obligations of
beneficence. We bounce back and forth between viewing actions as
charitable and as obligatory; and we may feel guilty for not doing more,
at the same time doubting that we are obligated to do more." [Beauchamp
and Childress, 200]

Nobody, after all, is likely to embrace all the consequences of the
MBA. Singer himself shied away from actually reducing his condition to

that of bare subsistence. The real danger is that people who take the MBA seriously will regard it as a *reductio ad absurdum* of the duty of beneficence. The MBA invites people to reject the notion that they have any positive duties of beneficence to others; in doing so, it appears to back up an all-too-common slippery slope argument. Once we say that Brown has a duty to help the beggar at hand, goes the argument, how can we refuse to allow that Brown has a duty to help beggars farther away? If Brown ought to give some money to the beggar, how can we keep from supposing that Brown ought to give even more? Apparently the only way to avoid beggaring poor Brown is to deny that persons have *any* positive duties of beneficence.

The slippery slope argument against duties of beneficence has affected practice as well as theory. If an experienced and able swimmer, on seeing a person drowning, can reasonably expect to save the victim without any danger to himself, the danger of the slippery slope has made both courts and legislators reluctant to attribute to the swimmer any positive obligation to rescue the victim. Instead, if the swimmer rescues the victim this is considered an act of supererogation: The rescuer has gone above and beyond the call of duty. Courts and legislators take this stand, I think, only because they see no other way to avoid sliding down the slippery slope. They want at all costs to avoid the conclusion that a poor swimmer has a positive duty to plunge into shark-infested waters in a probably fruitless attempt to rescue a victim. The lure of the slippery slope is seemingly irresistible: A tiny step leads inevitably to perdition.

Thus a report to British law commissioners in India in the last century reasoned as follows: "It is true that the man who, having abundance of wealth, suffers a fellow creature to die of hunger at his feet, is a bad man — a worse man, probably, than many of those for whom we have provided very severe punishment. But we are unable to see where, if we make such a man legally punishable, we can draw the line. . . . [T]he penal law must content itself with keeping men from doing positive harm and must leave to public opinion, and to the teachers of morality and religion, the office of furnishing men with motives for doing positive good."[12]

The MBA would validate the slippery slope argument if the MBA were itself valid. For the effect of the MBA is precisely to deny that a line can be drawn between acceptable and unacceptable positive duties of beneficence. If the MBA were right, we could not allow any positive duties of beneficence without allowing an indefinite proliferation of those duties. And the result, as I have suggested, is that people might deny any positive duties of beneficence at all — which is surely inconsistent with not only common morality but the common law. Victor Grassian cites a 1942 decision of the Indiana Supreme Court, *Jones* v. *State*. A man had raped a twelve-year-old girl, who immediately afterward stumbled into a nearby creek and drowned. The man could easily have saved the girl but chose not to do so. The court upheld his conviction for second-degree murder. Since the man's criminal action had led to the girl's drowning, the court could not stomach the thought that he had no positive legal duty to rescue her. [Grassian, 285] Few people, I imagine, would take issue with the court's conclusion. The rapist certainly did have a positive legal and moral duty to rescue the girl. We have positive duties of beneficence; to the extent the MBA leads people to deny such duties, the MBA is pernicious.

Slippery slopes are usually avoidable, and people should avoid the present one. We do have some positive duties of beneficence, but those duties cannot proliferate to the point of absurdity. By controverting the MBA, I am effectively suggesting that we can take enough precautions in our specification of positive duties of beneficence to avoid the slippery slope. I see no reason why legislators might not mandate that a capable swimmer must try to rescue drowning victims if there is no danger to the swimmer, and they might well choose to provide that those who fail in this duty will be punished. Again, a religious body might determine that its members are morally obligated to provide charity in certain situations, such as when a beggar is at hand. Neither the MBA nor the slippery slope it seems to license provides a valid basis for turning such duties into legal and moral chaos.

In general, we can conclude that a study of deontic logic has its uses. Even if the study provides no more than a prophylactic against bad moral or legal arguments and illegitimate moral or legal conclusions, it will be of use. Construction cannot be done well until the rubbish has been cleared away.

Chapter 13: Moral Realism and the Need for a New Semantics

Moral realism is the position that there are moral facts or truths which do not depend for their existence on the various ways in which we learn of, believe, or justify those facts or truths.[1] If it is a fact that we should not commit murder, the moral realist believes that the fact would stay the same however our attitudes and beliefs toward murder might change. If some or even all people should have what seem to them good reasons for permitting murder, that would not affect the moral facts of the matter, according to the moral realist.

Most opponents of moral realism nowadays do not deny the existence of moral facts or truths; rather, they deny the independent status of those facts or truths, or of their specifically moral components. A prescriptivist, for example, will claim that "You shall do no murder" is a prescription for how people are to behave, not — or not essentially — a description of any state of affairs. To say that "You shall do no murder" is true is to say that the prescription is warranted by the relevant evidence. Hence, for the prescriptivist, the truth of moral claims is dependent on the ways, if any, in which those claims can be justified.

Moral realism, after having been under something of a cloud for much of this century, has made a comeback in recent years. Philosophers have called attention to various features of moral language and of the use of that language; these features are thought to support a realist interpretation over non-realist alternatives. Later in this chapter, I shall take a brief look at some of those features.

But the travails of SDL semantics raise a formidable difficulty for moral realism. I shall argue that a non-realist has an apparently easy explanation for the intensionality and resulting opacity of 'ought to do' and 'ought to be' sentences. But a realist can account for opacity only by a possible world semantics. Therefore, if moral realism is to remain a plausible theory, much less the favored theory I believe it deserves to be, we must find a new possible world semantics for 'ought' statements.

This challenge to moral realism can be met by constructing a radically new type of semantics for 'ought' statements. In this chapter, I shall spell out in detail the nature of the challenge to moral realism. Then in Chapter 14, I shall present my new semantics for 'ought' statements and show that it escapes the criticisms I have leveled against SDL semantics. Finally, in Chapter 15, we will look at the nature and effectiveness of the deontic logic that falls out of the new semantics. If I am right, a pruned and chastened deontic logic will rest on a firmer foundation than ever before.

Most of us accept a correspondence theory of truth. According to Tarski's well-known convention T, the sentence "Snow is white" is true if and only if snow is white. The truth of the sentence is guaranteed by, and guarantees, the existence of the state of affairs reported in the sentence. But to say that a state of affairs exists is to say that the various objects spoken of in the sentence exist and have the qualities and relations the sentence says they have. "The cat is on the mat" is true if and only if the cat exists, the mat exists, and the first is on the second. Our standard account of true sentences thus commits us to the existence of objects named in those true sentences. But the existence of the cat, the existence of the mat, and the relation of the first to the second are all utterly independent of how the sentence happens to speak of them. If the same cat is called both Cicero and Tully, then "Cicero is on the mat" will have the same truth-value as "Tully is on the mat." We can substitute one name for the other and preserve truth-value.

The standard account of truth thus suggests that all true sentences are extensional and non-opaque. Existential quantification into a truth should yield a truth; substitutivity of equals for equals within a truth should yield a truth. If there are intensional and opaque sentences, there must be some special reason why they are exceptions to the extensional norm. But, of course, there are in fact intensional and opaque sentences. And theorists have provided two different types of explanation for the opacity of such sentences.

A large group of opaque contexts notoriously arises from what people *say* or *think*. From the truth of "John says, 'I will capture the Loch Ness monster'" or from that of "John expects he will capture the Loch Ness monster," we cannot infer the existence of the Loch Ness monster. That is only reasonable: Since Parmenides few have supposed that what a person meaningfully says or thinks must be true. That John exists is guaranteed by the truth of the sample sentences; that his statement and expectation exist is also guaranteed; and so is the fact that he made the statement and has the expectation. What is not guaranteed is the truth of the *content* of John's statement and expectation, or the existence of the state of affairs corresponding to that content. What follows verbs of expression or of mental attitude might look like, but is not, a group of individually referring expressions. All that refers is the entire context following the verb; that context cannot be broken up, quantified over, or substituted into if we are to be sure of preserving the truth of the original sentence.

This standard explanation of the origin of one sort of opacity was, until the rise of possible world semantics, the only sort of explanation available. As a result, many philosophers tended to assimilate other kinds of opaque sentences, such as counterfactuals or statements of possibility and necessity, to the model of sentences containing verbs of mental attitude. All probability is subjective probability, according to this way of thinking, for a state of affairs with a given probability might never actually exist. To say that it is probable must mean that somebody believes it will obtain. Similarly, to call a state of affairs possible is on this account to speak indirectly of someone's belief.[2]

One of the many virtues of modal semantics is that it provided a new and distinct explanation for the opacity of certain intensional sentences. "It is possible that a monster lives in the loch" was taken as true if and only if there is a world, not necessarily the real world, in which a monster lives in the loch. Quantifying existentially over the term 'monster' in "It is possible that a monster lives in the loch" is therefore obviously dangerous: "There is a monster that possibly lives in that loch" asserts that something exists in the real world, while "It is possible that a monster lives in the loch" asserts the existence of something in a possible world. The most we can infer is that in the world or worlds where "A monster lives in the loch" is true, there is a monster who lives in the loch; since we do not know if the real world is one of those worlds, we cannot infer that there is in the real world such a monster.

Similarly, assume the truth of the sentence "Necessarily the first person in a certain line is not the second person in that line." Suppose also that George is the first person in a certain line. We cannot infer "Necessarily George is not the second person in that line;" therefore, we cannot substitute equivalent terms in the original sentence *salva veritate*. Modal semantics has no trouble in explaining this failure of substitutivity: "Necessarily the first person in a certain line is not the second person in that line" means that in any possible world, not only this one, the first person in a certain line in that world is not the second person in that same line in that same world. Now George might be the first in the line in this world, but there are countless possible worlds in which he is not. Therefore, we have no reason to think that in some of those other worlds he might not be second in line; which means that we have no reason to think substitution in the original sentence will preserve its truth.

Causal conditionals receive the same sort of treatment. "If we place gold in *aqua regia* it will dissolve" is true if and only if, in all worlds with the same physical laws as this one and with gold placed in *aqua regia*, the gold dissolves. Now this world obviously has the same physical laws as itself, but it might not be a world in which any gold is placed in *aqua regia*. Hence the original causal conditional is non-trivially true even though the state of affairs <some gold is placed in *aqua regia* and dissolves> does not obtain.

Modal semantics thus accounts for the opacity of certain sentences by allowing their terms to refer to or speak of objects and states of affairs not in the real world. Thus terms in contexts following modal operators are individually capable of referring; it is not merely the entire context that refers.

Nor do we have to adopt a modal realist account of possible worlds to explain the opacity of modal and counterfactual statements. Even if a possible world is only a state description in this world, we can explain the opacity of "It is possible that a monster lives in that loch." All we need to say is that in some state description, the sentence "A monster lives in that loch" has the value 'true', as does "There is a monster such that it lives in that loch." Since we are not told whether the state description in question accurately describes this world, we cannot infer the truth or falsity of "There is a monster that possibly lives in that loch."

However we understand modal semantics, then, we can explain the opacity of certain contexts without supposing them to be merely an expression of our hopes, fears, thoughts, wishes, or the like. A non-subjectivist reading of some opaque sentences is legitimate.

In Chapter 5 I argued that both 'ought to do' and 'ought to be' contexts were intensional and opaque. We can explain their opacity by either of two routes: by supposing that these contexts report the contents of thoughts, wishes, and the like; or by supposing that terms in these contexts refer in whole or in part to items in other possible worlds. Someone who is not a moral realist would have little difficulty in choosing the first route. Most moral non-realists nowadays, because they take moral truths to be dependent on our thoughts and attitudes, suppose any moral truth implicitly prefaced by a verb of mental attitude. The collapse of SDL semantics would therefore seem no major concern to moral non-realists, for they do not need semantics to explain the odd logical behavior of 'ought' terms. But a moral realist, who believes that moral truths exist independently of our thoughts and attitudes, supposes no verb of mental attitude implicitly prefacing moral truths. "Slavery is wrong" does not, according to the moral realist, mean or imply "X, Y, and Z believe that slavery is wrong" — no matter who or how many X, Y, and Z might be. Hence, moral realists cannot explain the opacity of 'ought' contexts by assimilating them to contexts which follow verbs of mental attitude.

But the second route also looks closed to the moral realist. For it was my argument in the first part of this book that SDL semantics is riddled with faults; even if a truncated version can be constructed, it proves useless to us. An appeal to modal semantics, if directed at some form of SDL semantics, yields little or no explanation of the opacity of 'ought' statements.

There are only three possible courses of action for moral realists. They might give up moral realism altogether, or they might try to find a new explanation for the opacity of 'ought' contexts, or they might look for a better deontic semantics. The first alternative is obviously unattractive to the moral realist, and I shall argue that finding a new explanation of opacity is unlikely. Only the search for a better deontic semantics offers a plausible way for moral realists to escape from their predicament.

Finding a new way of explaining opacity is a forlorn hope. Of course, one can never rule out the possibility of finding something new. But explaining opacity as a normal consequence of verbs of mental attitudes and speech involved taking individual terms in the opaque clause as non-referential; explaining opacity by possible world semantics involved taking individual terms in the opaque clause as referring, but not necessarily to items in the real world. There seems only one other possibility: that individual terms in opaque clauses refer entirely to items in the real world. And so far as I can see, the only way that this third possibility could be true and yet clauses be opaque would be if the following were true: possible worlds are merely state descriptions, and to say that term 'n' succeeds in referring in a given world is to say that in a given state description the answer to the question "Is there an n?" is "Yes." But this way of letting individual terms in opaque clauses refer entirely to items in the real world is simply a non-realist version of our explanation of opacity through possible world semantics. To find a genuinely new method of explaining opacity, we need to discover a new way of transforming the concept of reference; and having done so, we need to show that the new method does not reduce to possible world semantics nonrealistically interpreted. Perhaps this program is possible, but it seems highly unlikely.

Giving up moral realism might appear the most plausible course. Many excellent philosophers, past and present, have denied moral realism, and not all have come to obvious moral or philosophic grief as a result. If neither semantics nor mental attitude gives a moral realist the needed explanation of opacity, perhaps we should conclude, "So much the worse for moral realism." But that is much too quick and dirty an answer, for four good reasons:

- If mental attitude is the sole explanation of the opacity of deontic sentences, unwanted results arise. Take again the passage from the American Declaration of Independence that I cited in Chapter 10: "That these United Colonies are, and of Right ought to be Free and Independent States." If one is to read an implicit "we think that" as prefaced to the claim that the colonies ought to be free and independent states, why is the same "we think that" not prefaced to the intertwined claim that the colonies are free and independent states? But there is no opacity in the passage at all: Since the colonies are free and independent states, there are colonies, there are free and independent states, and the first ought to be the second. Not all deontic speech is referentially opaque, as the mental attitude explanation suggests it is. As I argued in Chapter 4, the subject terms of 'ought to do' sentences are in purely referential position. In "John ought to cut the grass," we can quantify existentially over 'John' or substitute equivalent terms; as long as the original sentence is true, the resulting sentences will also be true. But in "X thinks John ought to cut the grass," the term 'John' is no longer in purely referential position. We can preserve the referentiality of 'John' only with such a reading as "John is such that X thinks he ought to cut the grass." But for John to have an obligation is clearly not the same as for John to be thought to have an obligation.

- A second reason for not jettisoning moral realism is that the opacity induced by mental attitude or speech is often of a different kind from that of deontic contexts. In Chapter 5, I argued that "Christopher ought to build St. Swithin's Cathedral in Little Gidding" is referentially opaque — primarily on the grounds that the sentence could be true and yet the cathedral would never be built. It is the possibility of failure in duty that makes creative 'ought to do' sentences opaque. If we construe the example as meaning "X thought that Christopher ought to build St. Swithin's Cathedral in Little Gidding," we would be explaining the failure of 'St. Swithin's Cathedral' to refer not by Christopher's failure but by X's mental processes. Change "X thought" to "X knew" and you remove any opacity introduced by a term of mental attitude — but the term 'St. Swithin's Cathedral' still fails to refer.

- A third reason for not giving up on moral realism is that, in complex sentences making use of 'ought' expressions, the scope of any implied verbs of mental attitude is far from clear. Take the statement "If Smith ought to do great deeds, Smith is a lucky person." On a moral non-realist interpretation, we can read that statement in either of two ways: "X thinks: if Smith ought to do great deeds, Smith is a lucky person"; or "If X thinks Smith ought to do great deeds, Smith is a lucky person." The second reading surely misconstrues the original: Smith's luck does not stem from what anyone thinks. But the first reading is no more likely. Surely, from "If Smith ought to do great deeds, Smith is a lucky person" and "Smith ought to do great deeds," *modus ponens* will let us conclude "Smith is a lucky person." But from "X thinks: if Smith ought to do great deeds, Smith is a lucky person" and from "Y thinks: Smith ought to do great deeds," we cannot infer "Smith is a lucky person." Even if X and Y are the same person, and even if X is aware that here is an opportunity for *modus ponens*, all we can conclude is that X will infer that Smith is a lucky person — not that "Smith is a lucky person" is true.

- A fourth reason for not getting rid of moral realism stems from Chapter 1: Some deontic inferences which we think valid are justifiable only if we can make use of information within deontic contexts. For instance, if a person ought to choose either A or B, and it turns out not to be the case that she ought to choose A, it seems only reasonable to say that she ought to choose B. A theory which allows no reference within a deontic context provides no way of justifying this inference. Therefore, even anti-realists must have recourse to semantics to justify certain acceptable deontic inferences. Therefore giving up moral realism and relying on the opacity induced by verbs of speech and mental attitude fails to provide a general explanation of opacity in deontic contexts. Even a moral non-realist needs a semantics.

Moreover, there are positive reasons for preferring moral realism to its non-realist competitors. A moral realist has an easy and obvious explanation of certain facts about moral discourse: we talk about making mistakes in moral matters, we distinguish learning to be moral from mere indoctrination in a set of opinions, we distinguish moral reasoning from mere attempts to persuade, and the like. According to a moral realist, we talk about moral mistakes because people sometimes get the moral facts wrong; we talk of a person's learning to be moral whenever the person is learning the moral facts; and we talk of moral reasoning whenever persons are using moral facts in their reasoning. A moral non-realist will be able to explain these phenomena, but the non-realist's explanations will be more complex and less perspicuous than those of the moral realist. Hence, other things being equal, the moral realist's explanations are preferable to those of the non-realist. The burden of proof, that is, rests with moral non-realists, not their realist opponents.

Giving up moral realism is therefore not a promising way of meeting the challenge which I have posed in this chapter. Should we be unable to find an acceptable semantics to explain the opacity of 'ought' statements, there would be no alternative but to give up moral realism. But even if we took that route, much of the opacity of 'ought' statements would remain unexplained and apparently inexplicable.

Hence, by far the best course of action is to look for a new semantics of 'ought' statements — a semantics that covers both 'ought to be' and 'ought to do' statements. The new semantics must be able to explain why both sorts of 'ought' statements are intensional and opaque; it must also be free from the objections which I raised in Part I against SDL semantics. And finally, the new semantics must give rise to a set of principles in deontic logic — principles which allow us to make the deontic inferences we want to make without assuming too much that is dubious.

In the next chapter, I shall present a deontic semantics that, I believe, meets these criteria.

Chapter 14:
A New Deontic Semantics

In this chapter, I shall introduce a new semantics for deontic logic.[1] My method of presentation will be informal. I shall begin with the basic intuitions that underlie the new semantics. I shall look next at a series of problems with those basic intuitions. In response to those problems, I shall expand, explain, and repair the intuitions. The result is a new deontic semantics, which I shall present as a block. Then I shall give a preliminary justification of the new semantics.

1. DEVELOPMENT OF THE NEW SEMANTICS

I begin with two basic intuitions:

O_1: To say that a state of affairs ought to be is to say that the world is or would be better off with that state of affairs than without it.

O_2: To say that people ought to perform a certain act is to say that the world is or would be better off if those who fail to perform the act in question suffer appropriate negative consequences than it would be if they do not suffer such consequences. That is, S ought to do F if and only if it ought to be that S suffers appropriate negative consequences for failing to do F.

I believe that O_1 and O_2 are a good first try at capturing what most people mean by their 'ought to be' and 'ought to do' statements. Note that both speak of what 'would be' the case if certain things were true; thus both O_1 and O_2, in their use of counterfactual conditionals, implicitly presuppose causal principles.

O_1 and O_2 are not the only intuitions on which one might found a non-standard deontic logic. Mary Gore Forrester, for instance, has in an unpublished manuscript based a system of deontic logic on the premiss that what an agent ought to do is what is necessary to meet a given standard. The resulting system is similar in many respects to the one I develop here. Hence, I cannot and do not claim that my logic and its founding intuitions are the only alternatives to SDL. I do think they are the best alternatives, however. I think it plausible that it ought to be that people have as duties only what is necessary to meet standards; but unfortunately, what ought to be the case is not always so.

O_1 and O_2, unlike principles of SDL semantics, do not generalize beyond the particular situation. On SDL semantics for monadic deontic logic, if you ought to do something, you do it in *all* deontically accessible worlds, no matter how much those worlds might differ from each other and from the real world. Similarly, what ought to be is, for SDL semantics, what is always optimal or always permissible. The SDL semantics for dyadic deontic logic also generalizes, although in a far less sweeping way: "Ought, given p" is explained as "true in all deontically accessible worlds where 'p' is true." With O_1 and O_2, on the other hand, a particular situation ought to be if and only if its occurrence would make the world better than its non-occurrence would; we cannot infer that its occurrence at other times, even under the same circumstances, would make the world better. I think that in this respect, O_1 and O_2 are closer to ordinary deontic thought than are the principles of SDL semantics; for when people ordinarily speak of what they ought to do and what ought to be, they do not always suppose that their 'ought' statements can be generalized. For that reason, I think deontic logic should commit its users to generalization only if there is no good alternative. If O_1 and O_2 can be the basis of a viable alternative to SDL semantics, that alternative has an important initial advantage over its competitor.

We can apply O_1 and O_2 to conditional as well as to unconditional obligation. To say that, given condition C, it ought to be that p is to say that the world would be better off if C obtains and 'p' is true than it would be if C obtains and 'p' is false. Likewise, to say that S ought to do F under condition C is to say that the world would be better off if C obtains, S does not do F, and S suffers appropriate negative consequences than it would be if C obtains, S does not do F, and S does not suffer such consequences. To introduce conditional obligation is simply to restrict the states of the world relevant in determining what is obligatory. As I noted in Chapter 4, 'ought to do' statements are generally but not invariably conditional, whereas 'ought to be' statements are often unconditional. Hence, the semantics of neither kind of obligation statement can require that the obligations in question be conditional.

O_1 represents a minor shift from my analysis of 'ought to be' statements in Chapters 4 and 10. There I had suggested that what ought to be is what is good; a reasonable corollary is that a state of affairs is permissible if its absence is not good. O_1 says instead that what ought to be is what makes the world better than it would otherwise be. Unlike my earlier account, then, O_1 implicitly brings in causality, and it considers not only states of affairs but their consequences.

I believe this change brings O_1 closer to the ordinary understanding of what ought to be. For a state of affairs might be neither good nor bad in itself, yet causally sufficient to bring about a highly valuable result. For instance, take the sexual act that produces a person who brings lasting peace and justice to the world. Surely most people would agree that the act ought to be, even though that act might itself have no moral dimension. On the other hand, some good deeds have disastrous results: The boy scout's helping the old lady across the street led to their both being killed by a runaway bus. Most people, I believe, would say that good deeds with disastrous outcomes ought not to take place. Hence, I think it right to make the definitions of 'ought to be' and 'may be' speak of good results as well as of good states of affairs.

The intuitive status of O_2 is more controversial.[2] I intend the notion of negative consequences to cover both the natural consequences of one's actions and sanctions imposed by humans or by God.[3] With moral and legal uses of the 'ought to do', the appropriate negative consequences are usually punishments imposed by a properly constituted authority.[4] But punishment is generally out of place when the 'ought to do' is one of prudence or of etiquette. Although you ought not to take foolish chances, it seems wrong to think that you should be punished for doing so. And punishment for using the wrong fork with fish seems bizarre.

Still, it does seem plausible that, when people violate 'oughts' of prudence or etiquette, they ought to pay somehow. It ought to be that violators suffer some sort of negative consequences, whether these be mild or harsh, natural or man-made. We think it ought to be that a person who continually takes senseless risks will eventually stumble, even though we might hope the consequences will not be too severe. And if a salesman loses a contract as a result of his poor table manners, the result seems appropriate if regrettable. In sum, if we allow the notion of negative consequences to cover everything from punishments to mishaps, the preliminary definition of 'ought to do' is plausible.

Because talk of negative consequences is clumsy, I shall from this point on use the terms 'penalty' and 'penalize' in my formulations of O_2.

The reader should keep in mind that my use of 'penalty' covers natural as well as man-made or God-made negative consequences.

O_2 might remind readers of Alan Ross Anderson's reading of 'oughts': if not, then a sanction.[5] [Anderson 1, 100-103] But this world is not one where penalties regularly follow the non-performance of duties; worse, all too often the penalties come after a person has done nothing wrong. That's the way life is. Hence I do not think that our intuitions support the claim that if persons do not do as they ought, then they will be penalized — even if one takes the 'if-then' to be a causal conditional. But Anderson had hold of an important point: There does seem to be an important connection between not doing as one should and being penalized; and this connection might well be the basis for an adequate account of doing what one should. O_2 says that the connection occurs through the 'ought to be': It ought to be the case that people are penalized appropriately if they fail to do as they ought.

I doubt that ordinary deontic thought would support the stronger claim that someone ought to penalize people in an appropriate way for failure to do as they ought. For nobody might be in a position to carry out any such punishment — as in a Hobbesian state of nature, for instance. It would be at best fatuous to suppose that anyone in that state of nature has the duty that Hobbes would ascribe only to a sovereign. But even in the state of nature, right-minded people eager for the advent of a sovereign would agree that it ought to be that evildoers are penalized properly.

O_2 turns our intuition that it ought to be that wrongdoers are penalized into a definition of 'ought to do'. Instead of stating that it ought to be that all who fail to do as they should are penalized, O_2 defines what persons ought to do as what it ought to be that they are appropriately penalized for failing to do. Thus O_2 seems to me largely in accord with how most people think about the sense of 'ought to do' expressions.

But as they stand, O_1 and O_2 are in radical need of greater precision, if they are to serve as semantic bases for a trouble-free deontic logic. Some parts of these principles will need to be explained, some call for expansion, others should be limited, and still others will require major revision. Let us then look at problems with O_1 and O_2, to see what changes are necessary.

In stating these objections, and in setting out NDL semantics as well as the new deontic logic itself, I shall adopt the following convention:

$<p>$, $<q>$, and $<r>$ are states of affairs; the statement 'p' says that state of affairs $<p>$ obtains, 'q' says that $<q>$ obtains, and 'r' says that $<r>$ obtains.

1. Just what does it mean to say, and by what criteria can we determine, that the world would be better or worse off for the occurrence of a state of affairs?

These are questions that I do not believe a deontic logic should try to answer. People assert many different 'ought to be' statements because there are many different and often conflicting views of the world. Neo-fascists might suppose that there ought to be Hitler-like rulers for their countries; democrats would vigorously disagree. The neo-fascists would no doubt claim that the world would be better off for the presence of Hitler-like rulers, the democrats would claim that the presence of such rulers would make the world worse. It is not, I believe, the province of any sort of logic to decide such quarrels. Rather, the term 'better off' should be left undefined: Whatever view of the world leads a person to claim that a state of affairs ought to be, that view of the world provides the standards by which the person judges that the world is better off with that state of affairs than without it. Whether a given set of standards is proper or not is a matter for ethics, law, prudence, or etiquette, but not for logic.

Similarly, in Chapter 7 I discussed the role of institutions in the assertion of 'ought to do' statements. Institutions do not always agree: there are often differences among church, state, institutional morality, universal morality, and etiquette on the topic of what we ought to do. Indeed, these institutions themselves rarely speak with a single voice. If the kinds of 'ought to do' statements issued are as diverse as the institutions issuing them, and if the notion of 'ought to do' is defined by O_2, clearly no single set of standards can determine whether the world is better or worse off for the occurrence of a state of affairs.

Still, the use of 'better off' in O_1 and O_2 suggests a kind of utilitarianism; unless there is no alternative, I do not want to tie deontic logic to any particular ethical theory. Hence, in succeeding versions of O_1 and O_2, I shall speak of one condition's being *preferable* to another. Although I shall treat the notion of preferability as a logically primitive term, there are certain conditions that apply on any reasonable understanding of that term. I shall discuss several of these conditions informally here; I shall reserve a more formal presentation for the next section of this chapter.

The relation of being preferable to, like the relation of being better off than, is a two-place relation between possible states of affairs. One cannot therefore ask meaningfully whether a state of affairs in which a logical contradiction occurs is or is not preferable to any other. If condition *a* is preferable to condition *b*, and condition *b* is preferable to condition *c*, clearly *a* is preferable to *c* on any reasonable interpretation of 'preferable'. Thus the preferability relation is transitive. If condition *d* is preferable to condition *e*, then on any reasonable interpretation *e* is not preferable to *d*. Therefore, the preferability relation is asymmetrical. And no condition is preferable to itself. Thus preferability is irreflexive. Hence, preferability is a transitive, asymmetrical, irreflexive two-place relation between possible states of the world.

Now it is clumsy at best to speak of the world's being preferable when it contains a given state of affairs to the way the world is when it does not contain that state of affairs. Provided that we restrict the set of possible worlds to actual or causally possible states of this world, it is easier to talk of one possible world's being preferable to another. That restriction will have to be formally written into our semantic principles, of course. But from now on, we will take preferability to be a relation between pairs of possible worlds.

There are two further rules of preferability, the rules which I will call AGGR and CONS. I will present and defend them in section 2 of this chapter.

Finally, preferability, as I use the term, is an all-things-considered relation. One world is either preferable to or not preferable to another world; we cannot say that it is preferable in one respect but not in another.

2. But if we are going to speak of one state of the world (or one possible world) as preferable to another state (or another possible world), we are implicitly assuming the reality of such states or worlds. That is modal realism, and it is a debatable point.

It is easiest and most convenient for anyone talking of possible worlds to use the language of modal realism. However, nothing I have said so far commits us to a realist interpretation. Even non-realists allow themselves to prefer the way the world would be if A were to happen over the way it would be if A were not to happen. A Carnapian, for example, could meaningfully prefer one state description to another. Thus the objection as it stands is weak.

However, the objection raises an important point. If 'preferable to' is defined as a relation that obtains between two possible worlds, then for "world₁ is preferable to world₂," to be true or even meaningful, both world₁ and world₂ must not only be possible but must be accessible to this world. Hence, the final version of our semantical principles must allow for accessibility.

3. What is an appropriate penalty, and how can we determine when a given penalty is appropriate?

As with the notion of preferability, people have many different views on what makes a penalty appropriate, and it hardly seems right to enshrine any particular view in the structure of deontic logic. We do better to leave the notion of appropriate penalty as an undefined primitive in the system.

However, once again some general characteristics constrain any definition of a primitive term. Appropriateness in a penalty is a broad notion: it includes not only the nature of the penalty as related to the nature of the offense and perhaps other considerations; it also includes the manner of imposing the penalty, the status of any people who are to exact the penalty, and the like. Further, there are many ways of not being penalized appropriately: one can be unpenalized; one can be penalized too leniently or too severely; one can be penalized by the wrong people or in the wrong way. Hence, O_2 does not presuppose that, for a failure to do one's duty, any penalty is better than no penalty. Rather, the right penalty, administered in the right way, by the right persons is preferable to the wrong penalty or to no penalty at all. Likewise, when bad natural consequences are involved, poetic justice is preferable to poetic injustice or poetic indifference.

4. Suppose that the world cannot get along without a certain state of affairs obtaining; or suppose that the world cannot get along without that state failing to obtain. In either case, how should we determine whether the world is better off with that state of affairs than without it?

What is the truth-value of the statement "State of affairs <p> ought to be," where <p>'s obtaining is either necessary or impossible? In ordinary deontic thought, the question looks strange: we have no reason even to consider whether it ought to be the case that $2 + 2 = 5$, for whatever we might want and do, it never will be the case that $2 + 2 = 5$. Similar remarks can be made of the proposition that it ought to be the case that $2 + 2 = 4$: it is idle even to wish that $2 + 2 \neq 4$.

Standard Deontic Logic, as we saw, gives the value 'true' to both "It ought to be the case that $2 + 2 = 4$" and "It ought to be the case that not: $2 + 2 = 5$." For what is true in all possible worlds is true in all deontically accessible worlds, as the latter are a subset of the former. I propose that the semantics of a new deontic logic follow ordinary deontic thought, by ensuring that statements that a necessary or impossible state of affairs ought to be do not have a truth-value.

There are two ways of accomplishing this objective. We might build into each of the assertions of the system a condition that any state of affairs which we say ought to be must be contingent. The result would be cumbersome assertions; even worse, as Kenith Sobel has shown, contingency claims would tend to drop out in proofs.[6] A better procedure is to put a provision into the formation rules for the syntax of our new deontic logic. I will define the expression "State of affairs <p> ought to be" only if 'p' is contingent. Thus any expression containing '<q> ought to be', where 'q' is not contingent, will be ill formed. What the syntax rules out cannot have a semantics and hence will lack a truth-value.

5. O_2 needs adjustment. As Chapter 4 argued, the truth of 'ought to do' statements, unlike that of 'ought to be' statements, presupposes the existence of agents named by the subject-term.

This objection needs no discussion beyond that of Chapter 4; I take it as perfectly correct.

As a result of the points made so far, we might revise O_1 and O_2 as follows:

O_1a: To say that a state of affairs <p> ought to be is to say that any world containing <p> is preferable to any world not containing <p>.

O_2a: To say that an agent S ought to perform a certain act F is to say both that S exists and that any world in which S fails to perform F and is appropriately penalized is preferable to any world in which S fails to perform F and is not appropriately penalized.

6. O_1a and O_2a speak only of 'oughts'. Deontic logic also includes permissibility.

The point is reasonable enough. We can model intuitive definitions of permissibility on O_1a and O_2a:

P_1a: To say that it is permissible for state of affairs <p> to exist is to say that there is at least one world in which <p> does not exist, there is at least one in which <p> does exist, and the first world is not preferable to the second.

P_2a: To say that it is permissible for agent S to perform act F is to say both that S exists and that there is a world in which if S performs F, S is appropriately penalized; there is a world in which if S performs F, S is not appropriately penalized; and the first world is not preferable to the second.

Although in framing these accounts I have used the common deontic principle that something is permissible if and only if its negation is not obligatory, this principle applies only in modified form to 'ought to do' statements. For both O_2a and P_2a are conjunctions, and the negation of a conjunction is a disjunction. The negation of an 'ought to do' or 'may do' statement is therefore: *either* the agent does not exist, *or* a preference relation between worlds does not hold. Hence, the statement that an agent ought to do a given act presupposes the agent's existence; the statement that it is not the case that it is permissible for the agent to fail to do that same act does not presuppose the agent's existence. Likewise, the statement that it is permissible for an agent to do a given act presupposes the agent's existence; but the statement that it is not the case that the agent ought to fail to perform that act does not presuppose the agent's existence.

So far as I can determine, the failure of equivalence between 'ought to do' and 'is not permissible not to do' is a reasonable consequence of our deontic intuitions, not a sign of failure or confusion among those intuitions.

7. The principles O_1a, O_2a, P_1a, and P_2a absolutely require that time-references be built in. For the world is not the same from moment to moment; what would make the world preferable at one time might well fail to do so at another.

Here is another good objection. I argued in Chapter 9 that a causal semantics provides the best way of avoiding Chisholm's contrary-to-duty paradox; for, given a causal semantics, the same act-type might be obligatory for an agent at one time and not at another. As we are now erecting a causal semantics, we are implicitly building in time-references; we should do so explicitly.

There are two time-spans relevant to an 'ought to do' statement: the time during which the agent has the obligation; and the time during which the act is to be performed. Often these coincide: I have an obligation for the next ten days to make a standard mortgage payment during the next ten days; should I not pay within that period, I will have the different obligation of making a late mortgage payment. Likewise, I have an obligation at all times not to kill others at any time. Sometimes, though, the time-spans do not coincide: I might have an obligation today to repay you tomorrow, and I might terminate that obligation today by an early repayment. The same is true of 'ought to be' statements: perhaps it ought to be today that something happen tomorrow, but events might prevent it from being true tomorrow that it ought to be that something happen that day.

Of these two time-spans, the more practically important is the one during which the agent ought to act or the state of affairs ought to be in existence. For it is the act and the state of affairs which, together with their consequences, do or do not make the world preferable, not the mere presence of an obligation.[7] Thus we should restate all 'ought' statements so that whatever falls within the scope of an 'ought' operator receives an explicit temporal index. However, we also need to time-index 'ought to be' and 'ought to do' operators as well, if we are to avoid problems such as Chisholm's paradox. In the final version of my semantical principles, although not in intermediate versions to follow, both sorts of time-indices will be present.

8. Sometimes good deeds have overall bad consequences. Surely if good deeds have sufficient intrinsic value, they ought to be, even though the world is the worse for their occurrence.

On this point, I believe, ordinary deontic thought and language make no definite pronouncement. If it were shown that saints inevitably cause more harm than good, would people generally conclude that there ought to be no saints? Perhaps, and perhaps not. Some would hold that the intrinsic value of sainthood outweighs any bad consequences, while others would draw the balance differently; still others, of course, would deny any intrinsic value to sainthood.

If ordinary deontic thought and language do not determine the matter, I am free to decide in the way that best fits the construction of a logic. Determining what ought to be on the basis of the act and its consequences seems the easiest way to proceed, as it does not involve weighing intrinsic against consequential value. Note again, however, that I have set in place no particular tests to determine whether the world is or is not better off for the occurrence of the act and its consequences. A person who claimed, for example, that the proper tests to use are universalizability and respect for persons could perfectly well accept O_1a or O_2a. Hence, although I am committing my deontic logic to considering consequences, I am not committing it to any variety of moral consequentialism.

9. Sometimes a state of affairs, good in itself, is brought about by means so bad that the world is no better off or is even worse for the occurrence of that state of affairs. But O_1a suggests that such a state of affairs ought not to be, no matter how much good it might cause under usual circumstances. This result seems counterintuitive.

This is the first of four objections that will necessitate major revisions to O_1a and O_2a, as well as to their 'permissibility' analogues. In each case, my examples and revisions will be aimed at O_1a; but since O_2a also uses the 'ought to be', similar revisions are needed for it. And one should also revise P_1a and P_2a along the same lines; but as with temporal subscripts, I shall not make such revisions until the final version of the semantics.

A vicious dictator promulgates a law that is good, but not good enough to make the dictatorship worth enduring. Hence, there is a circumstance in which it is not the case that the world is or would be the better for the law's promulgation. Therefore, by O_1a, it is not the case that it ought to be that the law is promulgated — even in circumstances where the evil dictatorship is not present. That seems highly unintuitive.

A fairly simple revision will remove this difficulty. To say that state of affairs <p> ought to be is to say that the world is or would be better off with <p> than without it, provided that nothing is changed except what is brought about by the occurrence or non-occurrence of <p>. To make this notion clearer, I shall introduce the notion of a *counterpart world*:

Definition A: A world w_1 is *a counterpart world to a world w_2 with respect to $<p>$* (in brief, *is a $<p>$-counterpart to w_2*) $=_{df}$ the truth-value of 'p' is different in w_2 from the truth-value of 'p' in w_1', and the only differences between w_2 and w_1 result, entirely or partially, from $<p>$'s obtaining in one world and not the other.

If 'p' is a tensed statement, then $<p>$-counterpart worlds share the same causal structure and the same history, but they branch from one another at the time of the state of affairs in question. Had Hooker won the battle of Chancellorsville, subsequent history would have been very different. The real world then has counterparts in those worlds where Hooker did win that battle, with all the consequences that stem from his victory.

Using the notion of $<p>$-counterpart worlds, we can formulate a new version of O_1a:

O_1b: To say that a state of affairs $<p>$ ought to be is to say that any world containing $<p>$ is preferable to $<p>$-counterpart worlds that do not contain $<p>$.

From the standpoint of our original intuition O_1, which spoke of the world being better than it would otherwise have been, O_1b is a major improvement over O_1a. To be sure, the last clause of O_1b is unnecessary; from this point on, whenever I say that 'p' is true in w_1 and that w_2 is a $<p>$-counterpart world to w_1, I shall not add the redundant information that 'p' is false in w_2. But in this and the next chapter, I shall sometimes suppose that a truth-functionally complex proposition '(. . . p . . .)' is true in world w_1; if w_2 is a $<p>$-counterpart to w_1, the truth-value of the other atomic components of '(. . . p . . .)' will not alter from w_1 to w_2. It will then be necessary to say specifically what proposition is true in w_2, and I shall do so.

O_1b seems sufficient to take care of cases where states of affairs which ought to be are brought about by nasty causes. In the case of the vicious dictator and the good law, we need to ask whether the world where the dictator promulgates the good law is better off than it would have been had the vicious dictator, in the same circumstances, not promulgated the law. If so, then by O_1b the present case presents no counterexample to the supposition that the law in question, along with its promulgation by the dictator, ought to be. Thus O_1b is sufficient to avoid the objection.

10. O_1b is counterintuitive. Suppose that the only ways of achieving a good outcome are by means far worse than that outcome. It is consistent with O_1b that such an outcome ought to be, which is absurd.

For instance, suppose that in this world, only a vicious dictator can promulgate a certain good law. Unfortunately, the law for all its goodness is not worth our suffering under the vicious dictatorship. It hardly seems reasonable to claim that the law ought to be; and yet, O_1b would back up such an unreasonable claim. By O_1b, so long as the law in a set of circumstances leaves things better off than would the absence of that law *in those same circumstances*, the law ought to be. So much the worse for O_1b!

Hence, we need to amend O_1b once again:

O_1c: To say that a state of affairs <p> ought to be is to say that any world containing <p> and its inevitable causal antecedents is preferable to <p>-counterpart worlds.

Obviously, if a <p>-counterpart world does not contain <p>, it does not contain inevitable causal antecedents for <p>.

Therefore, whenever we determine whether the presence of a complex state of affairs makes the world better off — and hence whether the state of affairs ought to be — O_1c bids us consider any inevitable causal antecedents of the state of affairs, together with the nature and consequences of the state.

11. Sometimes a good state of affairs <p> is part of, or is implied by, a not-so-good state of affairs <q>. In fact, it can happen that the evil of the complex state <q> outweighs the good of the simpler <p>. In that case, by O_1c, we cannot say that <p> ought to be. But surely that is wrong.

For instance, suppose the following, surely consistent, premises to be true:

(1) It ought to be that you give five dollars to a beggar;
(2) It ought not to be that you give all the money you own — which is more than five dollars — to the beggar; and

(3) The result of giving the beggar all you own would be no better than the result of failing to give the beggar five dollars.

If you do give all you own to the beggar, and if all you own is more than five dollars, it follows that you give five dollars to the beggar. Since there is at least one possible circumstance in which you give five dollars to the beggar, that in which you give all you own; and since, by 3, the result of giving the beggar five dollars *in this circumstance* is no better than the result of not giving him five dollars in this circumstance; then it follows from O_1c that it is not the case that it ought to be that you give the beggar five dollars. And that contradicts 1.

We can modify O_1c appropriately if we consider that O_1 and O_2, the two intuitions with which we began, are limited. Certainly, if something that ought to be actually happens, the world will be better off — *under normal conditions.* But if what ought to be comes accompanied by miserable attendant circumstances, nobody is likely to think that the world will be better off. Conversely, the failure of the world to be better off if $<p>$ obtains hardly impugns the claim of $<p>$ to be a situation that ought to be — so long as the reason for the failure lies not in $<p>$ itself but in the attendant circumstances.

How can we spell out the notion of normal conditions? In the system we are developing, we do so by restricting the possible worlds under consideration. For this purpose, a further definition is of use:

Definition B: A world w_0 is *normal with respect to* $<p>$ (or, for short, is $<p>$-*normal*) $=_{df}$ there is no proposition 'q' such that '⊢ q ¬ p' is true, $<q>$ obtains in w_0, and some world where $<q>$ obtains is not preferable to some counterpart where $<q>$ does not obtain.

Clearly, if a given world w_1 is $<p>$-normal, and if 'p' is true in w_1, all $<p>$-counterparts of w_1 are $<p>$-normal. For the counterparts will differ from w_1 only in that the state of affairs reported by 'p' and any causal consequences of that state of affairs do not obtain in the $<p>$-counterparts. But if 'p' is false in the $<p>$-counterparts, there can be no proposition 'q' such that '⊢ q ¬ p' is true and 'q' is true in $<p>$-counterparts.

I therefore revise O_1c to speak only of $<p>$-normal worlds:

O_1d: To say that the state of affairs $<p>$ ought to be is to say that any $<p>$-normal world containing $<p>$ and its inevitable causal antecedents is preferable to $<p>$-counterpart worlds.

That is, worlds which contain a nasty situation which implies a good situation are irrelevant in considering whether that good situation ought to be.

O_1d heads off a potentially damaging objection. For suppose that 'q → p' is a theorem, and suppose that 'OBp' is true in this world. By O_1c we would have to conclude that 'OBq' is true in this world — that is, that from '⊢ q → p' we could derive '⊢ OBp → OBq'. And that inference rule would lead to highly unintuitive results at best![8] By insisting on <p>-normal worlds, O_1d blocks this objection.

But O_1d is not quite the finished product we need. There is a major difficulty left to consider:

12. It seems perfectly possible that two states of affairs <p> and <q> each ought to be, but that their joint occurrence either is impossible or should not be. But according to O_1d, we cannot avoid concluding that <p.q> ought to be.

The difficulty is that, by O_1d, if <p> ought to be and if <q> ought to be, then any <p>-normal world where 'p' holds is preferable to its <p>-counterparts, and any <q>-normal world where 'q' holds is preferable to its <q>-counterparts. Now all worlds in which 'p.q' holds are worlds in which 'p' holds and worlds in which 'q' holds; and all worlds in which neither 'p' nor 'q' holds are worlds in which 'p.q' does not hold. Further, all <(p.q)>-normal worlds are <p>-normal and <q>-normal, for whatever implies 'p.q' implies 'p' and 'q'. Therefore, all <(p.q)>-normal worlds in which 'p.q' holds are preferable to their counterparts in which 'p.q' does not hold — whence, by O_1d, 'OB(p.q)' follows.

However, this result is counterintuitive. Suppose first that <p>'s occurrence logically excludes <q>'s occurrence: i.e., ⊢ p → ~q. Then the state of affairs <p.q> is logically impossible. Even if one supposes, with SDL, that the logically necessary ought to be, there seems no reason to add that the logically impossible shares that status!

More frequently, the joint occurrence of <p> and <q> is possible but just not something that ought to be. This is a point Leibniz would relish. On a cold winter's day you meet a shivering beggar. You can spare the money to let the beggar buy a new coat; you can give the beggar your coat and buy yourself a new one; but you cannot afford to give the beggar both your coat and the money for a new coat. If you did so, you would freeze and those dependent on you would starve. Giving the beggar both the coat and the money would make matters no better than failing to give the beggar the coat; likewise, it would make matters no better than failing to give him the money. If we deny that it ought to be that you give both the coat and the money, we must, by O_1d, deny either that it ought to be that you give the coat or that it ought to be that you give the money; if we affirm both that it ought to be that you give the coat and that it ought to be that you give the money, O_1d commits us to the unacceptable conclusion that it ought to be that you give both.

Remember the person who supposed that there ought to be a law against boom boxes in public places, but who would also assert that it ought to be that boom boxes were never invented at all. Had boom boxes never been invented, we would need no law against their use in public places; and if there is a law against their use in public places, it is false that they were never invented. Thus a person with tender ears might well assert that there ought to be a law against boom boxes in public places, but the same person might deny that all worlds where there is such a law are preferable to those counterparts where the law is missing.

We need to amend O_1d to allow for the possibility that any one of a number of alternative courses of action might make the world better, even though several occurring together — should that be possible — would not. To make the change, I first define a set of *OB-alternatives*:

Definition C: $\{<p>, <q>, <r>, \dots\}$ is a set of *OB-alternatives* $=_{df}$ Any world where one member of the set $\{<p>, <q>, <r>, \dots\}$ obtains is preferable to every world where no member of the set obtains; and for each pair of members of the set, either there is no world in which they jointly obtain, or some world in which they jointly obtain is not preferable to some world in which they both fail to obtain.

Then to say that OBp is to say that $<p>$ is a member of a set of OB-alternatives. If $<p>$ is a member of a set of OB-alternatives, I shall say that the members of the set, including $<p>$, are *$<p>$-alternatives*. If $<p>$ is the only member of a set of $<p>$-alternatives, then our account of 'OBp' reduces to the claim that all worlds in which 'p' is true are preferable to their $<p>$-counterparts. Our final version of O_1 therefore is:

O_1e: To say that the state of affairs $<p>$ ought to be is to say that any $<p>$-alternative-normal world containing a $<p>$-alternative is preferable to $<p>$-alternative-counterpart worlds.[9]

O_1e provides an easy answer to the twelfth objection. To say that there ought to be a law against boom boxes is to say that a world which has a law against boom boxes, or no boom boxes, or some other alternative would be preferable to its counterparts where none of those alternatives obtains. It does not license us to infer from "There ought to be a law against boom boxes" and "There ought to be no boom boxes" that "There ought to be both a law against boom boxes and no boom boxes." For the state of the world in which there are no boom boxes but in which there is a law against boom boxes might, for all we know, be either impossible or no improvement over the state of the world in which neither of these conditions obtains.

I have made a series of refinements in our original intuitions, O_1 and O_2, to meet various difficulties and objections. Next, I shall state the resulting semantics more formally.

2. STATEMENT OF THE NEW SEMANTICS

I begin with eleven definitions:

Definition 1: 'W_0 is a world' $=_{df}$ (1) W_0 is a possible world, accessible to the real world;[10] (2) W_0 has the same causal laws as the real world; (3) There is a time such that at least one event occurred prior to that time in W_0, and such that any event occurred prior to that time in W_0 if and only if it occurred in the real world.

Definition 2: Where w_1 and w_2 are worlds, '$w_1 \blacktriangleright w'_2 =_{df} w_1$ is preferable to w_2'.

Definition 3: A world w_1 is a $<p>$-*counterpart* to $w_2 =_{df}$ the truth-value of 'p' in w_2 is different from the truth-value of 'p' in w_1, and the only other differences between w_2 and w_1 are partially or entirely caused by $<p>$'s obtaining in one world and not the other.

Definition 4: A world w_0 is $<p>$-*normal* $=_{df}$ There is no proposition 'q' such that: '$\vdash q \to p$' is true, 'q' is true in w_0, and not every world where 'q' is true is preferable to some counterpart where 'q' is false.

Definition 5: $\{<p>, <q>, <r>, \ldots \}$ is a set of *OB-alternatives* $=_{df}$ any world w_0 in which any member of $\{<p>, <q>, <r>, \ldots \}$ obtains $\blacktriangleright$ all $<p>$-counterparts of w_0 in which no member of $\{<p>, <q>, <r>, \ldots \}$ obtains; and for any pairs $\langle <p>, <q> \rangle$ of members of

{<p>,<q>,<r>, . . . }, *either* ⊢ p ⁀ ~q *or* $(\exists w_1)(\exists w_2)$['p.q' is true in w_1, no member of {<p>, <q>, <r>, . . . } is true in w_2, and $w_1 \sim^{\blacktriangleright} w_2$]. If <p> and <q>' are members of a set of OB-alternatives, <q> is termed a *<p>-alternative* (in short, a *$<p^a>$*) to <p>; and if two worlds, w_1 and w_2, differ only as a result of containing different $<P^a>$'s, w_1 is a *$<P^a>$*-world to w_2.

Definition 6: A *$<p>$-alternative-normal* world (for short, a *$<p^a>$-normal* world) $=_{df}$ a <q>-normal world, and a *$<p>$-alternative-counterpart* world (for short, a *$<p^a>$-counterpart*) $=_{df}$ a <q>-counterpart world, where <q> is a $<p^a>$. If a certain $<p^a>$ is said either to obtain or not to obtain in a $<p^a>$-normal or $<p^a>$-counterpart world, the <p>-alternative is the same as the <p>-alternative that defines the world unless otherwise stated.

Definition 7: '$OB_{t1}p_{t2}$' $=_{df}$ 'It ought to be at time t_1 that p at time t_2'.

Definition 8: Where 'S' stands for an agent and 'F' for an action-type, '$OD_{t1}SF_{t2}$' $=_{df}$ 'S ought-at-time t_1 to do F at time t_2'.

Definition 9: '$PB_{t1}p_{t2}$' $=_{df}$ 'It is permissible at time t_1 that p be at t_2' (*or:* 'It may be at t_1 that p at t_2').

Definition 10: Where 'S' stands for an agent and 'F' for an action-type, '$PD_{t1}SF_{t2}$' $=_{df}$ 'It is permissible for S at time t_1 to do F at t_2' (*or:* 'S may at t_1 do F at t_2').

Definition 11: Where 'S' indicates an agent, 'AP_S' $=_{df}$ 'S suffers an appropriate penalty'.

From definition 5, it follows that any state of affairs <p> that ought to be is its own $<p^a>$, and any world containing <p> is its own $<p^a>$. Hence, included in all $<p^a>$-normal worlds containing a $<p^a>$ are all <p>-normal worlds containing <p>; the same for $<p^a>$-counterparts.

In definitions 7, 8, 9, and 10, time-references can be omitted where they are either unclear or universal. For instance, "You ought not to tell lies" might best be understood as: "You ought-not-at-any-time to tell-lies-at-any-time"; if so, it could be symbolized as '$\sim OD_Y L$', omitting any temporal subscripts.

The following rules are consequences of Definition 2:

1. TRAN (Rule of transitivity): The relation '$\blacktriangleright$' is transitive. That is, if $w_{0t} \blacktriangleright w_{1t}$ and if $w_{1t} \blacktriangleright w_{2t}$, then $w_{0t} \blacktriangleright w_{2t}$.

2. ASYM (Rule of asymmetricality): The relation '$\blacktriangleright$' is asymmetrical. That is, if $w_{0t} \blacktriangleright w_{1t}$, then $\sim(w_{1t} \blacktriangleright w_{0t})$ — or, as I shall write from now on, $w_{1t} \sim^{\blacktriangleright} w_{0t}$.

3. NONR (Rule of non-reflexivity): The relation '▸' is non-reflexive. That is, w_{0t} ~▸ w_{0t}.

4. AGGR (Rule of aggregation): If all worlds at t where 'p' is true ▸ all their <p>-counterparts at t in which 'r' is not true; and if all worlds at t where 'q' is true ▸ all their <p>-counterparts at t in which 's' is not true; then all worlds at t where 'p v q' is true ▸ their <p>-counterparts or <q>-counterparts at t in which 'r v s' is not true.

5. CONS (Rule of consequent change): If all worlds at t in which 'r' is true ▸ their r-counterparts at t in which 'p' is false; and if all worlds at t where 'p' is true are worlds where 'q' is true; then all worlds at t in which 'r' is true ▸ their r-counterparts at t in which 'q' is false.

6. POSS (Rule of possible worlds): '▸' is a two-place relation between worlds. Any expression of the form 'x ▸ y', where either 'x' or 'y' does not designate a world, in the sense given that term in Definition 1, is ill-formed.

The first five rules all have, and require, temporal subscripts. No world at a given time is preferable to itself at that time, but it can be preferable to itself at another time. One world can be preferable to another at one time but not at another. If w_0 is preferable to w_1 at 10 a.m., and w_1 is preferable to w_2 at 11 a.m., there might never be a time at which w_0 is preferable to w_2. We can aggregate and alter semantic claims by the rules AGGR and POSS only if ought-times in the aggregated and altered claims are all the same.

Earlier in this chapter I argued for four of these rules; I shall now give a brief justification of AGGR and CONS. I think the rule AGGR both appropriate and intuitive for the following reason: Assume that worlds where 'p' is true ▸ <p>-counterparts where 'r' is false, and that worlds where 'q' is true ▸ <q>-counterparts where 's' is false. Since worlds where 'r v s' is false are worlds where *both* 'r' and 's' are false, worlds where 'p' is true ▸ <p>-counterparts where 'r v s' is false. By the same token, worlds where 'q' is true ▸ <q>-counterparts where 'r v s' is false. Therefore, worlds where either 'p' or 'q' is true ▸ <p>- or <q>-counterparts where 'r v s' is false; and this is the rule AGGR.

As for the rule CONS, I think it appropriate and intuitive for the following reason: Suppose that every member of set N of worlds ▸ every member of set M of worlds. Then every member of N ▸ every member of any subset of M. Further, since for some p, every world in N is $<p>$-normal, every world in M is a $<p>$-normal $<p>$-counterpart to an N-world; hence, every world in any subset of M is a $<p>$-normal $<p>$-counterpart to an N-world. That gives us the rule CONS.

I am now in a position to state the semantical rules for NDL, my new deontic logic. There are five rules for the semantics of 'ought to be' statements and five rules for the semantics of 'ought to do' statements; each set of five is parallel to the five rules of SDL semantics. See Appendix 1 for a tabular comparison of the three sets of semantical rules.

First come the five NDL rules for the semantics of 'ought to be' statements:

NDLS1$_B$: The statement "It ought at time t_1 to be that p at t_2," is true in world w_0 only if every $<p^a>$-normal world w_1 (branching from w_0 at t_1 or identical to w_0) where a $<p^a>$ obtains at t_2 ▸ any $<p^a>$-counterpart world w_2.

NDLS2$_B$: The statement "It ought at time t_1 to be that p at t_2," is true in world w_0 if every $<p^a>$-normal world w_1 (branching from w_0 at t_1 or identical to w_0) where a $<p^a>$ obtains at t_2 ▸ any $<p^a>$-counterpart world w_2.

NDLS3$_B$: The statement "It is permissible at time t_1 to be that p at t_2," (*or*: "It may be at t_1 that p at t_2,") is true in world w_0 only if there is at least one $<\sim p^a>$-normal world w_1 (branching from w_0 at t_1 or identical to w_0) where no $<p^a>$ obtains at t_2, and there is at least one $<\sim p^a>$-counterpart world w_2, and $w_1 \sim ▸ w_2$.

NDLS4$_B$: The statement "It is permissible at time t_1 to be that p at t_2," (*or*: "It may be at t_1 that p at t_2,") is true in world w_0 if there is at least one $<\sim p^a>$-normal world w_1 (branching from w_0 at t_1 or identical to w_0) where no $<p^a>$ obtains at t_2, and there is at least one $<\sim p^a>$-counterpart world w_2, and $w_1 \sim ▸ w_2$.

NDLS5$_B$: For any world w_0 and any proposition 'p', such that 'p' is neither necessarily true nor necessarily false, if 'p' is true in w_0, there is a $<p>$-counterpart world w_1 accessible to w_0.

Next come the five NDL rules for the semantics of 'ought to do' statements:

NDLS1$_D$: "S ought at t_1 to do F at t_2," is true in world w_0 only if: (a) S exists in w_0; and (b) every $<AP_S^a>$-normal world w_1 (branching from w_0 at t_1 or identical to w_0) where either S does F at t_2 or some $<AP_S^a>$ obtains ▸ any $<AP_S^a>$-counterpart world w_2 where it is false that S does F at t_2 and it is false that any $<AP_S^a>$ obtains.

NDLS2$_D$: "S ought at t_1 to do F at t_2" is true in world w_0 if: (a) S exists in w_0; and (b) every $<AP_S^a>$-normal world w_1 (branching from w_0 at t_1 or identical to w_0) where either S does F at t_2 or some $<AP_S^a>$ obtains ▸ any $<AP_S^a>$-counterpart world w_2 where it is false that S does F at t_2 and it is false that any $<AP_S^a>$ obtains.

NDLS3$_D$: "It is permissible for S at t_1 to do F" is true in world w_0 only if: (a) S exists; and (b) there is at least one $<AP_S^a>$-normal world w_1 (branching from w_0 at t_1 or identical to w_0) where if S does F at t_2, some $<AP_S^a>$ obtains, and there is at least one $<AP_S^a>$-counterpart world w_2 where S does F at t_2 and no $<AP_S^a>$ obtains, and w_1 ~▸ w_2.

NDLS4$_D$: "It is permissible for S at t_1 to do F" is true in world w_0 if: (a) S exists; and (b) there is at least one $<AP_S^a>$-normal world w_1 (branching from w_0 at t_1 or identical to w_0) where if S does F at t_2, some $<AP_S^a>$ obtains, and there is at least one $<AP_S^a>$-counterpart world w_2 where S does F at t_2 and no $<AP_S^a>$ obtains, and w_1 ~▸ w_2.

NDLS5$_D$: For any world w_0 and any proposition 'p', such that 'p' is neither necessarily true nor necessarily false, if 'p' is true in w_0, there is a $<p>$-counterpart world w_1, accessible to w_0.

Note that NDLS5$_B$ is identical to NDLS5$_D$. Also, if 'p' is necessarily true or necessarily false, 'p' remains a well-formed formula (wff) of NDL, even though 'OBp' is not. Therefore, NDLS5 needs its provision banning necessarily true and necessarily false propositions.

NDLS1$_D$ and NDLS2$_D$ are more expansive than the original O_2. They assert that OD_SF if and only if all $<AP_S^a>$-normal worlds in which either S does F or S is appropriately penalized are preferable to all $<AP_S^a>$-counterparts in which S neither does F nor is appropriately penalized. In other words, both doing your duty and being appropriately penalized for not doing your duty are preferable to unpenalized failure for not doing your duty. O_2 had asserted only that being penalized for not doing your duty is preferable to not being penalized for not doing your duty. Also, NDLS1$_D$ and NDLS2$_D$, in allowing the possibility that S ought to do F, S does F, and S is appropriately penalized, make room inside the deontic tent for Augustinians who think that people should be punished whatever they do.

As a final point in setting out NDL semantics, I need to look briefly at the notion of validity in NDL.[11] As we shall see in Chapter 15, certain assertions follow from NDL semantics, even though the terms '▸' and 'appropriate penalty' remain undefined. The validity of these assertions, therefore, does not depend on any particular interpretation of '▸' and 'appropriate penalty'; they are logical truths for any deontic logic which uses NDL semantics. Thus a wff in any NDL system is valid if and only if it is true for all interpretations of its sentence letters, all values of its variables and of its non-logical constants, all readings of its function-letters, and all interpretations of '▸' and 'appropriate penalty'.

That completes my outline of the semantics of NDL. In Chapter 15, I shall explain what sort of deontic logic results from the semantics just given. The remainder of Chapter 14 is an informal justification of the semantics of NDL. But because a semantics is acceptable only if the logic that falls out of it is acceptable, a full justification of NDL semantics depends on the results of Chapter 15.

3. PRELIMINARY JUSTIFICATION OF NDL SEMANTICS

In the first part of this book, I had some harsh criticisms of SDL semantics, as it applied both to 'ought to be' and to 'ought to do' sentences. I shall try to show that these criticisms do not apply to NDL semantics. If I am right, we have good initial reason to prefer NDL semantics to the ordinary semantics of standard deontic logic.

SDL semantics made no distinction between the semantic counterparts of 'ought to be' and 'ought to do' statements. NDL provides distinct semantic counterparts for each of these two types of statement. If I was correct in arguing in Chapter 4 that 'ought to do' and 'ought to be' statements differ in meaning and logical structure, then NDL semantics is preferable to SDL semantics.

The SDL semantics of 'ought to be' statements reduced to a claim that n ought to be if and only if it is good that n. Since "It is good that n" is just as opaque as "n ought to be," SDL semantics is of no help whatsoever. NDL semantics claims instead that n ought to be if and only if n's existence would bring about a preferable state of affairs. This definition, by using a causal conditional, allows for the sort of semantics employed with such conditionals. And with that semantics, we have successful reference to events in other possible worlds. That is, the semantical explanation consists of non-opaque, extensional sentences. Advantage NDL.

Again, the SDL semantics of 'ought to be' statements requires that necessary truths ought to be and necessary falsehoods ought not to be. The same requirement is not present in NDL semantics, because of the rule POSS — itself a consequence of our decision that if 'p' is either logically necessary or logically impossible, 'OBp' is not a wff of NDL. A necessary truth holds in all possible and accessible worlds; there are no worlds in which it does not hold. Therefore, the very notion of a counterpart world in which any necessary truth does not hold is ill formed: It speaks in effect of an impossible possible world.[12] Therefore, the claim that worlds where the necessary truth holds are better than counterparts where it does not is senseless — not false, but ill formed. We therefore cannot use such a claim to infer that necessary truths ought to be.

Suppose that we face a difficult and unpleasant problem. There are two equally good ways out of the problem, A and B, but these ways are mutually exclusive. I think it reasonable to assert both that A ought to be and that B ought to be. To take my earlier example, there ought to be a law against boom boxes, and boom boxes ought never to have been invented. SDL semantics will not allow any such assertion, for any world in which B obtains is one in which A fails to obtain, and vice versa. Hence, on SDL semantics, if A ought to be, A obtains in all deontically accessible worlds; in which case, B obtains in no deontically accessible worlds; whence, since there is at least one such world, it is not the case that B ought to be. Thus SDL semantics will not allow us to assert both that A ought to be and that B ought to be. NDL semantics will allow this, for A and B are OB-alternatives.

Next, what about iterated 'ought to be' statements? In Chapter 10, I argued that causal and temporal considerations block us from being able to reduce 'OB(OBp)' to 'OBp', as SDL semantics requires. NDL semantics confirms this result: if the world would be made better in 2000 by its being better in 1950 that <p> obtains, it by no means follows that the world would be made better in 1950 by <p>'s obtaining. On NDL semantics, then, we cannot make a counterintuitive reduction of iterated 'ought to be' operators.

The NDL semantics of 'ought to be' statements therefore escapes the difficulties I posed for SDL semantics. Does the same happy fate await the NDL semantics of 'ought to do' statements? Start with Schotch and Jennings's problem left over from Chapter 3: surely "We ought to feed the starving poor" does not imply "There ought to be starving poor." [Schotch and Jennings, 151] On SDL semantics, the implication holds; on NDL semantics, it does not. For let us assume that all worlds where we do not feed the starving poor and receive an appropriate penalty are preferable to their counterparts in which we do not feed the starving poor and fail to receive an appropriate penalty. We cannot infer that all worlds which contain starving poor are preferable to their counterparts which do not contain starving poor. For "We ought to feed the starving poor," in NDL semantics, makes no claim about the existence in this world of anything but us. We cannot even infer that this world contains starving poor, much less that a world with starving poor is in any way preferable to a world without starving poor. Therefore, NDL semantics does not allow us to infer from "We ought to feed the starving poor" that "There ought to be starving poor." Nor can we infer that the poor ought to starve. For even if all worlds where we do not feed the starving poor and are appropriately penalized are preferable to counterparts where we do not feed the starving poor and are not appropriately penalized, it does not follow that all worlds where the poor do not starve and are appropriately penalized are preferable to counterparts where the poor do not starve and are not appropriately penalized. "We ought to feed the starving poor" implies our existence alone, whereas "The poor ought to starve" implies the existence only of the poor. NDL semantics, by disallowing the Schotch and Jennings inference, is clearly preferable to SDL semantics.

Someone might object at this point that among the worlds in which we do not feed the starving poor are worlds in which there are no starving poor — surely there is nothing good about our being punished in such worlds! But the objector forgets that the worlds of NDL semantics branch from a world in which we ought to feed the starving poor; and no world would contain that obligation without containing starving poor — unless people deserve punishment whatever they do. Hence, if indeed we ought to feed the starving poor, NDL semantics takes no cognizance of possible worlds without starving poor.

In Chapter 6, we looked at a series of objections that required us to narrow the set of deontically accessible worlds and change drastically SDL semantics. Deontically accessible worlds must branch from the real world, even though the morally impeccable behavior SDL ascribes to persons in those alternatives hardly resembles the behavior of those same persons in the real world. Further, events in branching worlds are relevant to what we ought to do in this world only during a very short period after the ought time — short enough that no new duties are contracted and no old ones lost or modified because of expected future behavior. For our expectations differ from world to world: in branching worlds we know people always behave well; in the real world, we know nothing of the sort.

NDL semantics also makes use of branching worlds, but it does not suppose that people in those branching worlds suddenly begin acting in ways quite foreign to their behavior in the real world. Nor does it require that a world be used in our semantics only in the brief span of time until duties are formed, lost, or modified. Rather, changes in the status of duties might well be part of the overall result which makes one set of worlds preferable to another. For example, on a deterrence theory of punishment, suffering a penalty for not doing one's duty causes others to perform their duty. Then among the worlds in which John is appropriately penalized for his failure to do F, his duty, there are worlds in which John's failure and penalty cause Mary to do G, her duty. Quite aside from deterrence, Mary's duty might be to punish those who fail to do F. In at least some worlds where John fails to do F and is not appropriately penalized, Mary is not caused to do G.[13] And other things being equal, worlds where Mary does her duty are morally preferable on most accounts to worlds where she does not. Hence, we have a partial account of why some worlds in which John fails to do his duty and is appropriately penalized are morally preferable to their counterparts in which John's failure is not appropriately penalized.

Hence, so far as I can see, we need not make so many restrictions on the set of worlds for NDL semantics as Chapter 6 required for SDL semantics. Moreover, those restrictions that I did make on NDL semantics — to wit, that the worlds in question branch from a given world at the ought time — require no sudden shifts in behavior patterns or other oddities in the makeup of the branching worlds. The objections of Chapter 6 leave the NDL semantics of 'ought to do' statements intact.

In Chapter 7, we looked at difficulties posed for SDL semantics by backward translation. Now according to NDLS2_D, NDL semantics also supposes that one can translate from certain statements concerning possible worlds to statements of what one ought to do; and this is a form of backward translation. Do the problems of backward translation for SDL semantics raise difficulties for NDL? I think not.

SDL semantics provided that if it is necessary for Jane not to square the circle, Jane ought not to square the circle; I saw no way of avoiding this conclusion in SDL without at least modifying backward translation. NDL easily avoids this difficulty. For since there can by definition be no possible worlds in which Jane does square the circle, there can be no possible worlds in which she squares the circle and is penalized, nor can there be possible worlds in which she squares the circle and is not penalized. So by the rule POSS, the statement "The set of worlds in which Jane squares the circle and is penalized is better than the set of worlds in which she squares the circle and is not penalized" is not false but ill formed. Hence, one cannot use NDLS rules to infer that Jane ought not to square the circle. That is a plus for NDL semantics.

In Chapter 7, I argued that "It ought to be that the secretary ought to keep the books" is not equivalent, as SDL semantics requires, to "The secretary ought to keep the books." NDL semantics confirms that '$OB(OD_SF)$' does not in fact imply 'OD_SF'; for, as we have seen, it confirms that '$OB(OBp)$' does not imply 'OBp' and hence that '$OB[OB(F_S \to AP_S)]$' does not imply '$OB(F_S \to AP_S)$'. If the world would be better in 2000 if it ought to be in 1950 that S is appropriately penalized for not doing F, we cannot infer that it ought to be in 1950 that S is appropriately penalized for not doing F. What would make the world better at one time might not make it better at another.

The example of our setting up a club, discussed in Chapter 7, confirms this analysis. You said that it ought to be that the vice-president ought to keep the books, while I said that it ought to be that the secretary has that duty. We obviously cannot infer that either of those officers actually has that duty. The reason we cannot do so has to do with time: If it ought to be during the period the club is being set up that the secretary ought to keep the books, it is false that during that time the secretary actually has that duty. The ought time for the 'ought to be' is therefore different from that of the 'ought to do', although the two might overlap to some extent. Reduction of iterated oughts in the example therefore fails because of temporal considerations, as the NDL analysis says it will. And we shall see in Chapter 15 that NDL agrees with Chapter 7 in disallowing the reduction of cotemporal iterated oughts. NDL analysis of iterated oughts is therefore much more plausible than the SDL counterpart.

The assertibility argument suggested that a person might be in a position to assert 'p' in all deontically accessible worlds but not in a position to assert 'Op' in this world. Hence, we cannot justify the SDL inference from the assertion of 'p' in all deontically accessible worlds to the assertion of 'Op' in this world. But the assertibility argument is no objection to NDL semantics, which does not infer an 'ought' statement from truth in any set of worlds.

Perhaps NDL semantics faces a variant of the assertibility argument. Might not someone be in a position to assert that all worlds where a person does not do F and is appropriately penalized are morally preferable to their counterparts where the person does not do F and is not appropriately penalized, and yet not be in a position to assert that the person ought to do F? But that cannot happen. Remember that the only worlds NDL considers are ones which branch from the real world: If potential actors are or should have been aware of relevant norms before the ought time in the real world, they are or should be aware of them in all the worlds that branch from it at the ought time. And if potential actors neither are nor should be aware of relevant norms in a given world, what sense can we make of the notion of an appropriate penalty in that world? Hence I can see no way in which anyone is in a position to assert that all worlds where a person does not do F and is appropriately penalized are morally preferable to their counterparts where the person does not do F and is not appropriately penalized, and yet is not in a position to assert that the person ought to do F. Objections to NDL semantics based on the assertibility problem do not offer any promise of success.

In Chapter 8, I considered a group of epistemic problems bedeviling SDL semantics. What access could we have to its deontically accessible worlds? There seemed no non-realist interpretation of deontically accessible worlds, and hence they seemed empty as explanations of deontic phenomena. NDL semantics does not presuppose those special worlds but instead posits a well-defined subset of the class of all possible worlds: namely, those which branch from a given world at a given time. A Carnapian equivalent of such worlds is easily constructed: One supposes that the questions giving rise to state descriptions all specify a specific time (e.g., "Is Cat X purple from 2 a.m. to 3 a.m., October 1,

2000, EDT?"). Branching worlds are for the Carnapian state descriptions with identical answers to all questions with time-references up to a given time. Our access to branching worlds allows us to determine the value of any causal conditionals; since we can determine that value, at least in some cases, we have the needed access. A person, perhaps even a computer, can project with some success what would happen if failure to act in a certain way both is and is not followed by appropriate penalties. Therefore, the worlds of NDL semantics face no special problems of accessibility. And for those with a taste for desert landscapes, the modal realist language in which I presented NDL semantics is merely a manner of speech.

Next, what about the more standard objections which I looked at in Chapter 9? These objections for the most part clustered around SDLT1 and SDLT5. In Chapter 15, I shall show that the NDL logic of 'ought to do' statements does contain counterparts to SDLT1 and SDLT5, but in each case the counterpart holds only under an important condition. And this condition, I shall argue, is sufficient to insure that the objections in question do not arise for NDL.

I argued that only a causal semantics of branching worlds can give an adequate solution of Chisholm's contrary-to-duty paradox. NDL semantics is causal, and it employs only branching worlds. We should therefore expect it to escape Chisholm's paradox, and indeed it does. For Chisholm's paradox was built on four assumptions:

(A) S ought to do F.
(B) S ought to do the following: if F then G.
(C) If S does not do F, it is not the case that S ought to do G.
(D) S does not do F.

Clearly, C is problematic in its formulation. In Chapter 9 I suggested briefly that we read C as a causal statement: S's failure to do F removes his obligation to do G. With a causal semantics, we can now make more sense of that brief suggestion.

Statements A and B have presumably the same implicit ought time, t. Let us read them, along with D, as follows:

(A') S ought at t_1 to do F at t_2 (where t_2 is later than t_1).
(B') S ought at t_1 to do the following: if F at t_2 then G at t_3 (where t_3 is the same time as or later than t_2).

(D') S does not do F at t_2.

Now we can take C to mean:

(C') S's failure to do F at t_2 causes it not to be the case that S ought at t_2 to do G at t_3.

Or semantically:

(C") Any world w in which S fails to do F at t_2 is such that there is some world w_1 branching from w at t_2, in which S does not do G at t_3 and AP_S, and there is a counterpart w_2 in which S does not do G at t_3 and $\sim AP_S$, and $w_1 \sim\blacktriangleright w_2$.

A' and B', as we shall see in Chapter 15, imply:

(E'): S ought at t_1 to do G at t_3.

C' and D' imply:

(E"): It is not the case that S ought at t_2 to do G at t_3.

Since a person often has a duty at one time and not at another, there is no paradox. Chisholm's four statements are consistent in NDL.

Several versions of the Good Samaritan paradox bedeviled SDL. To take the simple version of the paradox, if Sally ought now to help Joe, whom she is unjustly harming, does it follow from NDL semantics that Sally ought now to be harming Joe? Obviously not, for the NDL semantic equivalent of 'ought' statements is not that certain statements are true in different worlds but that certain worlds are related in a specific way. To say that Sally ought to help Joe is to say that all worlds where she does not help him and receives an appropriate penalty are morally preferable to counterpart worlds where she does not help him and receives no appropriate penalty. Adding that Sally is presently choking Joe tells us only that this is a world where she does not help him, at least at the present time. We cannot infer anything from the information provided about her supposed duty to harm him.

Similarly, Åqvist's variant and the paradox of gentle murders present no difficulties for NDL semantics. If George ought to know that Jessica does evil, then presumably it is true in this world and in any branching worlds that Jessica does evil. Hence, if 'ought to know' is an odd kind of 'ought to do', all worlds where George does not know the truth that Jessica does evil and is appropriately penalized ▶ their counterparts where

George does not know that truth and is not so penalized. These are all worlds where Jessica does evil. Nothing follows about worlds where Jessica does not do evil and is penalized for her righteousness. Hence, it does not follow from NDL semantics that Jessica ought to do evil.

Likewise with gentle murders. We say to someone, "You ought to do the following: if you murder, murder gently." That is to say, all worlds where you murder, do so non-gently, and are appropriately penalized ▸ their counterparts where you murder, do so non-gently, and are not so penalized. What is true of worlds where you do not murder, NDL semantics does not say. Hence, nothing can follow about a duty to murder, even if we add the premiss that you do in fact commit a murder.

I can sum matters up quite roundly: None of the problems that the first part of the book raised for SDL semantics creates the slightest difficulty for NDL semantics. Unless NDL itself can be shown to engender a new crop of problems, people have good reason to adopt the new system.

But perhaps NDL semantics suffers from its own set of problems which SDL semantics escapes. In particular, some readers might be uneasy at a semantic account that defines what one ought to do — in any sense of 'ought' — by the notion of an appropriate penalty. I raised this question earlier in the present chapter, but I need to discuss it more fully here.

There are, I think, two main reasons for being uneasy with my account of 'ought to do' expressions:

(1) Sometimes a person ought to do something, but we do not think that failure to do it calls for the person to be penalized;

(2) Sometimes we think penalties are in order for failures, even though these are not failures to do as one ought.

The first difficulty suggests that my definition of 'ought to do' is too narrow, the second that it is too broad. We must look at each.

(1) Often, especially when our 'ought to do' expressions have little moral flavor to them, the notion of a penalty, appropriate or not, looks fairly tenuous at best. If so, my definition of 'ought to do' would be too narrow, for it would not fit non-moral 'ought to do' expressions.

For instance, suppose I am teaching a novice to play bridge; like many novices, she plays second-hand high on a lead from her right. I tell her that she ought not to do that except in some very special circumstances.[14] Am I assuring her that it ought to be the case that if she keeps on playing second-hand high, the skies will open and fire and brimstone descend on her head? Obviously not. The only penalties in view are the mild ones of getting less than optimal results — and sometimes not even those penalties will obtain! We all know and have been stung by persons who make the right move for the wrong reasons, and we all think that to be beaten by such persons is a case of cosmic injustice. The duplicate bridge player's motto is surely, "Damn it, that should not happen!"

Here we need to remember that, as I suggested earlier in the chapter, I intend the notion of a penalty to be broad enough to cover not only deliberate punishments but also all sorts of unfortunate results. Although no drastic penalties are in order for bad bridge play, surely it ought to be that my novice bridge player gets a bad board as a result of her bad play. That would be, at least in the short run, an unfortunate consequence for her. And that is all I meant by saying that she ought, except in special circumstances, to avoid playing second-hand high.

For more serious infractions, there ought to be more severe penalties. Just what penalties are appropriate for failures to carry out moral 'oughts' depends on one's moral code or theory. Children ought not, on practically any moral code, to make fun of a man's baldness; but only a particular religious code thinks it an appropriate penalty for the children to be torn apart by bears.[15]

In a way, I have accepted Geoffrey Sayre-McCord's suggestion that deontic logic differs from one moral code to another. [Sayre-McCord, 193-194] I do think that the *structure* of that logic is the same for all moral codes. But one puts flesh on those bare bones by giving sense to such undefined terms as 'appropriate penalty' and 'preferable to'. And the sense that one gives to those terms depends on one's moral code or theory. Hence, the logic that one actually uses is specific to one's moral beliefs, but the structure of that logic is not.

By the NDL semantics of 'ought to do' statements, it ought to be that those who do not do as they ought will suffer an appropriate penalty. After having read Chapter 4, the reader will not be tempted to interpret that claim as requiring that someone else provide that penalty. Not just the fear of an infinite regress, or a regress to basic oughts, rules out such a reading. Stalin, in possession of nuclear weapons, did many things that he should not have done, but no one was in a position to penalize him. It would have been at best pointless to have said to someone, "You ought to punish Stalin;" there is no one to whom one could have assigned such a duty. Yet Stalin surely should have been penalized for his actions.

Again, people do what they should not do but no penalty seems appropriate in cases of excused improper behavior. Such excuses usually stem from ignorance, compulsion, disease, or defect. For instance, the law in some jurisdictions will not punish those criminals whose misbehavior is caused by mental disease or defect. We have no reason to suppose that all worlds where the mentally deficient commit such crimes and are penalized are better than counterpart worlds where they commit the crimes and remain unpenalized — and some would doubt that *any* world where they are penalized is better than its counterparts.

I see no way of explaining such cases as those of mentally deficient criminals except to say that an excuse is just that: Murderers are excused from their obligation not to murder. Those who ought to do something must be of reasonably sound mind, in possession of adequate information, and under no compulsion to do otherwise. No one would suppose that a bank cashier, on receiving a hold-up note from a man brandishing a pistol, ought to give him money only if the bank has approved a loan. Force and particular ignorance are, as Aristotle argued, usually valid excuses from responsibility for one's actions; if so, then it is idle to say that a compelled or relevantly ignorant person should have acted otherwise. Likewise, if one believes that mental disease or defect, when partially responsible for a criminal act, are valid excuses, one believes that the diseased or defective person, in committing the act in question, was not failing to do as he ought. In general, then, excused misbehavior does not provide reasonable counterexamples to NDL semantics.

(2) But even if all who fail to do as they ought deserve penalties, perhaps other kinds of failure also call for penalties. If so, my definition of 'ought to do' is too broad, for it holds of more expressions than the 'ought to do'. For instance, the law holds that violators of strict liability statutes, such as the Pure Food and Drug Act, should be penalized for the public good, even though the violators have not been negligent and have broken no obligations.

But if strict liability statutes are to be anything but immoral traps for the unlucky, they must presuppose that violators of such laws have not done as they ought. Confusion about such failures stems from the fact that we usually reserve the words 'duty' and 'obligation' for the most important cases of what a person ought to do. For example, the Russian poet Yevgeny Yevtushenko, in his telegram of protest to Brezhnev after the 1968 crushing of the Prague Spring, spoke of his 'moral duty' to speak out.[16] Only on such solemn occasions, when one faces the likelihood of the gulag, does the twentieth century find it appropriate to speak of duties. Hence, failing to do what one ought often does not count as a violation of obligation or a failure to carry out one's duty.[17] But in all cases I can think of where failure deserves a penalty, those who failed did not do what they ought to have done. If a child or a high university official thoughtlessly grabs for the first good-looking toy that he sees, without stopping to consider potential risks, we say, "You should not just grab; you should stop and think first." Not all grabbers get into trouble because of their actions, but we think it fitting if they do.

Hence, it does seem that all and only those persons who fail to do as they ought — whatever the variety of 'ought' one is using — should be penalized. NDL semantic principles concerning 'ought to do' statements seem reasonably in accord with the ordinary meanings of 'ought' and 'may', at least so far as the notion of 'appropriate penalty' is concerned.

To be sure, I cannot rule out the possibility that the NDL semantics of 'ought to do' statements will lead to paradoxes at least as damaging as those which beset SDL. Since I have provided no restrictions on what constitutes an appropriate penalty, I am in no position to rule out unwelcome consequences from a vicious moral or legal code, except when those consequences are inconsistent with NDL itself.[18] Just as it is consistent with the principles of SDL but not of most moral codes that I ought to murder next week the person whom I help today, so might various interpretations of '▸' and 'appropriate penalty' lead to unpleasant results which NDL could not block. Certainly, no logic can guarantee only welcome consequences.

Stephen Harris has suggested the following problem: Suppose that all worlds in which you murder, but not on a Monday, and are appropriately penalized are preferable to counterpart worlds in which you murder, but not on a Monday, and are not so penalized. Does it not follow from NDL semantics that if you murder, you should do it on a Monday? And since the same can be said of murders on all other days, does that not suggest that if you murder, you should do so daily? Like the Good Samaritan, that would not be an illogical result but it would surely be an unwelcome one!

But this unfortunate result does not follow from NDL semantics. Certainly we can infer that one ought not to murder on days other than Monday; and if the situation is the same for all other days, we can infer that one ought not to murder on days other than Tuesday, Wednesday, and so on. But if we put any two such principles together, the result is not that a murderer should murder daily. If one ought not to murder on days other than Monday, and if one ought not to murder on days other than Tuesday, then (since Tuesday is a day other than Monday, and vice versa) it follows that one ought not to murder at all. And that result is neither paradoxical nor unwelcome. Hence, I do not believe that Harris's problem causes difficulties for NDL semantics; whether worse problems might arise, I am unable to tell.

That ends my preliminary justification of NDL semantics. On the whole, I believe our results have shown that NDL semantics is preferable to SDL semantics. But whether NDL semantics is of any value in its own right, only the new deontic logic itself can determine. The proof of any semantic pudding is in the logical eating.

Chapter 15: Being Good and Being Logical: What Deontic Logic Ought to Be

With NDL semantics in place, I turn to the logic that falls out of that semantics. I shall first determine the formation rules for well-formed formulae in my new deontic logic (NDL). Then I shall state and argue for inference rules of NDL, while explaining why certain other possible inference rules are not part of NDL. Next I shall state and argue for some important theorems asserted by NDL, and I shall show why certain other possible theorems are not asserted by NDL. As I go along, I shall be trying to show how NDL, both in the rules and theorems that it accepts and in the rules and theorems that it rejects, is far closer than Standard Deontic Logic (SDL) to our ordinary deontic thoughts and statements. I shall close this chapter with a brief review of how NDL deals with some of the problems we found in SDL.

In Chapter 14 I set out the semantical rules of NDL in a way parallel to those of SDL. This parallelism will continue in the present chapter: I shall consider whether the 'ought to be' and 'ought to do' counterparts of *each* typical inference rule and commonly asserted proposition of standard deontic logic obtain in NDL. By this device, I hope to make the reader clearly aware of specific differences, not only between NDL and SDL, but between the logic of 'ought to be' statements and the logic of 'ought to do' statements.[1]

To make the comparisons easy for the reader, Appendix 1 contains a set of tables. The first column of these tables lists every normal semantical rule, typical inference rule, commonly asserted proposition, and usually unasserted proposition of SDL. Parallel to each listing in the first column, the second column gives a counterpart, if one exists, in the language of 'ought to be' statements. Counterparts to propositions not asserted in SDL are listed as non-assertions of NDL. Likewise, parallel to each listing in the first column, the third column gives an NDL counterpart, if any, in the language of 'ought to do' statements. Hence

Appendix 1 provides a useful summary of the results of Chapters 2, 14, and 15.

Wherever I find no counterpart — or only a restricted counterpart — for an SDL rule or assertion in either the NDL logic of 'ought to be' statements or the NDL logic of 'ought to do' statements, I shall first give an argument why no unrestricted counterpart follows from the semantics of NDL. I shall then give a counterexample, the purpose of which is to show that a deontic logic not containing an unrestricted counterpart of the SDL rule or assertion is closer to ordinary deontic thought and language than is a deontic logic which contains such a counterpart. For the most part I have already discussed these counterexamples at length earlier in the book, so that a brief mention and a chapter reference will be sufficient. Wherever NDL gives a modified, restricted version of an SDL rule or assertion, I shall argue that the restrictions are justified by ordinary deontic thought and language.

In arguing for inference rules and asserted propositions in SDL, I shall be using the rules of NDL semantics developed in Chapter 14 and reprinted in Part IV of Appendix 1. However, as the rule POSS, NDLS5$_B$, and NDLS5$_S$ all make clear, the semantical rules of NDL give truth-conditions for deontic claims only if the non-deontic bases for those claims are contingent propositions. If 'p' is a necessary truth, the semantics of NDL provides no truth-conditions for 'OBp'; if it is necessarily false that S does F, there are no truth-conditions in NDL for '~OD$_S$F'.

I usually do not state in each proposition and inference rule that, for 'OBp' and 'OD$_S$F' to be well-formed formulae (wffs), 'p' and 'F$_S$' must be contingent. However, explicit statements of contingency are needed in two instances:

(1) To employ NDL semantics on 'OD$_S$F', it is not enough that 'F$_S$' be contingent. In virtue of NDLS1$_D$, 'AP$_S$^{a}' must also be contingent — even though 'OD$_S$F' is not explicitly formed from a proposition that says that 'AP$_S$^{a}' is true.

(2) Sometimes it happens that two statements are separately contingent, but their conjunction is necessarily false. It is contingent that this sheet of paper is white all over and contingent that this sheet of paper is purple all over, but it is not contingent that this sheet of paper is both white all over and purple all over. Thus

from the fact that '$\sim F_S$' and '$\sim AP_S{}^a$' are contingent, it does not follow that '$\sim F_S. \sim AP_S{}^a$' is contingent, as must be the case if we are to apply NDLS2$_D$. NDLS 'ought to do' theorems therefore require an explicit condition that '$\sim F_S. \sim AP_S$' is contingent.

Where an explicit statement of contingency is needed, I have used the expression "CT'p'," meaning '$\sim \vdash p. \sim \vdash \sim p$'.[2]

In calling a proposition 'p' contingent, I mean more than that 'p' is logically contingent. For the possible worlds which NDL considers are the real world and its branches — that is to say, what the real world would have been like if certain events had occurred or would occur. And such branching from the real world assumes a continuity of physical laws between the branching worlds and the real one: We have no way of assigning truth-value to a counterfactual such as "If I could jump to the moon, I could jump back." To say, then, that something takes place in one such possible world is to say that it is not only logically but physically possible; "CT'p'" therefore means not only that both 'p' and '$\sim p$' are logically possible but that both are physically possible as well.

The most important preliminary point is that all the arguments for NDL rules and assertions presuppose synchronicity. That is, any 'ought' operators used in my arguments have the same time-reference, and all the worlds spoken of in statements employing NDL semantics are worlds that branch at that same single time. Not one of the assertions of NDL could be proved from NDL semantics if its operators could be given different ought times; at least some would produce counterintuitive results if that were so.

If operators in a given proposition have different time references, NDL semantics will not let us prove the proposition. For as Chapter 14 shows, the basic relation '▸' holds only between synchronous worlds. Any semantic arguments in NDL make use of the fact that '▸' is transitive, asymmetrical, and irreflexive; but the relation has these properties only between worlds at the same time. Asymmetry is the most important of these properties: if an argument shows or assumes that $w_0 \blacktriangleright w_1$, the argument will get nowhere if one cannot infer that $w_1 \sim \blacktriangleright w_0$. But worlds can change; as they do, their relative preferability might alter. World w_0 might ▸ w_1 at one moment and not at the next. Since the NDL semantics of both 'ought to do' and 'ought to be' statements is built on the relation '▸', the semantic proofs of rules and theorems of NDL employ only synchronous 'ought' operators and worlds — and therefore, those rules and theorems themselves employ only synchronous 'ought' operators.

With 'oughts' of different times, the assertions of NDL would be very dubious. Take, for instance, NDLT1_B: ⊢ ~(OBp.OB~p). In a changing world, what ought to be sometimes alters: there ought today to be a law against boom boxes, but before boom boxes were invented such a law would have been otiose and perhaps even harmful. There is neither contradiction nor implausibility in saying both: that all worlds branching in 1996 where there is a law against boom boxes or some alternative ▸ all counterparts where there is no law and no law-alternative; and that all worlds branching in 1850 where there is no law against boom boxes or some alternative ▸ all counterparts where there is a law or an alternative. Hence, '~(OBp.OB~p)' cannot be a theorem so long as the two 'OB' operators have different time-references.

Again, consider NDLT7_B: ⊢ OBp ↔ ~PB~p. This is a simple operator exchange. But if 'OB' and 'PB' could have different time-references, NDLT7_B would produce counterexamples. Something ought today to be, yet its non-existence might have been perfectly permissible in 1850.

Even truth-functional rules appear to fail when time-references differ. Take the seeming contradiction 'OBp.~OBp': If the time references of the 'OB' operators differ, the boom box example shows that not even this seeming contradiction is impossible in NDL. When operators have different time-references, they are different operators: '$\text{OB}_{t1}p.\sim\text{OB}_{t2}p$' is not a true contradiction.

Because all oughts and all worlds mentioned in an argument are synchronous, I shall make my arguments more readable by omitting all time-references. However, in the statement of each NDL inference rule and theorem, I shall place time-references. Thus 'OB_tp' says, "It ought to be at time t that p"; '$\text{OD}_{St}F$' says, "S ought at time t to do F."

1. FORMATION RULES OF NDL

NDL, like SDL, is built on the foundation of the propositional calculus. Hence, all well-formed formulae (wffs) of the propositional calculus are wffs of NDL. However, we need to add to the foundation some formation rules for any wffs of NDL which incorporate 'ought to be' and 'ought to do' operators.

As noted above and in the previous chapter, we need to restrict the basic rule for forming OB-expressions. If 'p' is a wff, then 'OBp' is a wff — provided that 'p' is neither logically necessary nor logically impossible. That is, if 'p' is a wff, and if neither ' ⊢p' nor '⊢~p', 'OBp' is a wff.

To determine other plausible formation rules for well-formed formulae in NDL, I shall look at iterated modalities. Consider the following expressions:

(A) OB(OBp);
(B) PB(OBp);
(C) $OD_S(OD_SF)$;
(D) $PD_S(OD_SF)$;
(E) $OB(OD_SF)$;
(F) $OD_S(OBp)$;
(G) L(OBp);
(H) OB(Lp);
(I) $M(OD_SF)$;
(J) $OD_S(Mp)$.

Do these expressions and ones similar to them make sense? And of those expressions that do make sense, is there any clear way of simplifying them? The answers to these questions will indicate any restrictions we need to place on the list of well-formed formulae in NDL.

Some of these ten expressions are clearly nonsensical. What someone ought to do or may do is to perform an action, but such expressions as 'OD_SF', 'OBp', and 'Mp' can hardly be read as standing for actions. Rather, they are statements that a person ought to do something, that a state of affairs ought to be, and that a state of affairs is possible. Therefore, C, D, F, and J, all of which state that a person ought to or may do something which is not an action, are ill formed. Even attempting to spell out a semantical equivalent for each of them leads to gibberish. An 'ought to do' operator therefore cannot be prefixed to an expression beginning with another operator, nor to a proposition containing a nested operator; for, as Chapter 4 showed, what follows an 'ought to do' operator is not a proposition but a predicate.

However, predicates can themselves be complex. John should either mow the grass or weed the garden today. What he should do is a disjunctive task; to say that he should perform this task does not imply that John either ought to mow the grass or he ought to weed the garden. Disjunctive tasks cannot therefore be simplified into disjunctions of oughts. Hence, formation rules for wffs in the NDL logic of 'ought to do' statements must allow for us to speak of complex tasks.

Turn next to 'ought to be' operators, beginning with sentence A. A semantical translation of A, using $NDLS1_B$ twice, would read: "All p-normal worlds such that (all p-normal worlds where p ▸ their p-counterpart worlds) ▸ their (it is not the case that all worlds where p ▸ their p-counterpart worlds)-counterparts." That looks like gibberish, but it is not. Recall that our semantics uses *only* world w — usually, but not necessarily, the real world — and worlds branching from w and with the same causal laws as w. We can divide any such set of worlds exhaustively into two subsets: (1) worlds in which 'OBp' holds; and (2) worlds in which 'OBp' does not hold. (We have, of course, a semantic account of what it is for 'OBp' to hold in a given world.) Now suppose that all 1)-type worlds ▸ all 2)-type worlds. If so, then 'OB(OBp)' would be true. Informally, 'OB(OBp)' says that the very fact that it ought to be that p makes the world better than it otherwise would be. Notice that there seems no less complex way of stating this informal claim. If A is reducible, it is not obviously so.[3]

Similar reasoning shows formulae G and I to be well-formed. Since the semantics of both 'ought to be' and 'ought to do' speaks of worlds that branch from w, not necessarily the real world, there is no problem in prefacing either kind of statement with either the 'L' operator ("In all possible worlds . . .") or the 'M' operator ("In no possible world. . ."). Again, if expression A is well formed, so must E be well formed; for E amounts to 'OB[OB $(\sim F_S \rightarrow AP_S^a)$]'. And similar reasoning to that which dealt with A leads to the conclusions that B and H are well formed.

To sum up, any well-formed formula, if preceded by 'OB' or 'PB', yields a well-formed formula — unless, of course, it or its negation is a theorem. Hence nested modalities, as well as iterated modalities, may occur in NDL.

Our brief look at iterated modalities has therefore indicated the following formation rules:

NDLF1: All wffs of the propositional calculus are wffs of NDL.

NDLF2: If 'S$^{1'}$ and 'S$^{2'}$ are terms designating agents, so are 'S^1.S$^{2'}$ and 'S^1 v S$^{2'}$. If 'F$_S$' and 'G$_S$' are terms designating actions, so are 'F$_S$.G$_S$', 'F$_S$ v G$_S$', 'F$_S$ → G$_S$', 'F$_S$ ↔ G$_S$', and '~F$_S$'.

NDLF3$_B$: If 'p' is a wff of NDL, and if ~⊢p and ~⊢~p, then 'OBp' and 'PBp' are wffs of NDL.

NDLF3$_D$: If 'F$_S$' is a term designating an action performed by agent S, and if ~⊢(F$_S$ v AP$_S$) and ~⊢(~F$_S$.~APS), 'OD$_S$F' and 'PD$_S$F' are wffs of NDL.

NDLF4: If 'p' and 'q' are wffs of NDL, '~p', 'p.q', 'p v q', 'p → q', and 'p ↔ q' are wffs of NDL.

NDLF5: These are the only wffs of NDL.

2. INFERENCE RULES OF NDL

In proving the inference rules and theorems of NDL, it is useful first to prove the fundamental theorem of NDL:

NDLT0: ⊢ OD$_S$F ↔ [E!S.OB(F$_S$ v AP$_S$)].

The expression 'E!S' is to be read: "S exists." The proof of NDLT0 is obvious from NDL semantics. By NDLS1$_D$ and NDLS2$_D$, 'OD$_S$F' is equivalent to "E!S. All <AP$_S$^{a}>-normal worlds in which 'F $_S$v AP $_S$'are true ► all <AP$_S$^{a}>-counterparts in which '~F$_S$.~AP$_S$^{a}' is true." And that, in turn, is by NDLS1$_B$ and NDLS2$_B$ equivalent to 'E!S.OB(F$_S$ v AP$_S$)'.

NDLT0 is the fundamental theorem of NDL because it alone connects 'ought to do' and 'ought to be' propositions. SDL, because it employs a single 'ought' operator, has no equivalent to NDLT0. However, a version of SDL could use NDLT0 as a definition, introducing a second deontic operator. Hence NDLT0, although not part of SDL, is not incompatible with SDL.

The practical value of NDLT0 in what follows is that, whenever a proposed rule or a theorem holds true for all 'ought to be' statements, it will hold true for all 'ought to do' statements, so long as the agent in question exists; and whenever it does not hold true for all 'ought to do' statements, it will not hold true for all 'ought to be' statements. For NDLT0 allows us to treat an 'ought to do' statement as a particular kind of 'ought to be' statement: one in which the agent exists and the argument of the OB-operator is a disjunction. Hence, I can often use a single argument to deal with both OD- and OB-counterparts of SDL rules and assertions.

However, matters are not quite so simple: sometimes the argument by which I prove an 'ought to be' theorem — or OB-theorem — will not work for the corresponding 'ought to do' theorem — or OD-theorem — without additional conditions. For instance, if 'OD_SF', which implies '$OB(F_S \vee AP_S)$', appears, our formation rules guarantee that 'F_S' and '$\sim F_S \rightarrow AP_S$' are contingent; but for all we know, 'AP_S' might not be contingent. Almost all OD-counterparts of OB-theorems and rules cannot be proved unless we assume that 'AP_S' is contingent. Hence, in this and the next section, whenever I prove an OB-theorem or an OB-rule, NDLT0 makes a separate argument for its OD-counterpart unnecessary, unless the proof of the OD-counterpart requires a condition beyond the contingency of 'AP_S'. Whenever I show a proposed OD-theorem or OD-rule not to be an assertion of NDL, NDLT0 proves that its OB-counterpart — and therefore, its OB-counterpart without special conditions — is not an assertion of NDL.

In this section we look at the inference rules of NDL. Inference rules from the propositional calculus are part of NDL, just as they are part of SDL. These include standard rules of substitutivity and *modus ponens*, as well as the standard derived inference rule: If 'B' follows from the axioms plus the assumption 'A', then 'A → B' follows from the axioms alone. These rules must, as usual, be relativized to specific possible worlds: if 'p' holds in w_1 and 'p → q' in w_2, *modus ponens* cannot uncover any world where 'q' holds.

SDLR1, an inference rule occurring in some standard deontic logics, is an amplified substitution rule. SDLR1 allows substitution of a term for any provably equivalent term, whether these terms are atomic or complex, in any theorem of SDL. Since some theorems of SDL contain occurrences of the deontic operator 'O', SDLR1 licenses the substitution of provable equivalents within deontic contexts. Does a parallel to SDLR1 hold for the NDL logic of 'ought to be' and 'ought to do' statements?

Assume first that '$OB(\ldots p \ldots)$' and 'p ↔ q' are theorems, and assume that neither 'p' nor '~p' is a theorem. By NDLS1$_B$, all $<p^a>$-normal worlds where 'p' is true ► $<p^a>$-counterparts; and by NDLS5$_B$ this is not an empty claim. But since 'p ↔ q' is a theorem, all and only worlds where 'p' is true are worlds where 'q' is true; and all and only worlds where 'p' is false are worlds where 'q' is false. Moreover, all $<p>$-normal worlds are $<q>$-normal, and all $<p>$-alternatives $<q>$-alternatives. Hence, all $<q^a>$-normal worlds where 'q' is true ▸ $<q^a>$-counterparts where 'q' is false and no $<q^a>$ obtains. By NDLS2$_B$, then, 'Oq' is true in this world. Hence we can assert the following rule:

NDLR1$_B$: If 'p ⇌ q' is a theorem, CT'p', and 'OB$_t$(. . . p . . .)' is a theorem; then 'OB$_t$(. . . q . . .)', the result of uniformly replacing 'p' by 'q' in 'OB(. . . p . . .)', is a theorem.

Notice the role played by NDLS5$_B$ in my argument for NDLR1$_B$. Suppose first that our assumptions allowed 'p' to be a theorem. Then there might be no counterpart worlds in which 'p' is false. Suppose instead that our assumptions allowed '~p' to be a theorem. Then '~p' might be true in all worlds, and there would be no counterpart worlds in which 'p' is true. Either assumption would debar us from using NDLS1$_B$ to derive a meaningful statement, because of the rule POSS (see Chapter 14, p. 223). Hence we must assume that neither 'p' nor '~p' is a theorem. But that assumption is not enough to allow us to use NDLS1$_B$ meaningfully; for even though 'p' is true in some worlds and '~p' in other worlds, it might be the case that no world in which '~p' is true is accessible to a given world in which 'p' is true. If that were the case, there would be no counterpart worlds in which 'p' is false; in which case, once again, NDLS1$_B$ could not meaningfully be used. Hence, NDLS5$_B$ is necessary to assure us that there is at least one counterpart world in which 'p' is false; without NDLS5$_B$ or an equivalent, the argument for NDLR1$_B$ could not proceed.

Is NDLR1$_B$ in full accordance with our intuitions? Suppose that necessarily all and only rational creatures have a moral dimension; and suppose that it ought to be that George has a moral dimension. Should we conclude that it ought to be that George be rational? One might think not, if one believes that it ought to be that George has a moral dimension because of some features of having a moral dimension, and that these features are not in any clear way dependent on rationality. That is, if OBp, 'p' ought to be for certain reasons; and those reasons might not apply to 'q', even though ⊢ p ⇌ q.[4]

This objection turns on the difference between meaning equivalence and extensional equivalence. Two extensionally equivalent propositions can have different meanings, and the objection presupposes that whether it ought to be that p is a function of the meaning of 'p'. I do not think the presupposition is correct. Rather, it ought to be that p only if it ought to be that state of affairs <p>, however referred to, actually obtains. It is wrong to suppose that in ordinary deontic thought, '⊢ p ⇀ q' and 'OBp' can hold, but the respect in which 'p' ought to be does not apply to 'q'. If '⊢ p ⇀ q' holds, state of affairs <p> just is state of affairs <q>, and if <p> ought to be, so ought <q>.

In Chapter Five I did argue that deontic contexts are intensional, and one cannot substitute at least extensional equivalents within an intensional context *salva veritate*. But having given in Chapter 14 a semantics for NDL, I have provided a vehicle for substitution in deontic contexts of meaning-equivalents and of expressions designating the same object.

Since NDLR1$_B$ holds, so must its OD-counterpart:

NDLR1$_D$: If 'OD$_{St}$F' and 'F$_S$ ⇀ G$_S$' are theorems, and if CT'AP$_S$' and CT'F$_S$', 'OD$_{St}$G' is a theorem.

We need an explicit condition stating that 'AP$_S$' is contingent, for if 'AP$_S$' should not be contingent, we could not derive 'OB(G$_S$ v AP$_S$)'.

NDL therefore contains counterparts to the inference rule SDLR1, both in the logic of 'ought to do' statements and in the logic of 'ought to be' statements. The opposite is true with counterparts to SDLR2, the rule of O-necessitation. SDLR2 states that if 'p' is a theorem, 'Op' is a theorem. Now suppose that 'F$_S$' is a theorem. Then 'F$_S$' is true in all possible and accessible worlds; there are no worlds in which S fails to do F and is appropriately penalized, nor are there worlds in which S fails to do F and is not appropriately penalized. Hence, by POSS, we cannot meaningfully state that all <AP$_S$^{a}>-normal worlds in which S fails to do F and is appropriately penalized ▸ <AP$_S$^{a}>-counterpart worlds in which S fails to do F and is not appropriately penalized; any such claim would violate NDLS5$_D$. Therefore, we cannot use NDLS2$_D$ to conclude that 'OD$_S$F' is true. Hence the semantics of NDL supports no counterpart in the logic of 'ought to do' statements for SDLR2; and for that reason, there is no OB counterpart for SDLR2, either.

These are reasonable results. As discussed in Chapter 3, people have tried to square the circle, to give a repeating decimal value of pi, and to construct more than five kinds of regular solids in Euclidean space. All of these projects are logically impossible. But it hardly seems reasonable to say that the people who worked on those projects were trying to do what ought not to be, or were trying to do what they should not do.

Turn next to SDLR3, which states that if 'p → q' is a theorem, 'Op → Oq' is a theorem. Suppose that 'p → q' is a theorem and 'OBp' is true. Does NDL semantics allow us to infer that 'OBq' is true? If so, then from the inference rules of the propositional calculus we could conclude that a counterpart of SDLR3 holds for the NDL logic of 'ought to be' statements.

Since we are assuming 'OBp', 'p' must be contingent. By NDLS1$_B$ and NDLS5$_B$ we can infer that all <p^a>-normal worlds in which 'p' is true ▸ <p^a>-counterparts. Since 'p → q' is a theorem, all worlds in which 'p' is true are worlds in which 'q' is true. But we cannot infer that all <q^a>-normal worlds in which 'q' is true ▸ <q^a>-counterparts; for all we know, there might be <q^a>-normal worlds in which 'q' but not 'p' is true, and we have no reason to think such worlds preferable to their counterparts. Moreover, on our assumptions, we do not know that all worlds in which 'p' is false are worlds in which 'q' is false; to know that, we would have to know that 'q → p' is a theorem. Hence, we do not have enough information to conclude that all <p^a>-normal worlds in which 'p' is true ▸ <p^a>-counterparts in which no <q^a> obtains. Nor do we know that <p^a>-normal worlds are <q^a>-normal. Hence, we are far from knowing that all <q^a>-normal worlds in which <q^a> obtains ▸ all <q^a>-counterparts; hence, we cannot apply NDLS2$_B$ to derive 'OBq'. That is, the semantics of NDL does not support a direct counterpart in the logic of 'ought to be' statements to SDLR3.

We can understand this result if we suppose that 'p' and '~q' are logically exclusive OB-alternatives: For instance, let 'p' be 'There is a law against boom boxes' and let 'q' be 'Boom boxes were invented'. In that case, by mutual exclusivity, we can assert that p → q. If OBp, could we conclude that OBq? That is, can we infer from the mere fact that there ought to be a law against boom boxes that it ought to be that those miserable devices were invented? Surely not. The Schotch and Jennings example of the starving poor shows the same point. Necessarily, if we feed the starving poor, then there are starving poor. If it ought to be that we feed the starving poor, we cannot infer that it ought to be that there are starving poor. (For yet another argument against a supposed NDLR3$_B$, see the discussion of NDLT1$_B$ in the next section of this chapter.) Therefore, there is no direct NDL 'ought to be' counterpart to SDLR3.

We might think to find an indirect counterpart, however. For suppose that 'p → q' is a theorem and 'OBq' is true; further, suppose that 'p' is contingent. If we did not confine ourselves to consideration of $<p^a>$-normal worlds, we would be able to infer 'OBp'. That is, from 'p → q', we could infer 'OBq → OBp'. For if we ignore the requirement of $<p^a>$-normality, by NDLS1$_B$ and NDLS5$_B$ we can infer from 'OBq' that all $<q^a>$-normal worlds where $<q^a>$ obtains ▸ $<q^a>$-counterparts, and that there are such worlds. Since 'p → q' is a theorem, we know that all worlds where 'q' is false are worlds where 'p' is false. That is, the set of p-true worlds is a subset of the set of q-true worlds; and the set of q-false worlds is a subset of the set of p-false worlds. Since all worlds where 'p' is true are worlds where 'q' is true, then all worlds where 'p' is true ▸ $<q^a>$-counterparts. And since all worlds where 'q' is false are worlds where 'p' is false, all worlds where 'p' is true ▸ $<q^a>$-counterparts where 'p' is false. By NDLS2$_B$, it follows that 'OBp' is true. This result, as I suggested in the preceding chapter, would be strongly counterintuitive. Among other things, it would mean that if a great evil has as a component part a small good, the fact that the small good ought to be entails that the great evil ought to be.

Hence, the requirement of $<p^a>$-normality should not be ignored. For world w_0 is $<q>$-normal only if there is no 'p' such that 'p → q' is a theorem, 'p' is true in w_0, and some world where 'p' is true is not preferable to some $<p^a>$-counterpart. Now we are assuming there is a $<p>$ such that '⊢ p → q'. Hence, either some world where 'p' is true is not preferable to some $<p^a>$-counterpart, or 'p' is false in every world under consideration. If the former alternative is true, by NDLS2$_B$ ~OBp; and if the latter alternative is true, then statements about all worlds where 'p' is true are empty. In either case, we cannot infer OBp. As Chapter 14 showed, that is a welcome result. For suppose an evil complex to have a good component; even if the good component ought to be, we hardly want to infer that the evil complex ought to be.

Both the semantics of NDL and the counterexamples I have brought lead to the conclusion that we cannot infer 'OBq' from 'OBp' if we are given only that 'p' is either a logically necessary or a logically sufficient condition for 'q'. As we shall see, though, if 'p' is both logically necessary and logically sufficient for 'q', we can infer 'OBp' from 'OBq'. That result will be NDLR4$_B$.

Turn next to the question whether there is an 'ought to do' counterpart of SDLR3. If '$F_s → G_s$' is a theorem and 'OD_sF' is true, can we infer that 'OD_sG' is true? We cannot do so from the information given; but some additional assumptions will allow us to make the inference. For suppose that 'G_S' and '$AP_S{}^a$' are contingent. Because we are assuming that OD_SF, then 'F_S' must be contingent. By our assumptions plus $NDLS1_D$ and $NDLS5_D$, we know that all $<AP_S{}^a>$ -normal worlds where '$\sim F_S.AP_S{}^a$' is true ▸ $<AP_S{}^a>$-counterparts where '$\sim F_S.\sim AP_S{}^a$' is true. Now since '$F_S \to G_S$' is a theorem, all worlds where '$\sim G_S$' is true are worlds where '$\sim F_S$' is true. But we do not know whether any worlds where '$\sim G_S$' is true are worlds in which '$AP_S{}^a$ ' is true. However, if there are $<AP_S{}^a>$-normal worlds where '$\sim G_S.AP_S{}^a$' is true, we know that they are preferable to all $<AP_S{}^a>$-counterparts in which '$\sim F_S.\sim AP_S{}^a$' is true. That includes all worlds in which '$\sim G_S.\sim AP_S{}^a$' is true — if any such worlds exist. Hence, if we knew that S's failure to do G is compatible both with S's being appropriately penalized and with S's not being appropriately penalized, we could infer an NDL_D counterpart of SDLR3, but not otherwise.

Therefore, the following is a rule of NDL:

NDLR3$_D$: $\dfrac{\vdash(F_S \to G_S).CT`AP_S{}'.\ CT`(\sim G_S \to AP_S)'}{\vdash(OD_{St}F \to OD_{St}G)}$

$NDLR3_D$ is closer to our deontic intuitions, I believe, than SDLR3. In the first place, $NDLR3_D$ allows us to infer only that the same agent who ought to do F ought to do G. It thus blocks us from inferring from our duty to feed the starving poor that the poor ought to starve.[5] Second, $NDLR3_D$, unlike SDLR3, does not suppose that S cannot fail to do G, even if S fails to do F. For instance, if George ought tomorrow to repay Joan tomorrow, George will stay alive until tomorrow whether he repays her then or not. $NDLR3_D$, unlike SDLR3, does not allow us to infer that George ought to stay alive until tomorrow. Third, if there is no way of appropriately penalizing George for not staying alive until tomorrow, $NDLR3_D$ will not license us to say that George ought to do so.[6] Fourth, if S's failure to do G is going to bring a penalty no matter what, it seems implausible to say that S ought to be penalized appropriately for not doing G. It is incoherent to suppose that the inevitable can also be appropriate, for appropriateness suggests a choice among alternatives. Thus if S's failure to do G is going to lead to an inevitable penalty, it seems implausible to say that S ought to do G. Hence $NDLR3_D$ is more intuitively plausible than SDLR3.

But $NDLR3_D$ is not free from all the problems that confront SDLR3. If I repay you $10, necessarily — by the meaning of the word 'repay' —

I have borrowed \$10 from you. I ought to repay you \$10. Does it follow that I ought to have borrowed \$10 from you? It does, according to SDLR3; and this result is strongly counterintuitive. But $NDLR3_D$ appears to countenance the same result, provided that at some time I both ought to borrow from you and ought to repay you. For I can indeed fail to have borrowed from you; and if I do, I might or might not be appropriately penalized. Thus the conditions of $NDLR3_D$ are met, and the inference goes through. If so, then NDL might be better off than SDL, but as a reflection of ordinary deontic thinking NDL too falls short.

But, as I argued ·in Chapter 4, most 'ought to do' statements are conditional. I do not have an unconditional obligation to repay you, for I might never have borrowed from you. I ought then to do as follows: given that I have borrowed \$10 from you, to pay you \$10. Then by $NDLS1_D$, we can infer that all $<AP_S^a>$ -normal worlds where I have borrowed the money from you, I do not pay you, and I am appropriately penalized are preferable to $<AP_S^a>$-counterparts where I have borrowed the money from you, I do not pay you, and I am not appropriately penalized. Since this tells us nothing of the relative preferability of worlds in which I do not borrow the money, we cannot infer that I ought to have borrowed the money. Thus the counterexample fails, and $NDLR3_D$ does not need further amendment.

The same strategy wards off a counterexample proposed by Mary Gore Forrester and discussed in Chapter 4. We are likely to assert that if George chews with his mouth closed, George chews; and many would say that George ought to chew with his mouth closed. The conclusion that George ought to chew is unwelcome. But what George ought to do is the following: given that he chews, to chew with his mouth closed. From this we cannot use $NDLR3_D$ to infer that he ought to chew.

Chisholm's contrary-to-duty paradox might seem to raise a difficulty for $NDLR3_D$. Suppose that Jane ought to do F, and that her doing F entails her doing G. By $NDLR3_D$, Jane ought to do G. But suppose further that if she does not do F, it is not the case that she ought to do G. Since she does not do F, it is not the case that she ought to do G. However, the premisses of Chisholm's paradox are plausible only if the time at which Jane ought to do F is different from the time at which she ought to do G; and $NDLR3_D$ applies only to synchronous oughts. $NDLR3_D$ seems safe from counterexamples.

SDL has one other standard inference rule: SDLR4. From the fact that 'p ↔ q' is a theorem, we can derive that 'Op ↔ Oq' is a theorem. This inference rule has an NDL counterpart in the logic of 'ought to be' statements. For suppose that 'p ↔ q' is a theorem and 'OBp' is true. Since 'p' is contingent, so must 'q' be. Since 'OBp' is true, by $NDLS1_B$ and $NDLS5_B$ all $<p^a>$-normal worlds where 'p' is true ▸ all $<p^a>$-counterparts. But since ⊢ p ↔ q, the class of $<p^a>$-normal worlds where 'p' is true is identical to the class of $<p^a>$-normal worlds where 'q' is true; hence, of course, the class of $<p^a>$-normal worlds where 'p' is false is identical to the class of $<p^a>$-normal worlds where 'q' is false. Moreover, since there is no baneful state of affairs that entails 'p', there is no baneful state of affairs that entails 'q'; so the class of $<p^a>$-normal worlds where 'q' is true is identical to the class of $<q^a>$-normal worlds where 'q' is true. And since 'p' and 'q' are true or false together in any given world, any $<p^a>$-counterpart world is a $<q^a>$-counterpart world. Hence, all $<q^a>$-normal worlds where $<q^a>$ obtains ▸ all $<q^a>$-counterparts. Hence, by $NDLS2_B$, 'OBq' is true. Likewise, by assuming the truth of 'OBq' we can prove that of 'OBp'. Therefore, the following is a rule of NDL:

$NDLR4_B$: $\underline{\vdash (p ↔ q)}$
$\vdash(Ob_tp ↔ OB_tq)$.

Since $NDLR4_B$ is a rule of NDL, so is the following:

$NDLR4_D$: $\underline{\vdash(F_S ↔ G_S).CT`AP_S'}$
$\vdash(OD_{St}F ↔ OD_{St}G)$.

Both inference rules are plausible, although neither appears to be particularly valuable.

That concludes our look at the inference rules of NDL. We turn next to the question whether typical asserted propositions of SDL have analogues in NDL.

3. ASSERTED PROPOSITIONS

In Chapter 2, I listed eleven asserted propositions of SDL. In this section of Chapter 15, I shall look at each of these propositions, to determine which of them has counterparts in the NDL logics of 'ought to be' and of 'ought to do' statements. Because of NDLT0, I need not argue for the 'ought to do' counterpart of any 'ought to be' theorem, unless the counterpart requires conditions beyond the contingency of 'AP$_S$'; and having disproved a proposed 'ought to do' theorem, I need not give an additional disproof of its 'ought to be' counterpart.

The eleven typical asserted propositions of standard deontic logic are as follows:

SDLT1. $\vdash \sim(Op.O\sim p)$.
SDLT2. $\vdash O(p \rightarrow q) \rightarrow (Op \rightarrow Oq)$.
SDLT3. $\vdash O(p.q) \rightarrow (Op.Oq)$.
SDLT4. $\vdash (Op.Oq) \rightarrow O(p.q)$.
SDLT5. $\vdash \sim O(p.\sim p)$.
SDLT6. $\vdash O(p \vee \sim p)$.
SDLT7. $\vdash Op \leftrightarrow \sim P\sim p$.
SDLT8. $\vdash Pp \leftrightarrow \sim O\sim p$.
SDLT9. $\vdash Op \rightarrow Pp$.
SDLT10. $\vdash OOp \leftrightarrow Op$.
SDLT11. $\vdash O(Op \rightarrow p)$.

To provide a road map through this section, I shall preface the number of each SDL asserted proposition, in boldface, to my discussion of possible NDL counterparts to that proposition.

1. The direct 'ought to be' NDL counterpart of SDLT1 is '$\sim(OBp.OB\sim p)$', which is a theorem of NDL. For if not, there is some sentence 'p' such that $OBp.OB\sim p$, whence both OBp and $OB\sim p$. Then, by NDLS1$_B$, 'p' is a member of a set $\{p, q, r, \ldots\}$ of OB-alternatives, such that all $<p^a>$-normal worlds containing any member of the set are preferable to their $<p^a>$-counterparts in which all members of the set are false. And similarly, '$\sim p$' is a member of a set of OB-alternatives. (Note that 'p' and '$\sim p$' are not members of the *same* set of OB-alternatives; for if they were, the rule POSS would mandate that there are worlds in which both 'p' and '$\sim p$' are false — which is impossible.) Now consider a $<p^a>$-normal world w_1 in which 'p' holds, as well as a $<\sim p^a>$-normal world w_2 which differs from w_1 only in the falsity of 'p' and in any facts which flow from that falsity. Clearly w_1 is a $<p^a>$-counterpart of w_2; but just as clearly, w_2 is a $<\sim p^a>$-counterpart of w_1. Hence, since OBp, $w_1 \blacktriangleright w_2$; but since $OB\sim p$, $w_2 \blacktriangleright w_1$. By the rule ASYM, the asymmetricality of the '$\blacktriangleright$' relation, this is impossible. Therefore, the assumption that there could be a value of 'p' such that $OBp.OB\sim p$ has led to an impossibility, and the theorem follows.

Hence, the following is a theorem of NDL:

NDLT1$_B$: $\vdash \sim(OB_t p . OB_t \sim p)$.

So, therefore, is an OD-counterpart of NDLT1$_D$; but as it requires a special condition, I need to argue for it separately.

It might look as if NDLT1$_B$ will run into difficulties with NDLR4$_B$:

$\vdash(p \rightarrow q)$

$\vdash(Ob_t p \rightarrow OB_t q)$.

For suppose that 'p' and '$\sim$q' are OB-alternatives and that $\vdash (p \rightarrow q)$. Then since '$\sim$q' is an OB-alternative, OB$\sim$q. And since 'p' is an OB-alternative, OBp; whence, by NDLR4$_B$, OBq — which contradicts NDLT1$_B$. But I derived the contradiction by the logical equivalent of dividing by zero. For if $\vdash (p \rightarrow q)$, then every world is either one in which 'p' holds or one in which '$\sim$q' holds, but not both. But then, 'p' and '$\sim$q' cannot be OB-alternatives. For on the assumption that OBp, all $<p^a>$-normal worlds in which $<p^a>$ obtains $\blacktriangleright$ all $<p^a>$-counterpart. If '$\sim$q' were an OB-alternative to 'p', then there would be no worlds which do not hold a $<p^a>$. And that would violate the rule POSS. Hence, our suppositions that $\vdash (p \rightarrow q)$ and that 'p' and '$\sim$q' are OB-alternatives turn out to contradict one another.

This result, I believe, fits with our intuitions. If the world must be in exactly one of two states, it hardly makes sense to claim that both of those states ought to be. The obvious question arises: "They ought to be instead of what?" In ordinary deontic speech, to say that a state of affairs ought to be at least suggests that it is not true that certain other states of affairs ought to be. The effect of the rule POSS is to draw NDL closer to that intuition.

It is worth noting that, if NDL semantics allowed a rule NDLR3$_B$,

$\vdash (p \rightarrow q)$

$\vdash (OB_t p \rightarrow OB_t q)$

we could derive a contradiction from NDLT1$_B$. For one OB-alternative often excludes another: If there ought to be a law against boom boxes, it is not the case that boom boxes were never invented. Hence '$\vdash(p \rightarrow q)$' is perfectly consistent with the claim that 'p' and '$\sim$q' are OB-alternatives; and we could derive 'OBq.OB$\sim$q'. Therefore, NDLT1$_B$ provides one more reason for rejecting NDLR3$_B$.

The OD-counterpart of SDLT1 would be '$\sim(OD_s F . OD_s \sim F)$'. If we use the same argument I gave for NDLT1$_B$, we start by assuming this false, in which case $OB(F_S \lor AP_S).OB \sim (F_S \lor AP_S)$. We would argue as before that $<(F_S \lor AP_S)^a>$-normal world w_1 where $<(F_S \lor AP_S)^a>$ obtains ▸ $<(F_S \lor AP_S)^a>$-counterpart w_2, and that w_2 ▸ w_1. But now let us assume that $OB(AP_S)$, in which case all $<AP_S^a>$-normal worlds in which 'AP_S' is true ▸ all $<AP_S^a>$-counterparts. Now 'F_S' is either true in w_1 and w_2 or it is false in both, since w_1 and w_2 differ only with respect to the truth or falsity of '$F_S \lor AP_S$' and its implications. If 'F_S' is true in w_1 and w_2, '$F_S \lor AP_S$' will be true in both worlds, and world w_2 will by definition not exist. If 'F_S' is false in w_1 and w_2, then in both worlds '$F_S \lor AP_S$' reduces to 'AP_S', in which case 'AP_S' will be true in w_1 and false in w_2. But in that case w_1 and w_2 will be $<AP_S^a>$-counterparts and it will be false that w_2 ▸ w_1. Hence, whether 'F_S' is true in both worlds or false in both worlds, if '$OB(AP_S)$' is true we cannot derive a contradiction. Therefore, the OD-counterpart of NDLT1$_B$ must specifically include a provision that '$OB(AP_S)$' is false. Hence, the following is an assertion of NDL:

NDLT1$_D$: ⊢ $\sim OB_t AP_S \to \sim(OD_{St}F.OD_{St}\sim F)$.

The assumption that 'AP_S' is contingent follows from the fact that the antecedent of an asserted conditional, NDLT1$_D$, must be a wff.

The fact that there is no simple assertion denying contradictory obligations is a plus, not a minus, for NDL. For as I discussed in Chapter 3, it is part of ordinary deontic thought that persons sometimes do have conflicting obligations. NDL, unlike SDL, does not rule out conflicting obligations; therefore, unlike the other system, NDL does not have to try to explain away a major discrepancy with our ordinary deontic thought.

However, NDLT1$_D$ does rule out contradictory obligations, so long as it is false that the person in question ought to be appropriately penalized no matter what. Now there is nothing illogical in the claim that someone ought to be penalized no matter what. Such a claim, given the usual goals for which we use deontic language, might be practically useless, but nothing prevents people from using 'ought' language for other than the usual goals. A religious legislator anxious to show that all people deserve damnation would have no difficulty accepting the proposition that people ought to be penalized whatever they do. Such religious legislators might well be considered immoral or even vicious, but they should not be considered illogical.[7]

In sum, then, NDLT1$_S$ bans conflicting obligations, but only if one's deontic code, on practical or ethical grounds, forbids the claim that people ought to be penalized, whatever they do. Since not all codes do in fact forbid that claim, NDL countenances the possibility of contradictory obligations. It is therefore closer to ordinary deontic thought than is SDL.

2. Turn next to SDLT2, '$O(p \to q) \to (Op \to Oq)$'. Here we start with the NDL logic of 'ought to do' statements. A direct OD-counterpart of SDLT2 would read: '$[OD_S(F \lor G).OD_S{\sim}F] \to OD_SG$'. If this is false, then $OD_S(F \lor G).OD_S{\sim}F.{\sim}OD_SG$. Assume that S's being appropriately penalized is a contingent matter. By $NDLS1_D$, $NDLS2_D$, and $NDLS5_D$ we know that: (1) all $<AP_S{}^a>$-normal worlds in which '${\sim}F_S.{\sim}G_S.APS^a$' is true ▸ all $<AP_S{}^a>$-counterparts in which '${\sim}F_S.{\sim}G_S.{\sim}AP_S{}^a$' is true; (2) all $<AP_S{}^a>$-normal worlds in which '$F_SAP_S{}^a$' is true ▸ all $<AP_S{}^a>$-counterparts in which '$F_S.{\sim}AP_S{}^a$' is true; and (3) some $<AP_S{}^a>$-normal world w_1 in which '${\sim}G_S.AP_S{}^a$' is true ~▸ some $<AP_S{}^a>$-counterpart w_2 in which '${\sim}G_S.{\sim}AP_S{}^a$' is true. Now since w_1 and w_2 are $<AP_S{}^a>$-counterparts, they do not differ with respect to the truth value of '${\sim}F_S$' — provided that neither '$F_S \to AP_S$' nor its negation is a theorem. Should '${\sim}F_S$' be true in w_1 and w_2, then '${\sim}F_S.{\sim}G_S.AP_S{}^a$' is true in w_1 and '${\sim}F_S.{\sim}G_S.{\sim}AP_S{}^a$' is true in w_2 — which contradicts (1); and should '${\sim}F_S$' be false in w_1 and w_2, then '$F_S.AP_S{}^a$' is true in w_1 and '$F_S.{\sim}AP_S{}^a$' is true in w_2 — which contradicts (2). Therefore, so long as $<AP_S>$ is contingent, the assumption that '$OD_S(F \lor G).OD_S{\sim}F.{\sim}OD_SG$' is false has led to a contradiction. NDL therefore asserts the following:

NDLT2$_D$: $\vdash OD_{St}(F \lor G).OD_{St}{\sim}F.CT'AP_S'.CT'(F_S \to AP_S)' \to OD_{St}G.$

NDLT2$_D$ allows an inference I said in Chapter 1 that any deontic logic needs: If Tamino ought to go through one of the three doors, and if he ought not to go through either of the first two, he ought to go through the third. However, Chapter 3 might seem to provide a counterexample to NDLT2$_D$. Suppose that there are two equally rotten candidates for election, one ought to vote in the election, and one ought not to vote for Candidate A. Surely we cannot infer that one ought to vote for Candidate B. But we can defang the counterexample if we recall, once again, that 'ought to do' statements are almost always conditional in form. What does it mean to say that one ought not to vote for Candidate A? If it means that one ought not to vote for A no matter what, or if it means that one ought not to vote for A given that the only other choice is B, then we surely can infer that one ought to vote for B. If, however, the supposition that one ought not to vote for A means only something like "One ought not to vote for A if there are better candidates," then the stipulation that A and B are equally rotten defeats the condition that there are better candidates than A, and the conditional obligation statement "One ought not to vote for A" would not be true. Whatever "One ought not to vote for A" means, then, the case fails as a counterexample to $NDLT2_D$.

The situation is not the same if we examine a proposed $NDLT2_B$, 'OB(p v q).OB~p → OBq'. If this is false, OB(p v q).OB~p.~OBq. Since 'p', 'q', and 'p v q' are all contingent propositions, we can use $NDLS1_B$ and $NDLS2_B$ to conclude the following: (1) All $<p^a>$-normal worlds where a $<p^a>$ does not obtain ► all $<p^a>$-counterparts; (2) All $<(p \text{ v } q)^a>$-normal worlds where $<(p \text{ v } q)^a>$ obtains ► all $<(p \text{ v } q)^a>$-counterparts; and (3) Some $<q^a>$-normal world w_1 where 'q' is true ~► some $<q^a>$-counterpart w_2. Now we can again note that, unless 'q' implies 'p', the truth-value of 'p' must be constant from w_1 to w_2. But suppose 'p' is true in both w_1 and w_2; we then know that some $<q^a>$-normal world where 'p' holds ~► some $<q^a>$ counterpart where 'p' holds. Even if the sets of $<p^a>$-normal, $<(p \text{ → } q)^a>$-normal, and $<q^a>$-normal worlds were identical, this result would obviously not violate (1). It would not violate (2), either, because 'p v q' would be true in both w_1 and w_2. Suppose again that 'p' is false in both w_1 and w_2. Then again, even if the sets of worlds were identical, we could derive no contradiction. For (1) tells us nothing about worlds in which 'p' does not hold; and (2) has nothing to add, because 'q' and hence 'p v q' is true in w_1 and false in w_2. Therefore, assuming that the proposed theorem is false does not lead to a contradiction, and $NDLT2_B$ fails. The specific OD-theorem therefore has no OB-counterpart.

This result should not be unexpected. Perhaps the world will be improved if $<\sim p>$ obtains, and perhaps the world will be improved if $<p \text{ v } q>$ obtains, but it need not be improved if $<\sim p.(p \text{ v } q)>$ obtains. And even if the world would be improved whenever $<\sim p.(p \text{ v } q)>$ obtains, it does not follow that the world would be improved whenever $<q>$ obtains. For 'q' can be true in $<q>$-normal worlds where '$\sim p.(p \text{ v } q)$' is not. We therefore have no reason to think $NDLT2_B$ correct.

We can see the difference between 'ought to do' and 'ought to be' on this point if we return to the example of voting for rotten candidates. It ought to be that I vote for A or for B, and it ought not to be that I vote for A — but it ought not to be that I vote for B, either. It is often best to have a choice, even if neither of the two choices deserves to be picked. From the mere fact that it ought to be that we do not pick the first, we can hardly infer that it ought to be that we do pick the second. We should remember that in SDL, quite rightly, 'O(p v q)' does not imply 'Op v Oq'. That it ought to be that either X is chosen or Y is chosen does not imply that either it ought to be that X is chosen or it ought to be that Y is chosen. And therefore, we cannot infer Y's fitness from X's unfitness to be chosen.

Notice that reinterpreting the example as we did in the case of NDLT2$_D$ does not help. "It ought not to be that one votes for A," "It ought not to be that one votes for B," and "It ought to be that one votes for A or for B" all seem unconditional.

3. I turn next to SDLT3: 'O(p.q) → (Op.Oq)', the direct counterpart of which is 'OB(p.q) → (OBp.OBq)'. If this is false, then OB(p.q).(~OBp v ~OBq), which is equivalent to [OB(p.q).~OBp] v [OB(p.q).~OBq]. Take the first disjunct. Since 'p.q' and 'p' are contingent, by NDLS1$_B$ and NDLS2$_B$: (1) all <(p.q)^a>-normal worlds in which a <(p.q)^a> obtains ▸ all <(p.q)^a>-counterpart worlds; and (2) at least one <p^a>-normal world w_1 in which a <p^a> obtains ~▸ some <p^a>-counterpart w_2. (1) and (2) entail no contradiction, so long as 'q' is not true in w_1 and w_2; and 'q' is not true in w_1 and w_2 only if 'p → q' is not a theorem. By a similar situation, the second disjunct is a possibility, but only if 'q → p' is not a theorem. Therefore, the following is a theorem of NDL:

NDLT3$_B$: ⊢ [⊢(p ↔ q).OB$_t$(p.q)] → (Ob$_t$p.OB$_t$q).

That is, if 'p ↔ q' is a theorem, and if OB(p.q), then OBp.OBq. NDLT3$_B$ is far more circumscribed than its SDL counterpart. From the fact that a complex state of affairs ought to be, we can derive that each of its components ought to be *only if* the proposition that one component exists is logically equivalent to the proposition that any of the other components exists. Hence, from the fact that it ought to be that you get up and get to work, we cannot infer that it ought to be that you get up, nor can we infer that it ought to be that you get to work; for getting up is not logically equivalent to getting to work. NDLT3$_B$ is therefore of very little use in our deontic reasoning.

But a stronger principle, such as SDLT3, would not accord well with ordinary deontic reasoning. Often, as both Leibniz and Chapters 3 and 10 remind us, a complex state of affairs ought to be, even though not all of the components are good in themselves. Perhaps the world is better off if it contains both poor people and charitable assistance than if it contained neither, but that hardly means that the world is always better off containing poor people than it would have been without poor people. To say that a complex whole ought to be then does not imply that each of the components ought to be — unless each of the components implies the others. Since there could be poor people without charitable assistance, $NDLT3_B$, unlike SDLT3, will not let us draw the counterintuitive conclusion that there ought to be poor people.

One implicit restriction of $NDLT3_B$ deserves some comment. It is not enough that 'p' and 'q' be contingent; so must 'p.q'. That means, in part, that we cannot substitute '~p' for 'q' in $NDLT3_B$, or make any similar maneuver. The provision that 'p ↔ q' be a theorem effectively disallows any such substitution, as does the fact that 'OB(p.q)' is a wff.

From the fact that $NDLT3_B$ is a theorem, we can infer that there must be a theorem $NDLT3_D$. The direct counterpart to $NDLT3_B$ would be: '$OD_S(F.G).(F_S ↔ G_S) → (OD_SF.OD_SG)$'. But in fact, we can prove a stronger theorem. Suppose that $OD_S(F.G)$. Provided that 'AP_S' is contingent, by $NDLS1_D$ and $NDLS5_D$ all $<AP_S^a>$-normal worlds where '$~(F_S.G_S).AP_S^a$' is true ► all $<AP_S^a>$-counterparts where '$~(F_S.G_S).~AP_S^a$' is true. That is, all $<AP_S^a>$-normal worlds where *either* '$~F_S.AP_S^a$' *or* '$~G_S.AP_S^a$' is true ► all $<AP_S^a>$-counterparts where *either* '$~F_S.~AP_S^a$' *or* '$~G_S.~AP_S^a$' is true. But, by the definition of '$<p^a>$-counterpart', the $<AP_S^a>$-counterparts to worlds where '$~F_S.AP_S^a$' is true are worlds where '$~F_S.~AP_S^a$' is true; and the $<AP_S^a>$-counterparts to worlds where '$~G_S.AP_S^a$' is true are worlds where '$~G_S.~AP_S^a$' is true. Hence, all $<AP_S^a>$-normal worlds where '$~F_S.AP_S^a$' is true ► all $<AP_S^a>$-counterparts where '$~F_S.~AP_S^a$' is true, and all $<AP_S^a>$-normal worlds where '$~G_S.AP_S^a$' is true ► all $<AP_S^a>$-counterparts where '$~G_S.~AP_S^a$' is true. Since 'F_S', 'G_S', and 'AP_S' are all contingent, we can invoke $NDLS2_D$ and conclude that 'OD_SF' and 'OD_SG' are both true. Discharging our premiss that $OD_S(F.G)$, we have the theorem:

$NDLT3_D$: ⊢ $[CT'AP_S'.OD_{St}(F.G)] → (OD_{St}F.OD_{St}G)$.

So long as it is contingent that S is appropriately penalized, then if S ought to do both F and G, S ought to do F and S ought to do G. Hence, with one added condition, $NDLT3_D$ is a direct counterpart to SDLT3. If you ought to do both chores, you ought to do each. Even if doing the first chore is worthless without doing the second, you still ought to do the first.

"After all," as Mary Gore Forrester once remarked, "'X ought to do A' does not imply that X ought to do A *only*."

$NDLT3_D$ seems highly plausible, whereas a less restricted version of $NDLT3_B$ is not. Perhaps it ought to be that you do two things, but one is only causally necessary and not sufficient for the other. For example, it ought to be that you both live and pay me the money that you owe me; for it ought to be that you pay me the money, and you could not do that unless you live. But if your obligation is to perform a pair of actions, then you are obligated to perform each of the pair.

4. To SDLT4, '$(Op.Oq) \to O(p.q)$' NDL asserts neither an 'ought to do' nor an 'ought to be' counterpart. The reason is the same in both cases: SDLT4 does not take account of OB-alternatives. Nor can we amend it to allow for OB-alternatives without turning it into a truth-functional platitude. Since the failure of an OD-version of SDLT4 implies the failure of an OB-version, we need disprove only the OD-version.

The NDL 'ought to do' version of SDLT4 would be '$(OD_S F. OD_S G) \to OD(F_S.G_S)$', the negation of which is '$OD_S F. OD_S G. \sim OD_S (F.G)$'. Suppose that '$F_S \vee AP_S$' and '$G_S \vee AP_S$' are OB-alternatives — that is, either '$\vdash (F_S \vee AP_S) \to \sim(G_S \vee AP_S)$' or '$OB(F_S \vee AP_S). OB(G_S \vee AP_S). \sim OB[(F_S \vee AP_S).(G_S \vee AP_S)]$' is correct. But '$F_S \to \sim G_S$' cannot be correct, for then '$\sim OD_S(F.G)$' would be ill formed. Therefore, '$OB(\sim F_S \to AP_S). OB(\sim G_S \to AP_S). \sim OB[(\sim F_S \to AP_S).(\sim G_S \to AP_S)]$' is correct. But '$OB(\sim F_S \to AP_S). OB(\sim G_S \to AP_S). \sim OB[(\sim F_S \to AP_S).(\sim G_S \to AP_S)$' is equivalent to '$OD_S F. OD_S G. \sim OD_S(F.G)$'. Therefore, if '$\sim F_S \to AP_S$' and '$\sim G_S \to AP_S$' are OB-alternatives, the supposed $NDLT4_D$ must be false. We might try to alter the supposed $NDLT4_D$ by adding as a condition that '$\sim F_S \to AP_S$' and '$\sim G_S \to AP_S$' are not OB-alternatives. But that condition, as we have seen, implies $NDLT4_D$. To be sure, we can infer any proposition from itself; but that is a mere truth-functional tautology, of no peculiarly deontic value. Therefore, an amended version of $NDLT4_D$ fails. And with the failure of $NDLT4_D$, of course, $NDLT4_B$ also bites the dust.

We can confirm these results by looking at a promising argument for $NDLT4_B$. Assume that '$OBp.OBq$' is true. Then since 'p' and 'q' are contingent, by $NDLS1_B$ and $NDLS5_B$ all $<p^a>$-normal worlds where $<p^a>$ obtains ► all $<p^a>$-counterparts; and all $<q^a>$-normal worlds where $<q^a>$ obtains ► all $<q^a>$-counterparts. Nothing, however, follows about $<p.q>^a$-normal worlds. For if $<p>$ and $<q>$ are OB-alternatives, it would follow from the definition of "OB-alternative" that either there are no worlds in which $<$p.q$>$ obtains, or else at least one $<$(p.q)$^a>$-normal world where $<$(p.q)$^a>$ obtains $\sim\triangleright$ all $<$(p.q)$^a>$- counterparts where no $<$(p.q)$^a>$ obtains. In either case, we cannot use NDLS2$_B$ to infer 'OB(p.q)' — which confirms that the supposed NDLT4$_B$ is false.

The failure of the supposed NDLT4$_B$ confirms the analysis of Chapter 14. If each two events ought at a certain time to be, the two might be OB-alternatives. They could be mutually exclusive solutions to a problem, or their joint occurrence might not improve the world. In neither case can we infer that it ought to be that both take place.

To confirm that NDLT4$_D$ fails, look at an argument for it. The NDL direct version of SDLT4 would be: '(OD$_S$F.OD$_S$G) $\rightarrow$ OD$_S$(F.G)'. Assume the contrary, 'OD$_S$F.OD$_S$G. $\sim$OD$_S$(F.G)'. If 'AP$_S$' is contingent, we can apply NDLS1$_D$ and NDLS5$_D$ to determine: (1) that all $<$AP$_S$$^a>$-normal worlds in which '$\sim$F$_S$.AP$_S$^{a}' is true $\triangleright$ all $<$AP$_S$$^a>$-counterparts in which '$\sim$F$_S$.$\sim$AP$_S$^{a}' is true; (2) that all $<$AP$_S$$^a>$-normal worlds in which '$\sim$G$_S$.AP$_S$^{a}' is true $\triangleright$ all $<$AP$_S$$^a>$-counterparts in which '$\sim$G$_S$.$\sim$AP$_S$^{a}' is true; (3) that some $<$AP$_S$$^a>$-normal world w_1 in which '$\sim$(F$_S$.G$_S$).AP$_S$^{a}' is true $\sim\triangleright$ some $<$AP$_S$$^a>$-counterpart w_2 in which '$\sim$(F$_S$.G$_S$).$\sim$AP$_S$^{a}' is true. Hence, '$\sim$(F$_S$.G$_S$)' is true in both w_1 and w_2. But since w_1 and w_2 are $<$AP$_S$$^a>$-normal counterparts, they differ only with respect to $<$AP$_S$$^a>$ and its effects and consequences. Hence, unless $<$F$_S>$ is an effect of $<$AP$_S$$^a>$ or 'F$_S$' a consequence of 'AP$_S$^{a}', if '$\sim$F$_S$' is true in w_1, it is true in w_2; and the same holds for '$\sim$G$_S$'. Therefore, either '$\sim$F$_S$' is true in both w_1 and w_2, or '$\sim$G$_S$' is true in both worlds. If the first is true, (1) and (3) contradict one another; if the second is true, (2) and (3) contradict one another. Therefore, assuming that '(OD$_S$F.OD$_S$G) $\rightarrow$ OD$_S$(F.G)' is false has led to a contradiction.

The argument might look good, but it assumed, among other things, that 'OD$_S$F.OD$_S$G' designates a possible state of affairs that can be assumed true. But if $<$F$_S>$ and $<$G$_S>$ are OB-alternatives, that assumption is false, and the argument fails. The argument cannot prove NDLT4$_D$, which confirms that NDLT4$_D$ is not an assertion of NDL.

This result seems reasonable to anyone who believes that a person S can have obligations both to do F and to do G, even though S's doing both F and G would be worse than doing neither — and who concludes that in such a case S should not do both F and G. If a cook-in-training is told by one superior that she should add a tablespoon of cayenne pepper to a dish and is told by another that she should add a tablespoon of red pepper oil, and if adding both would make the dish inedible, I find it entirely reasonable to assert that she should add the cayenne, that she should add the oil, but that she should not add both. Or, to use an example of Walter Sinnott-Armstrong, a professor ought to counsel student A at 3 p.m. and ought to counsel student B at 3 p.m., but ought not to counsel both at 3 p.m. [Sinnott-Armstrong 2, 130-133]

5. Next we turn to Kant's Principle, SDLT5: '~O(p.~p)'. The direct counterpart in NDL 'ought to be' logic would be '~OB(p.~p)', which by NDLF3$_B$ is ill formed. Hence, there cannot be an NDLT5$_B$.

Ordinary deontic intuitions are, I suspect, undetermined as to whether an explicit contradiction ought or ought not to be. There seems no practical stake in deciding the matter, since contradictions simply will not occur. However, a hidden contradiction is another matter. As I mentioned in Chapter 3, people have tried to do things that, unknown to them, were logically impossible — for example, to square the circle. Some such attempts were no doubt well intentioned, and others were no doubt wicked. There seems no reason to suppose either that failure in all such efforts ought to be, or that in all such efforts it is not the case that there should be success. Hence NDL, in refusing to assert an analogue of Kant's Principle for 'ought to be' statements, seems slightly closer to deontic intuitions than SDL.

As happened with SDLT2 and SDLT3, the 'ought to do' counterpart of Kant's Principle, '~OD$_S$(F.~F)', fares better. For if it is false, then 'OD$_S$(F.~F)', from which by NDLT0, 'OB[(F $_S$ v ~F)$_S$ v AP]$_S$' or 'OB(AP$_S$)' follows. Therefore, the following is a theorem of NDL:

NDLT5$_D$: ⊢ ~OB$_t$(AP$_S$) → ~OD$_{St}$(F.~F).

If it is false that S ought to be appropriately penalized whether S does F or not, then it is not the case that S ought to do both F and not-F. We do not need to build an explicit statement of the contingency of 'AP$_S$' into the antecedent of NDLT5$_D$, for '~OB$_t$(AP$_S$)' must be well formed.

NDLT5$_D$ is, I believe, considerably closer to ordinary deontic thought than is SDLT5. For, unfortunately for S, some people believe S ought to be appropriately penalized no matter what, and such people have no logical difficulty in assigning S conflicting obligations. A legal system out to entrap the innocent might provide for conflicting duties, because it assumes its victims ought to be punished whatever they do. Thus where

SDL finds logical inconsistency, NDL and common sense agree in finding a logically possible, if morally objectionable, position.

6. SDLT6 asserts that $O(p \lor \sim p)$, the NDL OD-counterpart of which is '$OD_S(F \lor \sim F)$'. But the semantical rules of NDL cannot be applied to this statement. We cannot use $NDLS1_D$ to say "All $\langle AP_S{}^a \rangle$-normal worlds where '$\sim (F_S \lor \sim F_S).AP_S{}^a$' is true $\blacktriangleright$ all $\langle AP_S{}^a \rangle$-counterparts where '$\sim (F_S \lor \sim F_S). \sim AP_S{}^a$' is true." For a world in which '$\sim (F_S \lor \sim F_S)$' obtains would be an impossible possible world; and the relation '$\blacktriangleright$' connects only possible worlds. Therefore, NDL semantics cannot be used to argue for an 'ought to do' counterpart of SDLT6. For that reason, then, it cannot be used to argue for an 'ought to be' counterpart of SDLT6; in fact, '$OB(p \lor \sim p)$' is not even a well-formed formula in NDL.

As with SDLT5, I see a small but genuine advantage to NDL in its refusal to assert an OB-counterpart to SDLT6. With explicit tautologies, ordinary deontic thought is unlikely to care whether we assert or deny that they ought to be; we usually reserve 'ought to be' claims for what we think might, but need not, be the case. But some hidden tautologies might look good and some bad; ordinary deontic thought is not likely to suppose that they all ought to be. Thus NDL, in not giving an 'ought to be' counterpart to SDLT6, has a slight advantage over SDL.

The advantage of NDL over SDL is greater with the failure of $NDLT6_D$. We ordinarily do not say that someone ought to do something unless we think he has a good, practical reason for doing it — whether that reason lies in his nature, his position, or the likely outcome of his action. SDLT6 says that we all have positive duties to do the tautologous; since we will do the tautologous anyway, how could anyone have a practical reason for so doing? Thus SDLT6, in saying that we ought to do a number of things which we have no reason to do, departs considerably from common deontic thought. NDL is much closer to ordinary thought in this regard.

7. SDLT7, SDLT8, and SDLT9 all concern the logical relations between obligation and permission. SDLT7 states that $Op \leftrightarrow \sim P\sim p$. Its direct counterpart in the NDL logic of 'ought to be' statements is '$OBp \leftrightarrow \sim PB\sim p$'. And, given the usual restriction to contingent propositions, this is an assertion of NDL. For by $NDLS3_B$ and $NDLS4_B$, 'PBp' is equivalent to "Some $\langle \sim p^a \rangle$-normal world w_1 where a $\langle \sim p^a \rangle$ obtains $\sim\blacktriangleright$ some $\langle \sim p^a \rangle$-counterpart w_2." Therefore, '$PB\sim p$' is equivalent to "Some $\langle p^a \rangle$-normal world w_1 where a $\langle p^a \rangle$ obtains $\sim\blacktriangleright$ some $\langle p^a \rangle$-counterpart w_2." Hence,

'~PB~p' is equivalent to "All $<p^a>$-normal worlds in which a $<p^a>$ obtains ► all $<p^a>$-counterparts;" which by $NDLS1_B$ and $NDLS2_B$ is equivalent to 'OBp'. Hence, the following is an assertion of NDL:

NDLT7$_B$: ⊢ $OB_t p → \sim PB_t \sim p$.

For any contingent proposition 'p', it ought to be that p if and only if it is not permissible that not-p.

Much the same result happens with the 'ought to do' analogue of SDLT7: $OD_S F → \sim PD_S \sim F$. But there is a difference: If S ought to do A or if S is permitted to do A, then S exists; but if it is not the case that S ought to do A, or if it is not the case that S is permitted to do A, we do not know whether S exists. ("Sorry, sir, you cannot order Jones to go on patrol tonight, because he's dead, sir.") Hence the analogue to SDLT7 is '$OD_S F → [E!S. \sim PD_S \sim F]$'. Assume that '$AP_S$' is contingent. Then by $NDLS3_D$ and $NDLS4_D$, '$PD_S F$' is equivalent to "E!S. Some $<AP_S{}^a>$-normal world w_1 in which $<F_S → AP_S{}^a>$ obtains ~► some $<AP_S{}^a>$-counterpart w_2 in which $<F_S. \sim AP_S{}^a>$ obtains." Therefore, 'PD $\sim$F' is equivalent to "E!S. Some $<AP_S{}^a>$-normal world w_1 in which $<F_S \vee AP_S{}^a>$ obtains ~► some $<AP_S{}^a>$-counterpart in which $<\sim F_S. \sim AP_S{}^a>$ obtains." Hence, '$\sim PD_S \sim F$' is equivalent to "E!S.All $<AP_S{}^a>$-normal worlds in which $<F_S \vee AP_S>$ obtains ► all $<AP_S{}^a>$-counterparts in which $<\sim F_S. \sim AP_S>$ obtains;" which, by $NDLS1_D$ and $NDLS2_D$, is equivalent to '$OD_S F$'. The following is therefore an assertion of NDL:

NDLT7$_D$: ⊢ CT'AP_S' → $[OD_{St} F → (E!S. \sim PD_{St} \sim F)]$.

So long as it is contingent that S does F and contingent that S is appropriately penalized, S ought to do F if and only if: (1) S exists; and (2) it is not permissible that S fail to do F.

The restrictions on $NDLT7_D$ and $NDLT7_B$ bring them closer to ordinary deontic thought than is SDLT7. Both versions of NDLT7 allow 'ought' operators only with contingent propositions; one would expect this restriction if, as I believe, ordinary deontic thought keeps silent on the appropriateness of terming necessary or impossible situations obligatory. Again, ordinary deontic thought allows it to be possible, as NDL does, that a person ought to do what that person is not permitted to do, provided that the person must be penalized no matter what. Finally, saying that S ought to do something implies S's existence, while saying that it is not the case that S is permitted to do something does not imply S's existence.

Now if 'q ⊣ r' and 'q ⊣ s' are asserted, so is 'r ⊣ s'. Therefore, it cannot be the case that 'OD$_S$F ⊣ ~PD$_S$~F' is a theorem of deontic logic; for if it were, since 'OD$_S$F' implies 'S exists', so would '~PD$_S$F'. Hence NDLT7$_D$ is more accurate as an account of ordinary deontic thought than SDLT7.

8. The same considerations apply to counterparts of SDLT8: 'Pp ⊣ ~O~p'. If we assume PBp, since 'p' is contingent, we can use NDLS3$_B$, NDLS5$_B$, and then NDLS2$_B$ to prove ~OB~p; whereas if we assume ~OB~p, since 'p' is contingent, we can use NDLS1$_B$, NDLS5$_B$ and then NDLS4$_B$ to prove PBp. Hence, the following is asserted in NDL:

NDLT8$_B$: ⊢ PB$_t$p ⊣ ~OB$_t$~p.

So long as 'p' is contingent, then it may be that p if and only if it is false that not-p ought to be.

Again, if we assume that 'PD$_S$F' is true and that 'F$_S$' and 'AP$_S$' are contingent, 'E!S' follows by NDLS3$_D$. By NDLS3$_D$, NDLS5$_D$, and NDLS2$_D$, '~OD$_S$~F' follows. If we assume instead that 'E!S.~OD$_S$~F' is true and 'F$_S$' and 'AP$_S$' contingent, by NDLS1$_D$, NDLS5$_D$, and NDLS4$_D$, it follows that PD$_S$F. Hence the following is asserted in NDL:

NDLT8$_D$: ⊢ CT'AP$_S$' → [PD$_{St}$F ⊣ E!S.~OD$_{St}$~F].

Provided that it is contingent that S is appropriately penalized, S may do F if and only if S exists and it is not the case that S ought to fail to do F.

The NDLT8 formulations have the same advantages over SDLT8 that the NDLT7 formulations have over SDLT7, with one change. With NDLT7, we considered what ordinary deontic thought would have to say in the case where it is necessary that a person be appropriately penalized; with NDLT8, we must consider the reaction of ordinary deontic thought where appropriate penalty is impossible. If a person cannot be penalized no matter what for doing A, ordinary deontic thought might well allow that the person is permitted to do A. This again represents a minuscule advantage for NDL over SDL.

9. Next, we come to SDLT9: 'Op → Pp'. The direct 'ought to be' counterpart to SDLT9 is 'OBp → PBp'. If OBp, then 'p' is contingent. Since by NDLT1$_B$ ~(OBp.OB~p), it follows truth-functionally that ~OB~p; which by NDLT8$_B$ is equivalent to PBp. Hence, discharging the premises, we have:

NDLT9$_B$: $\vdash OB_t p \rightarrow PB_t p$.

If 'p' is contingent and <p> ought to be, it is permissible that <p> obtain. This is surely a plausible principle.

There must therefore be an NDLT9$_D$; but, as with NDLT5$_D$ we must add an important condition. For suppose $\sim(OD_S F \rightarrow PD_S F)$, or $OD_S F. \sim PD_S F$. Since $OD_S F$, E!S and CT'AP$_S$'; therefore, by NDLT8$_D$, $OD_S \sim F$. By NDLT5$_D$, OB(AP$_S$). Hence, NDLT9$_D$ must read not as '$OD_S F \rightarrow PD_S F$' but as the following:

NDLT9$_D$: $\vdash \sim OB_t AP_S \rightarrow (OD_{St} F \rightarrow PD_{St} F)$.

Provided that it is not the case that S ought to be appropriately penalized no matter what, if S ought to do F, it is permissible for S to do F. Again, as with NDLT5$_D$, if S ought to be appropriately penalized, NDL formation rules for 'ought to be' statements require that 'S is appropriately punished' is contingent.

NDLT9$_D$ reflects the fact that persons do sometimes have conflicting obligations; the mere fact that you ought to stay on the farm to help your mother is compatible with the claim that doing so is not permissible. If you are in a genuine dilemma, then it ought to be that you are appropriately penalized whether you stay or not. But if it is false that it ought to be that you are appropriately penalized, your obligations do not conflict.

10. We come next to SDLT10: $OOp \leftrightarrow Op$. By our formation rules, the only possible NDL 'ought to do' counterpart to SDL10 would be '$OB(OD_S F) \leftrightarrow OD_S F$'. The semantic translation of '$OB(OD_S F)$' is "All $<OD_S F^a>$-normal worlds in which $<OD_S F^a>$ holds $\blacktriangleright$ all $<OD_S F^a>$-counterparts;" the semantic translation of '$OD_S F$' is "All $<AP_S^a>$-normal worlds in which '$\sim F_S. AP_S^a$' is true $\blacktriangleright$ all $<AP_S^a>$-counterparts in which '$\sim F_S. \sim AP_S$' is true." Since not everything is an obligation, some worlds in which S does F are not worlds in which S is appropriately punished for not doing F, and since some obligations are not performed, some worlds in which S is appropriately punished for not doing F are not worlds in which S does F. Therefore, nothing about $<OD_S F^a>$ worlds proves anything about $<AP_S^a>$ worlds, and vice versa. There is no NDLT10$_D$; and therefore, there is no NDLT10$_B$.

These are results we should have expected from the discussions in section 3 of Chapter 7 and in Chapter 10. We can assert that the world would be better if preaching would improve it, but it does not follow that preaching will in fact improve the world. Thus 'OB(OBp)' does not imply 'OBp'. And even if the sacraments are the means of grace, we need not assert that it ought to be that they are — i.e., we need not assert that it ought to be that it ought to be that people take the sacraments. Again, it ought to be that John ought to fight a sea battle tomorrow, but John is under no such obligation — perhaps because he does not exist! Jane ought to prepare to atone for her future sins; but in at least some better worlds, she will not commit those sins and thus need not prepare to atone for them.

11. SDLT11 stated that $\vdash O(Op \rightarrow p)$. The only possible OD-counterpart would be '$OB(OD_SF \rightarrow F_S)$'. Assume '$OB(OD_SF \rightarrow F_S)$' false; by $NDLT7_B$, '$PB(OD_SF . \sim F_S)$' holds. Then by $NDLS3_B$, some $<(OD_SF \rightarrow F_S)^a>$-normal world w_1 where a $<(OD_SF \rightarrow F_S)^a>$ obtains $\sim\blacktriangleright$ some $<(OD_SF \rightarrow F_S)^a>$-counterpart w_2 where $<(OD_SF . \sim F_S)^a>$ obtains. There is no absurdity in asserting that world w_1 is not preferable to w_2. Doing one's duty need not improve the world, nor does NDL semantics imply that it does. From '$OB(F_S \vee AP_S)$', we cannot infer 'OBF_S'; we could not make that inference even if we also assumed '$OB \sim AP_S$', for there is no $NDLT2_B$. Hence, no absurdity resulted from assuming it false that $OB(OD_SF \rightarrow F_S)$, and NDL asserts no 'ought to do' counterpart of SDLT11. Therefore, NDL contains no OB-counterpart either.

Nor should versions of SDLT11 hold in NDL, according to my argument in section 3 of Chapters 7 and in Chapter 10. The slothful person can deny that it ought to be that, if it ought to be that people take the sacraments they actually take them, as she can deny that it ought to be that, if people ought to take the sacraments they actually take them. We surely can deny that it ought to be that a concentration camp guard do whatever he ought, under his orders, to do.

That completes the list of important propositions which are asserted within NDL. Next we shall see whether NDL goes beyond SDL in asserting any of the important claims that SDL left unasserted.

4. UNASSERTED PROPOSITIONS

In Chapter 2, I listed six propositions which, for good reason, are not asserted in most standard deontic logics. The six are as follows:

SDLX1. p → Pp.
SDLX2. Pp → p.
SDLX3. p → Op.
SDLX4. Op → p.
SDLX5. O(p v q) → (Op v Oq).
SDLX6. (Pp.Pq) → P(p.q).

I shall argue in the present section that NDL, like SDL, does not assert versions of these six propositions. This result is to be expected, as all the propositions we have found to be asserted in NDL are restricted versions of asserted propositions in SDL, except for NDLT0; and NDLT0 could be added as a definition to SDL. Unless we can find some assertions peculiar to NDL, our examination indicates that NDL is a proper subset of SDL: Every assertion of NDL is an assertion of SDL, but not vice versa. If that is so, any consistency proof for SDL will serve as a consistency proof for NDL.

SDLX1 and SDLX2 together claim that Pp ↔ p. NDL obviously does not assert either side of the biconditional 'PB ↔ p'. From the fact that 'p' is true in this world, we cannot infer anything about preferability relations between two worlds; and from relations between two worlds, nothing about this world follows — even though the only worlds under consideration are the real world and its branches. The world might not be very evil, as the old hymn would have it, but it is false that the world logically must be very good.

Likewise, NDL clearly will not assert either side of the biconditional 'PD$_S$F ↔ F$_S$'. Even if some world where if S does F, S is appropriately penalized is not preferable to some world where S does F and is not appropriately penalized, that tells us nothing about whether S does F in the real world. Likewise, if we know that S does F in the real world, we do not know whether some world where S does F and is appropriately penalized is not preferable to some world where S does F and is not appropriately penalized. Hence, NDL, like SDL, asserts no version of SDLX1 or of SDLX2.

SDLX3 and SDLX4 together claim that Op ↔ p. NDL certainly will not assert either side of the biconditional 'OBp ↔ p'. For again, what obtains in this world does not establish preferability between two worlds, nor does preferability between two worlds tell us what is true in this world. Only an additional, Panglossian assumption that everything in this world is as it ought to be could justify such an assertion.

Similarly, NDL will not assert either side of the biconditional '$OD_SF \leftrightarrow F_S$'. If S does F in this world, it might or might not be the case that all worlds in which S fails to do F and is appropriately penalized are preferable to counterpart worlds in which S fails to do F and is not so penalized. Conversely, if all worlds in which S fails to do F and is appropriately penalized are preferable to counterpart worlds in which S fails to do F and is not so penalized, it might or might not be the case that S does F in the real world. Alas, we do not always do our duty in this world. Thus NDL, like SDL, refuses to assert versions of SDLX3 and SDLX4.

SDLX5 claims that 'ought' is distributed over disjunctions: '$O(p \lor q) \to (Op \lor Oq)$'. We need consider only the 'ought to do' analogue of SDLX5: $OD_S(F \lor G) \to (OD_SF \lor OD_SG)$. Suppose that $OD_S(F \lor G).\sim OD_SF.\sim OD_SG$. By $NDLS1_D$ and $NDLS2_D$, we know the following: All $<AP_S^a>$-normal worlds where if S does neither F nor G, S receives an appropriate-penalty-alternative $\triangleright$ all $<AP_S^a>$-counterparts where S does neither F nor G and does not receive an appropriate-penalty-alternative; some $<AP_S^a>$-normal world w_1 where if S does not do F, S receives an appropriate-penalty-alternative $\sim\triangleright$ some $<AP_S^a>$-counterpart world w_2 where S does not do F and receives no $<AP_S$-alternative$>$; and some $<AP_S^a>$-normal world w_3 where if S does not do G, S receives an appropriate-penalty-alternative $\sim\triangleright$ some $<AP_S^a>$-counterpart world w_4 where S does not do G and receives no $<AP_S>$-alternative. These three circumstances are all perfectly consistent, so long as S does G in w_1 and w_2, F in w_3 and w_4. Hence, assuming the negation of the NDL OD-counterpart of SDLX5 does not lead to a contradiction. NDL therefore does not assert an $NDLX5_D$, and hence it asserts no $NDLX5_B$ either.

Finally, SDLX6 states that if each of two states of affairs is permissible, they are jointly permissible. Given the equivalence between 'Op' and '$\sim P\sim p$' stated in SDLT7, SDLX6 is equivalent to SDLX5; to reject one is to reject the other. However, since NDL accepts only qualified versions of SDLT7, we should consider NDL counterparts to SDLX6 in their own right.

We need consider only the OD-counterpart of SDLX6: '$(PD_SF.PD_SG) \to PD_S(F.G)$'. Suppose this false; then $PD_SF.PD_SG.\sim PD_S(F.G)$. From $NDLS3_D$ and $NDLS4_D$ we can infer the following: Some $<AP_S^a>$-normal world w_1 where '$F_S \to AP_S^a$' is true $\sim\triangleright$ some $<AP_S^a>$-counterpart w_2 where

'$F_S. \sim AP_S{}^a$' is true; some $<AP_S{}^a>$-normal world w_3 where '$G_S \rightarrow AP_S{}^a$' is true $\sim\blacktriangleright$ some $<AP_S{}^a>$-counterpart w_4 where '$G_S. \sim AP_S{}^a$' is true; and every $<AP_S{}^a>$-normal world where '$(F_S.G_S) \rightarrow AP_S{}^a$' holds $\blacktriangleright$ every $<AP_S{}^a>$-counterpart where '$(F_S.G_S). \sim AP_S{}^a$' is true. Assume that 'G_S' is false in w_1 and w_2, 'F_S' false in w_3 and w_4. Then worlds w_2 and w_4 will not be worlds in which '$F_S.G_S$' is true; and the relations of worlds w_1, w_2, w_3, and w_4 will not contradict the claim that every $<AP_S{}^a>$-normal world where '$(F_S.G_S) \rightarrow AP_S{}^a$' is true $\blacktriangleright$ every $<AP_S{}^a>$-counterpart where '$(F_S.G_S). \sim AP_S{}^a$' is true. Hence, assuming the converse of an 'ought to do' analogue of SDLX6 does not lead to a contradiction; and NDL does not assert NDLX6$_D$. Therefore, neither does NDL assert NDLX6$_B$.

Hence, of the six propositions that standard deontic logics usually, and quite rightly, decline to assert, NDL asserts no analogues, either in the logic of 'ought to do' or in the logic of 'ought to be' statements.

In addition to counterparts of propositions not asserted in SDL, NDL does not assert a certain proposition which cannot even be formed in SDL. This is the point I argued in Chapter 4: that 'ought to do' statements neither imply nor are implied by corresponding 'ought to be' statements. In NDL, this would be:

NDLX0: $OBF_S \rightarrow OD_SF$.

Just as NDLT0 is the fundamental theorem of NDL, so is NDLX0 the fundamental non-theorem.

If NDLX0 is false, then $OBF_S. \sim OD_SF \vee \sim OBF_S OD_SF$. The first of these disjuncts is, by NDLT0, equivalent to '$OBF_S. \sim [E!S.OB(F_S \vee AP_S)]$', and thus to '$OBF_S. \sim E!S \vee OBF_S. \sim OB(F_S \vee AP_S)$'. We must consider three cases: '$OBF_S. \sim E!S$', '$OBF_S. \sim OB(F_S \vee AP_S)$', and '$\sim OBF_S. OD_SF$'. I shall show that none of the three entails a contradiction:

- '$OBF_S. \sim E!S$' entails no contradiction; for it could be true that all $<F_s{}^a>$-normal worlds in which '$F_s{}^a$' holds $\blacktriangleright$ all $<F_s{}^a>$-counterparts, even though S does not exist in the real world. So long as the real world is not an $<F_s{}^a>$-normal world in which S does F, there is no contradiction.
- '$OBF_S. \sim OB(F_S \vee AP_S)$' is equivalent by NDL semantics to "All $<F_s{}^a>$-normal worlds in which an $<F_s{}^a>$ obtains $\blacktriangleright$ all $<F_s{}^a>$-counterparts, and some $<(F_S \vee AP_S)^a>$-normal world w_1 in which an $<(F_S \vee AP_S)^a>$ obtains $\sim\blacktriangleright$ some $<(F_S \vee AP_S)^a>$-counterpart w_2." If no $<F_s{}^a>$ obtains in w_1 and w_2, then w_1 and w_2, even if they are $<F_s{}^a>$-normal, do not

contradict the hypothesis that all $\langle F_s^a \rangle$-normal worlds in which an $\langle F_s^a \rangle$ obtains ► all $\langle F_s^a \rangle$-counterparts. Hence, this case leads to no contradiction.

- '$\sim OBF_s.OD_SF$' is by NDLT0 equivalent to '$\sim OBF_S.E!S.OB(F_S$ v $AP_S)$', and by NDL semantics to "S exists, and some $\langle F_s^a \rangle$-normal world w_1 in which an $\langle F_s^a \rangle$ obtains $\sim$ ► some $\langle F_s^a \rangle$-counterpart w_2, and all $\langle (F_S$ v $AP_S)^a \rangle$-normal worlds in which an $\langle (F_S$ v $AP_S)^a \rangle$ obtains $\sim$ ► all $\langle (F_S$ v $AP_S)^a \rangle$-counterparts." If 'AP_S' is true in w_1 and w_2 there is no contradiction; for w_2 is not a world in which no $\langle (F_S$ v $AP_S)^a \rangle$ obtains.

Since assuming NDLX0 false does not lead in any of these three cases to a contradiction, NDL does not assert NDLX0.

This is an important result for NDL, for it confirms that NDL formalizes the non-equivalence between 'ought to be' and counterpart 'ought to do' expressions for which I argued in Chapter 4. Whereas SDL cannot even state NDLX0, NDL proves that NDLX0 is not a theorem.

That completes our look at the system NDL: definitions, semantics, formation rules, rules of inference, typical assertions, and non-asserted propositions. Now I must try to justify NDL.

5. JUSTIFICATION OF NDL

A system of logic needs two kinds of justification. The first is internal: the system must be free from contradictions, ambiguities, and paradoxes. The second is external: the system must give us all important inferences and not license any important bad inferences. Much of the internal justification has already been given. Those rules of inference and asserted propositions of NDL that we have examined are counterparts of rules, axioms, and theorems of Standard Deontic Logic; only NDLT0 has no counterpart in SDL. The rules and assertions of NDL are more restricted than those of SDL. For a tabular representation of these claims, see Appendix 1. Therefore, if SDL is consistent, so is NDL.

What about the various paradoxes? Alf Ross's paradox can be derived in NDL for 'ought to do' statements. For from NDLR3$_D$, '$(OD_SF$ v $OD_SG) \rightarrow OD_S(F$ v $G)$' follows, provided that 'F_S', 'G_S', '$\sim G_S.AP_S$', and '$\sim G_S.\sim AP_S$' are all contingent.[8] Suppose that these propositions are indeed contingent, and assume OD_SF. Then OD_SF v OD_SG, whence $OD_S(F$ v $G)$. But if S genuinely ought to do F, and if S's doing G is morally reprehensible, it seems as if S's duty to do the disjunctive act <F v G> can be fulfilled by his doing the reprehensible act G.

But Ross's paradox is not really a paradox. S can fulfill his obligation to do <F v G> by doing G, but that will not fulfill his duty to do F. S has, it seems, an unending list of disjunctive duties; he can perform each of those duties by doing F, his non-disjunctive duty, but he cannot perform F by doing any of the acts disjoined with F. If we assume, reasonably enough, that S ought to do *all* the things he ought to do, doing F is his only moral alternative; doing G will get him nowhere.

The four assumptions of Chisholm's contrary-to-duty paradox are:

(A) S ought to do F.
(B) S ought to do the following: if F then G.
(C) If S does not do F, it is not the case that S ought to do G.
(D) S does not do F.

As I argued in Chapter 9, these premisses generate a plausible contradiction only if they involve different ought times. S's duty to do G exists at one time, S's not having a duty to do G exists at another. Since NDL rules work only for synchronous obligations, Chisholm's paradox is no paradox in NDL.

The Good Samaritan is not derivable in NDL. Let 'Fsa' stand for 'S helps a' and 'Gsa' stand for 'S throttles a'. Then we can assert '(Fsa.Gsa) $\to$ Gsa'. If we could assert that OD_S(Fa.Ga), and if the usual contingencies hold, then by $NDLR3_D$ we would have the unwelcome '$\vdash OD_S Ga$'. But, of course, we have no reason to assert 'OD_S(Fa.Ga)'. That Jane does both help and throttle Richard does not mean that she should do both.

Åqvist's variant is also not derivable. If Smith knows Jones will rob the bank, Jones will rob the bank. But $NDLR3_D$ has as the operative portion of its premiss '$F_S \to G_S$', not '$F_S \to G_N$'. One might, however, try a variant on Åqvist's version: Smith, the person hired to find out about potential bank robbers, herself plans to rob the bank. Now if Smith knows Smith will rob the bank, Smith will rob the bank. And if Smith ought to know Smith will rob the bank, then it seems to follow that Smith ought to rob the bank. But with NDL semantics, it is easy to deny that Smith ought to know that Smith will rob the bank. For is it likely that all worlds where Smith does not know she will rob the bank and receives an appropriate penalty are morally preferable to counterparts where Smith does not know she will rob the bank and receives no such penalty? Certainly not: Among those worlds where Smith does not know she will rob the bank are worlds in which she does not rob the bank. And there is no reason to expect that even if she does not rob the bank, it is better for her to be penalized. Thus Åqvist's variant fails to disturb NDL.

My way of dealing with Åqvist's variant is of a piece with my earlier discussion of Chisholm's paradox. A genuine understanding of all such paradoxes requires the premiss that duties occur in a causal and changing world. Because the world changes, what one ought to do is not necessarily the same from moment to moment. Only a deontic semantics that incorporates causal and temporal structures can expect to tame these paradoxes. And NDL benefits from such a semantics.

If we remember from Chapter 4 that what we ought to do is usually only some aspect of a given action, my 'gentle murders' paradox holds no danger for NDL. To say that Smith ought to murder Jones gently is to say that Smith ought, given that she murders Jones, to do so gently. That is, all $<AP_s^a>$-normal worlds in which Smith murders Jones and either murders him gently or receives an appropriate penalty are preferable to all $<AP_s^a>$-counterpart worlds in which Smith murders Jones, does not murder him gently, and does not receive an appropriate penalty. One cannot infer from this that all $<AP_s^a>$-normal worlds in which either Smith murders Jones or she receives an appropriate penalty are preferable to all $<AP_s^a>$-counterparts in which she does not murder Jones and does not receive an appropriate penalty. One cannot, that is, infer that Smith ought to murder Jones. The 'gentle murders' inference simply does not follow in NDL.

However, the 'gentle murders' case, as well as my discussion of $NDLR3_D$ and $NDLT2_D$, suggests a warning. In applying NDL principles, one should remember that 'ought to do' statements are generally conditional. Many seemingly paradoxical inferences stem from taking a conditional obligation statement as unconditional. Those who make such inferences might blame deontic logic for the odd results, when the fault lies in their application of sound logical principles.

NDL has to this point shown no sign of producing unwelcome inferences. For the most part, NDL appears to be a stripped down version of Standard Deontic Logic. All the rules and assertions we have found for NDL are counterparts of rules and assertions in SDL, except for NDLT0. Hence, if NDL avoids the problems of SDL by forgoing some of the latter's rules and assertions, what NDL does assert should be acceptable.

The only likely problems people might have with NDL's rules and assertions concerns NDLR3$_D$.[9] Geoffrey Sayre-McCord, as I noted in Chapter 3, provides two objections to Bas van Fraassen's version of this principle. [Sayre-McCord and van Fraassen, *passim*] Sayre-McCord's first objection is that NDLR3$_D$ and similar rules allow the derivation of Alf Ross's paradox. [Sayre-McCord, 188] I argued above that Ross's paradox has no bite against NDL.

Sayre-McCord's second objection centers on a moral dilemma: S ought to do F and ought not to do F. Principle SDLT4 asserts that $(Op.Oq) \rightarrow O(p.q)$. Therefore S ought to do: F and not-F. But 'p.~p' implies any proposition whatsoever. Hence, '$F_S.~F_S$' implies any 'G_S'. By NDLR3$_D$, given the usual contingency requirements, S ought to do G. If there are moral dilemmas, then, everything is obligatory — and, Sayre-McCord might add, everything is forbidden. [Sayre-McCord, 190] However, since NDL contains no analogue of SDLT4, Sayre-McCord's argument does not arise in NDL.

Whether NDL is too stripped down to allow us all the inferences we want from a deontic logic is a far more difficult question. A full answer would require presentation of an axiomatic version of NDL, a task beyond the scope of a mere philosophic groundwork for a new deontic logic. But four considerations gives at least provisional reason to think NDL a sufficient system to meet our deontic needs:

(1) In each case where NDL asserts no parallel version of SDL rules or asserted propositions, I found good reason to reject candidates. That is, where NDL differs from standard deontic logic, I have found the advantage to lie with NDL. NDL, unlike SDL, can account adequately for Chisholm's paradox and various versions of the Good Samaritan, for the formation of new duties and the cessation of old ones, for moral codes that obligate us to do the impossible, for the differences in behavior between the two sorts of 'oughts', for moral dilemmas, and for a host of other features of ordinary deontic thought. What NDL does not give us in the way of inferences, then, we have some reason not to want.

(2) Where NDL does have parallels to SDL, those parallels are usually more hedged by restrictions than their SDL counterparts. The restrictions generally take the form of requiring that relevant non-deontic propositions be contingent, for the results of prefixing deontic

operators to logically necessary or logically impossible propositions
are not well formed. Also some NDL OD-assertions presuppose that
it not be the case that it ought to be that an agent is appropriately
penalized no matter what the agent does in a given situation. In
genuine decision-making, these restrictions pose no great problems.
I rarely find myself trying to decide whether I should do the
impossible, since whatever I decide I will not be able to do the
impossible; nor do I spend much time deciding to do the necessary,
since I will do it anyway. That NDL, unlike SDL, has no application
to non-contingent propositions is then no practical problem for NDL.
Likewise, non-Augustinians rarely assume that agents ought to be
penalized whatever they do. Hence, the restrictions NDL imposes
upon assertions of SDL should have no major impact on actual deontic
practice.

(3) As I argued in *Why You Should*, what looks like a matter of logic
is often better viewed as a matter of pragmatics. A supposed logical
implication might better be taken as a Gricean implicature. Although
Kant's Principle, 'Ought' implies 'Can', is not asserted or even
formulable in the NDL logic of 'ought to be' statements, there is under
normal conditions little point in supposing that a state of affairs ought
to be unless we think that state of affairs at least possible. A failure of
NDL to give us all the inferences we think we want might be best made
up by supplementing our logic with pragmatics, not by adding to our
logic.

   Needless to say, I would recommend the deontic pragmatics of my
Why You Should. But that self-serving recommendation aside, I need
only point out that apparent gaps in a logic need not be made up for by
that logic.

(4) Most of our specifically deontic reasoning — as opposed to
theoretical reasoning, or means-ends reasoning, or the calculation of
utilities — concerns what we ought to do, not what ought to be. What
we ought to do is almost always a directly practical matter; what ought
to be is, as Chapter 4 suggests, often a matter of wish. Intimately
connected with this fact is the fact that we find less structure in our
reasoning concerning what ought to be than we do in our reasoning
concerning what we ought to do. Our thought about wishes can be
amorphous in a way that our determination of our actions cannot be.
NDL captures this situation nicely. NDLT2_D, NDLT3_D, and NDLT5_D

are all important principles of deontic reasoning; the only one of the three that has even a severely restricted OB-counterpart is NDLT3$_D$. If deontic pragmatics must fill in the gaps NDL leaves in deontic logic, then, it will find those gaps where they belong: in the logic of 'ought to be' statements.

After a severe criticism of older versions of deontic logic, I have now presented a new system of deontic logic. NDL escapes the charges I brought against older deontic logics, and it presents some virtues of its own.

At long last, we are back to the Tertullian question with which I began this book: What does ethics have to do with logic? My answer is that there is indeed a logic of ethics. It is not peculiar to ethics, for it is a logic of all sorts of oughts. It contains no substantive moral claims. Locke's dream was a pipe dream. And yet the logic of ethics is more than the plain propositional calculus that structures other branches of study. At least so far as its logic goes, ethics is not merely a continuation of science by other means.

Athens is not a suburb of Jerusalem, nor is Jerusalem a suburb of Athens. But the two cities have more intercourse with one another than a skeptic might suppose. In this book, I have sought to give a map listing the roads between the cities.

But one big question remains: Even if NDL has gotten deontic logic right, what good is deontic logic? My argument throughout the book has assumed that the aim of those who do deontic logic is to codify at least a portion of our practical reasoning. In the final chapter of this book, I shall see how well that aim is met.

Part III

Deontic Logic and Practical Reasoning

Chapter 16: Deontic Logic and Practical Reasoning

I have now given an account of NDL, my new system of deontic logic. I have explained why I believe NDL is preferable to standard systems of deontic logic. One task remains: to explain why NDL should be of interest to philosophers. Because the task is both huge and somewhat tangential to the main purpose of this book, this chapter will be more a sketch than an exhaustive discussion. Perhaps another book is necessary to do justice to the issues I raise here.

I shall amplify and defend a position taken in Chapter 1: that NDL can serve as the basis for understanding practical reasoning. Deontic statements have truth values, so that some inferences that make use of deontic statements are deductively valid. But deontic statements are often used prescriptively, to get people to do certain actions, and the conclusion of a practical inference is usually considered a prescriptive statement. Therefore, deontic statements can serve as conclusions of valid practical inferences, and we should be able to use NDL to show the deductive validity of at least some practical reasoning. So I claimed at the book's outset; at the book's conclusion we are in a better position to assess my claim.

To begin with, the arguments of this book suggest that the 'ought' statements which have immediate practical force are 'ought to do' statements. Considerations of what ought to be are usually optative, as Chapter 4 suggested: They indicate what we would like to see happen. They carry with them no judgment as to whether what ought to be will or even can actually happen, and they ascribe no obligation to bring about what ought to be. If 'ought to be' statements are action-guiding, it is only by means of their pragmatic, non-logical connection with 'ought to do' statements.

Our thought of what we ought to do guides our actions. It is not our only guide, nor is it always a successful guide; but it is a guide. Therefore, considerations of what we ought to do are directly relevant to our choice of actions, whereas considerations of what ought to be are at most indirectly relevant, through the pragmatic tie between 'ought to be' and corresponding 'ought to do' statements.

Deontic logic, at least as it concerns 'ought to do' statements, is therefore part of the logic of practical decision-making. It is a practical logic that deontic logicians have, I believe, been after. The question of this chapter is whether the NDL logic of 'ought to do' statements can serve as a general logic of practical reasoning.

We all engage in practical reasoning, and we think we can tell good practical reasoning from bad. We consider various factors, whether moral, legal, or prudential, whether relevant or irrelevant, whether justifiable or unjustifiable, in determining what we or others are to do. Moreover, we have little hesitation in supposing that people sometimes make mistakes in practical reasoning: One person has failed to consider a factor, another has given a factor the wrong weight, and yet another has failed to see the full relevance of a factor. Nevertheless, as yet we have no agreed-upon logic of practical reasoning.

Before Aristotle the same situation obtained for theoretical reasoning. People argued, both well and badly, before they knew about logic, just as they spoke grammatically before anyone codified rules of grammar. It was the manifest success of some arguments and the clear failure of others that allowed Aristotle to discern and state the principles of syllogistic reasoning. Similarly, we might expect a latter-day Aristotle to codify the principles of practical reasoning. Some have indeed tried.

A large stumbling block stands in the way of any agreement on the logic of practical reasoning. Aristotle supposed that the conclusion of a piece of practical reason is an action; most theorists today think that practical reasoning ends in a decision or intention to act in a certain way, or an order or entreaty that another person act in a certain way. But whether practical reasoning leads to actions or to prescriptions, it does not seem on any account to lead to statements having a truth value.[1] Since only statements having truth-value can serve as conclusions of valid inferences, it follows that there can be no valid practical inferences, nor can there be a logic of practical reasoning.

The difficulty is not minor. First, suppose that Aristotle was right in thinking the conclusion of a piece of practical reasoning to be an action. Since an action is not a statement, the conclusion of a practical inference is neither true nor false. Next, suppose that the conclusion of practical reasoning is a prescriptive statement. To make a statement of one's decision or intention is not, or at least need not be, to report on a previous mental act; rather, to make the statement is, at least sometimes, to decide or to intend. Hence, "I *will* go to town tomorrow" is a performative utterance; and unlike a report, performatives are neither true nor false. Similarly, orders and entreaties are in the imperative mode and therefore have no truth-value. Hence, whether we adopt Aristotle's account of practical reasoning or modern alternatives, it seems that the conclusions of practical reasoning are neither true nor false. Therefore, practical reasoning cannot be valid or invalid.

The rules of deductive logic enable us to determine which arguments are valid and which are not. Without the concept of deductive validity, the notion of logical rules is empty at best. Further, a valid deductive argument is, by definition, one in which, if the premises are true, the conclusion must be true. An invalid deductive argument is one in which the truth of the premises does not guarantee the truth of the conclusion. Valid arguments are then truth-preserving; invalid arguments need not be so. But if the conclusion of a piece of practical reasoning is neither true nor false, then no truth present in the premises is preserved in the conclusion. Therefore, practical reasoning cannot be valid, and the notion of rules of practical reasoning is empty. We cannot hope to develop a logic of practical reasoning so long as practical reasoning issues only in actions, intentions, decisions, orders, or entreaties.

However, deontic statements provide a way in which practical reasoning can be both valid and prescriptive. If the conclusion of a piece of practical reasoning is a prescription, one can formulate that prescription as a deontic statement. I can cast my decisions or intentions in the form of first-person deontic statements: "I ought to help that old lady." Similarly, I can cast my orders or entreaties in the form of second- or third-person deontic statements: "You and he really ought to help those old ladies." The prescriptive conclusions of practical reasoning therefore seem to be equivalent to deontic statements. But deontic statements have truth value: Either it is true or it is false that I ought to help that old lady. Hence, arguments whose conclusions are deontic statements can be truth-preserving. Therefore, practical arguments, at least those which issue in deontic statements or their equivalents, can be valid. Thanks to deontic statements, there is indeed a logic of practical reasoning: deontic logic.

We might conclude that a properly formulated deontic logic, which I take to be NDL, is uniquely qualified to serve as the general logic of practical reasoning, because deontic conclusions alone have both truth value and prescriptive force. However, solving the problems of practical reasoning is not as easy as my argument suggests. At least three major problems stand in the way of our taking NDL as the logic of practical reasoning:

(1) Some non-cognitivists have argued that deontic statements do not in fact have a truth-value. An ethical emotivist, for example, would take my statement that you should not steal my money to be an expression of my negative attitudes toward your stealing my money. And expressions of attitudes are neither true nor false. If the emotivist is right, the very notion of deductively valid deontic reasoning is absurd.

(2) In *Why You Should*, I argued that deontic statements are not intrinsically prescriptive; it is obvious that deontic utterances regarding the past, for example, cannot be prescriptive.[2] Therefore, deontic statements cannot be equivalent to statements which are intrinsically prescriptive, such as imperatives.

(3) Most philosophers today would allow that deontic statements have a truth-value and can be used prescriptively. But prescriptive use is not determined by the meaning of deontic statements, for the same deontic statement can be used both prescriptively and non-prescriptively. Logical relations, on the other hand, depend on sentence meaning. Hence, although a deontic statement might follow deductively from a set of deontic premises, we cannot infer that the deontic conclusion is prescriptive — even if the premises are. But we are assuming that the conclusion of practical reasoning is prescriptive. Therefore, deontic logic does not provide a logic of practical reasoning; it does not even provide a logic of deontic practical reasoning.

The first of these problems does not need much discussion, as we can easily avoid giving a full post-mortem on non-cognitivism. In Chapter 15, I argued that certain reasonable patterns of argument unavailable in purely truth-functional logic are valid in NDL; defenders of other varieties of deontic logic would make the same claim for their preferred systems. Rigorous non-cognitivists must then shoulder the burden of proof, to show why none of these apparently valid patterns of argument can be trusted.

They must provide specific counterexamples; merely repeating their general metaethical principles will not do. Less rigorous non-cognitivists who accept some deontic inference patterns must show that those patterns they accept can be derived from ordinary non-deontic truth-functional logic, supplemented at most by certain definitions. Neither prospect looks promising.

The remaining two problems call for considerably more discussion. In *Why You Should*, I argued that there are three main uses of deontic speech: directive or prescriptive, judgmental, and informative. [J. Forrester 1, Chapter 3] The latter two senses are not in any straightforward way prescriptive: I can intelligibly assert that Caesar ought not to have crossed the Rubicon or that it is permissible for starving people to resort to cannibalism, although in neither case am I prescribing any actions for any persons. My purpose in making such assertions is simply to express my judgment on the matters I speak of, perhaps in order to apprise my listener of the extent of the moral law. Prescriptivity is therefore not built into the *meaning* of deontic statements. Rather, it is a feature of how those statements are often, but not always, *used*. Hence, prescriptivity has to do with the pragmatics of deontic statements, not with their semantics.

On the other hand, orders and entreaties are imperatives; they are by their very meaning attempts to influence actions. If any sentence means the same as "Please shut the door," uttering that sentence would surely be an attempt to get the listener to shut the door. Likewise, statements of decision and intention seem to be a kind of prescription to one's self. Thus "I *will* complete that project, although I am sure I will not complete it" is not self-contradictory but merely pathetic: The speaker is giving herself a prescription which she predicts she will not carry out. If decisions and intentions, like orders and entreaties, are by their very meaning prescriptive, they cannot be equivalent in meaning to deontic statements, which are not by their very meaning prescriptive.

NDLR3$_D$ validates the following inference:

(1) You ought to discover the criminal's identity.
    You ought to act as follows: if you discover the criminal's identity, to bring her to justice.
    Therefore, you ought to bring the criminal to justice.

Compare the following:

(II) Discover the criminal's identity.
     <u>If you discover the criminal's identity, bring her to justice.</u>
     Therefore, bring the criminal to justice.

Inference II seems little different from the valid inference I, yet II as it stands cannot be a piece of valid deductive reasoning, for neither its first premiss nor its conclusion is capable of truth or falsity. Moreover, even though II looks like *modus ponens*, the antecedent of the second premiss is not the same as the first premiss. Still, inference II seems reasonable enough: If the sheriff says to his deputy, "Discover the criminal's identity; and if you do so, bring her to justice," and if the deputy discovers the criminal's identity but does not bring her to justice, the deputy will get nowhere pleading that the sheriff gave no orders to bring the criminal to justice.

It makes sense to suppose that valid inference I sanctions our belief that II is likewise valid. But I's validity assures II's validity only if I and II are merely two ways of writing the same argument.[3] And the premisses and conclusion of inference II are necessarily prescriptive, whereas the premisses and conclusion of I might, but need not, be used prescriptively. A person who puts forward inference I might not be engaging in practical reasoning at all. Hence the premisses and conclusion of I are not truly equivalent to the premisses and conclusion of II, and NDLR3$_D$ provides us no help in understanding the logic, if any, of II. Deontic logic is therefore no use in understanding non-deontic practical reasoning.

The best way I know to meet this difficulty is to attempt to change our minds about the process of practical reasoning. Following R.M. Hare, I shall distinguish propositional (phrastic) and non-propositional (neustic) components of intrinsically prescriptive statements.[4] Unlike Hare, I take the phrastic, or propositional, component of an imperative or of a statement of intention to be logically equivalent to the corresponding first-, second-, or third-person deontic statement: The phrastic of "Shut the door" is "You ought to shut the door," and the phrastic of "I *will* go to the store tomorrow" is "I ought to go to the store tomorrow." The ought in these cases is an all-things-considered ought, not a *prima facie* ought. For I might intend to go to the store tomorrow even though I do not think I ought — in some sense of 'ought' — to do so.[5] Perhaps doing so strikes me as morally evil, or practically foolish, or impolite. But still, if I really intend to go, I will assert that I ought, all things considered, to go.

As Hare points out, logic, being propositional, can work only on the phrastic components of intrinsically prescriptive statements. From "If you go out, shut the door" and "You do go out," the imperative "Shut the door" does not follow. But what does follow is the phrastic component of "Shut the door": namely, "You ought to shut the door." Prescriptive premisses, even intrinsically prescriptive premisses, therefore never logically entail intrinsically prescriptive conclusions. For practical reasoning makes use only of the phrastic components of its premisses, in order to reach phrastic conclusions. The results of practical reasoning are not orders, entreaties, statements of intention, or statements of one's decision. Instead, the results of practical reasoning are true or false statements that *can* but *need not* be taken as orders, entreaties, statements of intention, or statements of one's decision.

If we do not separate phrastics from neustics, since logical operations concern only propositions, we have no way of explaining the seeming validity of argument II; if we make the separation, we need not hesitate to equate deontic statements to intrinsically prescriptive statements. Therefore, so far as logic is concerned, the operative portions of imperative premisses and conclusions are their phrastic components; unlike the entire imperative, phrastics are in fact equivalent to deontic statements. In this way, deontic logic can account for the logic of imperative inferences.

A more problematic mode of reasoning supports this conclusion. I have argued in an unpublished paper that sentence meaning is equivalent to non-attemptive illocutionary act potential. Ordering, entreating, and the like are all illocutionary acts, but they are attemptive illocutionary acts — i.e., speech acts that are attempts to get someone to behave in certain ways. Therefore, if my theory about meaning is correct, not even imperatives and the like are *intrinsically* prescriptive, for prescribing, as an attemptive act, is not part of sentence meaning. Therefore, neither the premisses nor the conclusions of practical reasoning are intrinsically prescriptive. Imperatives and deontic claims can, for all we know, be equivalent in meaning, for they might have the same non-attemptive illocutionary act potential.

However, recognizing that the prescriptivity of premisses does not entail prescriptivity of a conclusion only makes the third major problem worse. We had asked how deontic reasoning could be practical, since deontic conclusions need not be used prescriptively. But now we must

CHAPTER 16

ask: Where is the practicality in *any* kind of reasoning that does not issue in prescriptions?

Common sense suggests that prescriptive force does pass from premisses to conclusion. If at least one premiss is prescriptive in a certain way, and if no premiss is prescriptive in a different way, and if the conclusion is capable of being prescriptive, the conclusion is prescriptive in the same way as the premiss. If a premiss is an order, so is the conclusion; if a premiss is a statement of intention, so is the conclusion. In argument II, the deputy is told: "Discover the criminal's identity; and if you do so, bring her to justice." If the deputy succeeds in discovering the criminal's identity, surely he is under orders to bring her to justice. In a truly practical argument, prescriptivity flows from premisses to conclusions.

Moreover, the conclusion will have the same prescriptive force as the premiss. From "I *will* stick to my plan" and "If I stick to my plan, I must murder Banquo," most people would derive "I *will* murder Banquo" — not "I ought to murder Banquo," which might be used merely to express a judgment. "I ought to murder Banquo, but I'm not sure if I'll make the attempt" is coherent, if a bit lily-livered; "I *will* murder Banquo, but I'm not sure if I'll make the attempt" seems incoherent.[6]

The flow of prescriptivity in a practical argument is present even when the argument contains different sorts of prescriptions as premisses. In such cases, the rule seems to be that the conclusion takes on the prescriptivity of the least forceful premiss. For instance, from "Kill Pierre" and "I beg of you, if you kill Pierre, do so gently," what appears to follow is "I beg of you, kill Pierre gently."

However, I have argued that logic, deontic or otherwise, does not preserve prescriptivity in any argument. The principle that prescriptivity flows from premisses to conclusion is therefore not a logical axiom, theorem, or inference rule. That principle cannot be part of the proof of a practical conclusion, because no practical conclusion gains its prescriptive force by logical means. But if logic does not justify our common-sense belief in the flow of prescriptivity, what can?

I can see only one plausible answer to this difficulty. We must regard the principle that prescriptivity passes from premisses to conclusion as a general condition of successful practical reasoning. It is like the parallel but rarely stated principle that a conclusion from purely descriptive premisses will itself be descriptive. Neither principle can be said to be logically necessary: I may, without making a logical mistake, take the conclusion of descriptive premises to be prescriptively binding on me; and I may also regard the conclusion of prescriptive premises as having no prescriptive force. But in the long run, I will best perform my reasoning, theoretical as well as practical, if I take conclusions to have the same force as premises.

In Grice's language, I am arguing that the flow of prescriptivity from premisses to conclusions in practical arguments is a matter of *implicature*, not one of logical *implication*. [Grice, 65-66] And just as Grice derived conversational implicatures from our desire to fulfill as well as possible the general ends of conversation, so I contend that principles of the flow of prescriptivity stem from our desire to fulfill as well as possible the general ends of practical reasoning.

A strong indication that my position is correct is that, as with other implicatures, the principle of the flow of prescriptive force does not always apply. This is especially true when practical inferences require more than a few steps. For example, a mother tells her son: "Here's what I want you to do this morning: Pick up your toys; and if you finish doing that, vacuum your rug; and if you finish doing that, take out the trash." If prescriptivity flows unabated from premisses to conclusion, the son should infer that his orders to take out the trash are as much in force as his orders to pick up his room. But in fact, the son might well ask, "Do I have to do all those things?" The mother could consistently reply, "No, but at least pick up your toys." The longer the chain of inference, the more likely that the flow of prescriptivity will begin to dry up. That prescriptive force is not always the same in conclusions as in premisses shows that the principle of the flow of prescriptive force is not a matter of logical necessity. Rather, it can only be a general principle used by those who wish to employ practical reasoning well, a source of implicatures but not of implications.

Nor does the principle that prescriptivity passes from premisses to conclusion hold only for essentially prescriptive premisses. If a premiss of an argument represents an order, and all other conditions are met, then the conclusion represents an order — however that order might be expressed. When I was young, my mother used to express orders in the form of questions: "Would you like to do so-and-so?" When I answered "No," her invariable response was, "Well, *do* it." If "Would you like to go to the store?" expresses an order, then that plus the undisguised order "When you go to the store, pick up a quart of milk" surely imply "Pick up a quart of milk" — even if the conclusion is expressed as "Would you like to pick up a quart of milk?"

Hence an 'ought' statement used directively — that is to say, prescriptively — if it serves as a premiss of a piece of practical reasoning and if all other conditions are met, will normally lead to a prescriptive conclusion of the same kind as the premiss. "I ought to finish my tax return today," if used as a statement of intent, can help produce various conclusions which are themselves statements of intent. Similarly, "You ought to help your poor old mother," taken as an entreaty, can help produce various entreaties as conclusions.

If so, there seems no reason why we cannot substitute deontic expressions, *used directively*, for any intrinsically prescriptive expressions in practical reasoning. Prescriptivity will normally be preserved from premisses to conclusion — not as a matter of logic, but as a consequence of our intention to engage in good practical reasoning. And the preservation of prescriptivity was our only worry in letting deontic statements stand for imperatives and the like.

Hence, I believe I have justified the main claim of this chapter: that deontic logic can serve as a logic of practical reasoning. But there is much less to my conclusion than meets the eye, for practical reasoning comprises far more than determining what we ought to do and are permitted to do. More often than not, the role of deontic thoughts is only to set limits on our potential actions. Although most people generally do what they ought to do and avoid doing what they ought not to do, many possible actions are neither obligatory nor forbidden. Practical reason helps us decide which permissible action to take, but deontic logic is of little help in that portion of our decision-making.

Often we make our choice among permissible alternative actions on teleological grounds. Persons consider the goals they wish to accomplish, taking into account the relative importance of each goal. They also consider how likely each possible action will be in achieving their goals. The rational course of action is the one that seems most likely to achieve the most important goals. Now that much practical reasoning is teleological does not show that any practical reasoning ought to be teleological; but surely the burden of proof is on the upholder of deontic exclusivity. How is deontic logic useful in teleological practical reasoning?

We might compare the role of modal logic in theoretical reasoning. By modal reasoning, one can prove that a given proposition 'p' is necessary and that another proposition 'q' is equivalent to a logical contradiction; one does so by proving 'Lp' and 'L~q' to be theorems of one's modal system. In a strong modal system, one can infer that 'p' is true and 'q' false. But most propositions are neither necessarily true nor necessarily false. Modal logic can establish the truth-value of contingent propositions only when we add assumptions about the truth-values of other contingent propositions. In a similar manner, deontic logic would seem of no help in determining the practical value of most available actions.

On this way of thinking, deontic logic has an important but relatively small role to play in practical reasoning. Deontic logic helps us decide what we really should do, and it helps us rule out what we absolutely should not do; but it does not help us choose among the many possible actions that are neither obligatory nor forbidden. Such choices require us to engage in teleological reasoning.

I have deliberately overstated matters, but a partisan of deontic logic will not derive much joy from the fact. Often we reason with oughts that are not of the full-blooded, all-things-considered variety. Deontic reasoning, that is, often helps us reach practical decisions, even though the actions decided upon are not considered absolutely obligatory. But in such cases, deontic reasoning is usually far from sufficient to determine action. Other factors, including teleological reasoning, enter into the determination of action. If there is a sort of meta-reasoning to determine which sort of factor should win out in a given case, there seems no reason to suppose that the meta-reasoning in question should be deontic.

For example, I have made a promise, but keeping the promise would cause me a hardship that breaking the promise would avoid. Deontic reasoning leads me to the conclusion that I should keep the promise; teleological reasoning leads me to the conclusion that I should break the promise. If I try to decide the reasonable course of action, I will doubtless consider such factors as the amount of overall harm done by keeping my promise and the amount of overall good done by breaking my promise: if it costs little to keep my promise, I will have no qualms about doing so. But weighing overall good and harm is part of teleological reasoning, not a matter for deontic logic. The meta-reasoning by which I chose between applying deontic reasoning and applying teleological reasoning was therefore not, or at least not exclusively, deontic. The role of deontic reasoning in choosing my action is therefore very limited: even if I choose to follow deontic reasoning, I do so for largely non-deontic reasons.

Of course, what is the case often differs from what should be the case. That my meta-reasoning in the particular instance was teleological hardly shows that meta-reasoning in all such cases should be teleological. But my experience has been that practical meta-reasoning is generally teleological, in which case the burden of proof is surely on a deontic exclusivist to show, in a non-question-begging way, why we should change our ways of meta-reasoning.

Hence the fact that a proper deontic logic can be used in practical reasoning appears interesting but unimportant. Far more important is means-ends, teleological deliberation.

But we should not be too quick to dismiss the importance of deontic logic to practical reasoning. Three related points indicate that deontic logic has a more important role to play in practical reasoning than we have so far admitted:

(A) Determining that a course of action would fulfill some of my goals is rarely even close to being enough to prompt me to act. I must see no equally good reasons for alternative actions; moreover, I must be sure that the envisioned course of action will not cut me off from achieving more important goals. I need, that is, to be convinced that the projected course of action is the best one for me to take, all things considered.[7]

(B) NDL, unlike other systems of deontic logic, distinguishes between the logic of 'ought to be' statements and that of 'ought to do' statements. The NDL semantics of 'ought to be' statements amounts to the claim that state of affairs S ought to be if and only if the world with S is or would be preferable to the world without S.

(C) Even if I reach the conclusion that, all things considered, it is best for me to do F, and even though I have a prior commitment to do what is best for me to do, all things considered, I still might fail to do F. I might be weak-willed, or overcome by fear or greed or anger; habit or deontic scruples might get the better of me. A parallel result occurs with explicitly deontic reasoning: I might conclude that I absolutely ought to do G but might still fail to do G.

Neither deontic nor teleological reasoning, then, logically or causally necessitates that I act in a certain way. On the other hand, we often act without engaging in deontic reasoning, just as we often act without engaging in teleological reasoning; habitual actions, for example, require neither form of practical reasoning. Hence neither teleological nor deontic reasoning is necessary or sufficient for action.

I will not argue for these points here; A and C seem to me to be common sense, while B has been one of the themes of this book.

Let us put these three points together and see where they lead us. One might try to find a role for deontic logic in all practical reasoning by claiming that teleological reasoning brings about action only if one adds the specifically deontic premiss that we ought to do what is best for us to do, all things considered. But point C stands in the way of any such claim. Although teleological reasoning is not sufficient to bring about action, neither is deontic reasoning. The two sorts of practical reasoning appear to be on an equal footing: Each can contribute to a determination to act in a certain way, but neither is necessary for action and neither is sufficient for action.

However, even though it is wrong to read a hidden 'ought' into teleological reasoning, point A tells us that teleological reasoning to be effective must meet another condition: It must represent a global, all-things-considered judgment. I must know not only that my projected action will meet certain of my goals, but I must also be sure that the action will not prevent me from meeting certain other goals. That is, a good teleological reasoner will not act without concluding, in at least a rough and ready way, that matters will be better *as a whole* for his action. But as point B suggests, the teleological reasoner will therefore be making judgments about what ought to be the case; for NDL understands such judgments to concern how the world as a whole will be better. Of course, teleological reasoners might have purely selfish goals; even so, they will take only those actions which will, *from their standpoint*, make the world better. Their teleological reasoning will then conform to the logic of 'ought to be' judgments, even though a less selfish standpoint would condemn the premisses of that reasoning.

Deontic logic, I have argued, has two parts: the logic of 'ought to be' statements and the logic of 'ought to do' statements. The logic of 'ought to do' statements is crucial to effective deontic reasoning; I am arguing now that the logic of 'ought to be' statements is crucial to effective teleological reasoning. If teleological and deontic reasoning are the two co-equal forms of practical reasoning, and if NDL is the proper deontic logic, NDL has a strong claim to being the general logic of practical reasoning.

Deontic logic does indeed play the pivotal role in practical reasoning, but only if we include under the general heading of deontic logic both the logic of 'ought to be' statements and the logic of 'ought to do' statements, and so long as we do not confuse the two logics. NDL is, of course, a logic both of 'ought to do' and of 'ought to be' statements, and it is built on a clear distinction between these types of statements; as a result, an upholder of NDL or a related deontic logic has a good answer to the objection raised. Hence, I conclude that deontic logic in general, and NDL in particular, has a major role to play in practical reasoning.

Earlier in this book, I argued that NDL, or a similar deontic logic, is correct; in this chapter I have tried to show that NDL, or a similar deontic logic, is useful. It represents our best chance of realizing the dream of such figures as Aristotle and Locke: the dream of achieving a logic of practical reasoning.

Appendix 1: The Systems SDL and NDL

In this Appendix, I compare Standard Deontic Logic (SDL), as set out in Chapter 2, with my New Deontic Logic (NDL). NDL, as presented in Chapters 14 and 15, consists of two parts: a logic of 'ought to be' statements and rules, the names of which I designate by the subscript 'B'; and a logic of 'ought to do' statements and rules, the names of which I designate by the subscript 'D'.

In the first three sections, I present some basic information about NDL. Section I gives eleven definitions, while section II lists formation-rules for well-formed formulae of NDL. Section III contains six rules for use of the two-place relation '▸', as defined in Chapter 14 and in section I.

The final four sections make direct comparisons among SDL, the NDL logic of 'ought to be' statements, and the NDL logic of 'ought to do' statements. The first column in each of those sections gives an SDL statement or rule. Parallel to each SDL statement or rule, the second column lists an NDL_B counterpart if any, while the third column gives an NDL_D counterpart if any. Where there is no counterpart to an SDL statement or rule, I have indicated the fact by the letters 'NC'. In the case of NDLT0, I have listed 'NC' under the heading 'SDL'.

Section IV contains *semantical rules* of the three systems, section V contains the systems' *rules of inference*, and section VI contains *typical asserted propositions*. Thus the reader can tell at a glance how the structure of SDL, that of NDL_B, and that of NDL_D differ from one another. Section VII contains *propositions not asserted in SDL*; their NDL_B and NDL_D counterparts are not asserted in NDL.

I. Definitions of NDL

Definition 1: 'W_0 is a world' $=_{df}$ (1) W_0 is a possible world, accessible to the real world;[1] (2) W_0 has the same causal laws as the real world; (3) There is a time such that at least one event occurred prior to that time in W_0, and such that any event occurred prior to that time in W_0 if and only if it occurred in the real world.

Definition 2: Where w_1 and w_2 are worlds, '$w_1 ▸ w_2$' $=_{df}$ 'w_1 is preferable to w_2'.

Definition 3: A world w_1 is a *<p>-counterpart* to w_2 $=_{df}$ The truth-value of 'p' in w_2 is different from the truth-value of 'p' in w_1, and the only other differences between w_2 and w_1 are partially or entirely caused by <p>'s obtaining in one world and not the other.

295

Definition 4: A world w_0 is $<p>$-*normal* $=_{df}$ There is no proposition 'q' such that: '⊢ q → p' is true, 'q' is true in w_0, and not every world where 'q' is true is preferable to some counterpart where 'q' is false.

Definition 5: {$<p>$, $<q>$, $<r>$, . . . } is a set of *OB-alternatives* $=_{df}$ any world w_0 in which any member of {$<p>$, $<q>$, $<r>$, . . . } obtains ▸ all $<p>$-counterparts of w_0 in which no member of {$<p>$, $<q>$, $<r>$, . . . } obtains. If $<p>$ and $<q>$' are members of a set of OB-alternatives, $<q>$ is termed a $<p>$-*alternative* (in short, a $<p^a>$) to $<p>$; and if two worlds, w_1 and w_2, differ only as a result of containing different $<P^a>$'s, w_1 is a $<P^a>$-*world* to w_2.

Definition 6: A $<p>$-*alternative-normal* world (for short, a $<p^a>$-*normal* world) $=_{df}$ a $<q>$-normal world, and a $<p>$-*alternative-counterpart* world (for short, a $<p^a>$-*counterpart*) $=_{df}$ a $<q>$-counterpart world, where $<q>$ is a $<p^a>$. If a certain $<p^a>$ is said either to obtain or not to obtain in a $<p^a>$-normal or $<p^a>$-counterpart world, the $<p>$-alternative is the same as the $<p>$-alternative that defines the world unless otherwise stated.

Definition 7: '$OB_{t1}p_{t2}$' $=_{df}$ 'It ought to be at time t_1 that p at time t_2'.

Definition 8: Where 'S' stands for an agent and 'F' for an action-type, '$OD_{t1S}F_{t2}$' $=_{df}$ 'S ought-at-time t_1 to do F at time t_2'.

Definition 9: '$PB_{t1}p_{t2}$' $=_{df}$ 'It is permissible at time t_1 that p be at t_2' (*or:* 'It may be at t_1 that p at t_2').

Definition 10: Where 'S' stands for an agent and 'F' for an action-type, '$PD_{t1S}F_{t2}$' $=_{df}$ 'It is permissible for S at time t_1 to do F at t_2' (*or:* 'S may at t_1 do F at t_2').

Definition 11: Where 'S' indicates an agent, 'AP_S' $=_{df}$ 'S suffers an appropriate penalty'.

II. Formation-Rules for Expressions of NDL

NDLF1: All wffs of the propositional calculus are wffs of NDL.

NDLF2: If 'S¹' and 'S²' are terms designating agents, so are 'S¹.S²' and 'S¹ v S²'. If 'F_S' and 'G_S' are terms designating actions, so are '$F_S.G_S$', 'F_S v G_S', '$F_S → G_S$', '$F_S ↔ G_S$', and '~F_S'.

NDLF3$_B$: If 'p' is a wff of NDL, and if ~⊢p and ~⊢~p, then 'OB_tp' and 'PB_tp' are wffs of NDL.

NDLF3$_D$: If 'F_S' is a term designating an action performed by agent S, and if CT'(F_S v AP_S)', '$OD_{St}F$' and '$PD_{St}F$' are wffs of NDL.

NDLF4: If 'p' and 'q' are wffs of NDL, '~p', 'p.q', 'p v q', 'p → q', and 'p ↔ q' are wffs of NDL.

NDLF5: These are the only wffs of NDL.

III. Rules for the Relation '▸' in NDL

1. TRAN (Rule of transitivity): The relation '▸' is transitive. That is, if w_{0t} ▸ w_{1t} and if w_{1t} ▸ w_{2t}, then w_{0t} ▸ w_{2t}.

2. ASYM (Rule of asymmetricality): The relation '▸' is asymmetrical. That is, if w_{0t} ▸ w_{1t}, then ~(w_{1t} ▸ w_{0t}); that is, w_{1t} ~▸ w_{0t}.

3. NONR (Rule of non-reflexivity): The relation '$\blacktriangleright$' is non-reflexive. That is, $w_{0t} \sim\, \blacktriangleright\, w_{0t}$.

4. AGGR (Rule of aggregation): If all worlds at t where 'p' is true $\blacktriangleright$ all their <p>-counterparts at t in which 'r' s not true; and if all worlds at t where 'q' is true $\blacktriangleright$ all their <p>-counterparts at t in which 's' is not true; then all worlds at t where 'p v q' is true $\blacktriangleright$ their <p>-counterparts or <q>-counterparts at t in which 'r v s' is not true.

5. CONS (Rule of consequent change): If all worlds at t in which 'r' is true $\blacktriangleright$ their r-counterparts at t in which 'p' is false; and if all worlds at t where 'p' is true are worlds where 'q' is true; then all worlds at t in which 'r' is true $\blacktriangleright$ their r-counterparts at t in which 'q' is false.

6. POSS (Rule of possible worlds): '$\blacktriangleright$' is a two-place relation between worlds. Any expression of the form 'x $\blacktriangleright$ y', where either 'x' or 'y' does not designate a world, in the sense given that term in Definition 1, is ill-formed.

IV. Semantics

<u>**Standard Deontic Logic**</u>	<u>**NDL 'Ought to Be'**</u>	<u>**NDL 'Ought to Do'**</u>
SDLS1: If 'Op' is true in this world, 'p' is true in all possible and accessible worlds.	**NDLS1$_B$:** The statement "It ought at time t_1 to be that p at t_2," is true in world w_0 only if every <p^a>-normal world w_1 (branching from w_0 at t_1 or identical to w_0) where a <p^a> obtains at t_2 $\blacktriangleright$ any <p^a>-counterpart world w_2.	**NDLS1$_D$:** "S ought at t_1 to do F at t_2," is true in world w_0 only if: (a) S exists in w_0; and (b) every <AP$_s^a$ >-normal world w_1 (branching from w_0 at t_1 or identical to w_0) where S does F at t_2 or some <AP$_s^a$> obtains $\blacktriangleright$ any <AP$_s^a$>-counterpart world w_2 where neither S does F at t_2 nor does any <AP$_s^a$> obtain.
SDLS2: If 'p' is true in all possible and accessible worlds, 'Op' is true in this world.	**NDLS2$_B$:** The statement "It ought at time t_1 to be that p at t_2," is true in world w_0 if every <p^a>-normal world w_1 (branching from w_0 at t_1 or identical to w_0) where a <p^a> obtains at t_2 $\blacktriangleright$ any <p^a>-counterpart world w_2.	**NDLS2$_D$:** "S ought at t_1 to do F " is true in world w_0 if: (a) S exists in w_0; and (b) every <AP$_s^a$>-normal world w_1 (branching from w_0 at t_1 or identical to w_0) where S does F at t_2 or some <AP$_s^a$> obtains $\blacktriangleright$ any <AP$_s^a$>-counterpart world w_2 where neither S does F at t_2 nor does any <AP$_s^a$> obtain.

SDLS3: If 'Pp' is true in this world, 'p' is true in at least one possible and accessible world.

NDLS3$_B$: The statement "It is permissible at time t_1 to be that p at t_2" (*or:* "It may be at t_1 that p at t_2") is true in world w_0 only if there is at least one <~p^a>-normal world w_1 (branching from w_0 at t_1 or identical to w_0) where no <p^a> obtains at t_2, and there is at least one <~p^a>-counterpart world w_2, and w_1 ~▸ w_2.

NDLS3$_D$: "It is permissible for S at t_1 to do F" is true in world w_0 only if: (a) S exists; and (b) there is at least one <AP$_S$^{a}>-normal world w_1 (branching from w_0 at t_1 or identical to w_0) where if S does F at t_2, some <AP$_S$^{a}> obtains, and there is at least one <AP$_S$^{a}>-counterpart world w_2 where S does F at t_2 and no <AP$_S$^{a}> obtains, and w_1 ~▸ w_2.

SDLS4: If 'p' is true in at least one possible and accessible world, 'Pp' is true in this world.

NDLS4$_B$: The statement "It is permissible at time t_1 to be that p at t_2" (*or:* "It may be at t_1 that p at t_2") is true in world w_0 if there is at least one <~p^a>-normal world w_1 (branching from w_0 at t_1 or identical to w_0) where no <p^a> obtains at t_2, and there is at least one <~p^a>-counterpart world w_2, and w_1 ~▸ w_2.

NDLS4$_D$: "It is permissible for S at t_1 to do F" is true in world w_0 if: (a) S exists; and (b) there is at least one <AP$_S$^{a}>-normal world w_1 (branching from w_0 at t_1 or identical to w_0) where if S does F at t_2, some <AP$_S$^{a}> obtains, and there is at least one <AP$_S$^{a}>-counterpart world w_2 where S does F at t_2 and no <AP$_S$^{a}> obtains, and w_1 ~▸ w_2.

SDLS5: Every possible world is in fact accessible to at least one possible world.

NDLS5$_B$: For any world w_0 and any proposition 'p', such that 'p' is neither necessarily true nor necessarily false, if 'p' is true in w_0, there is a <p>-counterpart world w_1 accessible to w_0.

NDLS5$_D$: For any world w_0 and any proposition 'p', such that 'p' is neither necessarily true nor necessarily false, if 'p' is true in w_0, there is a <p>-counterpart world w_1, accessible to w_0.

V. Inference Rules

| **Standard Deontic Logic** | **NDL 'Ought to Be'** | **NDL 'Ought to Do'** |

SDLR1: If 'p ↔ q' is a theorem, and if '. . . p . . .' is a theorem, then '. . . q . . .', the result of uniformly replacing 'p' by 'q' in '. . . p . . .', is a theorem.

NDLR1$_B$: If 'p ↔ q' is a theorem, CT'p', and 'OB$_t$(. . . p . . .)' is a theorem, then 'OB$_t$(. . . q . . .)', the result of uniformly replacing 'p' by 'q' in 'OB$_t$(. . . p . . .)', is a theorem.

NDLR1$_D$: If 'OD$_{St}$F' and 'F$_S$ ↔ G$_S$' are theorems, and if CT'AP$_S$' and CT'F$_S$ v AP$_S$', 'OD$_{St}$G' is a theorem.

SDLR2: $\dfrac{\vdash p}{\vdash Op.}$ NC NC

SDLR3: $\dfrac{\vdash p \to q}{\vdash Op \to Oq.}$ NC

NDLR3$_D$:
$$\dfrac{\vdash (F_S \to G_S).CT`AP_S`.}{CT`(\sim G_S \leftrightarrow AP_S)`}$$
$$\vdash (OD_{St}F \to OD_{St}G).$$

SDLR4: $\dfrac{\vdash p \leftrightarrow q}{\vdash Op \leftrightarrow Oq.}$

NDLR4$_B$:
$$\dfrac{\vdash (p \leftrightarrow q)}{\vdash (OB_tp \leftrightarrow Ob_tq).}$$

NDLR4$_D$:
$$\dfrac{\vdash (F_S \leftrightarrow G_S).CT`AP_S`}{\vdash (OD_{St}F \leftrightarrow OD_{St}G).}$$

VI. Typical Assertions

Standard Deontic Logic	**NDL 'Ought to Be'**	**NDL 'Ought to Do'**
NC	**NDLT0:** $\vdash OD_SF \leftrightarrow [E!S.$ $OB(F_S \vee AP_S)].$	**NDLT0:** $\vdash OD_SF \leftrightarrow [E!S.$ $OB(F_S \vee AP_S)].$
SDLT1: $\vdash \sim(Op.O\sim p).$	**NDLT1$_B$:** $\vdash \sim(OB_tp.OB_t\sim p).$	**NDLT1$_D$:** $\vdash \sim OB_t(AP_S) \to$ $\sim[OD_{St}F.OD_{St}\sim F].$
SDLT2: $\vdash O(p \to q) \to (Op \to Oq).$	NC	**NDLT2$_D$:** $\vdash OD_{St}(F \vee G).$ $OD_{St}\sim F.CT`AP_S`.CT`(F_S \leftrightarrow AP_S)` \to OD_{St}G.$
SDLT3: $\vdash O(p.q) \to (Op.Oq).$	**NDLT3$_B$:** $\vdash [\vdash(p \leftrightarrow q).$ $OB_t(p.q)] \to (OB_tp.OB_tq).$	**NDLT3$_D$:** $\vdash [CT`AP_S`.$ OD_{St} $(F.G)$ $] \to (OD_{St}$ $F.$ $OD_{St}G).$
SDLT4: $\vdash(Op.Oq) \to O(p.q).$	NC	NC
SDLT5: $\vdash \sim O(p.\sim p).$	NC	**NDLT5$_D$:** $\vdash \sim OB_t(AP_S) \to$ $\sim OD_{St}(F.\sim F).$
SDLT6: $\vdash O(p \vee \sim p).$	NC	NC
SDLT7: $\vdash Op \leftrightarrow \sim P\sim p.$	**NDLT7$_B$:** $\vdash OB_tp \leftrightarrow \sim PB_t\sim p.$	**NDLT7$_D$:** $\vdash CT`AP_S` \to$ $[OD_{St}F \leftrightarrow (E!S.\sim PD_{St}\sim F)].$

SDLT8: ⊢ Pp ·· ~O~p.   **NDLT8$_B$:** ⊢ PB$_t$p ·· ~OB$_t$~p.   **NDLT8$_D$:** ⊢ CT'AP$_S$' → [PD$_{St}$F ·· E!S.~OD$_{St}$~F].

SDLT9: ⊢ Op → Pp.   **NDLT9$_B$:** ⊢ OB$_t$p → PB$_t$p.   **NDLT9$_D$:** ⊢ ~OB$_t$APS → (OD$_{St}$F → PD$_{St}$F).

SDLT10: ⊢ OOp ·· Op.   NC   NC

SDLT11: ⊢ O(Op → p).   NC   NC

VII. Non-Assertions

<u>Standard Deontic Logic</u>	<u>NDL 'Ought to Be'</u>	<u>NDL 'Ought to Do'</u>
SDLX1: p → Pp.	**NDLX1$_B$:** p → PBp.	**NDLX1$_D$:** F$_S$ → PD$_S$F.
SDLX2: Pp → p.	**NDLX2$_B$:** PBp → p.	**NDLX2$_D$:** PD$_S$F → F$_S$.
SDLX3: p → Op.	**NDLX3$_B$:** p → OBp.	**NDLX3$_D$:** F$_S$ → OD$_S$F.
SDLX4: Op → p.	**NDLX4$_B$:** OBp → p.	**NDLX4$_D$:** OD$_S$F → F$_S$.
SDLX5: O(p v q) → (Op v Oq).	**NDLX5$_B$:** OB(p v q) → (OBp v OBq).	**NDLX5$_D$:** OD$_S$(F v G) → (OD$_S$F v OD$_S$G).
SDLX6: (Pp.Pq) → P(p.q).	**NDLX6$_B$:** (Pbp . PBq) → PB(p.q).	**NDLX6$_D$:** (PD$_S$F. PD$_S$G) → PD$_S$(F.G).
Not formulable	**NDLX0:** OBF$_S$ ·· OD$_S$F.	**NDLX0:** OBF$_S$ ·· OD$_S$F.

Appendix 2: A Note on Quantification

NDL, as I have presented it, is based on the propositional calculus. But many of the deontic statements we make contain quantifiers. Moreover, as Stephen Harris has pointed out, NDL treats the 'ought to do' operator as having predicates, not entire propositions, in its scope; in so doing, NDL gives at least some room for quantification. Can NDL serve as the basis for a quantified deontic logic? In a highly qualified sense, it can.

The standard axioms for introducing quantifiers are the following:

QA1: ⊢ $(\forall x)Fx \rightarrow Fx$.
QA2: ⊢ $Fx \rightarrow (\exists x)Fx$.

Let us look at the effect of adding these axioms to NDL.

Consider first the NDL logic of 'ought to do' statements. I argued in Chapter 4 that the 'ought to do' operator is *de re*, so that the agent-term is in purely referential position. For that reason, standard quantification theory allows us to apply QA1 and QA2 whenever the instantial variable ranges over agent-terms in an 'ought to do' statement. If everybody ought to register to vote, Sarah ought to register to vote. Likewise, if it is true that Henry ought to shovel the snow, then it is true that somebody ought to shovel the snow. Because the subject of an 'ought to do' statement is outside the scope of the operator, ordinary rules apply to quantifications over that term. Applying QA1 and QA2 to sentence-terms of 'ought to do' statements therefore yields ordinary predicate logic with deontic predicates.

But what about quantification over terms in the predicates of 'ought to do' statements? Certainly we do sometimes take instances of quantified expressions in such contexts. From a mother's "You should give everybody a piece of your cake," a child is expected to infer "You should give your brother a piece of your cake." However, neither taking instances of universal quantifiers nor quantifying existentially over particular objects is safe. If Christopher ought to build St. Swithin's Cathedral, it might or might not be the case that there is such a thing as St. Swithin's Cathedral, which Christopher ought to build. All <AP$_s$^{a}>-

301

normal worlds in which he either builds St. Swithin's or receives an appropriate penalty are preferable to all $<AP_s^a>$-counterparts in which he does neither. But whether the real world falls into either of these two groups, we do not know. Therefore, QA2 is not plausible.

QA1 seems better, but even it raises problems: If Jane ought to help all the children on the list, and Tomas's name is on the list, does it follow that Jane ought to help Tomas? I argued in Chapter 12 that it does not. Quantification over predicate terms in 'ought to do' statements is therefore problematic at best.

'Ought to be' statements are similarly problematic. Certainly a quantified statement can occur within the scope of a deontic operator: It ought to be that everyone is better than Mother Teresa; it ought to be that someone builds St. Swithin's Cathedral. But one cannot make normal inferences from quantified statements within the scope of an 'ought to be' operator: One cannot infer, for instance, that it ought to be that Mother Teresa is better than Mother Teresa. All normal worlds in which everyone is better than Mother Teresa are preferable to counterparts in which not everyone is better than Mother Teresa; but again, whether the real world fits into either of those classes is not given.

Can an 'ought to be' operator occur within the scope of a quantifier? If I was right in asserting that 'ought to be' operators are *de dicto* and opaque, the answer must be no. For the terms occurring in a context introduced by 'ought to be' are not in purely referential position.

Modal semantics provides SDL an escape from these difficulties, so long as we allow a term in a deontic context to refer to objects not in this possible world. 'Op' is true if and only if 'p' is true in all deontic alternative worlds; therefore, 'Op' is true only if the terms of 'p' succeed in referring to objects in all deontic alternative worlds. Thus, if 'O(Fa)' is true, we can expect '$(\exists x)O(Fx)$' to be true — so long as the range of the variable 'x' includes values in other possible worlds. Hence, the semantics of SDL allows for QA2 and a quantified deontic logic.

Does NDL semantics likewise allow quantification into deontic contexts? It does for the logic of 'ought to be' statements. To say that state of affairs N ought to be is, according to NDL semantics, to say that all normal worlds containing N or an alternative (and there are some such worlds) > their counterparts not containing N or an alternative (and there are some such worlds). Hence, to say that N ought to be implies that there are possible worlds in which N is the case and in which, therefore, the referring terms of N actually do refer — although they might not refer in this world. Hence, as with SDL, QA2 holds. Hence, we could construct a quantified NDL logic of 'ought to be' statements, so long as we allow our variables to range over objects in other possible worlds.

However, the same cannot be said of contexts introduced by 'ought to do' operators. To say that agent S ought to build cathedral c is to say, roughly, that all worlds (and there are some) in which S does not build c and is appropriately sanctioned ▸ counterparts (and there are some) in which S does not build c and is not appropriately sanctioned. Now 'S' is, of course, a referring expression. Since the only worlds of which we are speaking are worlds in which S does not build c, we do not know from the truth of "S ought to build c" whether 'c' succeeds in referring in any of those worlds. Hence, we have no basis for quantifying existentially over 'c', and QA2 fails.

I suggest this result is plausible in itself and not just an artifact of NDL. If it really ought to be the case that Christopher builds a cathedral, then since 'ought to be' implies 'can be', clearly there is a possible world in which that cathedral does exist. However, it might be the case that Christopher ought to build a cathedral even if his doing so is impossible: 'ought to do' does not imply 'can do'. As NDL tells us, perhaps it ought to be that Christopher is appropriately penalized, whether he builds or not. If so, we cannot infer from the fact that he ought to build a cathedral that there is a possible world in which the cathedral exists.

Finally, consider the 'ought to be' sentence which takes a quantified expression as its argument: for instance, "It ought to be that all humans are happy." We cannot plausibly infer "It ought to be that human H is happy." For we could surely agree that it ought to be that all humans are happy, while agreeing as well that no particular human ought to be happy unless all humans are happy. Or else, one could suppose that only if humans were radically different from presently existing people could or should they all be happy. Perhaps a believer in original sin might claim that, although all humans were meant to lead happy lives, none of us actually deserves to do so. In that case, all humans ought to be happy, even though no existing human ought to be happy. Hence, we must be careful even of universal instantiation within the scope of an 'ought to be' operator.

Hence, I conclude that there can be a quantified deontic logic only in a restricted sense. The subjects of 'ought to do' statements are subject to normal quantificational rules, and the predicates of those statements can contain quantifiers. But the subjects of 'ought to do' statements are extensional, and the predicates cannot be unpacked for purposes of logical inference. We can quantify over the contents of an 'ought to be' statement, but only if we allow an extended meaning to existence claims. Further, a quantified statement might serve as the argument for an 'ought to be' operator, but the status of inferences within that operator's scope is dubious.

Notes

Notes to the Introduction

1. Simo Knuuttila has found the beginnings of deontic logic in late medieval thinking, although he does not suppose any direct influence of fourteenth-century deontic logic upon present-day work. See Knuuttila's "The Emergence of Deontic Logic in the Fourteenth Century," *passim*. [Information for this and other works cited in my text is listed in the Bibliography.]

2. Locke, 516. The italics in this and all subsequent quotations from Locke, as well as the rather dubious punctuation, are in the original.

3. For my understanding of Locke, as well as for pointing me to relevant passages in the *Essay*, I am indebted to John Colman's *John Locke's Moral Philosophy*.

4. Al-Hibri's reference is to Ernst Mally's *Grundgesetze des Sollens: Elemente der Logik der Willens*.

5. I owe a huge debt to Hector-Neri Castañeda, a great philosopher and a great person. Perhaps I am most greatly indebted to him for his teaching, by word and example, that it is never enough merely to tear down: one must always look for something better.

Notes to Chapter 1:

1. A more cautious version of this statement is necessary to comprehend those arguments which introduce a provisional premiss. Not every step in a *reductio ad absurdum* argument, for instance, is correct; what is correct, rather, is that if the premiss, then the step.

2. A moral realist believes, of course, that moral statements correspond to actual states of affairs. But if one assumes the truth of moral realism, Hume's question is not lost but only transmuted. It becomes: Can actual moral states of affairs be fully described by using only 'is' and not 'ought' language?

3. The problem is the little word 'can' in the second premiss. I may infer from Aristotle's premisses only that I *can* make a cloak. Since I fail to do many things that I can do, nothing like Aristotle's conclusion, "Straightway I make the cloak," will follow. Likewise, Aristotle's second premiss does not entail 'If I need a cloak, I make a cloak', which would yield a propositional version of Aristotle's conclusion. The only plausible course I can see is to take Aristotle's second premiss to imply: "I make a cloak only if I need a cloak"; but then, the inference pattern is that of affirming the consequent.

4. As I noted above, deontic statements need not be used prescriptively, although I have argued elsewhere that understanding their prescriptive use enables us to understand their other common uses. See my book *Why You Should*, Chapter 3, *passim*.

5. However, to take another parallel, the inference from "Something necessarily is F" to "Necessarily something is F" is counter-intuitive. An essentialist could believe that humans necessarily are animals without being committed to the necessary existence of animals.

6. For further discussion of Chisholm's paradox and the Good Samaritan paradox, see ahead, Chapter 9.

Notes to Chapter 2

1. Ruth Barcan Marcus raised this question in a private letter. I am grateful to her both for the question and for calling my attention to her 1966 article, "Iterated Deontic Modalities."

2. There are more reasons for construing deontic logic as a form of modal logic than the one I gave. For instance, "You cannot go that way" ($\sim$Mp) differs from "You can not go that way" (M$\sim$p); in just the same way, "You may not go that way" might mean "Your going that way is forbidden" ($\sim$Pp) or "You are allowed to fail to go that way" (P$\sim$p). Likewise, the common substitution of 'can' for 'may' suggests a close relation between possibility and permissibility.

3. Suppose 'Lp → p'. Substitute '$\sim$p' for 'p', and you have 'L$\sim$p → $\sim$p'. By contraposition, you have 'p → $\sim$L$\sim$p', and by the interdefinability of operators, you have 'p → Mp'. Hence 'p → Mp', the assertion that what is true is possible, is a theorem in any strong modal system. Now suppose 'p' is a statement true only in this world — for example, if this world and only this world is named 'Sam', let 'p' be the statement "The name of this world is 'Sam'." Since 'p' is true, in any strong modal system 'Mp' must be true, from which it follows that 'p' is true in at least one possible world accessible to this one. Since by hypothesis 'p' is true in this world only, then in any strong modal system this world must be a possible world accessible to itself.

4. For suppose it were the case that this world is a possible world, accessible to itself. Then any proposition 'p' which is true in this world would be true in at least one possible world accessible to this one. Hence, if 'p' is true, 'Mp' must be true; that is, we must assert 'p → Mp'. Substitute '$\sim$p' for 'p', and you have '$\sim$p → M$\sim$p', whence by contraposition '$\sim$M$\sim$p → p' and by interchanging operators 'Lp → p'. That is, if this world is a possible world, accessible to itself, a strong modal system is correct; and if a strong modal system is incorrect, then this world must not be a possible world, accessible to itself.

5. As far as I know, the first person to make this move was William H. Hanson [Hanson, 179-181]. However, the suggestion for the move was made two years earlier by Saul Kripke [Kripke, final paragraph, cited in Schotch and Jennings, 150].

6. Standard deontic logic, so far as I can determine, makes no pronouncements on the nature of possible worlds. One can employ modal semantics, for instance, without being committed to modal realism.

7. Clearly, all that I can provide at this point is an indication. From the fact that a set of propositions falls out of a given semantics, and from the fact that the semantics turns out to be no good, we can hardly infer that the set of propositions must itself be faulty.

8. Negating the antecedent of a conditional is not, of course, a good way of arguing deductively; but inductively, it has its uses.

9. Again, I must thank my anonymous reader for insisting that I include this condition in my account of SDL.

10. Of course, if deontic logic were more concerned with permission statements than obligation statements, I would reverse the designations and call SDLS2 and SDLS3 forward-translation principles, and SDLS1 and SDLS4 backward-translation rules.

11. Ruth Barcan Marcus's 1966 article, "Iterated Deontic Modalities," stimulated my thought on this topic.

12. K. Jaakko J. Hintikka explicitly adopts the principle that residents of a deontic alternative world fulfill all the obligations they have in that world. This is his principle $(C.O)_{rest}$: Hintikka 1, 185-6.

13. Arthur N. Prior, second edition, 225; cited in Marcus, 280, note 1. Prior and Marcus, of course, use the 'O' operator for both 'ought to do' and 'ought to be' expressions.

14. Von Wright's original rule is more restrictive than SDLR1. See al-Hibri's discussion [al-Hibri, 11-12].

15. Suppose first that O(p v q) → (Op v Oq). Substituting '~p' for 'p' and '~q' for 'q', we have 'O(~p v ~q) → (O~p v O~q)'. By de Morgan's Laws, the antecedent of this expression is equivalent to 'O~(p.q)', and by SDLT8, to '~P(p.q)'. The consequent of the expression, by a double application of SDLT8, is equivalent to '~Pp v ~Pq' and, by de Morgan's Laws, to '~(Pp.Pq)'. Thus the entire expression is equivalent to '~P(p.q) → ~(Pp.Pq)', from which by contraposition, (Pp.Pq) → P(p.q), or SDLX6. If instead we assume SDLX6, on substituting '~p' for 'p' and '~q' for 'q', we have '(P~p.P~q) → P(~p.~q)'. By SDLT7, (~Op.~Oq) → ~O~(~p.~q), whence ~(Op v Oq) → ~O(p v q), whence O(p v q) →(Op v Oq); which is SDLX5.

16. I am grateful to an anonymous reader for insisting that I follow this procedure explicitly; in an earlier version of the book, I had done so only implicitly.

17. Since the only inference rules used in the argument are substitution and *modus tollens*, both rules of the propositional calculus, we can hardly look in that direction for something to reject.

Notes to Chapter 3

1. Interestingly enough, one of those who has questioned the validity of Kant's Principle is the founding father of Standard Deontic Logic, G.H. von Wright: see von Wright 2, 28.

2. For a list of the assertions and rules of SDL, see Appendix 1.

3. Kant, no doubt, would have opted for a more full-blooded formula, that 'ought' implies the ability to perform. But since ability implies logical possibility, then if 'ought' implies ability, 'ought' implies logical possibility. Conversely, if it is not the case that 'ought' implies logical possibility, then it is not the case that 'ought' implies ability to perform. Hence if Kant's Principle in its weak sense is false, so is Kant's Principle in a stronger formulation.

4. Sayre-McCord notes that this 'paradox' was first put forward by Alf Ross, in [Ross].

5. Note that their example takes one operator as an 'ought to do' — "We ought to feed the starving poor" — and the other as an 'ought to be' — "There ought to be starving poor." It would be better not to beg the question whether 'ought to do' and 'ought to be' statements are identical. Schotch and Jennings could have made their point had they translated the first 'ought' claim as "It ought to be that we feed the starving poor," the second as "It ought to be that there are starving poor." Those who accept the first claim are hardly likely to accept the second.

6. SDLR1 I reserve for Chapter 5, which takes up the intensionality of deontic contexts (and thus the question of whether one can in fact substitute equals for equals in

those contexts *salva veritate*). SDLT7-9, being more in the nature of definitions than axioms, seem relatively harmless.

7. It is worth noting that the rule of O-necessitation is part of the definition of a normal modal system. See Hughes and Cresswell 1, 4-5. Hence, if we give up the rule of O-necessitation, deontic logic cannot be an application of such familiar normal modal systems as K, T, S4, or S5.

8. SDLT2, like SDLR2, is part of the definition of a normal modal system. See Hughes and Cresswell 1, loc. cit. Problems with SDLT2 thus reinforce the likelihood that deontic logic should not be an application of even a weak normal system such as K.

9. Åqvist 2, Chapters 5 and 6. James Tomberlin's review [Tomberlin] of Åqvist's book called my attention to this major work.

10. Van Fraassen, 17. I have substituted arrows for his horseshoes.

11. Castañeda 5, 259. I have added brackets and parentheses to make Castañeda's formulations a little easier to read. When, on p. 263, Castañeda gives a formal version of (1) as axiom A11, an unfortunate misprint leaves out a crucial negation-sign, making it seem as if he is committed to the proposition that if one ought to do A, one ought not to do A!

12. Castañeda 5, 264. Again, I have inserted parentheses for clarity.

13. On p. 249 of *Thinking and Doing*, Castañeda sketches a semantics in which, wherever there is a piece of rule-making in the real world, there is a set of other possible practical worlds with the same facts and laws of nature as this one but with different decisions and actions. He then contends that what is obligatory in one world is what is required in every relevant alternative practical world. But this last contention, plus the requirement that alternative practical worlds be possible worlds, entails that 'ought' implies 'can'.

14. Castañeda 5, 260. Again I have added parentheses and single quotes for clarity.

15. Castañeda could escape this consequence by noting that what follows an 'ought to do' (such as 'We ought to feed the starving poor) is a practition, while what follows an 'ought to be' (such as 'There ought to be starving poor') is a proposition, and by limiting the inference rule in question to forbid mixing of the two types of expression.

16. If, on the other hand, deontic logic of any sort gives rise to inescapable paradoxes, Sayre-McCord's proposal will not rescue it.

Notes to Chapter 4

1. This chapter had its origin in an unpublished paper which Mary Gore Forrester and I wrote. (Actually, the origin of that paper is somewhat romantic: we were taking a hike in a national forest on our wedding anniversary, and the talk turned — as always on such occasions — to deontic logic.) As I have revised the material several times for the purpose of including it in the present book, there might now be claims in the chapter that she would disassociate herself from. She has asked, as a result, that I not list her as co-author of this chapter.

2. The example is from an unpublished manuscript by Mary Gore Forrester.

3. Hector-Neri Castañeda also distinguishes between 'ought to do' and 'ought to be' [Castañeda 5, 45-46 and 207-208]. He deliberately leaves unsettled (p. 46) the question of the relation, if any, between the two forms.

4. The sentence says no more than this, but it is normally used to get people to act in certain ways. The normal use is not, I shall argue, part of the expression's meaning.

5. Perhaps Jones is legally barred from running for president. The person who says that it ought to be that Jones runs may then be expressing a desire that the legal barriers be removed.

6. Hector-Neri Castañeda would favor such a translation. See Castañeda 5, 201-203.

7. However, consider this example: "You ought to do the following: if you hurt Julie, to apologize to her." This can plausibly be taken as a complex 'ought to do' expression: "You ought either not to hurt Julie or to apologize to her."

8. We make somewhat more sense of SDLT2, using 'ought to do' expressions, if we substitute 'O(~p v q)' for 'O(p → q)': "George ought to do the following: either fail to clean the cat box or take out the garbage." Unfortunately, this makes it appear that George can fulfill his obligation by failing to clean the cat box; that hardly seems correct.

9. The distinction between 'ought to do' and 'ought to be' sentences is not a new one. Gilbert Harman, for instance, wrote in 1975: "There is another use of 'ought' which is normative and in a sense moral but which is distinct from what I am calling the moral 'ought'. This is the use which occurs when we say that something ought or ought not to be the case." [Harman, 6] It is noteworthy that Harman thought of all normative 'ought to do' expressions as moral, and of normative 'ought to be' expressions as only moral "in a sense." G.H. von Wright [von Wright 2] suggests the distinction between *Sein-Sollen* and *Tun-Sollen* is a well-established one. (I am indebted to Edward Sherline for calling my attention to Harman's article.)

10. Roderick Chisholm [Chisholm 2, 13] wrote, "We may now define 'the ought to do' by reference to 'the ought to be': D9: S ought to perform A =Df. It ought to be that S's performing A obtains." Von Wright [von Wright 3, 209] writes: "Norms, also norms obliging to or permitting certain actions, are a *Sein-Sollen* (-*Dürfen*) which in their application to the world of facts become connected with agents who are then said to be under an obligation or to hold a permission. Thus for both Chisholm and von Wright, 'It ought to be that S does F' is equivalent to 'S ought to do F'.

11. See J. Forrester 2, Chapter 3, *passim*.

12. These standards depend upon the metaethical theory one adopts. They might be objective or subjective; they might be expressed as statements or as imperatives. Mary Gore Forrester has discussed at length issues I can only allude to here. See M. Forrester, *passim*.

13. I shall suggest in Chapter 14 that, even if it ought to be that our obligations satisfy certain standards, this is not always so.

14. The logical underpinning for the following argument comes in Chapter 15, where I present my new system of deontic logic.

15. This example is clearly akin to the one from Schotch and Jennings that I discussed in Chapter 3. It ought to be that we feed the starving poor, but it is not the case that it ought to be that there are starving poor.

16. This is one of a number of problems that time-indexing of SDL 'ought' statements, and the introduction of appropriate rules for the cessation of duties, would alleviate. See especially my discussion of Chisholm's Paradox in Chapter 9.

17. Note that it would be a mistake to read SDLT6 as: Either it ought to be that p or it ought to be that not-p. That reading would require the forbidden SDLX5.

18. See Castañeda 5, 207-208. Castañeda does not flatly say that the object of an 'ought to be' is a state of affairs, but I think this a fairly obvious inference from his work.

19. Perhaps one can imagine a society which waits in vain for a deliverer named 'George' to take out the garbage.

20. The second version is meant to reflect Hector-Neri Castañeda's position that what follows an 'ought to do' is not a proposition but a practition. But a more faithful reflection of Castañeda's beliefs would have specified, by means of a subscript, the nature of the 'ought'.

21. I shall argue in Chapter 5 that *de dicto* 'ought to be' claims are in fact referentially opaque. As a result, one cannot quantify existentially over terms occurring in such contexts and be sure of preserving the truth of the original sentence.

22. Geach credits this type of example to St. Anselm, but he gives no reference.

23. This is Geach's own conclusion: that 'ought to do' operators attach to predicables of particular subjects. For if so, then the subject terms are not within the scope of the operators. See Geach, 2-3.

24. Gilbert Harman notes: "Thomas Nagel has observed that often, when we use the evaluative 'ought to be' to say that something ought to be the case, we imply that someone ought to do something or ought to have done something about it." (Harman, 6, n.2; Harman gives no reference for Nagel's observation.) I think Nagel is right in supposing that users of the 'ought to be' often imply that someone ought to do something. But that is far from supposing that 'ought to be' expressions themselves imply 'ought to do' counterparts.

25. Of course, that a duty is not assigned to a particular person does not mean that no duty is present. Often a duty can be fulfilled by any of a number of persons. But the makers of utopias do not seem to have in mind even such a distributed duty.

26. James Martin made this objection to an earlier version of this chapter.

27. A strict deontologist would, of course, find no place for teleological language as such. But most strict deontologists admit one or more duties of beneficence, of improvement, or of public welfare. I believe that in a strict deontological system, the 'ought to be' contexts find their place among such 'welfare duties'. If so, then a version of our point holds even for strict deontologists. After all, in Kant's moral argument for God's existence, he recognizes the logical possibility that people's doing what they ought might not lead to what ought to be. Hence, he believes, God is needed to ensure that those who do what they ought will receive their just rewards.

My rough definition is made somewhat smoother in Chapter 14.

28. I am indebted for this point to Matthias Steup.

29. Attempts to translate from 'ought to do' to 'ought to be', and vice versa, run into difficulties reminiscent of the troubles that arise in translating from sense-datum language into material object language and vice versa. Suppose we translate "It ought to be that p" as "If Condition C is met, then some agent A ought so to act that p." Obviously, the translation's viability depends on our specifying C; and it is easy to think up ways of multiplying the complexity of C indefinitely, making it unspecifiable. Similar problems arise for a reverse translation.

30. The first type of 'ought to be' statement asserts that a situation fits some standard, but a non-moral one. For example, it might be in accordance with our standards of reasoning to expect Smith to be dead by this time. Epistemic appropriateness thus

licenses the statement "Smith should be dead by now." With the second type of 'ought to be' statement, value is present. This value might be moral, although it need not be: aesthetic reasons might underlie an 'ought to be' of this sort. Judgments of this kind are not practical and have only a remote connection with action; at most they suggest that if the universe (or human society, or some subgroup of society) were arranged for the best, then a certain situation would obtain.

31. My argument goes only for counterpart 'ought' expressions. It might be possible to define one sort of 'ought' by means of the other sort, so long as the second expression is not a counterpart of the first. In Chapter 14, I shall put forward just such a definition of 'ought to do'. That definition, however, will be informal; in the formal version of the definition, the term 'ought to be' does not appear.

32. This statement holds, of course, only for the type of 'ought to be' statement which both involves value and generates a prescription for action.

33. I need to make two points clear here. First, I am talking about the third type of 'ought to be', which usually generates prescriptions for action but which does not always do so. Second, the reader should remember that not all 'ought to do' statements are used to guide action.

Notes to Chapter 5

1. Castañeda restricts this claim to 'ought to do' contexts, however.

2. The position for which I shall argue is therefore that of Peter Geach. See especially pp. 2-4 of [Geach].

3. These two are his *Deon.* 23 and *Deon.* 25, respectively. Castañeda is aware that existential generalization and substitutivity are not entirely separate questions; as he says on p. 231, the fundamental question in either case is whether the scope of a deontic operator affects the reference of expressions within that scope. I believe that Castañeda separates substitutivity from existential generalization only for the sake of orderly exposition.

4. James Martin has reminded me that existential generalization and substitutivity *salva veritate* are trustworthy tests for extensionality only on atomic sentences. For consider such a proposition as '$(p.{\sim}p) \to MFa$'. This conditional, having a necessarily false antecedent, is necessarily true. Substituting equivalents for 'a' or quantifying over 'a' will not affect the necessary truth of the proposition (at least, in the case of existential generalization, so long as anything exists at all). And yet 'M', the possibility operator, notoriously introduces an opaque context. Hence, I must apply the existential generalization and substitutivity tests only to sentences that are not truth-functional compounds.

5. I am grateful to Stephen Harris for convincing me of this point. Mary Gore Forrester had tried to show me the error of my earlier ways.

6. Mary Gore Forrester objects that Christopher ought only to build *some* cathedral on that location; if she is right, then 'St. Swithin's Cathedral' does not, in the sentence "Christopher ought to build St. Swithin's Cathedral," refer to a particular. Since in all clearly extensional contexts in which it appears that phrase does refer to a particular (e.g., "Christopher builds St. Swithin's Cathedral"), Ms. Forrester's objection only seems to reinforce my claim that "ought to build St. Swithin's Cathedral" is an intensional context.

At any rate, both on Ms. Forrester's reading and mine, one cannot infer from "Christopher ought to build St. Swithin's Cathedral" that there exists a building such that Christopher ought to build it. Hence, opacity with respect to existential quantification remains.

7. To be sure, Robinson can engage in certain actions which, were there such a person as Edith, might correctly be termed "getting the goods on Edith." But, as Mary Gore Forrester points out, 'getting the goods on' is a success-term, and one cannot succeed in getting the goods on a non-existent person.

8. Both this and the previous suggestion I owe to Mary Gore Forrester.

9. One might seek to rule out such incidental benefits by requiring that the value in question must accrue directly to the successful performance of the entire obligation. But in the first place, such a requirement appears rather *ad hoc*; I see no reason apart from the present discussion why one should suppose the requirement to hold. Second, the requirement seems to be a new application of the doubtful principle that 'ought' implies 'can'. For, as note 7 to Chapter 5 points out, Robinson is incapable of succeeding in getting the goods on Edith.

10. See my discussion of Chisholm's Paradox in Chapter 9.

11. Quine notes that the epigram, which he thoroughly approves, came from Ruth Barcan Marcus — who presumably did not approve!

12. I talk of 'counterparts' here so as not to beg the question whether the original sentence and its semantical counterpart are equivalent in meaning. So far as I can see, there is no need to try to settle that vexed question here — nor am I able to do so.

13. How this latter sentence is to be read, or whether its propositions should be replaced by practitions, is not to the point here. However the inference in this example is to be worded, a deontic logician would want the inference to be valid.

14. For the rules of SDL semantics, see Chapter 2 or Appendix 1.

15. Geach's attack on deontic semantics is on pp. 9-11. He calls the inference rule 'plausible' on p. 7; on p. 8, he calls it 'surely acceptable'. (I suspect in the latter passage there is a misprint: Geach says that principle (3) is acceptable, but the principle he uses is (3)', which I have quoted in the text.)

Notes to Chapter 6

1. We need to be cautious in the placement of time-indexes. I ought now to keep my promises, I ought at a given time in the past to have kept my promises, and I should have the obligation in the future to keep my promises. Is it therefore legitimate to conclude that, for every time t, I ought-at-t to keep my promises? No, for I am not around at every time t. But surely, for every time t such that I am alive and in possession of my faculties at t, I ought-at-t to keep my promises. But if quantification is possible over times, the time-reference cannot be within the scope of the opaque 'ought to do' operator. That is, there is a difference between saying that X ought-at-t to do F and saying that X ought to do F at t. In the latter case, the time reference is within the operator's scope.

2. Granted, Jane might choose to rob a bank and pay back John with the hot money. But since the law would not allow John to keep the bank's cash, Jane would not have made restitution to him.

3. I shall consider problems of circularity and empty claims more fully in Chapter 8.

Notes to Chapter 7

1. This point obviously does not hold for inference rules that SDL takes over from the propositional calculus. By *modus ponens* we can infer 'OB' from 'OA' and 'OA →OB'.

2. The theorem in question is Hintikka's cleaned-up version of a theorem which he quotes Arthur N. Prior as calling a 'quite plain truth' of logic. [Prior] is cited on p. 192 of Hintikka 1.

3. Note that the only portion of deontic logic *not* under attack in this chapter is the pair of principles I called into question in *Why You Should* and in Chapter 3 of this book.

4. This odd result should not be confused with the even odder "Either you ought to tie your shoes or you ought not to tie them," which does *not* follow in SDL.

5. I am grateful to Stephen Harris for calling my attention to Rantala's work on urn models and its relevance to the arguments of this chapter. (See p. 107 ff.)

6. Any proposition 'p' implies 'p v q'. Clearly there is a non-denumerable infinity of true propositions 'q' of the form 'n is greater than 0', where 'n' designates a real number; there is therefore a non-denumerably infinite set of true propositions 'p v q'. Therefore, if you know that p, you must know a non-denumerably infinite set of propositions.

7. My characterization of PLO, and in particular of the role played by the assumption that all epistemic worlds are possible worlds, is taken from Hintikka 3, 475-477.

8. As Hintikka notes, the worlds of Rantala's urn models are not actually inconsistent, merely changing.

9. Mary Gore Forrester pointed out the relevance of the Good Samaritan here. As she notes, some logical implications of duty-statements are merely neutral, not, as in the case of the Good Samaritan, vicious. For example, to repay a loan one must have borrowed. Most people would agree that one should repay without supposing that one should have borrowed. I shall discuss the Good Samaritan more fully in Chapter 9.

10. Curiously enough, Solt does not seem fully aware of the radical nature of his conclusion. An indication of his unawareness emerges from a brief note (note 3, p. 350) on Hintikka's model system, which does not explicitly provide for backward translation. [Hintikka 1, *passim*] Solt concludes that Hintikka means to deny backward translation. But Hintikka asserts that if 'Pp' is true in this world, then 'p' is true in at least one deontic alternative world; and this provision, as Chapter 2 argued, entails the principle of backward translation.

11. See, for instance, the first sentence of Solt's third paragraph on p. 349.

12. Solt himself considers the presence of a valid norm in this world both necessary and sufficient for the truth of a corresponding 'ought' statement. [Solt, 349-350] But Solt's argument requires only that norms are necessary conditions.

13. On that crucial question, Solt himself is of little help. He writes: "Let us suppose that everybody is drinking a cup of milk daily at the actual world. Does it mean that automatically it is obligatory to drink a cup of milk daily at our world, if there is not such a command? No, it does not." [Solt, 350, n. 2] This note suggests that Solt means by 'norm' a command, presumably by someone in a position of authority. Such a position is not tenable. A Nazi concentration camp commandant received no orders to avoid murdering the camp's inmates, but few would deny that he ought to have avoided doing

so. Only if the dictates of conscience count as commands is the point remotely plausible, and if they do, oughts would not hold of a conscienceless Nazi. As the law often says, if persons should have known better, they are responsible for not having done better.

14. As Mary Gore Forrester reminds me, a person at times should act in a certain way by virtue of his beliefs concerning the consequences of his potential actions. But such beliefs do not seem to be what Solt has in mind in speaking of norms.

15. The actual existence of an institution is not necessary for assertion of an 'ought to do' claim. A person who thinks reasonably but incorrectly that there is a law against nude bathing in backyard hot tubs is warranted in asserting that people ought not, under the law, engage in that activity.

16. As in Euripides' *Orestes*, where the existence of a court to try cases of murder is no innovation.

17. Ezekiel XVIII, 20; [Bible], 1023-1024.

18. A believer in biblical inerrancy would, I suppose, have to conclude that between the time of Exodus and that of Ezekiel, God changed his mind on the matter of personal responsibility.

19. The author of Ezekiel might not have been the first prophet to work out the notion of individual responsibility. Jeremiah XXXI, 29-30 makes the same point, and even quotes the same proverb, much more succinctly. But the author of Ezekiel is clearly struck by the idea of individual responsibility, and his care in working it out is beautiful.

20. The dependence of 'ought to do' statements on institutions does not entail ethical relativism. An ethical absolutist can allow the dependence of 'ought to do' statements on universal institutions, such as those provided by natural law theory. Alternatively, one might suppose that whenever a person considers conflicting institution-dependent 'ought to do' statements, one of those oughts, an all-things-considered ought, will always win out if the person is rational. Hector-Neri Castañeda put this position forward in *Thinking and Doing*: *"Thus the overriding ought, or the general structure of all individual overriding oughts, is a fundamental feature of reason."* [Castañeda 5, 304; his italics]

21. Mary Gore Forrester notes that the existence of sanctions might presuppose the presence of appropriate institutions, so that if 'ought to do' expressions presuppose sanctions, they would presuppose institutions. In Chapter 14, I shall argue that an 'ought to do' expression presupposes only that negative consequences for transgressors *ought to be*. If Smith ought to help his neighbor, there ought to be institutions punishing him for not doing so; but if Smith happens to live in Hobbes's state of nature, those institutions will not actually exist.

22. A decision that I ought to clean out the cat box is more than a decision to clean out the cat box. If, as I work on this book, the fumes rising from the cat box interfere with my ability to concentrate, I might well decide to clean the box out; but it would take consideration of what I owe to my wife and perhaps to the cats to convince me that I ought to clean out the cat box.

23. This is Hintikka's rule (C.OO*): if a person ought to do p in the real world, then the person ought to do p in every deontic alternative to the real world. [Hintikka 1, 185]

Notes to Chapter 8

1. Basing oughts on a ranking of worlds is the key concept of NDL semantics, to be presented in Chapter 14.

2. Of course, these are no restrictions on possible worlds as such. A modal realist might suppose that there are many worlds which we are not in a position to pick out by means of state descriptions; these worlds and perhaps others are inaccessible to us. But inaccessible worlds are of no use to the logician. Necessity, for instance, is not defined as truth in all possible worlds but as truth in all possible worlds to which we have access. Deontic logicians must either play by the rules of possible world semantics or enact and justify an alternative semantics.

3. Leibniz's point about compossibilities remains in force. This might be the best of possible worlds, but so long as duties remain undone, it cannot be deontically accessible to itself.

4. Hume, 32. Italics are in the original.

5. Strictly speaking, this type of argument does not usually prove circularity, for claim A might justify claim B, which justifies claim C, and so on. But in SDL semantics, SDLS1 and SDLS2 together say that 'ought' statements both imply and are implied by certain statements about deontically accessible worlds. If all that we know about the latter statements derives from the former, then we can hardly justify the former by the latter.

6. See, for example, the phrases from David Lewis and Lennart Åqvist cited above.

7. This is Hintikka's general procedure. For a modal example, see Hintikka 1, 57-58.

8. Hintikka finds no distinction between 'ought to be' and 'ought to do'; hence, there is no significance to his phrasing the definition of 'O' in 'ought to be' language.

Notes to Chapter 9

1. Although this chapter considers only the semantics of 'ought to do' statements, I shall take up in Chapter 10 the effects of standard arguments on the SDL semantics of 'ought to be' statements.

2. See his critique of Åqvist on this point: [Tomberlin], 113.

3. On Hintikka's rules, X's choking Y in all deontic alternative worlds entails not only that X ought to choke Y in this world, but that X ought to choke Y in each of the alternatives! This is a consequence of Hintikka's rules (C.P*) and (C.OO*): Hintikka 1, 185.

4. To meet Geach's second and third arguments, we must stipulate that F occurs only a brief time after t. Thus S, in deontically accessible worlds, has only a brief window of opportunity to do F; fortunately, in every world S succeeds. That is, not only do people always do as they should in alternative worlds after the branching — but they do as they should right away! This is yet another reason why Geach is right to ask how deontically accessible worlds can bear any relation to what one should do.

5. However, even if X cannot know what is false, why *ought* she not know it? Not having a duty to do the impossible sounds reasonable, but having a duty not to do the impossible does not: "George, squaring the circle is sinful!"

6. My paradox therefore raises difficulties only for those who accept some at least slightly non-standard version of deontic semantics and logic. Hence Hector-Neri Castañeda, whose semantics and deontic logic are non-standard, found my paradox an important difficulty. See Castañeda 2 and Castañeda 4.

Notes to Chapter 10

1. Hintikka's so-called impossible possible worlds are, thanks to his use of Rantala's urn models, not impossible but merely changing.

2. I am following a suggestion by Peter K. Schotch and Raymond E. Jennings. See Schotch and Jennings, 149-162 and 156-157.

3. Suppose it ought to be that I arrest any burglar who breaks in, and George is a burglar who breaks in. But I let him go, figuring that I cannot infer, because of opacity, that it ought to be that I arrest George, and realizing that George's being the burglar is something that would not happen in an ideal world, where no one burgles. Surely I have failed to do what it ought to be that I do. If SDL semantics will not license the necessary inference, so much the worse for SDL semantics.

4. Pascal, Letter IX (p. 442). Pascal adds, "Escobar afterwards remarks: 'I must confess that it is very rarely that a person falls into the sin of sloth'." Thus Escobar, at least, believed that there can be slothful people, and surely he was right — even on his sense of 'sloth'.

5. To be sure, a gentle murder might be reckoned an improvement over a ferocious one; but it would not be an improvement over no murder at all.

6. However, for the inference to go through we must stipulate that there is an improved world in which both "S does F" and "S does F → S does G" hold.

Notes to Chapter 11

1. CT is often taken as providing the *meaning* of 'rights'. For example, William Frankena wrote: "[T]he full correlativity of rights and duties is generally taken as axiomatic, so axiomatic that rights are usually defined in terms of duties, as ways in which the bearer ought to be treated." [Frankena, 196] But since CT as a thesis about meaning implies CT in a biconditional version, falsity of the latter implies falsity of the former. As I shall argue for falsity of CT as a biconditional, I therefore need not consider it as a meaning-claim.

2. For example, Article 1: "All human beings are born free and equal in dignity and rights. They are endowed with reason and conscience and *should* act towards one another in a spirit of brotherhood" — my italics.

3. Wills, 285, citing Sade, "Philosophy in the Bedroom;" in [Sade], 135.

4. Ibid; italics in the original.

5. This formulation of CT2 leaves open the question whether the duty to help belongs to each member of the group or whether the duty is a collective one. Mary Gore Forrester suggested a neutral formulation here.

6. See Frankena, 196-197, for a clear expression of the notion of a *prima facie* right. Frankena credits A.C. Ewing and E.F. Carritt for the idea.

7. This case shows the implausibility of the common belief that rights are always trumps, and that only invoking a stronger right can defeat the invocation of a right. That may be so for legal rights, although I do not see that it must be; it is certainly not true of natural rights.

8. I am not at all suggesting that ethical relativism is correct. Any ethical absolutist will allow that, although precepts do not vary with conditions, their applications will. To

send one's aged parents out to sea on an ice floe is not an approved practice in Tahiti, where ice floes are hard to come by.

9. To be sure, circumstances might make it unwise to invoke or impute rights. A relatively inconspicuous passenger on a hijacked airplane would do well not to proclaim her rights as an American citizen. But she nevertheless has those rights, even though they are not being respected by her captors.

10. I owe this suggestion to Mary Gore Forrester.

11. This argument is no better than a play on the word 'liberty'. Does it mean that one's actions *are* unimpeded or that they *ought to be* unimpeded? The argument I am imputing to Sade has it both ways. Alas, even philosophers in the bedroom are guilty of 'is'/'ought' confusions!

12. However, on some occasions the few preconditions for the practical value of negative rights do not occur. For example, if a natural catastrophe has caused a rescue worker to be able to save only some lives, she might draw up a list of those she will try to rescue. In leaving the name of one victim off the list, she is deliberately acting in a way that threatens to interfere with the victim's life. Yet one could hardly blame her for violating the right to life of those she fails to save, if her failure to interfere would be even more disastrous. As the catastrophe is unavoidable, it would seem silly for any but a believer in immediate divine causation of catastrophes to sigh that such a condition ought not to be.

13. Mary Gore Forrester raised this objection.

14. Obviously, if no one is able to give Jane a living wage, no one is in the best position to do so. If there is not enough food for anybody in the lifeboat, there is no best food distribution scheme.

15. I am not taking back my claim that what ought to be is largely independent of particular circumstances. If Jane has a right to a living wage, then it ought to be that someone who is able and best situated to give her a living wage, and who has no good reason not to do so, does so. If there is indeed such a someone, namely Smith, then we will most likely ascribe to him a duty to provide her with the living wage.

Notes to Chapter 12

1. Fishkin, 153. Much of Fishkin's book is a careful examination of the assumptions on which the MBA rests.

2. The term 'minimal altruism' is Fishkin's: Fishkin, 3.

3. By raising the question of the point of imposing such duties, I am suggesting that 'ought' implicates, rather than implies, 'can'. For argument on the point, see J. Forrester 1, Chapter 2.

4. James Fishkin discusses a number of such agent-specific principles and finds them wanting: Fishkin, 160-171.

5. Fishkin makes only the modest claim that the MBA, together with (1) and (2), *might* force a person to give up both (3a) and (3b). I think his analysis supports the stronger claim that a person could not under these conditions hold either (3a) or (3b).

6. It is more than just analogous if we understand deontic logic as a weak modal system, with 'ought' in the place of 'necessary'. However, this amounts to accepting a

version of standard deontic logic, and my argument in the first part of this book stands against our doing that.

7. The hypothesis is that in all possible worlds accessible to hers, Norma helps all those on the list. In the real world, Tomas is on the list; but there are worlds in which he is not on the list. In such worlds, Norma does not help him; therefore, she does not help him in all possible and accessible worlds. Someone might counter that the statement "It is necessary that Norma help everyone on the list" means that in every world Norma helps those who are on the list *in the real world*, rather than those who are on the list in that world. But that reading is thoroughly improbable. The counterfactual "If Tomas were not on the list, he would still be among those it is necessary for Norma to help" is at best counterintuitive.

8. In SDL semantics, we could derive "Norma ought to help Tomas" only if it is necessarily true or it ought to be that Tomas's name is on the list. Hence for all its problems. SDL does block the MBA.

9. It is tempting and perhaps reasonable to interpret "Norma ought to help the starving children" as "Norma ought to help *some* but not all of the starving children, since helping them all is impossible" rather than "Norma ought to help each of the starving children." But unless the 'ought to [do]' context is intensional, this maneuver does not escape the MBA. For suppose the context is extensional. Then from "Norma ought to help some, but not all, of the starving children" we can infer, "There is at least one starving child whom Norma ought to help and at least one whom it is false that she ought to help." But what is the difference between the fortunate ones and the unfortunate ones? There seems no morally relevant difference. Only if, by the intensionality of the 'ought to [do]' context, one can block the inference from general duties to particular duties does the MBA lack teeth.

10. SDL semantics does not justify this common-sense inference; for even if in all deontic alternative worlds Norma helps each child on her list, that list need not be the same in every deontic alternative world. Hence, we cannot infer from SDL semantics that Norma ought to help those three particular children, even though clearly she should. Thus although SDL semantics does good work in blocking the MBA, it is deficient in not recognizing that the MBA works in some restricted cases.

11. This might look like SDLR3: from "S ought to do F" and from "Necessarily, S does F → S does G," we infer "S ought to do G." But there is no necessity that, if Norma does her duty, she will help precisely those three children, for it is not logically necessary that only those names appear on her list. What *is* true in all possible worlds is that if Norma does her duty and if these three names comprise the list, then Norma helps those three children. Now Norma does her duty in all deontic alternative worlds, but it is false that those three names comprise the list in all deontic alternatives. Hence, we cannot conclude that Norma helps those three children in all deontic alternatives, and consequently we cannot use SDL semantics to conclude that she ought to help them.

12. The quotation is from an 1837 report. I drew it from Grassian, 284.

Notes to Chapter 13

1. This is essentially the position **MR** formulated by David O. Brink [Brink, 17] with one major difference: instead of saying that moral facts are independent of our epistemic relations to those facts, Brink speaks of the independence of our evidence for moral facts.

Brink suggests that **MR** provides important necessary but not sufficient conditions for moral realism. Whether it is sufficient or not, the principle does seem to capture what most authors have meant in speaking of moral realism. My brief discussion of moral realism in this chapter is heavily indebted to Brink's careful presentation.

2. Of course, before possible world semantics not everyone interpreted modalities subjectively. Carnap and others, for example, explained modalities *de dicto* by means of the concept of analyticity. But such explanations do not, without incorporating the notion of possible worlds, give a clear explanation of the opacity of modal sentences.

Notes to Chapter 14

1. Appendix 1 contains a summary of NDL, including its semantics.

2. Stephen Harris pointed out the confusion between punishment and negative consequences.

3. In a child-care book that I once read, the latter were described as 'logical consequences!'

4. This is not always so. An atheist might wish that an evildoer outside the reach of the authorities would contract a particularly nasty disease; this might be poetic justice but it would not be punishment.

5. Anderson later argued that the 'if/then' relation he needed was not the same even as strict implication; his espousal of a relevance logic is a close cousin to my insistence on a causal account. See Anderson 2, 345-360.

6. Mr. Sobel, in a private conversation, took as an example SDLT1: $\vdash \sim(Op.O\sim p)$. Suppose we add to SDLT1 the condition that 'p' be contingent: $\vdash CT'p' \rightarrow \sim(Op.O\sim p)$. Now NDL asserts that if 'p' ought to be, 'p' must be contingent: $\vdash Op \rightarrow CT'p'$. It follows truth-functionally that $\vdash Op \rightarrow \sim(Op.O\sim p)$, whence '$\vdash \sim Op \vee \sim Op \vee \sim O\sim p$', whence '$\vdash \sim Op \vee \sim O\sim p$', whence SDLT1. Thus the condition that 'p' be contingent has dropped out.

7. To be sure, the incurring or the presence of an obligation might itself have consequences for good or ill. For instance, my incurring an obligation to pay you $50,000 might cause me to have great anxiety. But those consequences would be relevant to determining whether one ought to incur that obligation or whether it ought to be that one is under that obligation. In the absence of a rule for reducing iterated modalities, we cannot suppose the consequences of incurring an obligation relevant to the obligation itself; and similarly for the consequences of an obligation's being present.

8. For instance, the Good Samaritan paradox would arise. From "Abner helps Esdras and Abner will kill Esdras" and "It ought to be that Abner helps Esdras," it is surely wrong to infer "It ought to be that both Abner helps Esdras and Abner will kill Esdras."

9. From this point on, I shall consider any inevitable causal antecedents of a <p>-alternative as part of that <p>-alternative.

10. This is not *deontic* accessibility, as in the semantics for SDL; the real world is a possible world under this definition.

11. I am grateful to Stephen Harris for pointing out the need for this discussion.

12. Stephen Harris notes that K. Jaakko J. Hintikka used urn models in order to allow for so-called impossible possible worlds. But as Hintikka makes clear, the point of his use of urn models is to show that such worlds are not impossible, after all — merely changing. See Hintikka 3, 478.

13. It is, of course, possible that in some worlds other factors will cause Mary to do G. Perhaps those factors are present but ineffective in worlds where John is appropriately penalized.

14. I owe this example to Mary Gore Forrester.

15. II Kings, II, 23-24. Of course the person whose baldness the children derided turned out to be a prophet, Elisha. Forty-two were killed for their temerity.

16. The text of the telegram is in Yevtushenko, 3-4.

17. I am suggesting that I see no difference *in kind* between duties, obligations, and what one ought to do. There are differences in degree of importance which people generally attach to these terms. 'Duty' and 'obligation' are rarely used words these days; now that the day of such Victorian moralists as George Eliot is over, they are reserved for special occasions. A bridge player who thoughtlessly plays second-hand high has not done as she ought, but no one would accuse her of failing in her duty — unless, say, the Army had assigned her to play good bridge as part of a mission vital to her country's welfare.

18. This point was made to me by Stephen Harris.

Notes to Chapter 15

1. This method of organization is my response to a valuable suggestion made by the anonymous reader credited in the Preface.

2. Brevity of expression is not the only reason for omitting statements of contingency. Constant use of a metalinguistic predicate "CT'p'" to mean "'p' is contingent" might seduce us into the belief that matters that belong properly to formation rules are assertions of the system. That is, we might suppose: "⊢ OBp → CT'p'" and "⊢ ~OBp → CT'p'." As Kenith Sobel has pointed out, from these two assertions "'⊢ Ct'p'" follows. And since the propositional calculus is included as part of NDL, that amounts to the claim that there are no necessary or impossible propositions!

3. Ruth Barcan Marcus has argued that if we read 'O~p' as 'p is forbidden', as some deontic logicians have done, (a) leads to paradoxical results. For 'OO~p' is equivalent to 'O~Pp' in SDL, whereas "It ought to be that it ought to be that not-p" is certainly not the same as "It is forbidden that p be permissible." Marcus analyzes the paradox as resulting from a confusion between evaluative and prescriptive uses of deontic operators. [Marcus, 581] I suggest instead that 'It is forbidden that' presents a possible state of affairs in this world, while 'It ought to be that not' presents a relation between two or more worlds.

4. I owe this objection to Mary Gore Forrester.

5. NDL semantics, of course, gives no basis for inferring that we ought to starve the starving poor.

6. To be sure, George could be penalized on his deathbed; but I fail to see how the penalty could be appropriate. Doing an obligatory action sometimes requires doing an innocuous action, and for failure to perform innocuous actions, there is no appropriate penalty.

7. See J. Forrester 2, Chapter 2.

8. The derivation is in al-Hibri, 13. My derivation of Ross's paradox here follows al-Hibri's account on p. 23.

9. Castañeda's argument that A.P.2 is inconsistent with rule-utilitarianism might be thought to raise a problem here. But I believe Castañeda's apparent paradox can be resolved by a better understanding of rule-utilitarianism.

Notes to Chapter 16

1. Consider this argument: "Everybody always does what is in his own interests. Saluting the flag is in my interests. Therefore, I will salute the flag." The conclusion is ambiguous: It either expresses an intention or states a prediction. If the conclusion expresses an intention, it does not follow from the premises, as expressions of intentions are neither true nor false; if the conclusion states a prediction of one's own behavior, it does follow from the premises. Hence the argument succeeds if and only if the conclusion is not prescriptive.

2. One might wish to allow for odd constructions, such as Hopkins's "Have fair fallen, O fair." But as Aristotle insisted, deliberation is about what agents can do. [Aristotle, 1112b 32]

3. More precisely, if the premises of inference II imply the premises of inference I, and the conclusion of I implies the conclusion of II, then the validity of I would entail the validity of II. However, the likelihood of proving these antecedents without meaning identity is small, and I must show in either case how a statement which is neither true nor false can imply or be implied by anything.

4. Hare 2, 17-31. As my concern in what follows is exclusively with the phrastic component, I shall not here worry about Hare's distinction between neustics and tropics.

5. Mary Gore Forrester made this point.

6. The distinction between *prima facie* and full-blown oughts is of no use here. That I ought, all things considered, to do my duty still does not imply that I will even make an effort to do my duty. Statements of intention, on the other hand, do seem to imply such an effort — although, of course, not necessarily a successful effort.

7. Many people trained in administration treat themselves as exceptions to this rule: Often administrators seem to think that if a proposal sounds good, it should be implemented. The messes that usually result from such carefree optimism suggest that we should take more care in teaching practical reasoning to those who should use that reasoning professionally.

Note to Appendices

1. This is not *deontic* accessibility, as in the semantics for SDL; the real world is a possible world under this definition.

Bibliography

In the text, I refer to the works listed below by the author's name. Where I have cited more than one work by the same author, I have used the author's name and a number, given in square brackets after each multiple entry. Thus "Aeschylus 1" refers to Aeschylus' *Choephoroe,* "Aeschylus 2" to his *Eumenides.*

Aeschylus: *Choephoroe.* [Aeschylus 1]

Aeschylus: *Eumenides.* [Aeschylus 2]

al-Hibri, Azizah: *Deontic Logic: A Comprehensive Appraisal and a New Proposal.* Washington, 1978.

Anderson, Alan Ross: "A Reduction of Deontic Logic to Alethic Modal Logic." *Mind* LXVII, 265 (January, 1958); 100-103. [Anderson 1]

Anderson, Alan Ross: "Some Nasty Problems in the Formal Logic of Ethics." *Nous* I, 4 (December, 1967); 345-360. [Anderson 2]

Anderson, Alan Ross: "The Formal Analysis of Normative Systems," In Rescher, 147-213. [Anderson 3]

Åqvist, Lennart: "Good Samaritans, Contrary-to Duty Imperatives, and Epistemic Obligations." *Nous* I (December, 1967); 361-379. [Åqvist 1]

Åqvist, Lennart: *Introduction to Deontic Logic and the Theory of Normative Systems.* Naples, 1987. [Åqvist 2]

Aristotle: *Nicomachean Ethics,* trans. Terence Irwin. Indianapolis, 1985.

Austin, John L.: "A Plea for Excuses." In his *Philosophical Papers.* Oxford, 1961; 123-152. Reprinted from *Proceedings of the Aristotelian Society* 1956-57.

Beauchamp, Tom L., and Childress, James F.: *Principles of Biomedical Ethics,* 3rd ed. New York & Oxford, 1989.

Bennett, Jonathan: "The Conscience of Huckleberry Finn." *Philosophy* 49 (1974); 123-134.

Brink, David O.: *Moral Realism and the Foundations of Ethics.* Cambridge, 1989.

Castañeda, Hector-Neri: "A Problem for Utilitarianism." *Analysis* 28 (March, 1968); 141-142. [Castañeda 1]

Castañeda, Hector-Neri: "Aspectual Actions and Davidson's Theory of Events." In *Actions and Events,* ed. Ernest Le Pore and Brian McLaughlin, 294-310. Oxford, 1985. [Castañeda 2]

Castañeda, Hector-Neri: "Ethics and Logic: Stevensonianism Revisited." *Journal of Philosophy* 64 (October 26, 1967); 671-683. [Castañeda 3]

Castañeda, Hector-Neri: "Obligations, Aspectual Actions, and Circumstances." *Philosophical Papers* 15 (November, 1986); 155-170. [Castañeda 4]

Castañeda, Hector-Neri: *Thinking and Doing.* Dordrecht, 1975. [Castañeda 5]

Chellas, Brian: *Modal Logic: An Introduction.* Cambridge, 1980.

Chisholm, Roderick: "Contrary-to-Duty Imperatives and Deontic Logic." *Analysis* 23 (1963); 33-36. [Chisholm 1]

Chisholm, Roderick: "Practical Reason and the Logic of Requirement." In *Practical Reason,* ed. Stephan Körner, 1-17. New Haven, 1974. [Chisholm 2]

Colman, John: *John Locke's Moral Philosophy.* Edinburgh, 1983.

Feinberg, Joel: "Voluntary Euthanasia and the Inalienable Right to Life." In *Medicine and Moral Philosophy*, ed. Marshall Cohen, Thomas Nagel, and Thomas Scanlon, 245-275. Princeton, 1981.

Fishkin, James: *The Limits of Obligation*. New Haven and London, 1982.

Forrester, James: "Gentle Murder, or the Adverbial Samaritan." *Journal of Philosophy* LXXI, 4 (April, 1984); 193-197. [J. Forrester 1]

Forrester, James: *Why You Should*. Hanover and London, 1989. [J. Forrester 2]

Forrester, James: "Conflicts of Obligation." *American Philosophical Quarterly* XXXII, 1 (January, 1995); 31-44. [J. Forrester 3]

Forrester, Mary Gore: *Moral Language*. Madison, 1982. [M. Forrester]

Frankena, William K.: "The Concept of Universal Human Rights." In *Science, Language, and Human Rights*, American Philosophical Association, Eastern Division, Vol. 1. Philadelphia, 1952; 189-207.

Geach, Peter: "Whatever Happened to Deontic Logic?" *Philosophia* XI (Fall, 1982), 1-12.

Goodman, Nelson: *Fact, Fiction, and Forecast*. London, 1955; 2nd ed. Indianapolis and New York, 1965.

Grassian, Victor: *Moral Reasoning: Ethical Theory and Some Contemporary Moral Problems*, 2nd ed. Englewood Cliffs, NJ, 1992 (1981).

Grice, H. Paul: "Logic and Conversation." In *The Logic of Grammar*, ed. G. Harman and D. Davidson, 64-75. Encino and Belmont, CA, 1975.

Hanson, William H.: "Semantics for Deontic Logic." *Logique et Analyse* 8 (1965); 177-190.

Hare, Richard M.: *Freedom and Reason*. Oxford, 1963. [Hare 1]

Hare, Richard M.: "Meaning and Speech Acts." *Philosophical Review* 79 (1970); 3-24. [Hare 2]

Hare, Richard M.: *The Language of Morals*. Oxford, 1952. [Hare 3]

Harman, Gilbert: "Moral Relativism Defended." *Philosophical Review* LXXXIV, 1 (January, 1975); 3-32.

Hilpinen, Risto (ed.): *Deontic Logic: Introductory and Systematic Readings*. Dordrecht, 1971. [Hilpinen 1]

Hilpinen, Risto (ed.): *New Studies in Deontic Logic*. Dordrecht, 1981. [Hilpinen 2]

Hintikka, K. Jaakko J.: *Models for Modalities*. Dordrecht, 1969. [Hintikka 1]

Hintikka, K. Jaakko J.: "Some Main Problems of Deontic Logic." In Hilpinen 1; 59-104. [Hintikka 2]

Hintikka, K. Jaakko J.: "Impossible Possible Worlds Vindicated." *Journal of Philosophical Logic* 4 (1975), 475-484. [Hintikka 3]

Hobbes, Thomas: *Leviathan*. Ed. Michael Oakeshott. Oxford, 1957.

Hughes, G.E., and Cresswell, M.J.: *A Companion to Modal Logic*. London, 1984. [Hughes and Cresswell 1]

Hughes, G.E., and Cresswell, M.J.: *An Introduction to Modal Logic*. London, 1968. [Hughes and Cresswell 2]

Hume, David: *A Treatise of Human Nature*, ed. L.A. Selby-Bigge. Oxford, 1888.

Knuuttila, Simo: "The Emergence of Deontic Logic in the Fourteenth Century." In Hilpinen 2; 225-248.

Kripke, Saul: "Semantic Analysis of Modal Logic. I." *Zeitschrift für mathematische Logik und Grundlagen der Mathematik* 9 (1963); 67-96.

Lemmon, E.J.: "Moral Dilemmas." *Philosophical Review* 71 (1962), 139-158.

Lewis, David: "Semantic Analyses for Dyadic Deontic Logic." In Stenlund, 1-14.

Locke, John: *An Essay Concerning Human Understanding*, ed. Peter Nidditch. Oxford, 1975.

Mally, Ernst: *Grundgesetze des Sollens: Elemente der Logik der Willens.* Graz, 1926.

Marcus, Ruth Barcan: "Iterated Deontic Modalities." *Mind* LXXV (October, 1966), 580-582.

The New English Bible [Bible]. Oxford, 1971.

Pascal, Blaise: *The Provincial Letters*, trans. Thomas M'Crie. New York, 1941.

Plato: *Republic*, ed. Ioannes Burnet. In *Platonis Opera* IV. Oxford, 1902.

Prior, Arthur N.: *Formal Logic.* 1st ed., Oxford, 1957; 2nd ed., Oxford, 1962.

Quine, Willard V.: *The Ways of Paradox.* New York, 1966. [Quine 1]

Quine, Willard V.: *Word and Object.* Cambridge, MA, 1960. [Quine 2]

Rescher, Nicholas (ed.): *The Logic of Decision and Action.* Pittsburgh, 1967.

Ross, Alf: "Imperatives and Logic." *Theoria*, VII (1941); 53-71.

Rantala, Veikko: "Urn Models: A New Kind of Non-Standard Model for First-Order Logic." *Journal of Philosophical Logic* 4 (1975) 455-474.

Sade, the Marquis de [Sade]: "Philosophy in the Bedroom." In Paul Dinnage: *The Marquis de Sade: Selections from His Writings.* John Calder, 1962.

Sayre-McCord, Geoffrey: "Deontic Logic and the Priority of Moral Theory." *Nous* XX, 2 (June, 1986).

Schotch, Peter K., and Jennings, Raymond E.: "Non-Kripkean Deontic Logic." In Hilpinen 2, 149-162.

Singer, Peter: "Famine, Affluence and Morality." In *Philosophy, Politics and Society*, ed. Peter Laslett and James Fishkin. 5th series. Oxford, 1979.

Sinnott-Armstrong, Walter: "'Ought' Conversationally Implies 'Can'." *Philosophical Review* XCII, 2 (April, 1984), 249-261. [Sinnott-Armstrong 1]

Sinnott-Armstrong, Walter: *Moral Dilemmas.* Oxford and New York, 1988. [Sinnott-Armstrong 2]

Solt, Kornel: "Deontic Alternative Worlds and the Truth-Value of 'OA'," *Logique et Analyse* (September, 1984), 349-351.

Stenlund, S. (ed.): *Logical Theory and Semantic Analysis.* Dordrecht, 1974.

Tomberlin, James E: Review of Lennart Åqvist: *Introduction to Deontic Logic and the Theory of Normative Systems. Nous* XXV, 1 (March, 1991), 109-116.

Trollope, Anthony: *Doctor Thorne*, with an introduction by Elizabeth Bowen. Boston, 1959.

van Fraassen, Bas C.: "Values and the Heart's Command." *Journal of Philosophy* LXX, 1 (January 11, 1973).

von Wright, Georg Henrik: "Deontic Logic." *Mind* 60 (1951), 1-15. [von Wright 1]

von Wright, Georg Henrik: "On the Logic of Norms and Actions." In Hilpinen 2, 3-35. Reprinted in von Wright, *Practical Reason: Philosophic Papers, vol. I.* Ithaca, NY, 1983; 100-129. [von Wright 2]

von Wright, Georg Henrik: "Norms, Truth and Logic." In von Wright, *Practical Reason: Philosophic Papers, vol. I.* Ithaca, NY, 1983; 130-209. [von Wright 3]

Wills, Garry: *Under God: Religion and American Politics.* New York, 1990.

Yevtushenko, Yevgeny: *Fatal Half-Measures: The Culture of Democracy in the Soviet Union*, ed. and trans. Antonina W. Bouis. Boston, 1991.

Index